SUITSWELL SOLUTIONS
INTERIOR DESIGN BIBLE

Mayannk

BlueRoseONE.com
Stories Matter
NewDelhi • London

BLUEROSE PUBLISHERS
India | U.K.

Copyright © Mayannk 2024

All rights reserved by author. No part of this publication may be reproduced, stored in a retrieval system or transmitted in any form or by any means, electronic, mechanical, photocopying, recording or otherwise, without the prior permission of the author. Although every precaution has been taken to verify the accuracy of the information contained herein, the publisher assumes no responsibility for any errors or omissions. No liability is assumed for damages that may result from the use of information contained within.

BlueRose Publishers takes no responsibility for any damages, losses, or liabilities that may arise from the use or misuse of the information, products, or services provided in this publication.

For permissions requests or inquiries regarding this publication,
please contact:

BLUEROSE PUBLISHERS
www.BlueRoseONE.com
info@bluerosepublishers.com
+91 8882 898 898
+4407342408967

ISBN: 978-93-5989-463-8

Cover Design: Muskan Sachdeva

First Edition: January 2024

PREFACE

Interior design is not just about creating a visually pleasing space, it is also about creating an environment that promotes comfort, functionality, and sustainability. The world is rapidly evolving and the need for sustainable living is more crucial now than ever before. This book is a reflection of the author's vision and experience in creating sustainable interior spaces, which are both visually appealing and environmentally responsible.

The author has dedicated over 15 years of his life to the real estate and design and build industry, creating numerous commercial and residential interior spaces. With each project, he has gained valuable insight and experience in the field of interior design. As a result, he has become an advocate for sustainable interior design, constantly striving to create spaces that are both aesthetically pleasing and environmentally friendly.

This book is a culmination of the author's years of experience in interior design and his passion for interior design & sustainability. It covers both residential and commercial interiors, highlighting the need for sustainable practices in both areas. The author delves into the latest trends and techniques used in sustainable interior design, sharing his expertise with readers.

This book aims to illuminate the intricacies of interior design while celebrating its profound impact on our daily lives. While sustainability plays an important role throughout the narrative, author strives to provide a holistic perspective that goes beyond any single aspect. The goal is to inspire and educate, showcasing the process of interior design from conceptualization to realization,. The book also offers practical tips and advice for incorporating sustainable practices in interior design.

The author's entire team has played a significant role in inspiring him to write this book. Their collective expertise, passion, and commitment to sustainability have motivated the author to share his knowledge with a wider audience. He hopes that this book will inspire readers to embrace sustainable interior design practices and create a better and more sustainable world for all.

In conclusion, this book is a must-read for anyone who wants to learn about interior design and the sustainable relations. It offers valuable insight and practical advice on how to create visually appealing and environmentally responsible interior spaces. The author's passion for sustainability and his years of experience in the field make this book is an essential guide for designers, architects, and anyone interested in creating sustainable interior spaces.

Content

A. Residential Interior Design

1. Why is there a need for Interior Designing
2. Understanding the "Space"
3. Creating a Livable Space
4. Elements of Interior Design
5. Fundamentals of Interior Design
6. Spectrum of Interior Design Styles
7. Sustainable HOME Design
8. Sustainability X Materials

B. Commercial Interior Design

1. Client Business Insight
2. The Dynamics of Commercial Interior Design
3. Factors Shaping Commercial Interior Spaces
4. Sustainable design
5. The Steps of Research and Project Implementation
6. Evidence-Based Design
7. The Office
8. Retail Facilities
9. Sustainability – The Indoor Environment
10. Charting a Sustainable Path: Overcoming Obstacles

RESIDENTIAL INTERIOR DESIGN.

In the realm of residential architecture, interior design stands as the creative and functional embodiment of the spaces we call home. It is an intricate balance of aesthetics, functionality, and personal expression, aimed at creating harmonious living environments. From selecting color schemes and furniture layouts to incorporating natural lighting and innovative materials, residential interior design has the power to transform a house into a warm and inviting home. In this essay, we will explore the key principles and elements that govern residential interior design, along with the latest trends shaping the industry.

The Essence of Residential Interior Design: Residential interior design is more than just superficial decoration; it encompasses the art and science of crafting spaces that accommodate the unique needs, preferences, and lifestyle of the inhabitants. Successful interior design merges creativity, functionality, and a deep understanding of human behavior to create spaces that evoke emotions, promote well-being, and enhance the quality of life.

WHY IS THERE A NEED FOR INTERIOR DESIGNING?

When it comes to designing interiors, it's all about elevating spaces to a whole new level of excellence. You see, it's not just about picking colors and furniture—it's about understanding the unique needs and desires of each client. And let me tell you, it's a big deal for them to find the perfect match for their home interiors. After all, for some, it's their forever sanctuary, while for others, it's a bustling hub for business or simply a place to unwind and relax. So, who they choose as their interior designer becomes a decision of utmost importance.

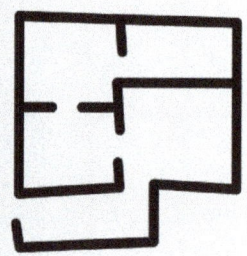

The demand for Interior Designing is ever-present, as people across the world aspire to have stunning and captivating interiors in their homes, offices, restaurants, and stores. In today's highly visual and design-oriented world, everyone desires spaces that look and feel exceptional. In this industry, your knowledge and skill-set play a crucial role in attracting clients of varying degrees. Your expertise sets you apart and positions you as a trusted partner in transforming their spaces into remarkable works of art. Whether you're already an experienced professional or dreaming of embarking on a career as an interior designer or starting your own interior business, this book can be a valuable resource for you.

- Excellent soft skills
- Team player / good leadership
- Resourceful & solution oriented
- Trending design knowledge
- Technical knowledge
- Softwares & presentation skills
- Customer oriented
- Sustainable design practices

- Effective communication skills can smooth your way & your relationships with others by helping you to understand others, and to be understood.
- To be resourceful means to provide & materialize your ideas & designs with the state of the art goods & services. To grow along the innovation.
- Designs needs to be put in a precise manner to be able to produce and execute and to do that, practicality & technicality aspects are the keys.
- Catering to your clients ethically and efficiently paves the path to a successful career. It is important to be sustainable conscious and actively choose to produce projects with the same

UNDERSTANDING THE "SPACE"

When referring to "space" in the context of interior design, it encompasses all the elements and factors associated with the project. This includes clients, designs, analysis, the site, and the overall project itself. The clients' input and vision play a vital role in shaping the design direction. The design process involves generating creative ideas and translating them into tangible plans, considering aesthetics, functionality, sustainability, and user experience. Analysis involves evaluating existing conditions, conducting research, and gathering data to inform the design decisions. The site refers to the physical location and its characteristics that influence the design. The project encompasses the entire process, including planning, designing, and executing the interior design project. By considering all these interconnected aspects, designers can create comprehensive and successful designs that meet clients' needs and optimize the potential of the space.

The initial phases of a project serve as the cornerstone upon which the entire design process will either thrive or fail. It is of utmost importance to allocate sufficient time during this stage, as it significantly impacts the project's potential for success. Devoting time to accurately identify and analyze each aspect of the project enhances your comprehension of the upcoming task, while also unveiling fresh possibilities for exploration as the design progresses.

Uncovering information within a brief regarding space can often be a time-consuming process that may not provide immediate satisfaction. However, it serves as a crucial step in conducting research and shaping a concept for spatial design. Strong concepts, which are the core ideas, are what drive the success of most spatial projects. To truly comprehend a space, several steps must be taken, starting from understanding the client's requirements and gathering insights, all the way to developing a comprehensive concept for the spatial design. This chapter delves into each of these steps, providing a more in-depth understanding of the process involved in designing and exploring space.

THE CLIENT

Clients can originate from various backgrounds and encompass a wide range of entities, including companies, organizations, or individuals. However, they all share a common need for the services of an interior designer, although their understanding of these needs can greatly differ. Some clients carefully evaluate their circumstances before deciding to engage a professional designer, while others may have a vague notion that a designer can provide better solutions than they could on their own. Certain clients may prioritize aesthetics as the main concern, overlooking the practical aspects that led them to seek the designer's expertise. Conversely, practical considerations may take precedence for other clients, with decorative concerns being of secondary importance.

For these reasons and many others, it is crucial for designers to possess the ability to communicate effectively with various personality types. Whether clients are forthright or timid, it is important to understand and respect their perspectives, emphasizing their essential role in the design process.

Establishing a strong rapport with clients is a fundamental requirement, as designers often strive to connect with them on an emotional level. In fact, building a solid client/designer relationship is sometimes even more significant than presenting an extensive curriculum vitae.

CLIENT PROFILE

The client profile serves as a valuable tool for better understanding the client's identity and lifestyle, whether in a residential or commercial context. While it may not directly align with the specific project brief, it provides insights that contribute to the design development process. In residential projects, the client profile aids in comprehending the daily utilization of the space, from morning to night, and offers indications of the client's stylistic preferences. Understanding the client's routine is crucial in creating a design that effectively caters to their needs. In commercial projects, it becomes vital to grasp the work practices of the organization that will ultimately occupy the space. This offers an opportunity to closely examine the existing work patterns and assess whether the space is being utilized optimally. It may reveal that the current practices are efficient, or it may allow for the exploration of alternative, improved ways of working. Commercial clients often engage designers not only to create comfortable work environments but also as catalysts for change when seeking to benefit the organization with a new direction.

THE BRIEFING IN INTERIOR DESIGN

The briefing process provides the first significant opportunity to gain an understanding of a project. Briefs can vary widely, ranging from carefully constructed documents that comprehensively convey the project's scope and details, to informal conversations over a cup of coffee. While a written brief may contain a substantial amount of information, the quantity alone does not guarantee quality. As French mathematician, physicist, and philosopher Blaise Pascal wrote in 1657, "I have made this letter longer than usual, only because I have not had the time to make it shorter." Succinct and relevant information is the essence of a successful briefing document. In fact, brevity is often desirable. A focused and clear brief enables designers to make decisive decisions and formulate effective design solutions more easily.

UNDERSTANDING THE BRIEF

Requesting the client to provide a written/ digital brief after their initial contact, prior to the briefing meeting, is a reasonable approach. This tactic encourages the client to carefully consider their requirements and confirms their seriousness about engaging an interior designer. Discussing the written brief at a later date allows both parties to address any issues or uncertainties that may arise from it. Utilizing this opportunity for mutual agreement is crucial, as it enables a better understanding of each other's perspectives and positively impacts the business relationship.

While a more comprehensive brief facilitates the designer's job, it's important to acknowledge that the client's initial ideas and desires for the project may be abstract or vague rather than a definitive list of specific needs. It is possible that the "brief" may consist of the client expressing a desire for "a great place to come back to after a hard day's work."

Even with a vague brief, it's important to establish constraints such as time, budget, aesthetic style, and project scope. Constraints, despite their limitations, actually help define the project. By understanding these constraints, designers can plan effectively, discarding options that fall outside the boundaries and focusing on those that align with the brief. Embracing constraints leads to more focused and successful design outcomes.

In many projects, whether residential or commercial, there are multiple individuals involved as clients. It is important to ensure that the final brief has been agreed upon by all stakeholders, regardless of who initially wrote it or who was present in the meetings. Face-to-face meetings provide an opportunity to ensure explicit understanding between the designer and the client. It is crucial to clarify any potential misunderstandings, such as differing interpretations of terms like "contemporary." This is the time to address and resolve any disparities in understanding.

DECODING DESIGN

After meeting the client and gathering the initial brief, it is crucial to commence the detailed analysis phase. The primary objective is to ensure a comprehensive understanding of all the client's needs. While some requirements may have been explicitly stated, there may be instances where you need to infer additional information from the available data. Thoroughly analyzing the brief and related information will help you gain a deeper understanding of the client's expectations and requirements.

GATHERING INSIGHTS

finding the right balance with the raw information is a crucial aspect, and your judgment plays a significant role in determining whether the client truly understands their own needs. It's important to remember that clients have sought your expertise precisely because they are not experts themselves. Therefore, some of their assumptions may be incorrect, and it becomes your responsibility to correct them. While delivering a finished design solution that meets all the specified requirements may satisfy the client, your aim should be higher than mere contentment.

Extraordinary and revolutionary outcomes often emerge when you go beyond providing the expected answer. It is through insights and innovative thinking that ideas can be challenged, turned upside down, or approached in unconventional ways. By doing so, you can address the brief in a superior, more efficient, or more aesthetically pleasing manner. While unconventional ideas will require thorough testing and resolution during the later stages of the design process, it is these ideas that have the potential to delight the client, rather than just leaving them content.

Within the brief, clients may express practical considerations that require attention, while others may discuss the desired emotional response they want their space to evoke, using more abstract language. Even if the brief lacks clarity, it is still possible to identify certain constraints such as time, budget, style, and more. Although the term "constraint" may have a negative connotation, it is important to actively seek out these constraints as they serve a beneficial purpose. Constraints play a positive role in the design analysis process as they help define the scope of the project. When faced with a complex or daunting brief, identifying the natural constraints can be one of the initial steps in understanding the project's shape and boundaries. Rather than hindering the design process, constraints serve as guiding factors that assist in defining the project's parameters and finding innovative solutions within them.

UNVEILING DESIGN INSIGHTS THROUGH INFORMATION ANALYSIS

The term "analysis" often brings to mind an intellectual and academic examination of the data provided in the brief. While this is indeed a significant aspect of analysis, it can also be a visual exercise alongside the literary one. As an interior designer, you will be exploring both the practical and aesthetic aspects of the brief. Engaging in visual activities such as collage, sketching, and photography allows you to establish connections and develop aesthetic ideas in a free and potentially unrestrained manner.

Working visually in this way enables creative minds to access new ideas as they emerge from the brief. It also complements the later stages of building and site research. Ultimately, to conduct an effective analysis, you should feel comfortable working in any medium or approach that suits you best. This skill may require practice, but it is highly rewarding and yields significant benefits.

Brainstorming and mind-mapping are two well-recognized techniques that aid the process of analysis and evaluation. Brainstorming, typically conducted in group settings, aims to generate a large number of ideas. However, the principles of brainstorming can also be applied during individual sessions. There are four fundamental rules that underpin the process:

1. Quantity matters: More ideas increase the chance of finding a solution.
2. No criticism: Avoid judging ideas initially; criticism can come later.
3. Embrace uniqueness: Encourage unconventional ideas for fresh perspectives.
4. Combine ideas: Build upon and merge ideas to create better solutions.

Mind maps are visual diagrams that represent ideas and associations related to a central concept or problem. They allow for flexible organization and linking of information in a way that feels natural. Mind maps incorporate images, doodles, and color alongside words, enhancing the visualization of ideas. The visual pattern of a mind map aids in easier processing and contemplation compared to a simple list, facilitating subconscious understanding. Extracting comprehensive information from the brief establishes a solid foundation for conducting project research, which will be discussed further in the subsequent sections.

EXPLORING BUILIDNG AND SITE RESEARCH

It is essential for any space design to consider the existing building it is integrated into. Understanding the current structure is crucial in determining the necessary modifications to accommodate its intended functions.

When designing interiors within newly constructed buildings, there is significant freedom to define the interior's appearance and atmosphere. However, when working within an existing building, the designer must appreciate how the building's past contributes to its character. Factors such as the volume proportions, placement of windows and doorways, and other architectural elements impose a sense of order on the space. The new design should respond to these factors and allow them to influence the design process. Additionally, understanding a building's history may extend beyond its physical boundaries to include the local area and its surroundings. However, this does not mean that the design should simply mimic the existing style of the building. The best designs honor the existing structure and may reference it through materials, construction techniques, craftsmanship, patterns, forms, and other design elements. It is about finding a balance between respecting the building's history and incorporating innovative design solutions.

CONCEPT DEVELOPMENT

Through thorough research and analysis, you will gain a comprehensive understanding of the essential factors that will influence the design:

- The existing structure: Familiarize yourself with the physical aspects and architectural characteristics of the space.
- Functions and activities: Determine the intended uses of the space and how practical considerations, such as furniture requirements, will be addressed.
- Possibilities and limitations: Identify what is feasible within the space, considering factors such as time, technical constraints, and budget limitations.
- Space functionality and interaction: Understand how the space functions and how it relates to its surrounding environment or other interconnected areas.
- Desired emotional response and aesthetic style: Explore the client's vision for the user's emotional experience within the space and their preferences for the overall aesthetic style.

While understanding these key points is essential, it's crucial to go beyond a mere collection of elements. To create a cohesive and considered design, you need to establish a unifying idea that ties together the different aspects. This central concept sets the stylistic tone of the design and ensures that all elements work harmoniously together.

THE ROLE OF RESEARCH IN CONCEPT DEVELOPMENT

Concepts can take various forms, whether visual or literary, and they can be discovered or created. They serve as a guiding idea that encapsulates the essence of the project. Concepts can be represented by a range of mediums, such as stories, images, poems, collages, or patterns. The key is to find something that sparks your imagination and conveys a strong and compelling idea that encompasses the project's visual aesthetic, sensory experience, and historical context.

The most powerful concepts often go beyond literal references to the specific elements of the project. Instead, they abstractly represent the ideas of form, texture, color, style, and mood expressed in the client's brief.

Concepts serve as a reference point for the designer throughout the design development process. Every decision made, whether regarding the spatial layout or the selection of materials and finishes, can be evaluated against the concept. By checking whether a design element aligns with the concept, designers can ensure consistency and coherence in achieving the desired look and feel of the space. For example, does a proposed furniture arrangement harmonize with the concept? Which fabric choice enhances the desired sense of sophistication and elegance? By referring back to the concept, these questions can be answered.

COMMUNICATING CONCEPTS

During the initial stages of a project, some designers prefer to work in an abstract manner, allowing ideas to come together around a central concept. They may create "mood boards" or "concept boards" that visually capture the desired atmosphere and aesthetic. Others may have clear ideas from the beginning and express them through "concept sketches," which are not meant to be finalized designs but serve as initial visualizations of how a space might function. Clients may request to see initial concept work to gain confidence that the design is heading in a direction they are comfortable with. However, these concept boards and sketches may appear raw, instinctual, and unfinished. While this can be exciting for the designer, it may confuse the client. It's important to assess the client's personality and potentially refine the work before presenting it to them.

Carefully executed line drawings, organized in a coherent yet tentative and unfinished representation of the space, possibly with added colors to define form, can be a highly evocative and persuasive tool for the designer. The aim of concept work is not to achieve perfection but to capture and communicate the essence and character of a space.

CREATING A
LIVABLE SPACE

Creating a livable space is all about designing an environment that is not only visually appealing but also functional and comfortable. Whether it's a home, an office, or any other type of interior, the goal is to transform it into a place where people can truly thrive.
When it comes to residential spaces, the concept of a livable space takes on added significance. It involves careful consideration of the needs and preferences of the individuals or families who will inhabit the space. A livable home should reflect their unique lifestyles, providing them with a sense of belonging, relaxation, and well-being.

Key elements that contribute to a livable space include efficient space planning, optimal lighting, appropriate color schemes, comfortable and ergonomic furniture, and the integration of natural elements. A well-designed livable space takes into account the flow of movement, ensuring that it is easy and intuitive for occupants to navigate and interact within the environment.
Furthermore, a livable space should promote a healthy and sustainable lifestyle. This involves incorporating elements such as proper ventilation, access to natural light, and the use of eco-friendly materials and practices. A focus on creating spaces that support physical and mental well-being is paramount, allowing occupants to thrive and find solace within their surroundings.
Ultimately, the art of creating a livable space lies in finding the perfect balance between aesthetics and functionality. It requires an understanding of the unique needs and aspirations of the people who will inhabit the space and translating that understanding into a design that enhances their quality of life.

Whether it's through thoughtful interior design, smart organization, or the incorporation of technology, the aim is to create a space that not only meets basic human needs but also inspires, uplifts, and fosters a sense of joy and harmony. Creating a truly livable space is a testament to the transformative power of design, where the environments we inhabit can positively impact our lives every single day.

Let's delve into the essentials of Interior Design for a while, where we'll uncover the foundational principles that bring balance, style, and functionality to every room.

ELEMENTS OF INTERIOR DESIGN

The 7 elements of design are designed to help you balance an interior scheme so that the finished look is aesthetically pleasing, as well as functional. Design is a science, after all, as well as an art. Addressing each of the elements that make up every design can enhance a room's best features, compensate for any flaws, and create an interior that satisfies the eye, the sense of touch, and fulfils its practical role.

A balance of these 7 elements is vital to every scheme.

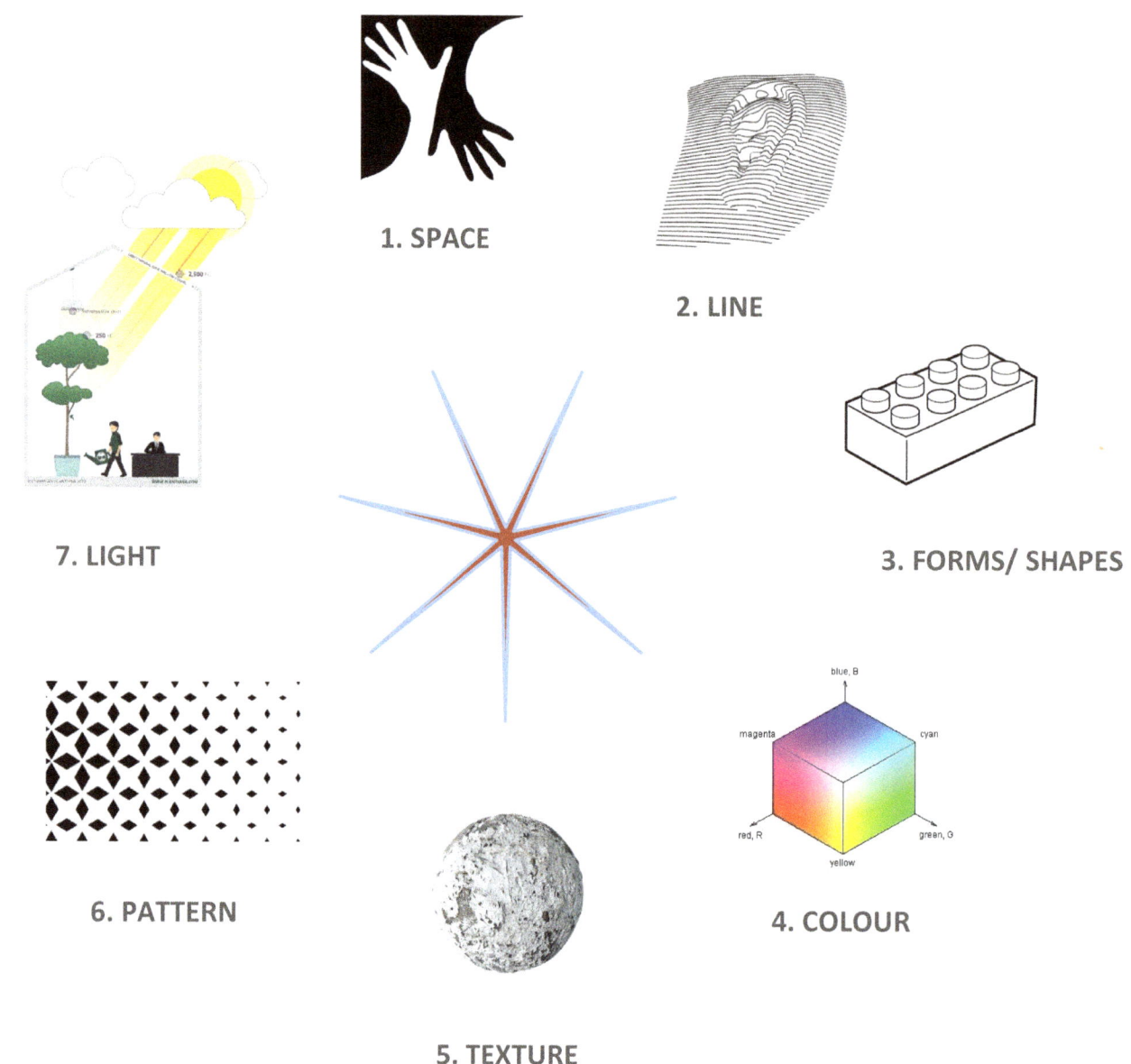

1. SPACE
2. LINE
3. FORMS/ SHAPES
4. COLOUR
5. TEXTURE
6. PATTERN
7. LIGHT

1. SPACE

'Space' encompasses the distance and arrangement of furniture and objects within a room, along with their proportions. Achieving the right balance in a room relies on effectively utilizing both 'positive' and 'negative' space.

Positive space refers to the placement of objects like sofas and armchairs, while negative space pertains to the gaps between them and includes circulation areas for movement and open spaces that prevent a room from appearing cluttered. Striking an appropriate balance between the two is crucial for a well-designed room. A higher proportion of negative space creates a sense of openness, spaciousness, and grandeur, but an excessive amount can make the room feel sparsely furnished and impersonal. Conversely, an overcrowded room with too much positive space occupied may give a feeling of being cramped and overly furnished.

How can we achieve this? Well, the perception of beauty is subjective, and what may feel cozy and comforting to one person might appear cluttered to another. If you prefer a more intimate and cluttered aesthetic, embracing additional negative space might be your preference. However, as a general guideline, it's important to ensure that pathways in a room are at least 1 meter wide, while gaps between furniture pieces like sofas and coffee tables should ideally be around 50 cm for comfortable movement.

At the core of all design concepts lies space planning, the essential foundation for bringing ideas to life. From conceptualizing floor plans to crafting living spaces, it all revolves around this key factor. While 2D modeling can provide a basic understanding of space and how design elements can achieve symmetry, we highly recommend utilizing 3D programming for a more precise visualization of different interior spaces and their potential. Through 3D rendering and modeling, you can ignite the client's visual interest and explore various possibilities. Space planning involves determining the desired amount of open space, allocating furniture placement, and achieving the desired balance in your floor plan.

Too little space can create a feeling of being exposed

Very large rooms designed for many people can produce a lonely feeling when it is occupied by one person

Space is affected by the number and size of objects in it

Many objects scattered throughout the room will most likely destroy the design effect because the space will have no apparent organization or unity

shape of subjects across diverse media
harmony, contrast, and unity.

Lines come into play through the structural characteristics of a space, as well as the furnishings within it, shaping the overall ambiance. They possess the ability to draw attention to focal points and create a sense of visual interest. Beyond the conventional horizontal and vertical lines, they can also take on dynamic and energetic forms, adding an extra dimension to the design composition.

A line can be defined as a stroke or mark that possesses a greater length than width, tracing the path of a point as it moves through space. Lines serve as the means through which objects and elements are visually perceived, capturing their essence and describing their form.

Characteristics of line include :
Width - Thick, thin, tapering, uneven
Length - Long, short, continuous, broken
Focus- Sharp, blurry, fuzzy, choppy
Feeling - Sharp, jagged, graceful, smooth
Direction - Horizontal, vertical, diagonal, curving, perpendicular, oblique, parallel, radial, zig-zag

Vertical lines of the room come from features like windows and doors. They're prized for giving a feeling of freedom and can make a room seem taller. Choosing a tall piece of furniture, for example, can lead the eye upwards and visually heighten the room.

Elevating verticality, infusing sophistication, symbolizing growth, embodying spirituality, exuding magnificence, and bestowing strength to a design.

Horizontal lines, like those found in tables, contribute a feeling of solidity and balance to an interior space, while also creating the illusion of increased width in a room.

Introducing visual expansiveness, tranquility, serenity, relaxation, gentleness, and a sense of grounded stability.

...curves, these lines can be found in architectural features... ...id tiles. T... ...ture injects vi...

Lines serve multiple purposes in design. They can be used complementary elements, or they can be intentionally employed to achieve asymmetry and create vis... interest. Lines have the power to evoke different moods and atmospheres, ranging from playful a... subdued and tranquil. Regardless of the chosen approach, lines play a crucial role in shaping th... aesthetic and impact of a design project.

The manner in which lines are utilized can greatly influence the effectiveness of a design's mess... solid, continuous line, for example, can create a sense of impact and urgency, effectively emphasizing a... conveying a particular message. Understanding and skillfully incorporating line aspects allows designers to harness their communicative powers and enhance the overall visual experience for the viewer.

DIAGONAL LINES

- Action
- Activity
- Movement
- Excitement
- Creates a sense of speed

Diagonal lines move the eye in a direction and indicate movement and fluidity.

ZIG-ZAG LINES

- Sharp
- Safety
- Illusive
- Dependent
- Busy Connection

Zig-zag lines are extremely active & evoke feelings. Horizontal zig zags are less active than vertical ones.

CURVED LINES

- Drama
- Soothing
- Natural flow
- Freedom & Graceful
- Appearance of softness

Curved lines can be seen in doorways arches, ruffled curtains, furniture, staircase & accessories.

3. FORMS/ SHAPES

Forms or shapes are the cornerstone of interior design, encompassing the fundamental structure and silhouette of three-dimensional objects within a space. They provide the essential framework, which can be achieved through the combination of various shapes and further elevated by the incorporation of complementary elements such as patterns, colors, and textures. By skillfully manipulating forms and shapes, designers can create visually captivating and cohesive environments that engage and inspire.

In order to understand the arrangement of visual elements within a space, we instinctively categorize them into positive shapes, which are perceived as figures, and negative shapes, which function as the background for these figures. This interplay between positive and negative shapes allows us to perceive and comprehend the overall structure of the visual field.

For instance, when we encounter letters like 'f' and 'g', we not only recognize them as individual characters but also perceive them as distinct figures with their own unique profiles, set against a background that provides contrast. As these figures increase in size in relation to their surrounding field, other elements within and around them start vying for our attention, challenging their prominence as the main figures within the composition.

Commonly known forms and shapes :

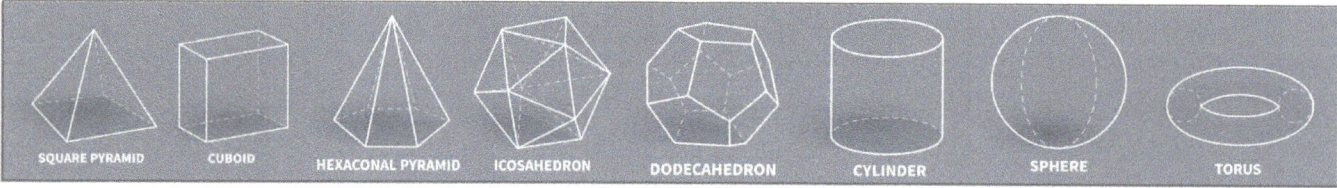

In interior design, form follows function, enhancing the aesthetic value of design trends. Forms include the shape of the room and the objects within it, such as furniture, artwork, and accessories. These forms can be geometric or natural, with precise lines or curvaceous elements. Natural forms, often requested by homeowners, incorporate natural colors and elements, creating a rustic or classic theme. As an interior designer, you can experiment with different forms to create visually appealing and functional spaces.

Shapes in interior design hold the power to convey meaning and evoke emotions. The size of a shape can communicate significance or insignificance, as well as strength or weakness. When a colored shape is placed on a white background, it creates a positive shape within the negative space. By exploring various types of shapes, we can unravel their unique characteristics and understand their impact on the overall composition. In the realm of interior design, shapes shape our perception and contribute to the visual language of a space.

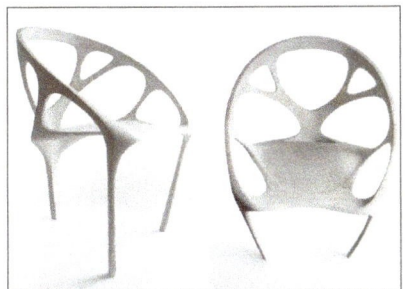

Organic - Natural, living form

Inorganic or formal - Man Made, non-living shapes

Free form - irregular, amorphic

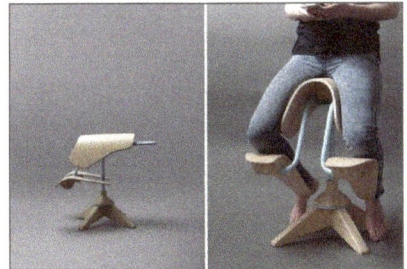

Open forms - Forms that are free & unconventional

Closed forms - Self contained, structured, elemental

Geometric form - Sphere, cube, pyramid, cone, cylinder

Achieving balance is key when working with different forms. Natural shapes add softness and contrast to interiors, while geometric forms are popular for contemporary spaces, adding diversity and complexity. Embracing these forms brings innovation and sophistication to interior design.

Geometric Shapes: Geometric shapes are those that can be constructed using a ruler or compass. They exhibit clean lines and a sense of order, providing a visually neat and controlled look.

Organic Shapes: Organic shapes, in contrast, are freeform and often complex, resembling shapes found in nature. They evoke a sense of naturalness and add an organic feel to the design.

Shape may be
Shiny and reflect images - Mirror
Transparent and create visual effects - Glass
Textured and absorb light & sound - Carpets

4. COLOUR

Color plays a vital role in interior design as it enables the creation of visually appealing combinations and influences us on a psychological level. It has the power to emphasize hierarchy and enhance the overall artistic expression. Furthermore, each color possesses three distinct characteristics: hue, saturation, and value.

1. Hue: Hue refers to the actual color itself, such as red, blue, green, etc. It represents the dominant wavelength of light that is reflected or emitted by an object.
2. Saturation: Saturation, also known as intensity or chroma, describes the purity or vividness of a color. A highly saturated color appears vibrant and intense, while a desaturated color appears more muted or grayish.
3. Value: Value, also known as brightness or lightness, refers to how light or dark a color appears. It is determined by the amount of white or black added to a pure hue. A high-value color is lighter, closer to white, while a low-value color is darker, closer to black.

Considering color and light as a cohesive entity is crucial in interior design because color can have a profound impact under varying lighting conditions. Therefore, before determining the color scheme for a space, an interior designer must possess the ability to recognize and understand the specific lighting conditions that will be present. By doing so, they can ensure that the chosen colors will harmonize effectively with the lighting, resulting in the desired visual atmosphere and ambiance.

Color Theory

Color theory is a blending of artistic and scientific principles, which serves to identify harmonious color combinations. Isaac Newton devised the color wheel in 1666, wherein he represented the spectrum of colors in a circular form. The color wheel forms the foundation of color theory, as it illustrates the connections between various hues.

A color harmony refers to a captivating blend of colors that complement each other. These harmonies are harnessed by artists and designers to evoke specific aesthetics or emotions. To discover these harmonies, one can rely on a color wheel, which applies the principles of color combinations. By considering the relative positions of various colors, one can uncover delightful color combinations that produce an appealing impact. Two main types of color wheels exist: the RYB (red, yellow, blue) wheel, favored by artists for mixing paint colors, and the RGB (red, green, blue) wheel, which serves as another valuable tool.

Color theory is a field of study that explores how colors interact, combine, and are perceived by the human eye. It encompasses various principles and concepts that help artists, designers, and individuals understand and work with colors effectively. Color theory examines the properties, psychology, and harmony of colors, providing a framework for color selection, combinations, and visual communication.

Color Wheel: The color wheel is a visual representation of color relationships. It consists of a circular arrangement of colors that demonstrates their organization and interaction. The traditional color wheel consists of twelve hues: the primary, secondary, and tertiary colors. It serves as a tool for understanding color harmonies, contrasts, and schemes.

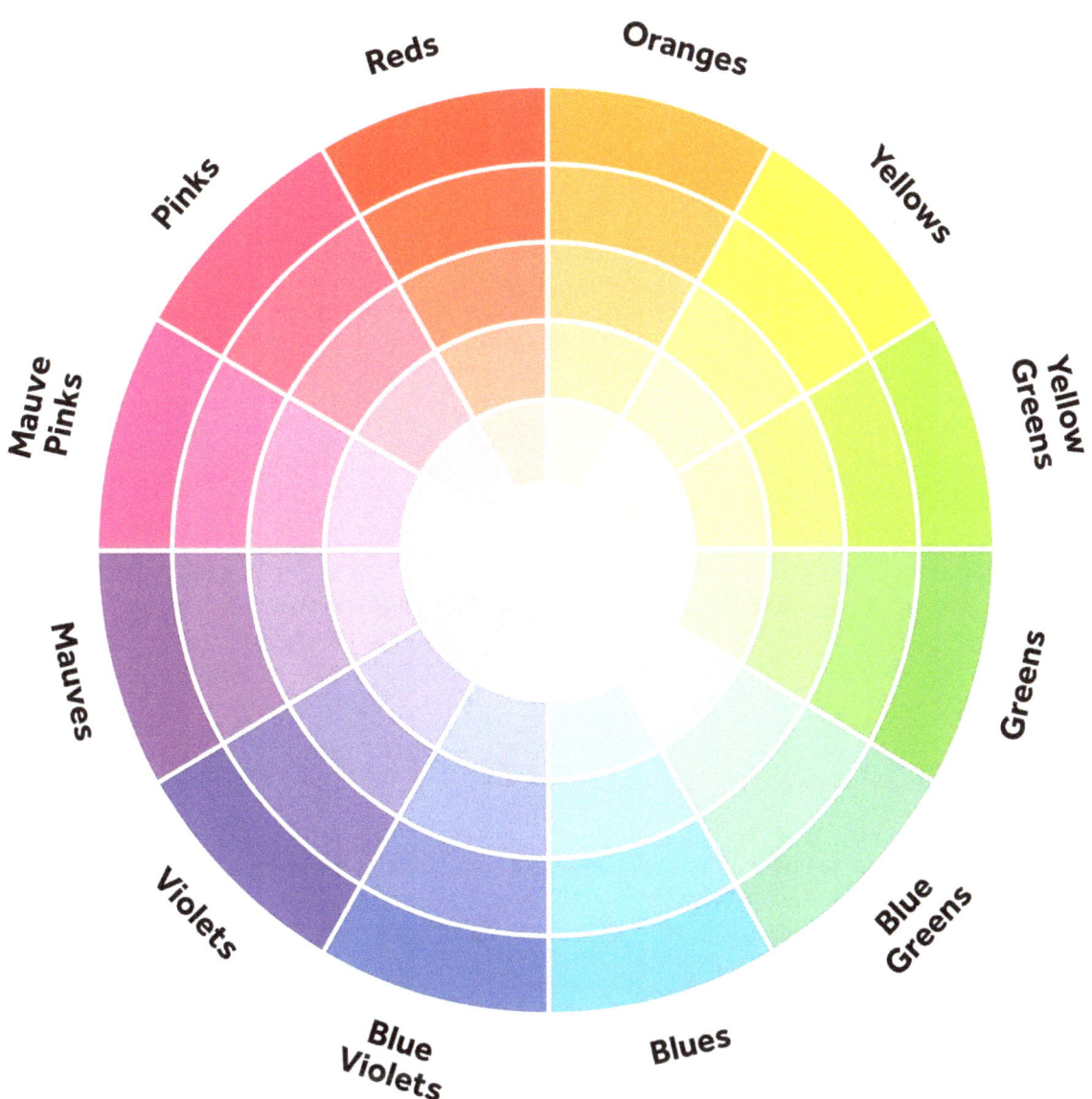

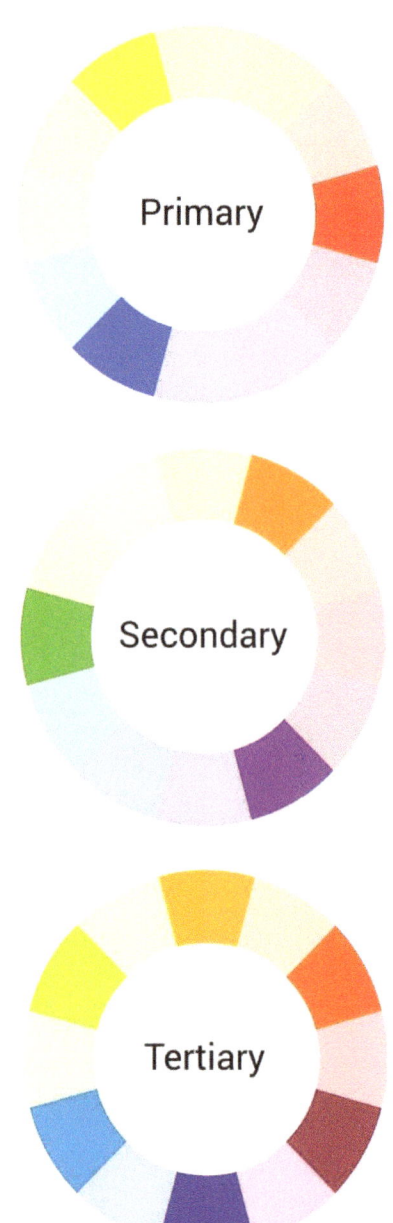

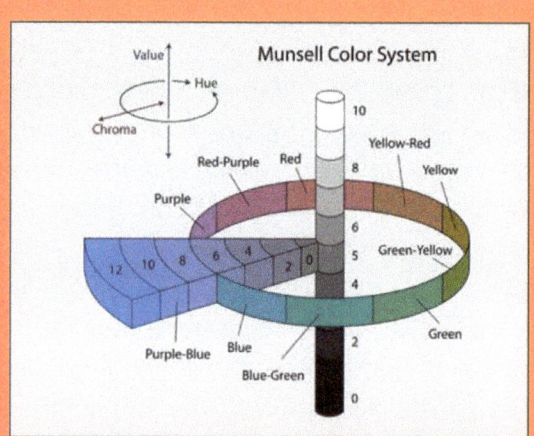

Primary Colors: The primary colors are the foundation of color theory. They are hues that cannot be created by mixing other colors. In traditional color theory, the primary colors are red, blue, and yellow. These colors serve as the base for all other colors in the color spectrum.

Secondary Colors: Secondary colors are created by mixing two primary colors together. The three secondary colors are orange (red + yellow), green (yellow + blue), and violet (blue + red). They sit between the primary colors on the color wheel.

Tertiary Colors: Tertiary colors are formed by mixing a primary color with a neighboring secondary color. For example, red-orange, yellow-orange, yellow-green, blue-green, blue-violet, and red-violet are all tertiary colors. Tertiary colors provide a wide range of hues and allow for more nuanced color combinations.

Color Harmony: Color harmony refers to the pleasing arrangement of colors in a composition. Different color combinations can evoke specific moods, emotions, and visual effects. Some common color harmonies include:

1. **Complementary Colors**: Complementary colors are pairs of colors that are opposite each other on the color wheel, such as red and green, or blue and orange. They create high contrast and vibrancy when used together.

2. **Analogous Colors**: Analogous colors are hues that are adjacent to each other on the color wheel, such as red and orange, or blue and green. They produce a harmonious and cohesive effect, often used for a soothing or unified color scheme.

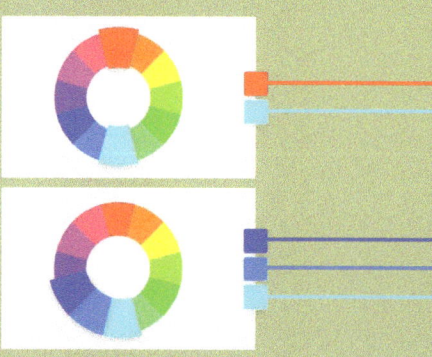

3. **Triadic Colors**: Triadic color schemes involve three colors that are evenly spaced around the color wheel, forming an equilateral triangle. For example, a triadic color scheme could consist of red, yellow, and blue. Triadic combinations offer a balanced and vibrant appearance.

4. **Split Complementary Colors**: Split complementary colors use a base color and the two colors adjacent to its complement. For instance, if the base color is red, the split complementary scheme would involve yellow-green and blue-green. This scheme maintains contrast while providing more variety than a complementary color pairing.

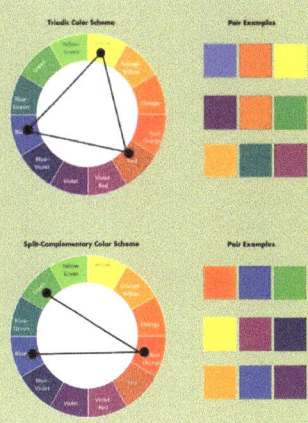

Color Temperature: Color temperature describes the perceived warmth or coolness of a color. It is often associated with lighting conditions and has a significant impact on the overall mood and atmosphere. Warm colors, such as red, orange, and yellow, are associated with energy, passion, and vibrancy. Cool colors, like blue, green, and violet, evoke calmness, serenity, and tranquility.

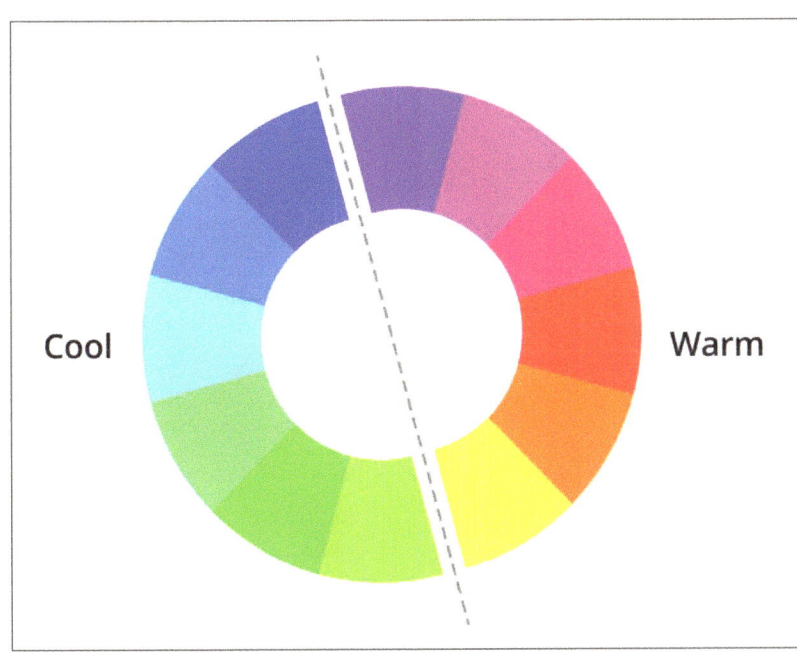

The color wheel can be categorized into warm and cool colors, each possessing a distinct color temperature. Color temperature refers to the perceived warmth or coolness of a color. When exploring the color combinations on a color wheel, one often encounters a harmonious blend of warm and cool colors. Color psychology suggests that different color temperatures evoke varied emotions and sensations. Warm colors, ranging from red to yellow, evoke feelings of coziness and energy, akin to the warmth of sunlight. On the other hand, cool colors encompass shades of blue, green, and purple, evoking a sense of serenity and solitude, reminiscent of the cooling qualities of water.

Color Mixing: Color mixing involves combining different hues to create new colors. In traditional art, primary colors are mixed to produce secondary and tertiary colors. In the subtractive color model (used in printing and painting), colors are created by subtracting wavelengths of light from white. Mixing all primary colors together results in black. In the additive color model (used in digital displays), colors are created by adding different wavelengths of light together. Mixing all primary colors in the additive model produces white.

Color in Design: Color theory plays a crucial role in various design disciplines, including graphic design, interior design, fashion design, and more. Understanding color harmonies, contrasts, and the psychology of colors helps designers create visually appealing and effective compositions. Color choices can influence brand identity, user experience, and visual hierarchy.

Color is important not just because it creates a mood in a room, but because it has the power to make a room feel larger, lighter, or cozier.

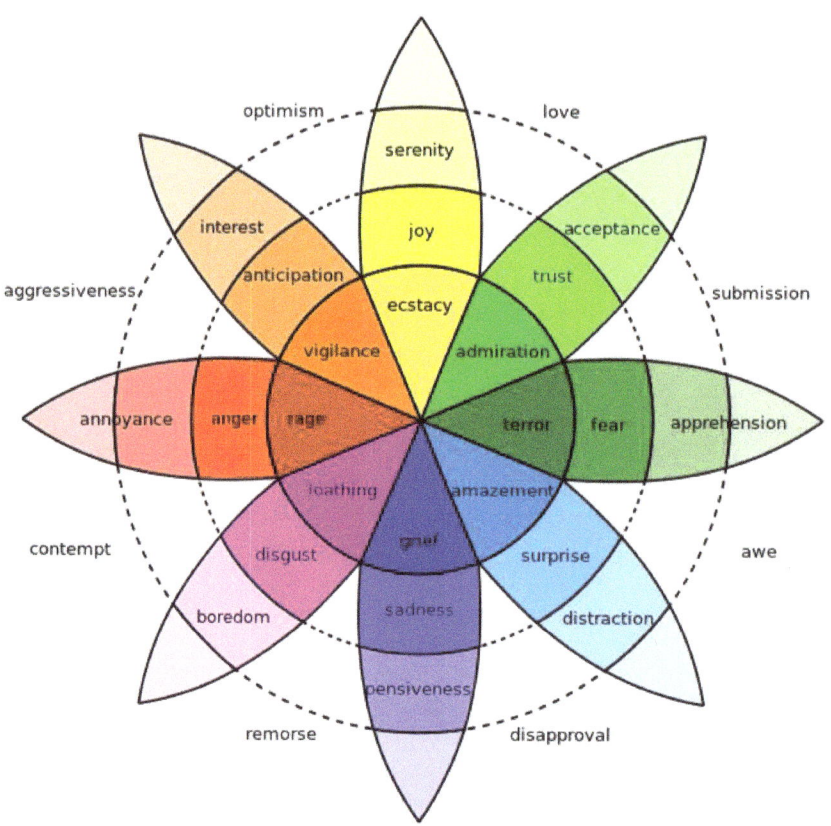

Color Psychology: Color psychology examines the emotional, cultural, and psychological effects of colors on individuals. Different colors can evoke specific feelings or associations. For example, red is often associated with passion and excitement, while blue is associated with tranquility and trust. Understanding color psychology can aid in effective communication and visual messaging.

Color psychology plays a major role in elevating or decimating the inhabitants disposition. Different colors tend to have different effects on the human mind. This is also to say that the perception and effects of these colors differ from person to person. While some people may find it beneficial to be surrounded by a bright, vibrant color scheme, others may find it to be palpitating. Their mood will also change based on the colors used in the room. This is why it is best to combine vibrant and dull colors to maintain a balance in the living space.

As mentioned, red has a motivating effect on the human brain. It makes people passionate about their life, their career, their loved ones, and their self. But too much red can also make them hyperventilate, lose their temper, or even become violent. Therefore, if you choose to add red to the walls of a room, then you must balance it out with more neutral colors in furniture. You can also use red in patterns, lines, or a piece of art and use neutral colors on the walls.

5. TEXTURE

Texture is the quality that encompasses the touch, appearance, and consistency of a surface. It refers to the tactile experience one has through sight, touch, and feel.

Texture holds significance beyond being a mere visual component that adds personality to interior design concepts. The selection of textures in living spaces directly reflects the homeowner's personality and interests. While visual textures, like captivating paintings by Caravaggio, can enhance the room's appeal, it is the subtle aspects of tangible texture that infuse a more authentic ambiance into the living space. By skillfully combining contrasting textures, a harmonious equilibrium can be achieved.

Texture is recognized through 2 perceptions :

Visual texture in interior design pertains to the surface quality that is visually perceived but may not be physically felt. It involves creating the illusion of texture through graphic details, giving the appearance of protrusions or variations on a flat surface.

On the other hand**, Physical or tactile texture** refers to the surface quality that can be both seen and felt. It involves the actual physical characteristics of the surface that are tangible to the senses.

While physical texture is more evident in architecture and sculpture, visual texture still plays a role. An excellent example is St. Peter's Cathedral in Rome, where a diverse selection of marble is used, providing a visually rich texture while the surfaces themselves remain hard and smooth to the touch.

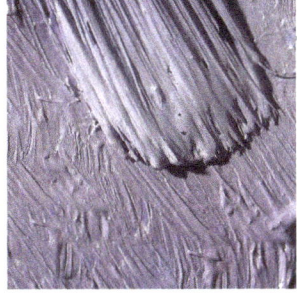

The left image creates the illusion of a substantial texture, despite actually being flat and smooth. On the other hand, the right image demonstrates the tangible and pronounced physical texture achieved through the application of thick oil paint.

Texture can be experienced as ;
- Rough or Smooth
- Wet or Dry
- Hard or Soft
- Shiny or Matte
- Slick or Sticky
- Slippery or Abrasive
- Coarse or Porous

Texture perception is not solely determined by individual surface characteristics. Surrounding textures, viewing distance, and lighting conditions also play a role. For example, rough surfaces appear more textured when placed next to smooth surfaces, viewed up close, and illuminated from the side. Mixing and contrasting textures enhances depth, visual appeal, and overall interest in room design.

Where & How Texture can be Placed in Interior Design?

- Architectural Components: If you're fortunate to have crown forming, seat rails, and plate roofs in the home, make them a point of convergence.
- Furniture: Wooden seats, glossy silk seats, and marble tabletops all carry a particular vibe to the space.
- Stylistic layout Items: Shadow Boxes, trinkets or even blossoms could be utilised.
- Floor and Wall Coverings: A painstakingly positioned carpet or even some designed divider configuration will carry huge loads of profundity to the room.
- Textile Materials: Use fabrics like slipcovers, toss cushions, and even covers to make the room stand out.

1. Use Texture with Light – Rough textures proffer a warm feeling as they reflect less light and hence make the object look more rustic and add weight. On the other side, smooth and shiny textures give a pristine and modern look as they reflect more light and offer a cool impression to the living space.

2. Use Texture with Scale – Scale is another component that you can use with texture. It will make the room look lighter and give the right kind of texture.

3. Use Texture with Color – Color and texture, when utilized properly, supplement and complete each other impeccably. Intensely finished items will ricochet less light, and, in that capacity, they give a dim shade to the color plan of the room.

6. PATTERN

Patterns can be incorporated in various ways, such as adorning walls, furniture pieces, or even through lighting arrangements. They are characterized by repeated elements or designs that create noticeable directional movements, adding a remarkable touch to your living space.

Patterns come in diverse shapes, forms, and sizes, allowing for endless possibilities. A pattern consists of recurring motifs, where lines, shapes, forms, or colors are replicated. These motifs can be organized in regular or irregular arrangements, further enhancing the visual interest and dynamic appeal of the pattern. By carefully selecting and implementing patterns, you can elevate the aesthetics of your home and create a captivating atmosphere.

Patterns are abundant in nature, art, and design, encompassing a wide array of intricate and repetitive arrangements that captivate our eyes and inspire creative expressions.

Jaguar skin — Cracked Earth

A pattern begins with a single element known as a motif, which serves as the foundation for repetition. The motif can be repeated and arranged in various configurations to generate different types of patterns. In the specific example provided, the motif is mirrored, occasionally twisting to the left or right. Furthermore, the colors undergo changes, resulting in different variations of the motif known as "buta." Despite these alterations, the essential motif remains recognizable throughout the various iterations of the pattern.

An irregular pattern is characterized by unpredictable changes in the motif or the manner in which it is repeated. It deviates from a regular, predictable sequence, resulting in a unique and dynamic visual arrangement.

In Parc Guell, Barcelona, Antoni Gaudi showcased his creativity by crafting benches using fragmented tiles arranged in an irregular pattern. While there is no defined repetition, we can discern motifs dispersed throughout, creating the illusion of repetition and adding a unique charm to the overall design.

Repeating shapes

Repeating objects

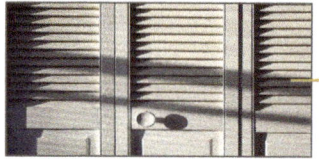

Repeating direction

Regular patterns exhibit a predictable repetition of motifs. The motif or motifs are repeated consistently, either in an identical manner each time or with regular variations that follow a specific pattern. This regularity in the arrangement creates a sense of order and harmony within the pattern.

Radial patterns, straight lines, and geometric shapes can be utilized to introduce depth and visual intrigue into your design concepts. Patterns can be incorporated into various materials, expanding the possibilities for creative implementation. Patterns, akin to texture, infuse a room with interest and vitality. They can be derived from elements such as area rugs, wallpapers, soft furnishings, and artwork. When selecting a pattern, it is crucial to ensure its style, be it floral, geometric, abstract, or another design, harmonizes with the overall scheme. Additionally, considering the scale of the pattern in relation to the space and the extent of its coverage is essential to prevent an overly busy or chaotic interior ambiance.

7. LIGHT

In interior design, the interplay between natural daylight and artificial illumination is crucial. Although the availability and quality of daylight may appear fixed, there are ways to control and enhance it. Drapery and window coverings can filter daylight, while techniques like hanging mirrors and borrowing light from adjacent rooms can boost it. Using window treatments that maximize the entry of light can also be effective in brightening up a space.

Light Influences Mood

- The psychological factors should not be overlooked.
- People need to change perspective in order to relax the eyes and mood.
- Lack of natural light makes people feel depressed and tensed.

Light Creates Atmosphere

- Many factors affect the atmosphere of a space, light being the most important.
- Interior designer needs to use light to create a different order and rhythm change the spatial effect gives different atmosphere.
- Natural light for the space is like the air for life, these two have symbiotic relationship.

Kelvin Color Temperature	2700K	3000K	3500K	4100K	5000K	6500K
Associated Effects and Moods	Ambiant Intimate Personal	Calm Warm	Friendly Inviting	Precise Clean Efficient	Daylight Vibrant	Daylight Alert
Appropriate Applications	Living/Family Rooms Commercial/ Hospitality	Living/Family Rooms Commercial/ Hospitality	Kitchen/Bath Light Commercial	Garage Commercial	Commercial Industrial Institutional	Commercial Industrial Institutional

The amount and type of lighting directly affect concentration, appetite, mood, and many other aspects of daily life.

Artificial lighting in interior design serves various purposes. Ambient or background lighting illuminates the overall space, while accent lighting highlights specific objects or features. Task lighting ensures functional areas like kitchens and offices are well-lit for specific tasks. Dimmer switches provide flexibility in creating different atmospheres, and the selection of light fixtures and fittings plays a significant role in enhancing the room's aesthetics. Together, these lighting elements contribute to the overall appearance and functionality of the space.

An example of how different structural elements can lead to light distribution is illustrated in the attached image. The strategic placement of windows, skylights, and architectural features allows natural light to permeate the space, creating a balance between lighter and darker areas. In addition to natural light, carefully positioned artificial lighting fixtures are used to further enhance the illumination and cater to the specific needs of the residents. By consciously allocating and combining both natural and artificial light sources, interior designers achieve a harmonious and visually appealing environment.

Efficiently allowing natural light in a space begins during the construction phase. From the outset, the interior designer must carefully consider the selection of window systems, including frames, protection grills, window shutter frame design, and the type of glass used to regulate the amount of light entering the space. There are various methods to bring in natural light, such as incorporating large windows, provisions for skylights, and implementing unique roofing solutions.

A prime example of optimizing natural light is the use of light shelves, which effectively distribute and reflect sunlight deeper into the room, enhancing the overall brightness and ambiance.

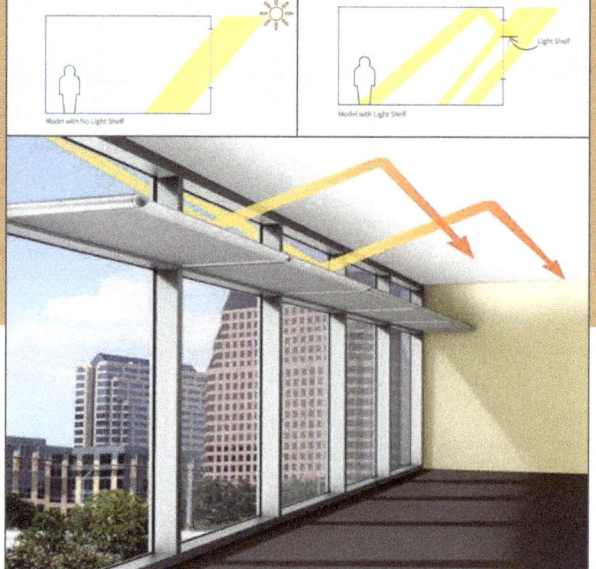

A light shelf is a horizontal surface that reflects daylight deep into a building. Bouncing' sunlight off a horizontal surface distributes it more evenly and deeply within a space, whereas direct sunlight can cause glare near an opening, whilst leaving dark areas further in.

- These design strategies aim to achieve an increase in illuminance, especially in non-daylit areas, to ensure adequate lighting throughout the space.
- They contribute to the improvement of uniformity in light distribution, creating a balanced and consistent lighting environment.
- By enhancing visual comfort, these measures promote a pleasant and visually satisfying experience for the occupants.
- The provision of sufficient shading helps control glare and maintain privacy, ensuring a comfortable and functional lighting atmosphere.

FUNDAMENTALS OF INTERIOR DESIGN

Interior design is the artistic process of crafting exquisite homes, where skilled designers breathe life into each space through their creative transformations. Creativity, deeply rooted in the human psyche, is a skill that thrives when pursued passionately, leading to success in creative industries like interior design. To embark on this rewarding journey, aspiring interior designers must acquire a range of fundamental skills. To simplify your decision-making process, we have curated a comprehensive list of these essential skills.

Fundamentals serve as the guiding principles for interior designers, forming the bedrock of creating effective and visually captivating designs for clients. They establish the foundation upon which interior design is built. This curated list of 8 fundamentals offers essential insights and knowledge, providing you with a solid understanding of the core aspects of interior design.

UNITY		All parts of an image are connected in a way so as to be seen as one. Sense of oneness / wholeness in an interior space
BALANCE		A feeling of balance results when the elements of design are arranged symmetrically or asymmetrically to create the impression of equality
RHYTHM		The use of recurring elements to direct the eye through the image. The way the elements are organized to lead the eye to the focal area
EMPHASIS		Special attention or importance given to one part of the content. Emphasis can be achieved through use of design elements or other principles
CONTRAST		The juxtaposition of different elements of design in order to highlight their differences and or create visual interest or a focal point
SCALE		The relationship between objects with respect to size, number, proportion & so on, including the relation between parts of a whole space
HARMONY		The arrangements of elements to give the viewer the feeling that all the parts of the piece form a coherent whole
DETAILS		Effort to bring perfection to achieve aesthetics & functionality

Unity takes center stage in home design, where every furniture piece, pattern, and decorative item should harmoniously complement one another. Achieving a cohesive and visually pleasing interior design relies on the unity and uniformity of all design elements. It is crucial to ensure a seamless flow in the use of patterns, colors, textures, and more, as any disruptions can create negative space within the overall design. Simply put, unity is the art of repeating elements to achieve a harmonious whole.

When unity and harmony come into play, the arrangement of furniture, color palette, and decorative elements blend together, creating a serene and cohesive ambiance in the room.

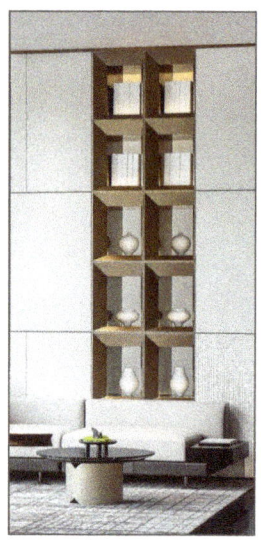

Balance. Achieving balance in interior design involves a careful interplay of various elements. It encompasses the distribution of visual weight, the arrangement of furniture, the selection of contrasting textures, and the establishment of focal points. The aim is to create a harmonious equilibrium where no single element dominates the overall composition. By skillfully balancing these elements, you can cultivate a space that exudes both visual appeal and a welcoming atmosphere. Balance serves as the linchpin of a well-composed and aesthetically pleasing interior design, ensuring a sense of coherence and unity throughout the space.

Rhythm, interior design embraces the concept of rhythm. Just as everything in the universe has a vibration, you can harness these vibrations to create a rhythmic feel in your design. Colors, textures, and shapes play a pivotal role in adding character to your home. To infuse rhythm, consider employing techniques like Progression, Alteration, or repetition. For example, adorn your living room walls with captivating radial patterns. Complement this with singular radial accent lighting suspended from the ceiling, repeating the pattern in a striking manner. Additionally, repeated colors or shapes can also be used to establish a rhythmic flow within your design. By incorporating these elements, you'll create a visually engaging space with a sense of rhythm that resonates throughout.

Emphasis In interior design, there are instances when clients desire to showcase their cherished possessions. As a designer, it's your task to create an arrangement that highlights these special objects, capturing the attention of anyone who enters the room. Whether it's a curated artwork, a personally crafted DIY piece, or a standout furniture item, emphasis is key. By strategically placing the object and incorporating contrasting designs and patterns, you can ensure it becomes the focal point of the overall design scheme. Let the beauty and impact of the object shine by designing the surrounding space to enhance its presence.

Contrast. While it is pivotal to create a flow in interior design, decorators sometimes overlook the importance of contrast. It is obviously necessary to follow a color scheme and definitive space planning. But if you keep a single color or just variations on a theme, then the entire design will end up looking bland. That is where contrast comes into the picture. You must always use colors and patterns that balance each other out but also have a contrasting effect so your design ideas aren't muted. Contrast can be implemented by choosing striking pieces of artwork, or decorations, or even lighting.

Scale and Proportion are vital principles in interior design, ensuring a harmonious and visually pleasing space. By carefully considering the size and dimensions of furniture and decor, as well as their arrangement and distribution, designers achieve the right balance and proportion. A well-scaled design creates a sense of cohesion and balance, avoiding objects that feel too large or too small for the space. The proper application of Scale and Proportion enhances the visual appeal and functionality of an interior, resulting in a well-designed and balanced environment.

Harmony is not just for singing anymore. Defined as a pleasant combination of things, music, or people, harmony is at its core sameness, one thing belonging with another. It's a feeling. It also happens to be a crucial tool to wield for a successful interior design.

Harmony is a crucial principle in interior design, responsible for creating a sense of unity and cohesion within a space. It is the art of bringing together various elements, such as furniture, decor, colors, and textures, in a way that they complement and enhance each other. When harmony is achieved, there is a seamless flow and balance throughout the room, creating a visually pleasing and inviting atmosphere. It is not about strict matching, but rather finding a common thread that ties everything together. A harmonious interior design evokes a feeling of completeness and harmony, where every piece has its place and contributes to the overall aesthetic. By carefully considering the relationship between different elements, designers can achieve a harmonious balance that elevates the overall look and feel of the space.

Attention to **Detail** is crucial in interior design as it is the key to achieving a well-designed and polished space. From the floor plan and space planning to the smallest elements, such as bedding patterns, curtains, doorknobs, and switchboards, every detail plays a significant role in tying the place together harmoniously. These details may seem small individually, but when combined thoughtfully, they contribute to the overall aesthetic and completeness of a room. Neglecting the importance of details can result in a space that feels haphazard and incomplete. By paying close attention to these finer points, you can elevate the look of a room and create a finished design that exudes sophistication and unity. The intricate details serve as the final touch, adding significance and enhancing the overall visual impact. So, embrace the power of details in interior design and unlock the potential to transform your space into a beautifully composed and fully realized environment.

Interior design details cover various aspects such as flooring, lighting, furniture accents, accessories, wall treatments, pillows, plants, window treatments, and architectural trim. These elements play a significant role in enhancing the overall design and adding character to the space.

SPECTRUM OF INTERIOR DESIGN STYLES

There exist numerous categories of interior design, continually evolving over time. While some styles may be temporary trends, others are enduring classics that withstand the passage of time. Each style incorporates unique furnishings, decorations, lighting, and accessories that contribute to its distinctive appearance. By familiarizing yourself with some of the most popular design styles, you can gain a deeper understanding of your own preferences and effectively meet the preferences of your clients.

Traditional Interior Design Style

When it comes to categorizing various types of interior design, one prominent style that stands out is traditional interior design. In traditional interiors, furniture like tables and chairs is crafted from dark wood and showcases intricate detailing. This design approach finds its roots in 18th and 19th Century England and France, which explains the prevalent use of luxurious textiles such as silk, velvet, and linen. These opulent fabrics can be found adorning upholstery and window treatments throughout traditional spaces. Moreover, traditional design embraces a diverse range of patterns, including damask, florals, stripes, and plaids. Additionally, traditional homes often incorporate a touch of glamour through the inclusion of crystal chandeliers.

Traditional interiors are significantly influenced by European décor. These timeless design schemes often feature a predominantly neutral color palette, with occasional vibrant accents introduced through oil paintings or floral arrangements. One of the essential aspects of traditional design is maintaining consistency, which is why it is common to encounter matching furniture sets in these spaces.

Transitional Interior Design Style

Transitional design is currently one of the most sought-after styles in the design industry. It represents a harmonious balance between traditional and contemporary aesthetics, often referred to as the "happy medium" of interior design. For those who find traditional design too formal and contemporary design too unconventional, transitional design offers an ideal solution. It combines the timeless elegance of traditional elements with the clean lines and modern textiles of contemporary design. In transitional interiors, the focus is on keeping accessories to a minimum, allowing the furniture and textiles to take center stage. Area rugs, throw pillows, and blankets can be strategically utilized to add stylish accents to the space.

One of the most visually appealing features of the transitional design style is the skillful blend of masculine and feminine elements. This fusion is often achieved through the incorporation of curved furniture and a diverse range of finishes, such as wood, rattan, steel, and lacquer. The combination of these contrasting styles results in an intriguing and inviting home design, particularly well-suited for entryways and various rooms throughout the house.

Contemporary Interior Design Style

Contemporary interior design embodies a sleek and minimalist aesthetic, characterized by its clean and uncluttered spaces. It incorporates various features such as intricate moldings on walls and windows, as well as open layouts, to create a distinctive and captivating environment. Typical contemporary furniture showcases exposed legs and clean lines, contributing to a sense of lightness and airiness. Materials like metal and glass are commonly used due to their light-reflecting properties. Contemporary design represents the ultimate fusion of different home décor styles. Neutral color palettes are prevalent in contemporary interiors, often accompanied by textured fabrics to add visual interest. This combination results in the creation of a luxurious and modern interior.

Modern Interior Design Style

The distinction between modern and contemporary lies in their temporal characteristics, although they do share several similarities. When examining an interior, certain prominent indications can help identify it as modern. Modern design is associated with a specific historical period, whereas contemporary design is continuously evolving. Modern interior design emerged during the early to mid-20th century and was shaped by a blend of Scandinavian, mid-century modern, and post-modern influences, ultimately shaping our current understanding of modern design.

In terms of furniture, modern interiors exhibit clean lines and feature smooth, sleek surfaces. Designers often favor materials such as metal, chrome, and glass. However, modern interiors adopt a minimalist approach to decor, eschewing clutter and prioritizing art as the primary decorative element. It is common to encounter vibrant, bold accents in both artwork and furniture within predominantly neutral spaces.

In terms of furniture, modern interiors exhibit clean lines and feature smooth, sleek surfaces. Designers often favor materials such as metal, chrome, and glass. However, modern interiors adopt a minimalist approach to decor, eschewing clutter and prioritizing art as the primary decorative element. It is common to encounter vibrant, bold accents in both artwork and furniture within predominantly neutral spaces.

Eclectic Interior Design Style

Eclectic interior design is characterized by carefully selected pieces that create a culturally rich and vibrant atmosphere. It strikes a balance between a layered aesthetic and avoiding overwhelming clutter. By using a neutral color palette with a few accent colors, an eclectic space exudes a worldly vibe. This style seamlessly blends old and new elements, combining color and texture harmoniously.

Minimalist Interior Design Style

Minimalist interiors typically embrace a neutral color scheme, but primary colors can be incorporated as accent colors for added visual interest. Patterns are generally avoided, while texture becomes a crucial element in creating depth and tactile appeal. The "less is more" philosophy is central to minimalist design, with functional furniture taking precedence as the essential design element. Storage is also a key consideration in minimalist interior design, leading to innovative solutions where furniture doubles as hidden storage. For instance, coffee tables that can be lifted to reveal concealed storage compartments exemplify the creative approaches employed in minimalist interiors.

Contemporary design and minimalist design share many qualities, including uncomplicated forms, clean lines, and simple finishes. However, the minimalist decorating style draws inspiration from Japanese design principles and focuses on the concept of "less is more." It emphasizes the idea of decluttering and reducing elements to their essential forms. In contrast, contemporary design encompasses a broader range of influences and allows for more creative expression while still maintaining a clean and uncluttered aesthetic. Nonetheless, both styles appreciate the beauty of empty space and understand its importance in creating a sense of calm and tranquility within a space.

Hollywood Glam Interior Design Style

Hollywood glam, an upcoming decorating style for 2023, has been a cherished trend primarily in California since the mid-twentieth century, tracing its roots back to Hollywood's golden age in the 1930s. It combines elements of art deco and mid-century modern to create a chic and glamorous interior design style that demands attention. High contrast color schemes are favored, with popular combinations including hot pink and green, as well as classic black and white. Opulent chandeliers paired with high gloss or mirrored furniture are often featured, contributing to a luxurious and glamorous ambiance.

This style exudes both sensuality and sophistication, making it an alluring choice for those seeking an elevated and refined interior design aesthetic.

Mid-Century Modern Interior Design Style

Mid-century modern homes are renowned for their effortless and uninterrupted flow, as they strongly emphasize indoor-outdoor living. To enhance the connection with nature, sliding doors and picture windows are often left uncovered, allowing natural light and scenery to take center stage. Rich and luxurious woods like teak, rosewood, and walnut are frequently utilized in mid-century modern design. In terms of color, accents of mustard yellow, chartreuse, or avocado are incorporated to provide vibrant pops of color amidst the overall scheme.

The current revival of mid-century modern design in the contemporary design industry has made this popular interior style more accessible and attainable than ever before.

Mid-century interiors have proven to be a timeless classic that remains relevant across decades. Originating in the 1950s and '60s in post-war America, mid-century design emerged as a means for the design industry to break away from traditional conventions and embrace the modern era. Remarkably, many iconic mid-century modern furniture pieces from that time are still widely used in contemporary homes, attesting to the enduring appeal of this style. Keep a lookout for modern versions of renowned furniture pieces like the Eames lounge chair, the egg chair, or the wishbone chair, as they continue to make a statement in interior design today.

Bohemian Interior Design Style

Bohemian interiors, much like mid-century style, are experiencing a surge in popularity. With numerous retailers embracing the boho trend, now is the perfect time to embrace your bohemian side. Bohemian design is characterized by a free-spirited aesthetic that blends diverse cultures and artistic expressions to create an eclectic style that defies conventions. The boho atmosphere exudes a laid-back vibe and often emphasizes the presence of nature. It is common to encounter bold patterns and vibrant colors in furniture and accents, adding a lively and energetic touch to the space. Embracing the bohemian style allows for a creative and unconventional approach to interior design.

Stepping into a home adorned with a bohemian design style immediately immerses you in a rich tapestry of diverse cultures. Trinkets and treasures from various travels are proudly displayed, creating an ambiance that feels nomadic and well-traveled.

In contrast to many other design styles, bohemian design embraces a sense of organic disorder. Mixing patterns, colors, and textures is not only accepted but actively encouraged. Moreover, there is a growing trend of modern boho style, where elements like animal hides, metallic accents, and rich wood are incorporated to add a contemporary touch to this eclectic aesthetic. One of the delightful aspects of bohemian style is its ability to repurpose and use items in unconventional ways. For instance, hanging a vintage rug on the wall can offer a fresh and unique take on artwork, enhancing the charm and individuality of the living room.

Modern Farmhouse Interior Design Style

Modern farmhouse interiors retain many of the classic elements of traditional farmhouse design while embracing a simplified and clean aesthetic. The timeless appeal of shiplap and the charm of barn doors continue to be prominent features in modern farmhouse spaces. However, modern updates bring a fresh twist to this style, such as wide plank floors, open concept living areas, and sleek lighting fixtures. These elements serve as common identifiers of the modern farmhouse decorating style, blending the warmth and rusticity of traditional farmhouses with contemporary design elements for a stylish and inviting home.

Farmhouse interiors mix metals for a contrasting effect and prioritize a strong connection to nature. Raw wood elements and greenery are essential in every room. Color palettes lean towards neutrals, but pops of deep navy, sage green, or burnt orange can be added for a touch of vibrancy.

Shabby Chic Interior Design Style

Shabby chic, a style with its roots in the 18th century, has evolved into the vintage-loving aesthetic we see today. At the heart of shabby chic design is vintage furniture, often passed down through generations, each adding their own unique touch. This design style shares a soft and feminine feel with its design counterpart, French country.

In the shabby chic interior design style, furniture is often adorned with painted or distressed finishes, adding a touch of rustic charm. The color palettes used are typically pale and complemented by delicate floral patterns. Whitewashed floors and walls further enhance the light and airy aesthetic. One of the captivating aspects of shabby chic interiors is the beautiful contrast between the distressed and rustic elements and the inclusion of glamorous accents, such as crystal chandeliers. This combination creates an elegant and cozy atmosphere that exudes a unique charm.

Coastal Interior Design Style

The coastal interior design style is not exclusive to beachfront living; it can be appreciated anywhere. Distinct from nautical décor, coastal decorating has its own unique charm. Coastal spaces draw inspiration from their natural surroundings, evident in their color palette and choice of materials. Neutrals, particularly whites and beiges, mimic the sandy shores, while pops of blues evoke the calming ocean waves and sunny skies. Brightness and airiness are essential in coastal homes, creating a seamless connection between indoors and outdoors. As a result, window treatments are kept minimal, often featuring light sheer fabrics that gently sway in the breeze, capturing the coastal vibe.

The coastal interior design style goes beyond cliché elements like anchors and seashells. Instead, it incorporates subtle yet effective elements to evoke the coastal ambiance. Blue glass vases, striped wallpaper, and abstract paintings are used to capture the coastal feeling. In terms of furniture, coastal interiors prioritize a comfortable and lived-in aesthetic. Painted and distressed furniture, along with the pairing of wicker or jute materials, create a harmonious combination. Emphasizing the connection to nature, indoor plants are a must-have in coastal design, adding a touch of freshness and greenery to the space.

Industrial Interior Design Style

Industrial interior design, although considered trendy by some, has its roots in the past. With the closure of factories in Western Europe at the end of the second industrial revolution, numerous large vacant buildings were left behind. As the population increased, people began transforming these industrial areas into residential neighborhoods, giving rise to the concept of industrial interior design.

The industrial interior design style embraces the aesthetic appeal of exposed pipes and beams, showcasing the raw elements of a space. Materials such as brick and concrete are commonly used to infuse character into the design. Descriptors like "soft" or "intimate" are not typically associated with this style, as it leans towards a more masculine aesthetic. However, ample texture is incorporated to add depth and visual interest. Oversized artwork and cozy textiles serve as perfect additions to soften the industrial vibe. Furniture is often chosen in raw or unfinished forms, and antique pieces may be paired to create a unique juxtaposition of old and new elements.

Southwestern Interior Design Style

The southwestern style, which has evolved over time, continues to undergo changes as years go by. Southwestern interiors draw inspiration from the gentle curves of adobe houses, Spanish textiles, ironwork, and the surrounding nature. The color palette used reflects the hues found in the American desert, with favorites among designers including rust, terracotta, and cactus green. Furniture in southwestern interiors tends to have a heavier appearance, often featuring thick legs and bulky finishes. Texture plays a vital role in southwestern interior design, with leather and suede being popular choices for upholstery materials, adding depth and tactile appeal to the space.

Rustic Interior Design Style

Rustic interior design is characterized by several key features that define its aesthetic. Natural materials, industrial elements, and farmhouse charm are prevalent in this style. Inspired by the Romantic movement, rustic design emphasizes the simplicity and inherent beauty of nature. In rustic interiors, it is common to find living room designs centered around a prominent fireplace, which serves as a focal point of the space and adds to the cozy ambiance.

In rustic interior design, the use of wood is complemented by the addition of cowhides and sheepskin, creating a warm and cozy atmosphere. Fabrics in rustic interiors tend to have subdued patterns, allowing texture to take center stage. Unexpected elements, such as an industrial pendant light, are incorporated to enhance the overall sophistication of the rustic design style. These elements work together to create a harmonious and inviting space that embraces the rustic charm while adding a touch of refinement.

Scandinavian Interior Design Style

Scandinavian design is known for its distinctive and easily recognizable characteristics. It embodies a light, airy, and organic aesthetic. In Scandinavian interiors, wood is often featured in an ashy color tone, contributing to the overall natural feel. These spaces exude a sense of relaxation and warmth, creating an inviting atmosphere. Key elements of Scandinavian design include white walls, large mirrors, and the use of cozy textiles. Embracing the Danish concept of hygge, Scandinavian spaces incorporate layered fabrics, glass furniture, clean lines, and a variety of textures to achieve a perfect balance of comfort and style.

Art Deco Interior Design Style

The iconic design style that emerged in the early twentieth century originally originated in France and later spread to the United States during the period from the 1910s to the 1940s.

The art deco design style drew significant inspiration from the industrial revolution, resulting in the prevalent use of metal as a popular material during that era. Art deco pieces are often characterized by pointed edges and jagged corners, making them easily identifiable. The style commonly featured oversized furniture, including armories and sofas. Presently, Florida, particularly Miami Beach, stands out as a prime destination to witness the art deco interior design style embraced and find inspiration.

Mediterranean Interior Design Style

Mediterranean design, originating from countries bordering the Mediterranean Sea such as Spain, Greece, and Italy, exudes a culturally rich aesthetic. This style is characterized by architectural elements like arches, columns, and interior balconies, reminiscent of the typical architecture found in those regions. Furniture in Mediterranean design showcases rich wood tones and ornate features, adding to its distinctive charm.

Mediterranean design embraces color palettes inspired by the sea and sky, featuring shades of blue alongside warm hues like terracotta and yellow. The goal is to capture the essence of the Mediterranean landscape. Large picture windows are commonly used to connect the interior with the outdoors, often adorned with minimal sheer draperies to maximize natural light. This design approach creates a bright and airy atmosphere in Mediterranean-inspired spaces.

Asian Zen Interior Design Style

Asian Zen interiors draw inspiration from contemporary design principles, emphasizing clean lines, intriguing shapes, and a tranquil ambiance. Nature plays a crucial role in creating the ultimate Zen space, with elements that evoke a sense of calm and serenity. This can be achieved through the use of natural materials like bamboo, stone, and wood, as well as incorporating indoor plants and water features. The color palette tends to be subdued and earthy, with shades of white, beige, gray, and muted greens. Overall, Asian Zen interiors strive to create a harmonious and peaceful environment for relaxation and meditation.

Asian interiors embrace asymmetry and favor circular shapes over squares, creating a sense of balance and harmony. Curtain walls or door panels are frequently used to divide larger spaces and provide a sense of privacy while maintaining an open feel. The color palette draws inspiration exclusively from nature, incorporating soothing tones such as soft greens, gentle blues, earthy browns, and subtle neutrals. This color scheme helps to enhance the serene and calm atmosphere that is characteristic of Asian interior design.

SUSTAINABLE HOME DESIGN

In recent times, the concept of sustainability has gained significant popularity in the realm of building and interior design. This surge in interest can be attributed to the growing recognition of the urgent need for environmental conservation. As a result, many homeowners and developers have embraced sustainable interior design as a means to mitigate their impact on the environment. Sustainable design, in essence, refers to an environmentally-conscious approach to interior design, where the principles of sustainability are integrated into every aspect of the design process.

This involves a careful assessment and selection of materials and products, taking into consideration their ecological interaction with residents, in order to contribute to a more sustainable future. Sustainable design adopts a holistic approach that encompasses the deliberate use of renewable and recycled materials, as well as the implementation of energy-conserving building systems and appliances. Moreover, it prioritizes design choices that foster the healthiest possible environment for occupants. By adopting sustainable design principles, not only can designers reduce the environmental impact of their projects, but they can also achieve cost savings in operational expenses. Furthermore, sustainable interiors have the potential to enhance productivity and overall well-being of occupants. This comprehensive approach to interior design paves the way for a more sustainable future while creating spaces that promote a harmonious coexistence between humans and nature.

Interior Design's Impact on Energy Consumption and Environmental Change

Energy consumption is a major contributor to environmental change, with buildings being responsible for a significant portion of greenhouse gas emissions resulting from energy usage. However, architects and interior designers play a crucial role in improving a building's energy efficiency and reducing its environmental impact. When it comes to energy efficiency, interior designers have influence over heating and lighting systems, among other factors. High-quality windows with good insulation are essential, as a significant amount of heat can escape through windows. Properly chosen curtains and drapes can help keep out cold air and excessive heat from the sun. By strategically opening and closing window coverings, such as blinds or shades, one can control the building's temperature in an energy-efficient manner. Additionally, carpets serve as excellent thermal insulators, retaining up to 10% of a room's heat.

Color selection also plays a role in energy conservation. Lighter colors reflect more natural light, reducing the need for artificial lighting. Conversely, rooms with darker walls and furnishings require more artificial lighting. Incorporating reflective surfaces, such as mirrors or metallic finishes, can help increase the amount of natural light in a room, thereby decreasing reliance on artificial lighting.

"Green gadgets" or home automation systems offer convenient solutions for energy control. For instance, remotely controlling heating and lighting systems can optimize energy usage. Home automated lighting systems, including dimmers, are particularly useful in areas like dining and living rooms, where adjustable lighting output is desirable. These technologies enable residents and occupants to save energy more efficiently and economically.

By employing these interior design strategies, architects and designers can contribute to reducing a building's energy consumption and carbon footprint. Creating energy-efficient spaces not only benefits the environment but also promotes sustainable living for the occupants.

> Designing a sustainable home involves a meticulous focus on detail and a comprehensive understanding of green practices. It goes beyond merely recognizing the concept of being "green" and requires a commitment to reducing the carbon footprint of your home. By adopting sustainable practices, you not only contribute to the well-being of the planet but also enjoy long-term benefits such as energy savings and reduced maintenance expenses.

Designing a sustainable home requires a meticulous focus on detail and a deep understanding of environmentally friendly practices. It goes beyond a superficial appreciation of the "green" concept and requires a genuine commitment to reducing the carbon footprint of your residence. By embracing sustainable practices, you actively contribute to the well-being of the planet while also enjoying long-term benefits, including enhanced energy efficiency and reduced maintenance expenses.

Constructing a sustainable home mandates a comprehensive approach that encompasses a range of eco-conscious practices. It involves a profound understanding of sustainability principles and their integration into every facet of your home's design and operations. By incorporating these principles, you not only make a positive impact on the environment but also benefit from financial savings and the creation of a more robust and comfortable living environment.

Let's explore some of the aspects that designers and architects can take into consideration when designing a residential space.

1. Durability and Flexibility in Design

When interior designers plan spaces, it is important to consider the lifespan of the materials used, especially for elements that endure significant wear and tear. The aim should be to create timeless spaces that avoid unnecessary disposal of materials and products. As individuals evolve and their preferences change, they desire spaces that can grow and adapt with them, reflecting their transformations. Therefore, interior designers should prioritize the flexibility of spaces, ensuring they can accommodate the changing needs of their users. To achieve longevity, several key principles should be considered. Designing flexible spaces is crucial, allowing for easy modifications and adjustments. Opting for timeless design choices rather than following passing trends, and emphasizing quality over quantity are also important considerations. Additionally, prioritizing simplicity and functionality over excessive embellishments contributes to the longevity of a design. Incorporating innovative elements adds further options for flexible design. For example, utilizing walls that can be modified or adjusted, along with modular furniture suitable for modern workplaces (as remote work becomes more prevalent), can greatly enhance adaptability. Modular flooring systems that allow personalization are another way to incorporate flexibility. Investing in sturdy, durable, and easy-to-clean or replace elements not only saves money but also minimizes the need for frequent renovations. Furthermore, such choices facilitate ease of maintenance, providing an additional benefit. By considering the lifespan of materials, designing for flexibility, and investing in durable and adaptable elements, interior designers can create timeless spaces that evolve with their users while minimizing waste and promoting sustainability.

2. Water-efficient Design :

Water conservation is a crucial aspect of sustainability in interior design, especially considering the widespread water shortage crisis prevalent today. To promote water efficiency, sustainable interior design incorporates various strategies, such as the implementation of built-in water recycling systems and the utilization of tools and technologies to prevent water wastage.

One effective approach is the installation of rainwater storage systems, which collect and recycle accumulated rainwater for household use. This reduces reliance on traditional water sources and helps conserve precious freshwater resources. Additionally, implementing a water-use feedback system can raise awareness and encourage conscious water consumption by providing real-time feedback on water usage to residents.

Furthermore, incorporating water-saving features such as no-leak tap systems, drip irrigation systems, pressure regulating devices, and high-efficiency nozzles contributes to reducing water consumption. Installing low-flow toilets and washrooms also plays a significant role, potentially saving up to 50% of daily water usage.

By integrating these water conservation measures into sustainable interior design, individuals can make a meaningful impact in mitigating the water shortage crisis and promoting a more environmentally responsible lifestyle.

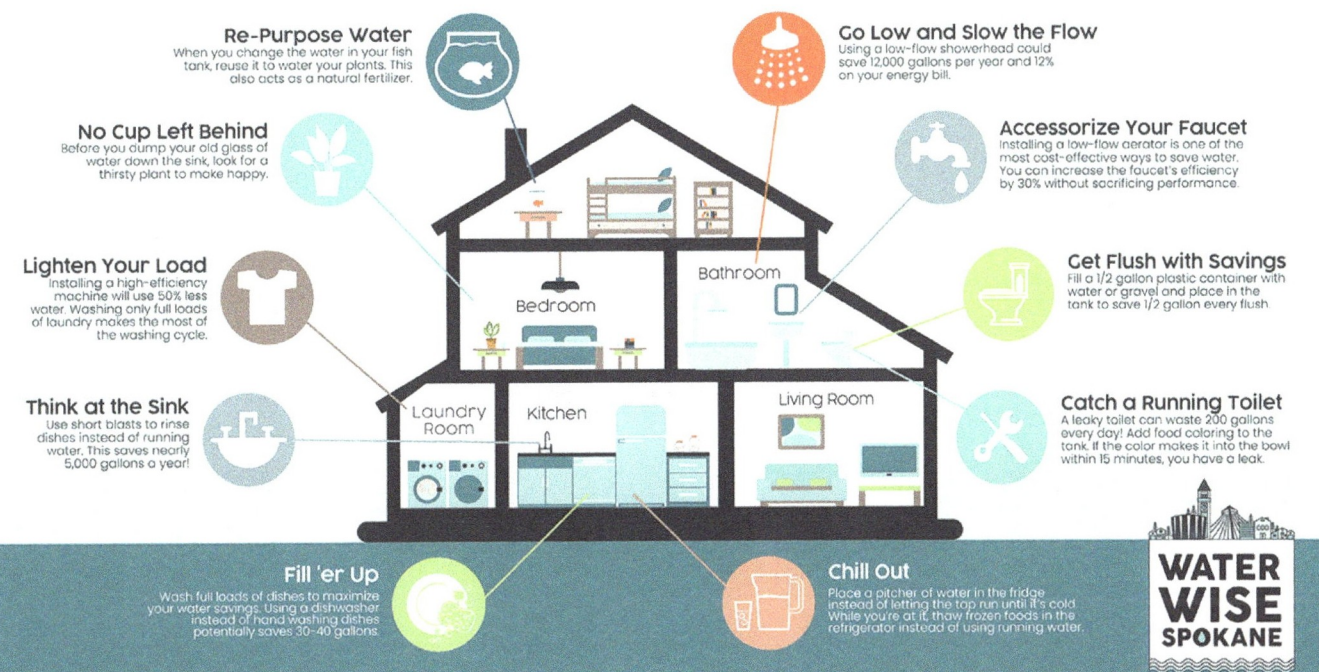

Diagram courtesy : spokanecity.org

3. Design for longevity and flexibility

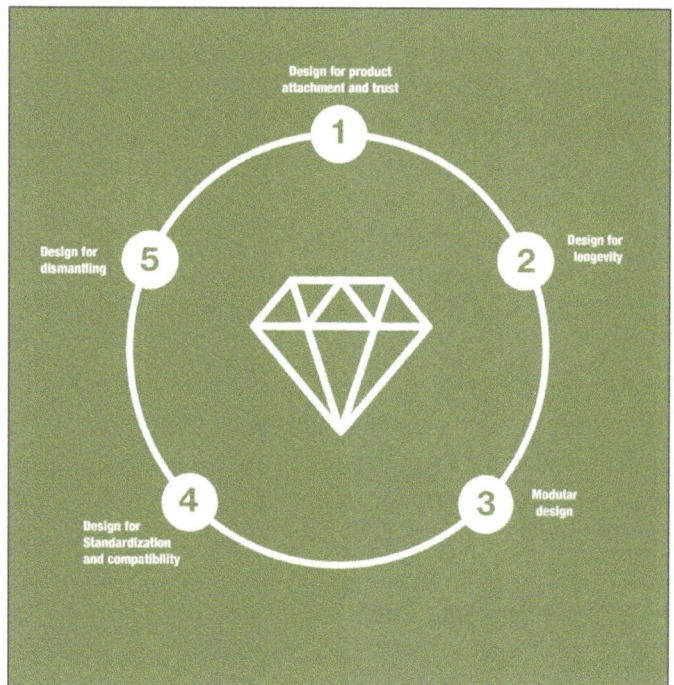

To minimize the frequent discarding of materials and products, interior designers should prioritize considering the lifespan of the materials they choose, particularly for elements that endure significant wear and tear, such as flooring. The ultimate goal is to design spaces that are durable, timeless, and resist the temptation of complete redesigns every few years. Achieving timelessness involves making choices that prioritize quality over quantity, classics over trends, and simplicity and functionality over excessive embellishments.

However, it's important to acknowledge that people evolve and change over time, and they desire their surrounding spaces to evolve with them and reflect those changes. In anticipation of this, interior designers should take into account the flexibility of spaces and how well they can be adapted to accommodate the changing needs of the occupants.

Designing flexible spaces is a key factor in promoting longevity. By incorporating elements that can be easily replaced or adapted within a room, there is no need for extensive demolition or complete renovations. Innovative solutions have provided numerous options for flexible design. For example, walls that can be modified allow for the creation of additional spaces as children grow and require their own rooms. Adjustable and mobile furniture can be reconfigured to suit the flexible demands of the modern workplace. Modular flooring systems enable personalization and simple replacement of individual pieces, ensuring easy maintenance and updates.

By embracing these flexible design concepts and utilizing innovative solutions, interior designers can create spaces that adapt to the changing needs of occupants, thereby extending the lifespan of the design. This approach not only reduces waste and unnecessary renovations but also promotes sustainability and cost-effectiveness.

4. Design for waste reduction

Interior designers hold significant power and responsibility in waste reduction and sustainable practices. With limited and precious resources on our planet, the mindset of discarding products as soon as they go out of style and replacing them with trendy alternatives is no longer justifiable. Fortunately, the design industry is increasingly recognizing the importance of sustainable thinking and embracing trends such as recycling, upcycling, and repurposing. Rather than disposing of functional yet "old-fashioned" objects, designers can unleash their creativity to give them a new lease on life.

Another effective strategy for interior designers to reduce resource depletion and divert waste from landfills is to choose synthetic materials that are made from recycled waste or can be renewed and recycled at the end of their life cycle. This cradle-to-cradle approach ensures that waste becomes a raw material for new products, forming a circular loop of manufacturing that minimizes or even eliminates waste altogether.

By embracing sustainable practices, interior designers actively contribute to the conservation of resources and the reduction of waste. Through recycling, upcycling, and repurposing, they can breathe new life into existing objects and materials. Additionally, by opting for synthetic materials that are environmentally friendly and can be recycled, they foster a circular economy that minimizes the extraction of new resources.

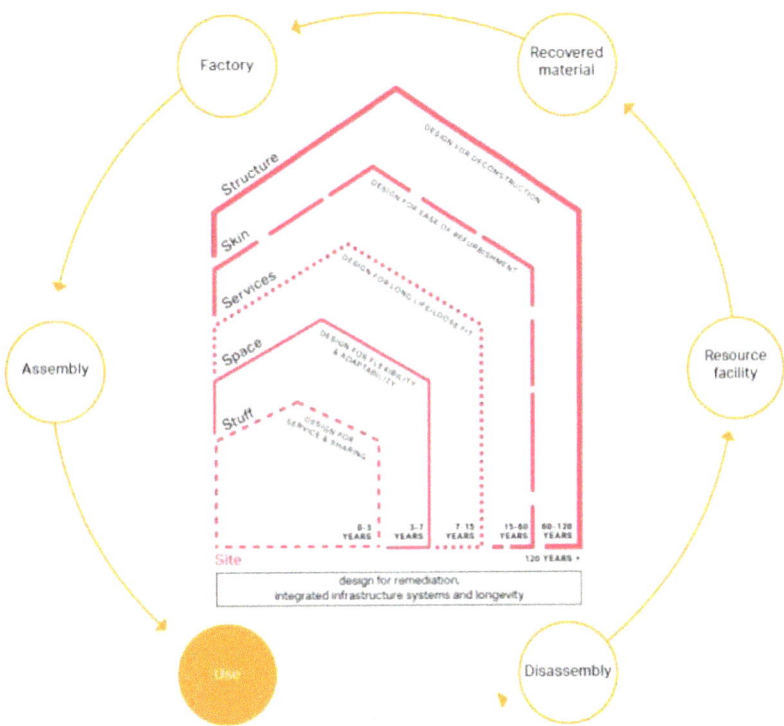

Illustration 2 - 'Building in layers diagram', diagram courtesy of Useful Projects

The power of interior designers in waste reduction lies not only in their material choices but also in their ability to inspire and educate clients and the wider community about sustainable design practices. By leading by example and promoting sustainable trends, interior designers can drive positive change in the industry and contribute to a more sustainable future for our planet.

5. Eco-Conscious Interior Styling

If you are a design professional who prioritizes eco-consciousness, here are some design aesthetics that not only create visually appealing interiors but also offer environmental benefits:

- Green Country Look: Embrace a rustic style that incorporates eco-friendly materials. Utilize reclaimed wood flooring sourced from recyclable materials, which adds a touch of beauty to the space. Instead of purchasing new items, consider sourcing furniture and decor from antique stores or flea markets. By repurposing old items, you contribute to a greener planet by avoiding the harmful manufacturing processes involved in creating new products. Transform your home into a unique and sustainable space with a wide range of items suitable for a rustic interior.

- Minimal Interiors: Adopting the principle of "Less is More," you can create interiors that are both ergonomic and environmentally conscious. Minimalism focuses on decluttering, organizing, and simplifying, resulting in fewer possessions and reduced manufacturing, which minimizes the negative impact on the environment. Scandinavian design is renowned for its minimalist approach, emphasizing the use of earthy, organic materials. By adhering to the bare essentials, you can limit the number of items in your home that rely on non-renewable resources. Opt for natural materials such as organic cotton, linen, and hemp for bedding and upholstery, and consider using small area rugs made from sustainable jute fibers. Furthermore, replacing electricity-based heating gadgets with biofuel-powered fireplaces during colder months can provide a more natural and sustainable heating source.

By incorporating these design aesthetics into your projects, you can create visually appealing interiors while prioritizing sustainability and minimizing the environmental footprint.

Kitchen by **PaperStone** Products : Crafted using sustainable materials

With the advancements in technology and manufacturing processes, sustainability no longer requires compromising the style or aesthetic value of interior design. Today, cork and bamboo floors are available in a variety of colors and textures, utilizing non-toxic dyes and materials. As a result, these eco-friendly flooring options are not only visually impressive like conventional wooden floors but also offer enhanced durability while significantly reducing their environmental impact.

Furthermore, numerous brands are actively engaged in developing a diverse range of recycled and environmentally conscious materials that are both stylish and sustainable. An excellent example is the emergence of PaperStone products, which are crafted from 100% post-consumer recycled paper and a non-petroleum resin. These innovative materials are gradually replacing conventional alternatives and are being used to create exquisite countertops, sinks, decorative accessories, and more, adding a touch of elegance to eco-friendly interior design.

6. Sustainable Furniture:

Furniture plays a crucial role in interior design, greatly influencing both the aesthetics and functionality of a home. To create an eco-friendly interior, it is essential to prioritize furniture made from natural wood or other organic and sustainable materials. These materials can include recycled or repurposed elements that have been transformed into new furniture pieces. While fast-growing bamboo has gained popularity as a sustainable furniture material, there are other excellent choices such as recycled metal and plastic, rattan, cork, and repurposed industrial waste.

The interior design of a home holds significant importance in shaping its most intimate spaces. By embracing sustainability and prioritizing efficiency, we can not only enhance convenience and comfort but also make a positive impact on the future. This approach ensures a healthy and responsible lifestyle, which is currently a pressing need in today's world.

Nicholas Karlovasitis and Sarah Gibson's aptly named **Confetti furniture collection** includes everything from recycled plastic tables and chairs to sofas and planters.

The WRECK series by Bentu Design represents a remarkable transformation of ceramic waste sourced from Chaozhou, China. Instead of being discarded as trash, these materials are repurposed and given new life, becoming treasures in the form of a unique collection. Bentu Design's innovative approach highlights the beauty and potential of utilizing waste materials, demonstrating how creativity and sustainability can go hand in hand. The WRECK series serves as a testament to the power of upcycling and the ability to turn what may have been considered waste into valuable and aesthetically pleasing design pieces.

A jaw-dropping 80 percent of plastic toys end up in landfills, waste incinerators, or even the ocean. **Ecobirdy** collects these playthings and recycles them into beautiful furniture.

7. Alternative Green Home Solutions:

Antiques - Recycle and Refurbish:

Incorporating antique furnishings into your home is an excellent way to embrace sustainability. Whether you have inherited antiques or enjoy collecting them, they offer a sustainable option for your interior design. By giving new life to vintage items such as tables, mirrors, or furniture sets, you extend their lifespan and contribute to reducing waste. Antiques add a touch of tradition and rustic charm to your home while also providing an attractive upgrade. Instead of purchasing new furniture from stores, consider shopping for old and vintage pieces, and give them a practical and aesthetically pleasing refurbishment for a long-lasting and sustainable addition to your space. In many cases, purchasing antiques can be more cost-effective than buying new furniture of comparable quality. While some rare and highly sought-after antiques can be expensive, there is a wide range of affordable options available.

By opting for antique and vintage items, you not only reduce the demand for new furniture production but also preserve the craftsmanship and history associated with these unique pieces. Refurbishing them allows you to personalize their appearance while retaining their inherent character, resulting in a sustainable and visually appealing home interior.

When it comes to interior design, the selection of materials is a key factor in determining the sustainability of our living spaces. Every decision we make regarding the materials we choose for furniture, flooring, walls, and decor has a profound impact on the environment. From the sourcing of raw resources to the manufacturing processes and the eventual disposal of products, each step in a material's lifecycle has far-reaching ecological consequences.

In the next chapter, we will explore the crucial topic of sustainable materials in interior design. The focus will be on highlighting eco-friendly options that prioritize renewable resources, minimize energy consumption, reduce waste generation, and prioritize non-toxicity.

SUSTAINABILITY X MATERIALS

FIRST, BASICS

Materials refer to the substances used or capable of being used in the creation of various objects or for specific purposes. In the context of interior design, interior materials are those utilized within a space to serve different functions. Finishes, on the other hand, encompass the techniques applied to provide a final touch to a product, endowing it with specific attributes such as shine, texture, color, as well as practical features like protection and durability. For example, applying polish to wood enhances its appearance and imparts the mentioned characteristics. While materials can be categorized as either natural or man-made, it is important to note that man-made or synthetic materials are essentially derived from natural sources and undergo treatments, mixing, processing, or reshaping. Natural materials typically hold prominence over non-natural or synthetic counterparts. Furthermore, materials that require minimal treatment, mixing, processing, or reshaping tend to exhibit greater refinement compared to those subjected to extensive modification.

Materials are utilized in interior design for a variety of purposes, including:

1. **Structural Elements:** Materials such as stones, bricks, cement, wood, plywood, and metal sections are utilized to provide the necessary structural framework and stability to interior spaces.
2. **Fillers:** Materials like bricks, cement blocks, lightweight blocks, and plywood are used as fillers to create partitions or fill empty spaces within the interior.
3. **Softness:** Cotton-wool, rubber, rubberized coir, foam, carpet, and durries are employed to introduce softness and comfort in areas such as seating, flooring, and cushions.
4. **Protection from Heat/Sound/Water:** Heat reflecting tiles, thermocol, fiberglass, sound-absorbing boards, and waterproofing agents are utilized to protect interior spaces from heat, sound, and water damage.
5. **Safety:** Materials such as grills, locks, and metal edges on furniture are incorporated to enhance safety and security within the interior.
6. **Maintenance:** Strong and durable materials like laminates and glass are chosen for surfaces to facilitate easy maintenance and cleaning.
7. **Privacy:** Partitions, grills, screens, blinds, and curtains are used to create privacy and separation between different areas within the interior.
8. **Visual Increase in Space:** The strategic use of materials like glass, mirrors, paint, paintings, and wallpaper can visually enhance the perception of space and make it appear larger.
9. **Visual Appeal:** Materials with color and texture, such as paints, fabrics, and mattings, are employed to add visual interest and aesthetic appeal to the interior.
10. **Economy of Size Strength**: Hinges, locks, aldrops, and other metal and alloy components are chosen to enhance the strength and functionality of doors and furniture, allowing for efficient use of space.
11. **Providing Services:** Materials required for plumbing, sanitation, electrical installations, telephone/intercom systems, air conditioning, and computer networking are integrated to support the necessary services within the interior.

Materials for Interior Design

Achieving the right balance between creativity and practicality is crucial when selecting materials for interior design. While some designers are brimming with inspiration, others may feel overwhelmed by the abundance of choices available. In this segment, we will explore the various aspects of material selection in interior design, including commonly used materials and effective tips for combining them. Materials play a vital role in shaping the aesthetics, functionality, and overall experience of an interior space, serving specific purposes from structural elements to decorative finishes.

A successful interior design process begins by addressing key elements like layout, flow, focal points, and preferred styles. As the project progresses, designers reach a stage where they need to make precise recommendations for selecting interior details and materials.

Sustainability takes center stage when it comes to material choice in interior design. Prioritizing materials with minimal environmental impact is essential for creating eco-friendly and responsible spaces. Designers should focus on renewable, recyclable materials with a low carbon footprint. Opting for sustainable options helps reduce carbon emissions, conserve natural resources, and promote environmentally friendly practices. Evaluating the lifecycle of materials, from sourcing to disposal, is crucial. Additionally, designers should seek materials that can be recycled or reused, contributing to a circular economy. Ethical considerations are also important, such as supporting fair trade and responsible sourcing practices that uphold workers' rights and social well-being.

Let's explore the details of sustainable materials commonly incorporated in interior design.

THE SOLIDS : CONCRETE

Reducing the carbon footprint of concrete is a crucial objective that the building industry should focus on. By implementing measures to mitigate the environmental impact of concrete production, the sector can make significant strides towards sustainability.

Throughout history, concrete has been an essential building material, dating back to ancient civilizations that used a combination of lime, chalk, oyster shells, and gypsum to create a durable substance. The Romans further advanced concrete technology by using volcanic rock, lime, and aggregates to develop a material known as pozzolana, which was used in iconic structures like the Parthenon. In more recent times, the introduction of Portland cement in the 19th century paved the way for modern concrete.

Today, concrete is the most widely used building material, known for its strength and longevity. However, its widespread use comes with a significant carbon footprint. Concrete production now contributes approximately 5 percent of global CO_2 emissions annually.

Despite its environmental impact, concrete offers several advantages. Its durability and long lifespan make it an eco-friendly choice compared to shorter-lived alternatives for walls, floors, fireplaces, and countertops. Additionally, utilizing the concrete structure itself as a visible finish eliminates the need for additional floor coverings, reducing waste and maintenance requirements. Concrete exhibits rock-like properties, making it resistant to off-gassing, rust, mold, and rot. Its inherent thermal mass allows for efficient temperature regulation, with light-colored concrete providing natural cooling in hot climates and darker colors effectively capturing heat in colder regions. Structures with a high concrete content may even require less energy for heating and cooling. Furthermore, concrete is highly versatile, easily molded and poured to meet specific design requirements. Additionally, it can be recycled indefinitely by crushing it into aggregate, contributing to a more sustainable construction industry.

Decorative enhancements can transform basic concrete into visually appealing surfaces. Mineral pigments, stains, texture treatments, and polishing techniques can be applied to make concrete shine. Additionally, concrete serves as an excellent matrix for incorporating aggregates such as recycled glass, creating stunning terrazzo-like finishes for floors and countertops. By using a higher percentage of recycled materials, the environmental value of concrete is further enhanced. The substitution of post-industrial waste for some of the aggregate or cement in concrete not only increases the strength of the product but also conserves raw materials.

While concrete offers several positive environmental attributes, it is primarily composed of non-renewable resources. Aggregates like sand and gravel comprise a significant portion (60 to 80 percent) of the mixture, while Portland cement, a complex combination of calcium, silicon, aluminum, iron, and gypsum, makes up around 10 to 15 percent. Obtaining the minerals required for Portland cement production involves mining various sources such as limestone, chalk, seashells, marl, shale, clay, slate, and silica sand. The process of grinding and firing these minerals at high temperatures results in a high embodied energy for concrete.

In some cases, post-industrial waste materials are incorporated into the concrete mixture. While many of these compounds are considered safe, there have been concerns about potential contaminants present in fly ash, which contains trace amounts of heavy metals like arsenic, cadmium, chromium, mercury, and selenium, as well as compounds from hydrocarbons and sulfur. However, preliminary testing conducted by various organizations suggests that leaching of heavy-metal contaminants from fly ash is minimal, with trace amounts ranging from 1 to 3 percent.

If you are dealing with clients who have chemical sensitivities, it is advisable to take a precautionary approach and avoid concrete ingredients that may potentially be toxic. However, it is widely accepted that the toxins present in post-industrial additives are minimal and become bound within the concrete, making it unlikely for them to leach or release gases once the concrete has hardened. While the complete safety assessment is still ongoing, incorporating fly ash and other recycled materials in concrete significantly reduces waste going to landfills and decreases the reliance on energy-intensive cement production. Admixtures, which are chemical additives used to enhance certain properties of concrete such as drying time, flow, bond, finish, or appearance, are commonly used in concrete mixes. They are particularly important for outdoor applications where the concrete is exposed to harsh environmental conditions that can impact curing and the lifespan of the material. However, for interior projects, admixtures are typically unnecessary if optimal pouring and curing conditions, including temperature control, are specified.

Concrete offsets its environmental impact through its durability, long lifespan, and low maintenance requirements. It surpasses the longevity of many interior finishes, lasting two to three times longer or even more. Additionally, for clients with chemical sensitivities, concrete can provide an inert and easy-to-clean surface that does not trap allergens or irritants, provided it does not contain questionable aggregates or admixtures.

While concrete is a permanent interior design element, it is also flexible enough to be covered with alternative finishes if desired. When considering concrete as an option, it is important to carefully evaluate the pros and cons with the client. Ultimately, concrete offers exceptional longevity, albeit with some environmental considerations.

Sustainable Mix: Repurposed Ingredients

Scientists and manufacturers have discovered that various by-products, which would typically end up in landfills, can be incorporated into concrete. This practice not only reduces waste but also improves the strength, plasticity, and impermeability of concrete. Furthermore, the addition of certain recycled materials allows for a significant reduction in the amount of cement required. Common postindustrial ingredients used in concrete include:

- Blast furnace slag: The residue remaining after the production of pig iron or other metal ores.
- Cement kiln dust (CKD): Collected from cement firing and reused as raw material.
- Fly ash: A by-product of coal-fired power plants containing trace amounts of heavy metals. It enhances concrete strength, reduces absorbency, and decreases water usage during production.
- Foundry sand: Waste material generated from metal casting.
- Lime sludge: Produced during paper recycling, this sludge exhibits cement-like properties due to its silica and magnesium content.
- Rice hull ash: Leftover material from rice milling, with approximately 85 to 90 percent amorphous silica content, obtained from the use of rice husks as fuel in the parboiling process.
- Silica fume: Waste product from the production of silicon alloys, which used to be released into the atmosphere prior to the implementation of air-quality controls.

The ingredients of concrete originate from various sources:

- Sand, gravel, water, and cement form the basic composition of concrete.
- Cement is predominantly made from limestone and a combination of minerals such as calcium, silicon, aluminum, and iron. These minerals are subjected to high temperatures, ground, and mixed with gypsum.
- Concrete can incorporate postindustrial waste as a partial substitute for cement or aggregates.
- Aggregates in concrete can include recycled glass, stones, or other natural or manufactured materials for decorative purposes.
- Chemical admixtures may be added to concrete, although it is possible to create concrete without them.
- Natural or synthetic pigments can be introduced into wet concrete to add color.

- Concrete can be left unfinished or treated with epoxy, polyurethane, or other chemical sealants.
- Alternatively, finishes like linseed oil and beeswax can be applied to concrete.
- Acid staining is another option where water-based acidic liquids containing metallic salts are used to impart color to the concrete.

Maintenance

Once concrete is sealed, it can be easily cleaned with mild detergent and water. Unsealed concrete should be dusted or gently scrubbed with a nonmetallic brush and water. It is important to avoid using cleansers or detergent on both sealed and unsealed concrete.

However, it's worth noting that sealants and finishes, as well as the concrete underneath, can be susceptible to scratches and abrasion from dirt, shoes, and cutlery. As a result, periodic resealing may be necessary every few years, depending on the type of sealant used and the amount of wear on the concrete surface.

Specification

To ensure sustainable and environmentally responsible interior design, it is essential to engage manufacturers who provide Environmental Product Declarations (EPDs) considering carbon footprint reduction and environmental impact. Develop guidelines for life-cycle assessments to compare concrete suppliers based on embodied carbon, energy, and water, with third-party verification of environmental impacts. Seek suppliers with multi-attribute environmental certifications.

- Produce solid structures and cement mixtures without the use of additives and harmful chemicals.
- Utilize aggregates (or "seeding") and cement derived from natural materials or verified-safe recycled materials.
- If necessary, employ natural mineral pigments.
- Employ potable water for the process of curing.
- Opt for factory-finished slabs for countertops and smaller applications.
- Choose biobased, low-VOC (Volatile Organic Compound), water-based or water-reducible, low-solvent, and formaldehyde-free stains, sealants, and finishes.
- Apply silicate dispersion paint.

Things to avoid:

- Avoid using aggregates or recycled ingredients that might introduce environmental contaminants or pose health hazards.
- Refrain from using admixtures, except for sucrose-based retardants, if necessary.
- Avoid chemical pigments or paints containing chromium, aniline, or heavy metals.
- Do not use acid stains.
- Avoid seeding with manufactured materials such as computer chips, which could potentially be hazardous.

THE MASONRY

The definition of masonry encompasses a wide range of work performed by masons. In interior applications, masons may work with materials such as rock, brick, stone, tile, and veneer. The specific project can vary, including dry stack (without mortar), mortar bed, grouted, glued in place, or simply cut to fit.

Stone, which serves as the fundamental building block for all masonry, undergoes a natural formation process spanning millions of years. This process involves volcanic eruptions (igneous rock), sediment sifting and settling (sedimentary rock), and significant geological changes (metamorphic rock).

Masonry has a long history that dates back to the earliest days of human civilization. It originated when our ancestors began constructing shelters by stacking stones. Initially, mortar was made from clay, and primitive forms of concrete were developed to enhance the grip of the masonry. Bricks were created by baking or drying clay under the hot sun. Over time, masonry evolved beyond mere structural purposes and became an art form. Ancient temples, pyramids, monuments, and other symbolic structures were crafted from rock and clay, imparting permanence and authority to these edifices.

Masonry stands out as a clear choice when durability is a priority for a structure intended to last for centuries. The Great Wall of China, an astonishing feat of engineering, extends over 4,000 miles and consists of countless individual stone and brick blocks. The majority of the world's remarkable government, cultural, and religious buildings, along with numerous monuments, are constructed using stone and brick. Cities like Chicago, Denver, and London, which suffered devastating fires in the past, rebuilt using masonry materials and even incorporated masonry requirements into their building codes.

In residential settings, natural masonry offers a timeless and traditional design option known for its longevity. Stone and brick do not emit volatile organic compounds (VOCs), outlasting materials like wood or bamboo. They are resistant to water, fire, insects, and mold. Maintenance typically involves simple dusting or cleaning with soap and water, although occasional sealing can enhance stain and scratch resistance. Moreover, these materials can be reused or recycled.

Both stone and brick are excellent choices when thermal qualities are crucial, such as for fireplaces, flooring over radiant heat, or walls and floors that benefit from passive solar radiation. Masonry has the capacity to store heat and release it gradually. Similarly, if kept away from direct sunlight or heat sources, masonry retains a cool temperature. Strategically incorporating stone or brick in design can actually reduce heating and cooling expenses.

When stone for interior design is sourced from the site or locally available rather than being mined, its ecological impact is minimal. Reclaimed stone from deconstruction is another environmentally friendly option. However, the environmental value of new masonry diminishes when considering activities like quarrying, mining, manufacturing, firing, and long-distance transportation. Quarried stone is obtained through cutting or excavation, typically resulting in less waste compared to mining.

On the other hand, mining involves extracting relatively small quantities of ore from larger rock formations. Methods include blasting, stripping, open pits, underground mines, hydraulic operations, or the use of augers. After extraction, the desired minerals must be separated from the ore. Although mined rock requires more energy compared to quarried rock, both methods leave permanent scars on the land and disrupt ecosystems. They impact runoff and water downstream, soil composition, and the local flora and fauna. Moreover, changes in slope or soil affect rain absorption, which can further damage the landscape through erosion, landslides, fallen trees, and flooding.

Mining operations not only have adverse environmental impacts but also pose risks to human health. Both quarrying and mining workers are exposed to various hazards, including inhalation of dust, poor air quality, chemical exposure, injuries, and repetitive motion disabilities. This is particularly prevalent in developing countries where labor standards may be lax. In residential settings, it is important to note that most of the stone used is quarried rather than mined. If the design application is intended to last for generations and can be recycled or reused afterward, or if the stone is locally sourced, it can be a wise and environmentally friendly choice.

Brick, on the other hand, offers a distinct advantage over stone as it is made from common clay that can be easily extracted from local pits. However, the process of transforming clay into brick involves processing, pressing, and firing at high temperatures. This significantly increases the embodied energy required for production and the pollution generated during the manufacturing process.

Salvaged brick is often readily available in many locations, and its use helps conserve natural resources and raw materials. However, salvaged or reclaimed stone from deconstruction projects may be less accessible. It is worthwhile to research local land resources, such as properties where field stones or flagstone can be easily gathered. Obtaining stone from a quarry in the same region as the construction site also makes ecological sense. Whenever feasible, relying on local sources greatly reduces the embodied energy associated with transportation and supports sustainability efforts.

Radon emission and Hazardous effects

Radon gas poses risks to human health and can be emitted by certain types of stone. It is a tasteless, odorless, and colorless gas that is believed to be a leading cause of lung cancer, second only to smoking. Radon can enter homes through well water and the foundation, as lower air pressure draws the gas in from the surrounding soil. While less common, radon emissions can also occur from concrete or specific types of stone, such as granite, used in construction or design applications.

The good news is that radon exposure in the home can be prevented and detected. It is essential to test the entire house for radon, or alternatively, check individual building materials before their use. If a small surface area is found to emit radon gas, using a water-based, low-VOC sealer may help prevent its release.

If dangerous levels of radon are present within the home, mitigation measures should be pursued. This typically involves the installation of abatement systems or, in rare cases, the removal of the material responsible for emitting radon. It's worth noting that the specific requirements for mitigation licensing can be very subjective across countries.

Maintenance

Masonry design elements are known for their low maintenance requirements, and in some cases, they can be left without any protective finish. However, certain masonry installations, such as countertops and floors, may benefit from regular reapplication of sealants to preserve stain and scratch resistance or to protect the grout between tiles. It is recommended to consult the supplier or installer to determine the frequency of sealant reapplication for specific surfaces. When selecting sealants, it is advisable to avoid spray-on sealants if future applications are anticipated. Spray-on sealants can create a barrier that makes it challenging to reapply sealants effectively. Opting for alternative sealant application methods will allow for easier maintenance and resealing when necessary.

Brick and stone have the advantage of being reusable or salvageable for new purposes. If a masonry application has been damaged beyond use in its original form, it can be downcycled into various applications such as roadbeds, landscaping, or even transformed into tile or terrazzo. Ultimately, all types of masonry will decompose over time and become part of the natural geological process. This highlights how masonry is a truly cradle-to-cradle resource, contributing to sustainable practices.

It's important to note that natural grouts and mortars, typically made with lime or sand, will also follow the natural cycle of deterioration. These materials will gradually break down over time as part of the natural aging process. On the other hand, synthetic grouts, adhesives, and mortars are designed to be more durable and may not decompose as easily.

Specification

Recommended:
- Utilize reclaimed, salvaged, or recycled brick and stone to minimize environmental impact.
- Source stone or brick from local suppliers to support the local economy and reduce transportation-related emissions.
- Prior to installation, perform radon testing on materials to ensure they do not emit hazardous gases.
- Use natural mortars and grouts made with lime or sand, which align with sustainable practices.
- Opt for low-VOC (Volatile Organic Compounds), low-solvent, water-based sealants, adhesives, and finishes that are free from toxic chemicals like formaldehyde.
- Choose wipe-on or brush-on sealants for easier maintenance and reapplication.

Avoid:

- Avoid imported stone or brick to reduce carbon footprint associated with long-distance transportation.
- Steer clear of adhesives, grout, mortar, or sealants that contain solvents, additives, or toxic chemicals such as formaldehyde, biocides, and isocyanates.
- Refrain from using spray-on sealants as they may hinder future reapplication and maintenance efforts.

METALS

Metals encompass a wide range of elements and alloys that possess distinct properties such as high electrical and thermal conductivity, malleability, ductility, and reflectivity of light. This category includes well-known metals like copper, aluminum, iron, and gold, as well as alloys such as steel and bronze. For the purpose of this discussion, we will focus on the common definition of metals, excluding elements like calcium, sodium, and potassium, which are metallic in the scientific sense.

Metals hold great significance in human civilization, as evident from historical periods like the Bronze Age and Iron Age, named after the discovery and early utilization of these materials. Many metals and alloys are incredibly durable, making them highly resistant to damage. Their enduring beauty has also made them a preferred material for coins worldwide.

In modern residential construction, metals play a vital role due to their exceptional strength. They are commonly used in joists, supports, flashing, shields, plumbing, and essential hardware. Metal can be shaped through various processes like stamping, pouring, hammering, and extrusion. It is frequently employed in the production of railings, fireplace surrounds, castings, decorative hardware, appliances, kitchen hoods, and countertops. Metals are not only utilitarian but also possess unique lusters and textures. They can be utilized as delicate powders or thin leaf forms, ideal for creating faux finishes and intricate detailing.

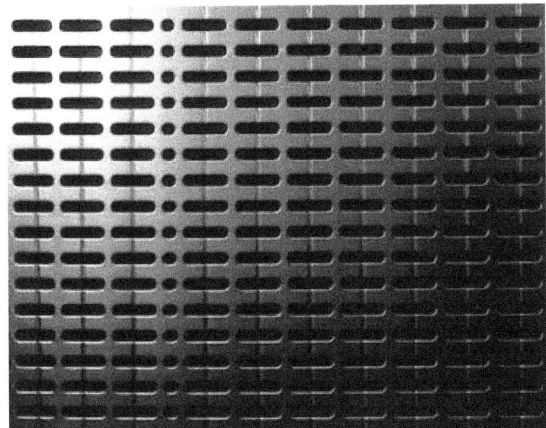

From an ecological perspective, the use of metal in homes offers significant advantages. In its unfinished state, metal does not emit harmful gases or trigger chemical sensitivities. Depending on the specific metal used, it can outlast the lifespan of the house itself. Metals are resistant to pests, fire, and mold. They generally require minimal maintenance. Moreover, metals can be recycled repeatedly, contributing to sustainable practices. While recycled metal has yet to become commonplace in residential design products, some factory-made hardware may already contain recycled metal, and many custom fabricators rely on it for their craftsmanship.

The process of obtaining metals from the earth through mining has significant environmental consequences, regardless of the mining method employed. Mining operations leave lasting scars on the land, pollute water sources, consume substantial amounts of fossil fuels for machinery, and contribute to poor air quality. For instance, the extraction of approximately one ton of copper requires the excavation of around 220 tons of earth. Mining leads to the destruction of plant and animal habitats, causing permanent disruptions to the local ecology.

Once the raw metal is extracted from the earth, additional energy-intensive steps are necessary to transform it into usable products. These steps involve transportation, mechanization, power usage, and heating processes from the mining site to the smelter and eventually to the fabrication facilities or retailers. This journey incurs significant energy costs, resulting in potentially the highest embodied energy among natural resources. In comparison to materials like wood, tile, or stone, metals generally have a higher energy footprint due to the complex extraction and processing involved.

Once elemental metals are extracted from the earth, they cannot naturally return to their original state. Unlike organic materials such as wood or straw, which biodegrade and contribute to the earth's natural cycles, the geological processes that formed metals take an extremely long time, spanning millennia. Additionally, some metals are scarce and not as abundant as others. While aluminium and iron are relatively abundant in the Earth's crust, metals like zinc, tin, nickel, and manganese are more limited in supply.

Given these considerations, designers and individuals involved in metal applications must carefully weigh the environmental cost against the longevity of the intended use. It becomes crucial to ask whether the extended lifespan of a metal application justifies its significant ecological impact.

To minimize the heavy environmental impacts of metals, recycling is an essential practice. Architectural salvage shops and metalworks can be valuable sources for reclaimed metal, particularly for interior design purposes rather than structural or protective applications. By reusing metals that are already in circulation, the additional embodied energy primarily comes from transportation or potential modifications, significantly reducing the overall environmental impact.

Metals have the potential to be reused and recycled multiple times, making them valuable and sustainable resources in various industries. Recycling metal plays a crucial role in promoting their sustainable nature. Interestingly, the amount of steel recycled annually surpasses the combined recycling figures of aluminum, paper, glass, and plastic. By specifying the use of recycled metal, we actively contribute to reducing energy consumption, minimizing waste, and avoiding the environmental consequences associated with mining. Opting for recycled metal has significant positive implications for sustainability.

When selecting metal products, prioritize those that have a substantial proportion of recycled metal, such as steel, aluminum, and copper. It is advisable to seek third-party certifications that verify the recycled content of these products. Additionally, pay attention to the coatings, finishes, or paints applied to the metal, whether during manufacturing or on-site. Whenever feasible, opt for metals like stainless steel that do not require any finishes or chemical cleaning solutions to prevent rust, oxidation, or to preserve their luster.

In some cases, a metal element like a kitchen hood may be shipped with a protective coating of natural or synthetic oil. It is important to remove this coating before installation, as synthetic oils can potentially trigger chemical sensitivities. It is recommended to consult the manufacturer or dealer to determine if the coating is standard and if it is possible to avoid using synthetic oil. Additionally, inquire about the appropriate method for removing the coating, which may involve simple soap and water. If the metal element is already finished or painted, it is best to let the manufacturer or fabricator handle the removal process, particularly if a client has chemical sensitivities. It should be noted that most paints and permanent finishes for metals are solvent-based and emit a significant amount of volatile organic compounds (VOCs), especially when wet. While manufacturers control the application conditions and allow for outgassing before the product reaches the home, it is still important to consider the environmental impact. Performing the outgassing process outdoors reduces the potential harm to sensitive clients.

Avoid using chromium, cadmium, brass, and nickel plating in metal applications as they can emit toxic emissions and by-products, posing risks to both workers and the environment. Galvanized metals, which have zinc coatings, may have relatively low emissions but require significant amounts of energy during production. Additionally, the process of galvanizing zinc can result in harmful discharge that can negatively impact aquatic life. Zinc itself is also relatively scarce, although some recovery efforts are in place for other industries. Instead of traditional plating, consider using plastic polymer or powder coatings, which are highly durable and can be applied through a heat-fusion process that minimizes outgassing after the initial drying.

When inquiring about finishes and patinas from manufacturers or artisans, ensure that they avoid using acidic or caustic toxic chemicals. Instead, request methods that employ low or zero volatile organic compounds (VOCs). It's important to understand the natural tendencies of different metals, as some are prone to rust or discoloration when exposed to elements. Specify patinas created through less toxic methods and inquire about the waste or wastewater generated during the process, as it can serve as an indicator of the method's toxicity.

Origins of Metal:

- Metal is mined from various locations around the globe.
- Some metals require intensive manufacturing processes to extract them from ore, while others, like silver and gold, are found in veins and require less energy-intensive separation methods.
- Metals are often combined into alloys to enhance their strength, sheen, or resistance to oxidation.
- Various factory coatings and finishes can be applied to metal, including paint, powder coating, protective oils (natural or chemical), metal platings, and zinc galvanizations.
- Metal has excellent recyclability and can be easily recovered from recycling processes and fabricated into new products.

Maintenance

Understanding the client's preferences and expectations regarding the appearance and maintenance of metal design elements is crucial. Different types of metals have varying requirements to maintain their desired condition. For example, copper and silver tend to oxidize quickly, while iron and certain types of steel are prone to rust.

It is worth noting that many commercial polishes and cleaning solutions often contain toxic chemicals such as kerosene, naphtha, perchloroethylene, chromic acid, silver nitrate, and solvents. To promote healthier and more environmentally friendly practices, it is advisable to substitute these harsh chemicals with alternatives like vinegar and food-grade oils. Additionally, using traditional methods of manual cleaning with some elbow grease can be effective in maintaining the desired appearance of metal elements.

If feasible, choose a type of metal that requires minimal maintenance. Certain metals, like copper or bronze, can develop a natural patina, such as a verdigris, as they age. If this patina aligns with the design aesthetic, there may be no need for regular polishing or cleaning.

Most metals have the ability to be recycled repeatedly. However, the actual amount of metal that gets recycled depends largely on consumer behavior, and unfortunately, a significant portion still ends up in landfills. Theoretically, over time, metal waste will undergo geological processes and become part of the earth's crust once again.

Specification

- Reclaimed or salvaged architectural metal pieces.
- Metal with a high percentage of recycled content, ideally with third-party verification.
- Local fabricators to minimize transportation impact.
- Metal that naturally develops a patina or verdigris over time.
- Metal that requires minimal or no upkeep with cleansers and polishes.
- Natural and non-outgassing protective oil coatings, or no coatings at all.
- Avoidance of paint or finishes on the metal.
- Consider factory-finished options like powder coating, galvanization, or paint.
- Consider the use of silicate dispersion paint for metal.
- Ensure that all scrap metal is recycled.

Avoid:

- Pieces made with virgin metal.
- Synthetic oil coatings. Imported fabrications.
- On-site painting or finishing of metal.
- Chemical polishes, treatments, or cleansers.
- Poor placement of the metal design element leading to unwanted thermal bridging, reflectivity, condensation, or electromagnetic field disturbances.

WOOD & COMPOSITE MATERIALS

Throughout history, wood has been a fundamental construction material, widely used in various forms of architecture. It possesses unique properties such as tensile strength comparable to mild steel and a favorable strength-to-weight ratio similar to reinforced concrete. Wood is known for its flexibility, adjusting to environmental changes, absorbing sound, and offering a durable solution. There are examples of wooden structures, like the Horyu-ji monument in Japan, that have stood for centuries, demonstrating its longevity.

Wood is also considered a renewable resource, provided that sustainable practices are implemented to maintain the supply and manage demand. Unfortunately, forests worldwide are facing rapid depletion, particularly the large and old-growth trees. Approximately half of the world's forests have already been lost, and at the current rate, the remaining undisturbed tropical forests may disappear within the next fifty years. This alarming trend can be attributed to factors such as booming commercial and residential construction, mining expansion, and the need for fuel and agricultural land.

The issue extends beyond clear-cutting practices. While a single oak tree may take centuries to reach maturity, it takes thousands of years for a complete forest ecosystem to fully develop. Careless felling of trees disrupts the complex biodiversity that surrounds them. Clear-cutting is widely recognized as disastrous in most settings, but even selective logging that targets only the largest and best trees can have detrimental effects. The remaining trees become susceptible to erosion, soil compaction, and high winds. Even the removal of a small percentage of trees can cause damage or destruction to those that remain.

Deforestation has local and global impacts. Trees play a crucial role in the carbon cycle by absorbing carbon dioxide and releasing oxygen. The increase in carbon dioxide concentration in the atmosphere contributes to climate change. Deforestation disrupts this natural process, leading to higher carbon dioxide levels and environmental challenges. Preserving forests is essential for biodiversity, ecological balance, and mitigating climate change.

Once trees have been harvested, the wood cannot be recycled in the same way as metals. Unlike metals that can be melted down and reformed without losing their integrity, most wood is downcycled when it is no longer useful. It is cut up, chopped up, or ground into sawdust to make lower-grade materials. For example, wood posts may become particleboard, board may become paper, and paper may be shredded for insulation. However, the positive aspect is that this cycle can continue for decades or even centuries. Ultimately, wood and paper will biodegrade, returning to the earth as long as toxic binders, adhesives, and glues are not used in the manufacturing process.

While cutting down trees carries significant costs, it is hard to find a material better suited for many aspects of home construction and design. Wood is a renewable resource that can be replenished in far fewer years compared to alternatives like stone or metal. It biodegrades naturally and completely, contributing to the formation of new soil that fosters the growth of more trees. When properly protected, the lifespan of cut timber can even exceed that of the standing trees. By growing, harvesting, and using wood sustainably, it can genuinely be considered a green choice.

Making Sustainable Wood Choices

When choosing wood for various interior design elements, it is important to prioritize sustainability. While framing consumes a significant amount of wood in home construction, other components such as casework, paneling, trim, flooring, and cabinetry also contribute to overall wood consumption. Design teams should be mindful of their wood choices and take into account the environmental impact, setting a positive example for contractors and clients alike.

One option is to specify reclaimed wood, which involves using wood salvaged from previous structures or sources. This reduces the demand for new wood and gives new life to old materials. Another approach is to select sustainable wood species that are known for their responsible sourcing and growth rates. Local availability is also a crucial factor to consider, as it reduces transportation distances and supports the local economy. Third-party certifications provide assurance that the wood products meet specific sustainability criteria. By choosing certified products, designers can contribute to the promotion of sustainable wood production practices. Additionally, careful calculation of dimensions and optimization of efficiency can help minimize waste during the construction process. By maximizing the use of wood and reducing waste, the detrimental effects on forests can be limited.

By prioritizing reclaimed wood, sustainable species, local sources, and third-party certifications, designers can make a positive impact on forest conservation, encourage sustainable wood production, and offer clients renewable, visually appealing, and durable materials.

Reclaimed Wood

Reclaimed wood is a popular choice for its environmental benefits and unique characteristics. It involves repurposing wood that has been previously used for other purposes, such as old buildings, railroad ties, or submerged timber. Reclaimed wood can be sourced from various locations, including dismantled structures like warehouses, barns, and homes, as well as from underwater environments where sunken or submerged wood is recovered.

The process of reclaiming submerged wood can result in high-quality timber, as the resins are washed away and the wood density is increased. However, it's important to consider the potential ecological impact of reclaiming wood from natural bodies of water, as it may disrupt established ecosystems for extended periods of time. The Rainforest Alliance offers a standard and lists businesses that hold "rediscovered wood" certificates, which attest to responsible salvage from bodies of water. Opting for reclaimed wood is an excellent ecological choice for many interior wood applications, especially when acquired locally. Using reclaimed wood sourced from nearby areas eliminates the need for long-distance transportation, reducing embodied energy and carbon emissions associated with shipping. Furthermore, choosing local reclaimed wood allows trees to be spared from logging and prevents the disposal of usable wood in landfills.

Local reclaimed wood often consists of species that are native to or historically grown in the region, making them well-suited for local use. These woods have undergone decades of acclimatization, reducing the risk of warping, shrinking, or expansion when used in homes. In addition, reclaimed wood often exhibits higher quality compared to new wood. While it is not recommended to cut down old-growth trees, reclaimed wood may have originated from such trees, offering wider planks and a tighter grain pattern than newly harvested wood.

In addition to its environmental benefits, reclaimed wood also offers aesthetic advantages. There is a unique joy in incorporating a "historic" product into a home, where it can be appreciated visually and through touch. When sourcing reclaimed wood for indoor applications, it is important to look for certifications that ensure the wood's origin and environmental integrity.

The Forest Stewardship Council (FSC) is a reputable organization that defines reclaimed wood as recycled material and provides certifications such as "FSC Recycled" or "FSC Mixed" labels. The Rainforest Alliance also offers certifications for "rediscovered wood" and "underwater salvage," verifying that the reclaimed wood has been sourced using measures that prioritize environmental preservation and the well-being of workers and communities.

Certifications are valuable because they provide transparency and accountability in the sourcing process. Without certifications, it can be challenging to trace the origin of reclaimed wood. It is advisable to inquire about the specific details of the wood's source and ensure that it is free from hazardous substances like arsenic (used in lumber treatment) and lead (found in older, chipped paint), both of which are known carcinogens. Additionally, it is important to verify the safety of wood originating from industrial or agricultural sites, as it may have been exposed to chemicals. While certified reclaimed wood may have limited availability, noncertified reclaimed wood can still be considered if sourced from reputable "rediscovered wood operators" (RWOs) who recover and sell wood locally. These operators often have a thorough understanding of the wood's source and may have personally deconstructed the site. They can provide information about the species, origin, and safety of the reclaimed wood for indoor use.

Certified Wood

The Forest Stewardship Council (FSC) was established in the mid-1990s as an independent nonprofit organization with the mission to promote environmentally appropriate, socially beneficial, and economically viable management of the world's forests. The FSC logo is widely recognized and serves as a symbol of responsible forest management. The FSC is a global leader in third-party chain-of-custody certification. They have stringent requirements for verifying the source(s) of wood products and ensuring quality and environmental controls throughout the supply chain. The FSC also emphasizes fair labor practices and responsible tree farming. By choosing FSC-certified wood products, individuals can be assured that the particular tree species used is not endangered and that the forestry practices employed are eco-friendly and sustainable. The certification also guarantees that the processing or manufacturing of the wood products adheres to strict guidelines. When specifying FSC-certified wood products, there are various options available, allowing individuals to select the most suitable and sustainable choice for their specific project.

In addition to FSC certification, there are other third-party certifications available that provide eco-labels for wood and forestry products. These certifications may be regionally based or recognized only within specific countries. Some certifications are affiliated with forestry, wood, or paper industries. While the FSC certification system is considered the best available and has strict standards, it is important to acknowledge that it is not flawless. The FSC continues to raise its standards and strives to represent the interests of various stakeholders, including loggers, indigenous peoples, consumers, and conservation groups. It's worth noting that wood sourced from suppressed trees, which are small undergrowth trees thinned and culled for forest fire prevention on public lands, is not currently certified by the FSC. However, if the source of such wood can be verified, it can still be considered an environmentally positive choice.

Two types of wood that are considered more environmentally friendly than many tropical woods are bamboo and palmwood. Bamboo, which is a type of grass, is often used as a wood substitute and can be harvested in a shorter time frame compared to traditional trees. Palmwood, obtained from mature coconut trees, is a new-wood option with characteristics similar to reclaimed wood. Both bamboo and palmwood offer sustainable alternatives due to their renewable nature and potential to reduce waste.

Sheet Materials from Wood

Wood-based sheet goods, including particleboard, engineered wood products, fiberboard, medium-density fiberboard (MDF), and plywood, are commonly used in the construction of cabinet boxes, faces, shelving, and furnishings. While architects and contractors typically specify these materials, designers can play a role in promoting eco-friendly choices. One approach is to use smaller and younger trees, as well as waste products like sawdust, wood chips, and old pallets, as alternatives to solid wood. This reduces the reliance on older-growth trees. When opting for engineered wood, it is advisable to specify products that are formaldehyde- and isocyanate-free, have FSC certification, and contain 100 percent recycled content.

However, it is important to note that some engineered boards used in cabinetry, shelving, and millwork may contain urea-formaldehyde binders and solvent-based finishes that emit harmful gases. These emissions can pose risks, especially for individuals with chemical sensitivities. Efforts have been made to develop improved substitutes, such as methylene diphenyl isocyanate (MDI), which is a particleboard binder that does not emit gases but still carries risks for factory workers. It is recommended to specify compliance with California 93120 Phase 2 emission standards, which limit formaldehyde emissions to .05 parts per million (ppm) for plywood. Additionally, opting for formaldehyde-free and low-VOC adhesives, binders, finishes, and naturally derived, biobased adhesives can help mitigate potential health and environmental concerns.

It might be feasible to eliminate the use of wood entirely by considering bio composite boards, which are made from renewable agricultural by-products. These boards can serve as an alternative for cabinets, doors, trim, and even floors. Bio composites are comparable to wood in terms of performance and provide an environmentally friendly solution.

Wood Sourcing: Exploring the Origins

- Wood products come from domestic and exotic trees.
- Reclaimed wood is sourced from residential, commercial, agricultural structures, fallen trees, and bodies of water.
- Some wood products are made from recycled wood scraps or sawdust, mixed with acrylics or resins.
- Wood sealants typically use polyurethane, but resin-oil primers are a more environmentally friendly option.
- Wood finishes or stains can contain natural oils, resins, pigments, solvents, chemical compounds, petroleum distillates, metal drying agents, formaldehyde, and sometimes water.

Maintenance

Proper care is essential for maintaining wood surfaces. The susceptibility of wood to scratches, dents, stains, and other marks depends on its hardness. Therefore, if heavy wear is expected, a harder finish may be necessary. To promote healthy indoor air quality and minimize wear issues, it is recommended to discuss a "no shoes" policy with the client, particularly in areas with wood floors. Providing shoe storage at primary entry points can help reinforce this policy. Clients should also be advised to use mild detergents and minimal water when cleaning wood surfaces.

If the client desires a weathered or aged appearance, the wood can be intentionally distressed or patinated either before installation or on-site through sanding and intentional marking. This approach reduces the need for frequent maintenance to preserve its desired appearance.

Biobased Composites: Sustainable Alternatives to Wood

Advancements in the green building industry have led to the development of biobased composite boards as an alternative to wood. These boards, also known as wheat board, agricultural board, crop board, or straw board, are produced by pressing pulp from crop residue with adhesive into sheets, which are then cut into boards. This manufacturing process is similar to that of wood-based particleboard, oriented-strand board (OSB), and medium-density fiberboard (MDF).

Wheat straw is the most commonly used fiber in these agricultural-based composites, but other materials such as sunflower hulls, rice, barley, oat straw, bluegrass, rye grass stubble, cornhusks, sorghum stalks, hemp, soybean plants, and bagasse (sugar cane pulp) are also being utilized. Designers specify these bio composites for various applications, including shelving, flooring, paneling, furniture, cabinetry boxes, frames, and doors.

While crop-based bio composites are not yet widely adopted, they hold great potential for both design and construction purposes. The crops used in their production can be harvested annually, making them a truly renewable resource. In comparison, trees require several decades to mature before they can be used in construction. By using biobased composite boards, significantly less land is needed, as an entire home can be constructed using only 15 to 20 acres of wheat instead of relying on almost an acre of forest.

Manufacturers of agricultural-based composite boards prioritize eco-conscious practices and use low-VOC, formaldehyde-free binders. Borate is a common preservative used, but pesticide-free and non-GMO bio composites are not yet available. Finishing options may vary, and the boards may have different appearances. Crop boards are lighter but not recommended for constant moisture exposure due to potential warping.

Maintenance

Biobased composites are a newer option in the market, and their long-term suitability for specific design applications and maintenance needs is not well established. It is advisable to consult with the manufacturer for recommendations regarding their use.

Specification

When specifying biobased composites, consider the following:

- Choose boards made from 100 percent renewable crop residue or agricultural by-products without added plastics.
- Specify formaldehyde- and isocyanate-free, low-VOC, water-based binders, sealants, adhesives, and stains.
- If necessary, include borate for preservative qualities or pest resistance.

Avoid the following:

- Formaldehyde and/or isocyanate in the binder or finish.
- Preservatives or pesticides, except for borate.

SURFACE FINISHES

When it comes to finishes for walls, ceilings, and floors, responsible designers aim to select materials that are healthy, high-performing, and have minimal environmental impact. Collaboration with the contractor and architect is essential to ensure the use of eco-friendly finishes, especially if the building envelope was not initially designed to green standards.

State and municipal regulations are increasingly adopting high-performing and healthy building standards, providing guidance for eco-friendly finishes. Various considerations need to be addressed before specifying finishes, such as the type of drywall and plaster to be used, the availability of preferred materials like recycled glass tile and the ability to specify the substrate, and whether the structure itself, such as exposed wood beams or unpainted plaster, can serve as the finish.

Green finishes offer versatility and can be adapted for multiple applications. Reclaimed flooring can be used as paneling, recycled glass bottles find their way into countertops, floors, or shower surrounds, and repurposed cardboard boxes can be transformed into countertops. This chapter serves as a foundation for understanding the basics of interior finishes for floors, walls, and ceilings, allowing designers to explore the ever-evolving market of eco-friendly interior finishes.

Plaster and Gypsum Board

Plaster has been a trusted building material for centuries, offering both structural support and a polished appearance to interiors and exteriors. It can be made from earth, gypsum, or lime, and has proven to withstand natural disasters across the globe. Plaster possesses excellent thermal properties, providing insulation against cold and remaining cool in hot conditions. Its fireproof nature makes it particularly suitable for high-risk fire areas like mountain and desert communities. Mineral-based plaster, free from synthetic additives, is an ideal choice for clients with chemical sensitivities, as it is inert once dry. Plaster walls are breathable, allowing for the exchange of water vapor and improving indoor air quality. However, it's important to specify non-toxic materials to prevent the release of harmful chemicals. Mixing plaster on-site minimizes waste that would otherwise end up in landfills. Depending on the type of plaster used, there are various environmentally friendly finish options available, including painting, tinting, applying a clear-coat finish or beeswax, or leaving it in its natural state. Choosing plaster that allows the structure itself to serve as the finish aligns with waste reduction and eco-friendly principles.

Gypsum board, also known as drywall, emerged as a popular alternative to gypsum plaster due to its convenient preformed and ready-to-finish nature. It has become the primary material used in new construction for walls, thanks to its smooth surface that accepts various finishes effectively. However, the convenience of gypsum board comes with environmental implications, as on-site construction waste and post-industrial debris contribute to landfill accumulation.

Most gypsum board contains chemicals and additives intended to enhance specific properties, but these may have unintended environmental and health effects. The manufacturing process involves using waste products from air pollution control technology in coal-fired power plants or other manufacturing processes.

Some manufacturers recycle scrap drywall, incorporating it into the production of new drywall along with their own post-manufacturing leftovers. Additionally, post-consumer gypsum wallboard recycling initiatives exist in certain areas of the United States. However, the recycling options for post-consumer scrap drywall may be limited depending on the synthetic content of the drywall in your specific location. While mineral-based plasters and wallboards share some eco-friendly characteristics, their embodied energy and waste generation can vary significantly. To determine the best options available, it is essential to consider these factors carefully.

Gypsum Plaster

Gypsum plaster, commonly known as plaster of Paris, has been used since ancient Egyptian times and is still widely recognized as a plaster material. It is named after the gypsum beds found in Paris. The primary component of gypsum plaster is hydrous calcium sulfate, a mineral that is abundant but nonrenewable. It is mined and then dehydrated at around 300°F to create a powdery substance known as hemihydrate gypsum. When mixed with water, it forms a workable plaster for application to walls or as joint compound. However, the mining and transportation of crude gypsum can have environmental drawbacks.

Synthetic gypsum plaster, also known as recycled or by-product gypsum, is derived from the mandated scrubbing of fossil fuels in power plants and the production of titanium dioxide. Recovering gypsum in this way reduces waste and minimizes landscape destruction. However, these products are not regulated and may not be as durable, so it's important to inquire about the source material.

Both crude gypsum and synthetic gypsum require hydration to become plaster. These plasters are suitable only for interior use as they are susceptible to erosion from rain and weather. Gypsum plaster can be applied as a veneer on top of structures like gypsum board or built up on a lath to serve as a structural wall element. One of the advantages of gypsum plaster is that natural mineral- or vegetable-based pigments can be added directly to the mix, eliminating the need for additional finishes like paint. Once set, gypsum plaster is essentially inert and provides a durable surface for various wall treatments, contributing to the longevity of the finish.

To enhance the properties of gypsum plaster, additional minerals like lime can be incorporated to prevent shrinkage and cracks. Another ingredient that is commonly found in gypsum plaster is crystalline silica, which acts as a drying agent. It's important to note that prolonged and heavy exposure to silica dust can lead to health issues such as silicosis, a form of cancer. However, the risk to occupants of a home with plaster walls is minimal.

Nevertheless, it is worth mentioning that many modern gypsum plasters contain harmful fungicides, setting agents, and other chemicals, which can offset some of the eco-friendly benefits. When specifying gypsum plaster, it is advisable to opt for natural variants that have little to no volatile organic compound (VOC) additives, if possible. This helps to minimize potential health and environmental impacts associated with chemical additives.

Origins of Gypsum Plaster:

- Gypsum plaster is primarily made by mixing powdered gypsum with water in different formulations. The gypsum used can be obtained from natural sources.
- Synthetic gypsum, on the other hand, may include coal ash derived from the scrubbing process used to remove sulfur dioxide from emissions in coal-fired power plants.
- In addition to gypsum, plaster formulations may also contain various chemical additives such as epoxies, plastics, fungicides, setting agents, drying agents, binders, and fillers. These additives can affect the performance and environmental characteristics of the plaster.
- Crystalline silica, often sourced from quartz, is commonly used as a drying agent in gypsum plaster mixes.
- Lime and other inert minerals may be incorporated into plaster to help prevent shrinkage and cracking, enhancing the overall stability of the material.

Maintenance

It is important to maintain dry and clean conditions for gypsum plaster walls, as they can deteriorate if exposed to moisture and may become chalky if scuffed. However, any damage can be easily patched or sanded to restore the appearance of the walls. Opting for natural or low-VOC gypsum plaster is a wise choice for creating an eco-friendly home with good indoor air quality. These types of plaster minimize the release of harmful volatile organic compounds (VOCs) and contribute to a healthier living environment.

Leftover plaster mix can be repurposed for other applications or taken to a construction salvage exchange to minimize waste. The mineral gypsum itself is not considered harmful to the environment, but caution should be exercised regarding any chemical additives present in the plaster as they could potentially leach into the land or water upon disposal. When it comes to recycling plastered walls, it can be challenging due to the difficulty of separating the plaster from paint and wallcoverings, as well as the complexity of separating plaster from the wall itself. Currently, plaster deconstruction and recycling are not widely feasible. However, the lath used in plaster walls can be recycled through appropriate wood or steel recycling resources. If the plaster does not contain arsenic, which is sometimes found in older plaster, it may be compostable.

Specification

- Use natural gypsum plaster mix or recycled/synthetic/by-product gypsum mix with no additives.
- Choose wooden lath, preferably reclaimed or FSC-certified, or recycled steel or metal lath.
- Opt for natural gypsum or recycled gypsum lath with a recycled paper face.
- If additives are necessary, select low-VOC options.
- Allow adequate dry time between coats for proper curing.

Avoid:
- Avoid remodeling, sanding, demolition, or cutting existing plaster without first testing for hazards such as

arsenic, vermiculite, or lead paint.
- Avoid the use of fungicides, chemical agents, or synthetic additives in the plaster mix.
- Prevent direct contact of water or high humidity with the plastered walls to avoid deterioration.

Gypsum Board: Drywall, Wallboard

After World War II, labor-intensive gypsum plaster was replaced by prefabricated wallboard, also known as gypsum board or drywall, which became the primary choice for American homes and offices. Architects or builders typically specify this material, but if possible, select the most eco-friendly type available.

Gypsum board, also referred to as plasterboard, plaster sandwiched between paper, or sheetrock, is a widely used wall and ceiling material. It consists of compressed gypsum plaster formed into rigid sheets. The standard sheet size is 4-by-8 feet, but custom lengths up to 16 feet are available to minimize seams and waste. The gypsum core is noncombustible, while the paper surfaces are often made from recycled newsprint. Installation involves screws, fasteners, and joint tape for seamless joints.

When specifying gypsum board for interior applications, it's important to consider the specific varieties and their characteristics. Here are the technical names and descriptions of different types of gypsum board:

- Gypsum Wallboard: Primarily used for interior surfacing, it has a manila-colored face paper. It comes in various thicknesses and can have a regular or fire-resistant core.
- Gypsum Ceiling Board: Specifically designed for interior ceilings, it shares the same characteristics as wallboard. The thickness is typically ½ inch, and it's suitable for water-based textured finishes with sag resistance equivalent to ⅝-inch-thick gypsum wallboard.
- Pre-decorated Gypsum Board: This type of board comes with a prefinished surface, such as paint, texture, print, or wallcovering. It is available in different thicknesses and can have a standard or fire-resistant core.
- Water-Resistant Gypsum Board (Greenboard): Used as a base for ceramic or plastic tile applications on walls, it has a green-tinted face paper. It features a water-resistant core and breathable face and back paper for drying support.
- Gypsum Base for Veneer Plaster: With a blue-tinted face paper, this board is treated to promote adherence and bonding with thin coats of plaster. It comes in standard sheet sizes and can have a fire-resistive core.
- Sound Board: Designed to reduce noise transmission, sound board incorporates viscoelastic polymers into conventional gypsum cores.
- Cement Board: Although not technically drywall, cementitious-based boards have comparable uses and characteristics. They are strong and moisture-resistant, commonly used for subflooring and tile substrates, especially in wet areas prone to mold and mildew. Various sizes and thicknesses are available.

Consider the specific requirements of your project to determine the appropriate type of gypsum board for each application.

Origins of Gypsum Board:

- Gypsum board is typically manufactured using mined calcium sulfate, which is a naturally occurring mineral.
- The board is composed of a gypsum core with a paper face.
- Chemical additives may be incorporated into the gypsum board formulation. These additives can include fungicides, adhesives, vinyl, naphthalene, or formaldehyde, depending on the specific product and manufacturer.
- Some types of gypsum board are labeled as "recycled" or "synthetic." These boards are made from industrial by-product gypsum, flue gas desulfurized gypsum, or other industrial by-products. These alternative sources help reduce the reliance on virgin gypsum mined directly from natural deposits.

Note: The specific composition and sourcing of gypsum board may vary depending on the manufacturer and the region.

Despite being made from an abundant natural material, can have environmental drawbacks. The accumulation of gypsum board scrap in landfills and the leaching of chemical additives into the earth are concerning issues. To mitigate these environmental impacts, it's important to specify eco-friendly options and promote sustainable practices. Here are some considerations:

- Specify Recycled Content: Look for gypsum board with a high percentage of recycled content. Recycled gypsum board utilizes post-consumer or post-industrial waste, reducing the demand for virgin materials and diverting waste from landfills.
- Low-VOC and Chemical-Free: Specify gypsum board that is free from harmful additives, such as volatile organic compounds (VOCs), fungicides, and synthetic chemicals. Opting for low-VOC products contributes to better indoor air quality and minimizes the release of harmful substances into the environment.
- Responsible Disposal: Encourage responsible disposal of gypsum board scrap. Explore recycling options for gypsum board in your area or consider partnering with construction salvage exchanges that can repurpose or recycle the waste material.
- Minimize Waste: Specify gypsum board in appropriate sizes to minimize waste and the need for excessive cutting and trimming. Proper planning and accurate measurements can help optimize material usage.
- Consider Alternative Materials: In certain applications, explore alternative materials that have lower environmental impacts. For example, in areas prone to moisture, consider using cement board or other moisture-resistant substrates instead of water-resistant gypsum board.

By prioritizing these considerations and advocating for eco-friendly practices, you can help reduce the environmental impact associated with gypsum board use.

Maintenance

Drywall is always finished because leaving it unfinished would result in visible joints and increased vulnerability to moisture. If exposed to standing water, high moisture, or constant humidity, drywall can warp or degrade. Therefore, it is crucial to provide a quality finish to protect the drywall. Various options, such as drywall texture, plaster, paint, or wallcovering, can be applied to the drywall surface to both enhance its appearance and safeguard it. Minor damage can be easily patched with taping and additional plaster or joint compound. However, if any sections of drywall become moldy, they should be promptly replaced to prevent further mold growth and maintain a healthy indoor environment.

In certain areas with suitable soil conditions, crushed gypsum can be utilized as a soil conditioner. If there is no available construction waste recycling for wallboard in the region, it is advisable to discuss with the contractor the possibility of pulverizing leftover wallboard into smaller pieces, less than half an inch in size, either manually or using power tools. These pulverized pieces can then be mixed into the topsoil.

Currently, the recycling of wallboard after it has been used in homes presents challenges. However, as the pressure on landfills increases, there may be a growing demand for more recycling options for wallboard in the future. When disposed of in landfills, gypsum board and the paper envelope will eventually break down. However, it is important to note that paint, chemical adhesives, and other manufactured materials present in the wallboard may introduce potential risks of toxic off-gassing and contamination.

Specification

- Purchase wallboard in precise measurements, aligning with the room height, to minimize waste.
- Opt for wallboard with a high gypsum content, whether natural or synthetic/recycled.
- Look for wallboard with high natural material content in addition to gypsum, such as sand or quartz.
- Choose wallboard with recycled paper sheathing or consider options with minimal additives or no paper sheathing.
- Use hypoallergenic or low-VOC joint compound, preferably gypsum-based plaster.
- Use joint tape and/or acoustical sealant made from recycled content paper.
- Reuse construction scrap on-site whenever possible.
- If allowed by local regulations, incorporate small amounts of ground scrap into topsoil.
- Explore wallboard recycling programs available in your region for proper disposal of scrap.

Avoid:

- Avoid powdered joint compounds that contain antifreeze, vinyls, preservatives, biocides, or those that emit VOCs.
- Avoid wallboard with chemical additives, particularly those that may release VOCs.
- Minimize wasteful purchases or installation methods for drywall to reduce unnecessary material consumption.

Tiles

Tile is a versatile material used in various applications, including flooring, shower surrounds, walls, ceilings, and backsplashes. It encompasses a wide range of materials, such as ceramic, porcelain, terra-cotta, earthenware (all types of fired clay), glass (new or recycled), cement, stone, and terrazzo (a resin-based conglomerate containing minerals and/or reclaimed components).

The durability of tile is one of its key characteristics, often requiring infrequent replacement. It can be easily maintained by washing with water and contributes to a healthy indoor environment due to its inert properties. Tile typically resists mold and stains, is fireproof, does not release harmful gases, and remains stable when exposed to water.

While tile offers durability and a healthy indoor environment, it does have some environmental drawbacks. The raw materials used in tile production, such as clay, sand, and stone, are non-renewable resources. The excavation of these materials can have negative impacts on water quality and landscape integrity. Additionally, the transportation of raw materials to manufacturing facilities, as well as the firing process itself, contribute to high embodied energy and carbon emissions.

The glazing process of tiles can also pose environmental risks. Although radioactive materials, asbestos, and lead-based glazes are now banned in many countries, there may still be traces of these substances in older tiles. Modern glazes may contain toxic chemicals that can be harmful to workers, the environment, and the atmosphere.

Despite these concerns, tile can still be a suitable choice for environmentally conscious homes for a couple of reasons. Firstly, when installed with healthy materials, tile does not emit contaminants or act as a sink for indoor pollutants. Secondly, tile is highly durable and has the potential to outlast the lifespan of a house, reducing the need for replacement and waste generation.

To ensure environmentally responsible tile choices, it is advisable to look for third-party certifications. The Green Squared certification, for example, provides a comprehensive evaluation of tile products, considering their characteristics, manufacturing processes, end-of-life management, corporate governance, and manufacturing innovation. These certifications aim to establish sustainability criteria throughout the product's lifecycle and promote the use of sustainable tile systems.

In addition to third-party certifications, it is beneficial to seek out tiles that are manufactured regionally, using raw materials sourced from nearby locations. This helps reduce the environmental impact associated with long-distance transportation. However, if regional options are not available, it may be necessary to expand the search.

When selecting tiles, prioritize those made from natural materials or those that have a positive environmental impact, such as recycled glass tiles. It is also important to consider the environmental implications of the underlayment, mortar, mastic, grout, and sealants used during installation, as these products can contain harmful chemicals. To make the best choice for both the client and the environment, it is necessary to carefully weigh various factors. This includes evaluating the tile's composition, manufacturing processes, transportation distances, and the methods and substances required for installation. By considering all these aspects, it is possible to make a more informed decision that minimizes environmental impacts.

Ceramic and Quarry Tiles

The terms "ceramic" and "quarry" are now used interchangeably and broadly refer to tiles made of clay that have been fired. In the past, the definitions were more distinct, with porcelain and ceramic tiles made from finer clay and glazed, quarry tiles being larger than 6 inches square, and terra-cotta tiles being unglazed and reddish in color. However, nowadays, the term "ceramic" is used for almost any tile made from fired clay, regardless of the specific type.

Ceramic and quarry tiles offer a durable, water-resistant, and low-maintenance surface. They are fireproof, resistant to bugs and mold, and do not emit VOCs in their unsealed state. Glazed tiles, in particular, do not absorb contaminants and reemit them. They are also suitable for energy-efficient passive solar storage or radiant heat systems. Tiles have a long lifespan and can outlast multiple installations of other materials. The enduring beauty of ancient mosaics created by Islamic and Roman artists centuries ago is a testament to their longevity.

For most residential applications, unglazed surfaces of ceramic or quarry tiles will require a sealant to protect them from dirt and stains. The porosity of the tile will determine the extent to which it absorbs contaminants, albeit in small amounts.

In general, designers often face challenges in obtaining precise information about the composition of ceramic tiles, as most manufacturers consider the specific ingredients and processes as proprietary information. The only available details typically pertain to the hazardous components mentioned in the Material Safety Data Sheets (MSDS). To address this, it is recommended to select tiles from manufacturers or dealers who have established strong environmental policies. By researching online, designers can find published company guidelines that outline internal standards aimed at reducing factory emissions and waste, enhancing recycling rates for raw and scrap materials, and prioritizing human safety. Choosing companies with transparent environmental practices can contribute to sustainable design choices in ceramic tile selection.

Glass Tile:

Glass is an excellent material for making tiles due to its abundant source, primarily derived from sand (silicon dioxide). It offers an inert surface that is easy to clean and maintain. Recycled glass tiles have gained popularity in recent years, as they are produced from postconsumer and postindustrial waste such as bottles, windshields, and windowpanes. The amount of recycled glass content in these tiles can vary widely, ranging from a small percentage to 100 percent.

The concept of recycled glass tile is appealing because it diverts used glass from the waste stream and transforms it into durable design materials. The manufacturing process for glass tiles is relatively straightforward. Ground-up glass, known as cullet, is poured into molds and may be mixed with metallic oxides to achieve desired colors. The glass is then fired or melted, shaped, and no glaze is necessary as glass is naturally impervious. The slight variations in color that occur in glass tiles add to their unique charm. Compared to ceramic tiles, manufacturing pure glass tiles typically requires less energy as the glass is melted or sintered at lower temperatures. Glass tiles are also commonly used in terrazzo-like designs that combine glass with concrete as the matrix material.

Origins of Ceramic and Glass Tiles:

- Traditional ceramic tiles are primarily made of fired clay, which provides the base material.
- Additional minerals such as talc, cement, or other additives may be incorporated during the ceramic tile manufacturing process.
- To enhance specific properties or incorporate sustainable elements, manufacturers may introduce manufactured or recycled materials like fly ash or glass into the tile composition.
- Ceramic tiles can be either glazed or unglazed. Glazes consist of metals, pigments, various chemicals, and silicon dioxide (sand), which become inert when fired.
- Glass tiles are predominantly composed of silicon dioxide (sand). Recycled glass tiles are often produced using post-consumer waste, such as bottles and windshields.
- The recycled glass content can vary significantly among manufacturers and even between different colors of tiles.
- For color and texture variations, small amounts of metals and chemicals may be added to glass tiles.

Note: The specific composition and proportions of these materials may differ based on the manufacturer, product line, and desired characteristics of the tile.

Maintenance

Tile, particularly when glazed, is highly durable and requires minimal maintenance, usually just soap and water for cleaning. However, the grout lines between tiles are susceptible to expansion and contraction caused by water and heat, leading to deterioration over time. If the tile and the room are not kept dry, mold and mildew can thrive in the grout. It is essential to ensure good ventilation through windows and exhaust fans, as well as regular cleaning of the tiled surface.

Unglazed ceramic, terra-cotta, frosted glass, and other porous tiles are more prone to damage from stains, scratches, and general wear and tear, whether used on floors or countertops. The porous nature of unglazed surfaces also makes them more susceptible to absorbing contaminants and harboring bacteria. In contrast, glazed tiles are resistant to most forms of damage.

However, it's important to note that the grout surrounding both glazed and unglazed tiles is more vulnerable and should be sealed on-site after installation to prevent mold and stains. It is advisable to specify a low-VOC, water-based, wipe-on sealant instead of a spray-on variety to minimize negative impacts on indoor air quality.

While it may be tempting to avoid using sealants, it's crucial to consider that both the grout and the tile itself will deteriorate more quickly and require replacement without proper sealing. Ultimately, if the tile becomes damaged and needs to be disposed of in a landfill, it would have a more significant environmental impact than the use of sealants. Sealants also play a vital role in preventing mold growth, which is crucial for maintaining sanitary conditions and indoor air quality. To prevent tile degradation, it is recommended to apply a sealant immediately after the tile installation and reapply it as per the manufacturer's recommendations.

Broken pieces of tile can find various uses to minimize waste and promote sustainability. They can be utilized in mosaic art, placed underneath soil in potted plants to improve drainage, or incorporated into the garden as decorative elements. Any extra tiles can be saved as replacements for future repairs or taken to construction recycling or exchange sites.

Tiles, along with mortar and grout, are similar to metamorphosed rock and will eventually break down into inert rock-like pieces at the end of their life cycle. The glaze on the tile is also inert. In certain areas, recycling programs exist for porcelain and ceramic fixtures such as old toilets, and tile may be accepted for recycling in those facilities. Glass tiles offer significant potential for recycling. Those made entirely of glass can be recycled repeatedly, ultimately being transformed back into sand. This makes them a particularly sustainable choice for reducing waste and promoting circularity.

Specification

When selecting tile, consider the following specifications to prioritize sustainability and environmental friendliness:

- Look for tile that has third-party certifications and full life-cycle assessments to ensure it meets rigorous environmental standards.
- Choose unprocessed, all-natural tile made from clays or safe recycled materials like glass.
- Prioritize domestic tile, especially those produced locally, to reduce the carbon footprint associated with transportation.
- Opt for factory-glazed ceramic tiles, which provide a durable and low-maintenance surface.
- Consider using one-hundred-percent recycled glass tile or tiles with a high recycled-glass content.
- Use natural backerboard, such as FSC-certified wood, plaster, gypsum, or concrete, as underlayment.
- Select simple mortar made from cement, sand, water, and possibly lime, without any additives.
- Look for third-party certification to ensure its environmental credentials.
- Choose grout without added fungicides and certified by a reputable third party.
- Use a low-VOC, water-based, wipe-on sealant to protect the tile.
- Avoid sealants with VOCs, solvents, or harmful additives.
- Opt for low-VOC, low-solvent, additive-free, and latex-free mortar and grout to minimize indoor air pollution.

To promote sustainability, avoid the following:

- Unregulated import tile, as it may not meet adequate environmental standards.

- Excessive amounts of new glass added to glass tiles, as it increases the demand for virgin materials.
- Mortar, grout, and sealants containing VOCs, solvents, fungicides, vinyls, or latex additives, as these can have harmful effects on indoor air quality and the environment.

Flooring

- Bamboo as flooring

Bamboo is a popular choice for sustainable flooring, cabinets, wall paneling, and furniture due to its rapid renewability and versatility. However, it's important to consider the following factors when selecting bamboo products:

- Not all bamboo products are created equal, as some may have been coated with harmful chemicals like pesticides, fungicides, biocides, and fireproofing agents. Additionally, some manufacturers use urea-formaldehyde as a binder, which is a known carcinogen. Look for formaldehyde-free options and consult the manufacturer for details on chemical contents.
- Bamboo flooring types vary, including solid bamboo, engineered bamboo, veneer bamboo, and strand bamboo. Strand bamboo products use individual fibers bound with pressure, heat, and resin, which typically contains formaldehyde. Engineered and veneer bamboo flooring may have a core wood sourced from certified sustainable forests.
- Moisture and humidity can affect bamboo, causing warping or weakening. It is not recommended for use in bathrooms or very wet climates where humidity levels exceed 60 percent.
- Bamboo has limitations when it comes to color choices, as it doesn't take stain easily. However, some manufacturers using water-based stains have had success in expanding color options.
- Carbonized bamboo is an alternative with a darker color achieved through extended steaming. However, it is about 20 percent less durable than natural bamboo and may show color variation if scratched.

While domestic bamboo production is not yet reliable, it's important to consider the environmental impact of transporting raw materials from overseas. Look for manufacturers with third-party certifications for other products as a guideline for selecting reliable bamboo sources. As demand for bamboo continues to grow, it is likely that domestic sources will emerge in the future.

Origins of Bamboo:

- Bamboo is a type of grass with a woody stalk and over a thousand species worldwide. While most bamboo is grown in Asia, there are emerging sources in the United States to meet increasing demand.
- Solid and engineered bamboo can be used for flooring, wallcoverings, and other residential purposes.
- Sustainable and ethical practices in bamboo plantations vary, and currently, there is no certification available from the Forest Stewardship Council (FSC) or third-party organizations specifically for bamboo.
- Engineered bamboo typically consists of layers, similar to laminate flooring, with a core made of rubberwood or another type of wood. Look for FSC-certified core wood for increased sustainability.
- In some countries with less regulated pesticide use, bamboo farms may employ harmful pesticides like DDT. However, borate, a pest-inhibiting treatment considered safe around humans, is also used.
- Urea-formaldehyde is commonly used as a bonding agent in bamboo flooring, although formaldehyde-free options are less common.
- Additional chemicals may be added for purposes such as mildew control, fireproofing, and pest resistance.
- Standard factory finishes for bamboo products often include aluminum oxide and polyurethane. Water-based acrylic stain may also be used in finishes.

Maintenance

Bamboo can experience discoloration when exposed to direct sunlight, particularly in high-altitude areas with intense solar radiation. To minimize this effect, it is recommended to use window coverings or UV-coated window treatments that provide protection against harmful UV rays. When it comes to cleaning bamboo flooring, it is best to use mild, nonabrasive, and environmentally friendly cleaners on an occasional basis. Regular vacuuming and/or sweeping will help keep the floor free of dust and debris. However, it is important to avoid using oil soaps and damp mopping, as excessive moisture can damage bamboo flooring.

Bamboo that has been manufactured with minimal amounts of binding adhesives, contaminants in the topcoat, or chemical treatments will biodegrade safely and relatively quickly, similar to wood. It can be disposed of in an environmentally friendly manner, such as through composting or natural decomposition processes.

However, it's worth noting that engineered bamboo, which typically involves the use of chemical binders, may not biodegrade as easily or quickly. The presence of these chemical binders can affect the natural decomposition process.

Another sustainable option for bamboo is to reclaim and refinish it for reuse in other applications. This promotes resource conservation and reduces waste. When considering the end-of-life disposal of bamboo products, it is important to check the specific manufacturing processes and materials used in their production. Opting for bamboo products that prioritize environmental sustainability and minimal chemical treatments will support their safe disposal and potential reuse.

Specification

When specifying bamboo products, consider the following:

- Look for formaldehyde-free bamboo options to minimize exposure to harmful chemicals.
- Prioritize bamboo products with third-party certifications like the Forest Stewardship Council (FSC), which ensures responsible and sustainable sourcing.
- Check if the bamboo products comply with California Section 01350, a standard for low-emitting materials.
- Choose bamboo products with low-VOC (Volatile Organic Compounds) finishes, preferably factory-finished, to minimize off-gassing of harmful chemicals.
- Select low-VOC underlayment, adhesives, and binders to further reduce indoor air pollution.
- Opt for bamboo products that minimize the use of adhesives, as excessive adhesive use can introduce more chemicals into the environment.
- Ensure that the subflooring is perfectly dry before bamboo installation to prevent moisture-related issues.

On the other hand, it is advisable to avoid:

Bamboo products that contain formaldehyde in the underlayment, binder, or finish, as formaldehyde is a known harmful chemical. Installing bamboo in high-humidity weather conditions, as excessive moisture can lead to warping, weakening, or other damage. Bamboo products that contain chemicals added for mildew control, fireproofing, pest resistance, or in finishes, as these additives may introduce harmful substances into the environment.

Biocomposite flooring

Biocomposites, made from agricultural by-products, are increasingly popular in home construction and design. These materials utilize leftovers from crops such as wheat or sorghum chaff, bagasse (sugar cane pulp), sunflower hulls, and other agricultural waste. They are commonly used as substitutes for plywood, medium-density fiberboard (MDF), oriented strand board (OSB), paneling, cabinet bodies and faces, and veneer.

Agriculture-based biocomposites offer the advantage of utilizing annually renewable resources that are readily available as by-products of crop production. While they may not possess the same hardness or water resistance as solid wood, many varieties of biocomposites compare favorably to their engineered wood counterparts for applications such as millwork, underlayments, backings, and casework. When used as finish materials, the natural grains, speckles, and color variations of biocomposite boards add unique beauty to environmentally conscious homes.

Biocomposites can be employed in flooring, cabinetry, and wall paneling applications. However, it's important to note that these materials are still somewhat experimental, and their long-term performance is not fully established. Some biocomposite boards made from sorghum waste fiber are being marketed as durable enough for flooring. Sorghum crops, known for their drought tolerance and minimal fertilizer and pesticide requirements, are primarily harvested in northern China. Sorghum is already cultivated worldwide for various purposes, including ethanol production, sweeteners, and livestock feed enhancers.

Origins of Biocomposites:

- Biocomposite boards are crafted from diverse agricultural residues and by-products, such as wheat, rice, barley, oat straw, sunflower hulls, bluegrass or rye grass stubble, cornhusks, sorghum stalks, hemp, soybean plants, and bagasse (sugar cane pulp).
- Adhesives and binders used in biocomposite boards may consist of low-VOC glues, outgassing solvents, formaldehyde, soy-based products, and natural or synthetic resins.
- Borate, which is occasionally employed as a pesticide in the manufacturing process, may be present. Other residual pesticides from the cropland might also be present.
- Finished biocomposite boards may feature water-based finishes or solvent-based polyurethanes.
- Formaldehyde can be used as a preservative during manufacturing or as an ingredient in the finish.

Maintenance

Maintenance requirements for biocomposites may differ based on their specific composition. It is advisable to consult the manufacturer for guidance on periodic resealing, if necessary. Generally, biocomposites should be cared for similar to wood. In areas with heavy foot traffic or the presence of pets, using rugs can significantly extend the lifespan of the floor.

Biocomposite boards, like wood, have the ability to decompose naturally and return to the soil. However, the decomposition process of the small amounts of binders, resins, stains, and finishes used in or on the boards may be slower. It is important to confirm the toxic content of these chemicals to prevent their re-entry into the soil during decomposition. Ensuring that the chemicals used are environmentally safe will help maintain the ecological integrity of the soil.

Specification

When selecting biocomposite boards, consider the following specifications:

- Choose boards made from 100 percent renewable grain, without the addition of plastics or other non-renewable materials.
- Opt for products that use formaldehyde-free binders, sealants, adhesives, and stains. Look for zero- to low-VOC (volatile organic compound) water-based options to minimize off-gassing and indoor air pollution.
- If necessary, ensure that any added preservative or pest resistance is in the form of borate, which is considered safe for human health and the environment.

On the other hand, it is advisable to avoid:

- Biocomposite boards that contain formaldehyde in their binders or finishes, as formaldehyde is a known toxin.
- Boards treated with preservatives or pesticides other than borate, as they may have adverse effects on human health and the environment.

By considering these specifications and avoiding potentially harmful substances, you can choose biocomposite boards that are environmentally friendly and promote a healthier indoor environment.

Wooden flooring

Wood is a popular natural element in home construction and design due to its simplicity to clean and maintain compared to other flooring options like carpet. It is particularly suitable for homes with children, pets, or individuals with allergies as it does not collect mold, dust, or pet hair. With proper maintenance and occasional refinishing, wood flooring can last a lifetime, making it a valuable long-term investment. One advantage of wood is its lower embodied energy compared to nonrenewable materials like stone or tile. Wood requires minimal processing and finishing to be suitable for home flooring. However, it is important to recognize that most wood grows slowly over many decades, making it a slow-renewable resource. Unfortunately, previous generations often disregarded this fact and contributed to the rapid depletion of old-growth trees.

Forestry practices, although improved in recent years, still face controversies and problems. Single-species tree plantations, an attempt by forest product companies to meet consumer demand, lack the biodiversity necessary for a healthy and sustainable ecosystem. The rapid destruction of tropical rainforests, equivalent to an area the size of six football fields per minute according to Greenpeace, is a concerning issue.

To address these environmental challenges associated with traditional forestry practices, the Forest Stewardship Council (FSC) has introduced chain-of-custody certification and environmentally friendly standards for the industry. Look for the FSC symbol on new wood flooring as it signifies that the wood has been sourced sustainably and meets stringent environmental criteria. Choosing FSC-certified wood helps promote responsible forestry practices and supports the preservation of healthy forests.

Reclaimed Wood Flooring

To ensure eco-friendly wood flooring, choose reclaimed wood from local sources such as construction salvage yards, dealers, or buildings slated for remodeling, deconstruction, or demolition. Opting for locally sourced repurposed wood minimizes new logging, eliminates long-distance transportation, and reduces wood waste. For added sustainability, consider specifying SmartWood-certified options that guarantee environmentally friendly species, logging practices, and remanufacturing methods.

It is crucial to verify the source of the reclaimed wood and ensure that the company does not encourage the dismantling of historical structures. Look for responsibly salvaged products with third-party certifications like "rediscovered wood" and "underwater salvage" from the Rainforest Alliance. These certifications validate the wood's sourcing and take into account procedures that prioritize environmental preservation and the well-being of workers and communities.

Conduct a thorough investigation into the reclaimed wood's suitability for indoor use. Determine whether the flooring has been exposed to industrial chemicals or agricultural pesticides, as such exposure would make it unsafe for residential applications. Reclaimed wood from older homes is a widely available and often ideal choice for residential flooring. Additionally, various unique woods are now being repurposed, including those sourced from wine and whiskey barrels, old fishing boats, or pallets, offering distinct options for flooring.

New Wood Flooring

When selecting new wood flooring, it can be environmentally friendly if the chosen species is not endangered and sustainable forestry practices are employed. Consider the project's sustainable objectives to guide the research and specifications for the flooring. For instance, while domestic wood may seem more eco-friendly due to lower transportation energy, it's crucial to check if the species is endangered. In some cases, exotic or foreign wood may be a better choice. The Forest Stewardship Council (FSC) provides guidance by certifying sustainably forested wood that does not deplete endangered ecosystems. The FSC evaluates tree species availability, monitors conservation efforts throughout the supply chain, and prohibits the use of genetically modified organisms (GMOs) and certain pesticides. While other certification organizations exist, the FSC is widely recognized for its thorough and impartial methods.

There are three primary types of new wood flooring: solid wood, engineered wood, and acrylic-impregnated wood.

1. **Solid wood flooring**: It is available in prefinished or unfinished options. When specifying FSC-certified solid wood with an eco-friendly finish, it becomes an excellent green choice. Suppressed wood, which refers to small undergrowth trees thinned and culled to prevent forest fires on public lands, may not yet be certified but is another wise selection from an environmental standpoint.

2. Engineered wood flooring: This type of flooring involves the use of various chemicals during manufacturing. It consists of pressed layers, typically three-ply or five-ply, that run in different directions, providing enhanced dimensional stability in humid conditions such as near bathtubs or sinks. When choosing engineered wood, look for products that are formaldehyde-free and FSC-certified.

3. Acrylic-impregnated wood: While acrylic-impregnated wood is commonly used for commercial installations like gym floors, it is not considered an ideal green choice for homes due to the significant presence of synthetics. However, there are a few manufacturers of acrylic-impregnated products that utilize FSC-certified wood, which can be a more sustainable option if desired.

Origins of Wooden flooring:

- Wood flooring can be sourced from both domestic and exotic trees, and there are different types available.
- Reclaimed wood is obtained from various sources such as residential, commercial, and agricultural structures, as well as natural sources like rivers and fallen trees.
- Some wood floors are made from recycled wood scraps or sawdust, which are combined with acrylics or resins.
- Common sealants for wood flooring include polyurethane and resin-oil primers.
- Floor finishes and stains may contain a range of components such as natural oils, resins, pigments, solvents, chemical compounds, petroleum distillates, metal drying agents, formaldehyde, and water.

Maintenance

To preserve the beauty and integrity of a wood floor, there are simple maintenance practices to follow. For both reclaimed and new wood flooring, it is advisable to:
- Apply penetrating oils and waxes occasionally, followed by thorough buffing.
- Use stripping as a last resort if layers of grime have accumulated.
- Take preventive measures to avoid scratches and marks, such as placing felt or floor protectors under furniture, rugs, and appliances.
- Encourage the removal of shoes inside the house.
- Use rugs in high-traffic or play areas, ensuring they are secured with nonslip backing or padding.
- Regularly sweep with a soft broom or vacuum with the rotating bristles turned off to prevent scratches.
- For more thorough cleaning, use a small amount of soap specifically designed for wood floors and minimal water.
- Avoid letting water pool on the floor, and use a mop with a towel underneath to handle spills.
- Replace any damaged flooring promptly to prevent the spread of damage.
- When refinishing the entire floor, if the existing finish is compatible, specify an eco-friendly product that adheres with minimal or no sanding. Stripping the floor completely can create a messy environment and pose risks to the health of workers and clients.

> Wood floors can undergo deconstruction to salvage the wood for various purposes. The salvaged wood can be used for similar flooring applications or repurposed for different uses. In some cases, the wood may be downcycled, meaning it is transformed into a wood-based product with a lower value or functionality. It's important to note that wood that is rotten or contaminated with toxic substances is not suitable for reuse. Such wood should be properly disposed of in an environmentally responsible manner. However, wood that is in good condition and free from contaminants can be salvaged and given a new life, contributing to sustainable practices and reducing waste.

Specification

When selecting wood for flooring, consider the following specifications:

Wood:
- Fallen or thinned wood from the property
- Reclaimed wood from reliable sources
- Locally or domestically harvested wood that is FSC-certified and comes from nonthreatened species
- Suppressed wood (no certification available)
- Rapidly renewable wood species

Finishes and stains (for prefinished wood or on-site application):

- Water-based finishes Finishes made of natural oils, resins, pigments, and waxes (sometimes referred to as food-grade)
- Low-VOC (volatile organic compound) finishes
- Formaldehyde-free finishes
- Finishes free of metallic hardening or drying agents (such as zinc)
- Solvent-free finishes
- Proper protection of wood from moisture before and during installation

Avoid:

- Reclaimed wood of uncertain origin
- Wood tainted with lead, arsenic, factory chemicals, or fungicides
- Uncertified wood
- Rare or threatened wood species
- Solvent-based finishes
- Presence of formaldehyde or other preservatives in the wood or finish
- Finishes containing metal-based drying agents

Rubber Flooring

Recycled "rubber" flooring, which is made from synthetic, petroleum-based latex recycled from tires, is still under scrutiny regarding its safety for residential applications. While many companies claim low-VOC levels that meet indoor air quality standards, there are concerns about the distinct odor and the exposure of the source latex to toxins from being used on roads. While recycling is valuable and the product is often marketed as eco-friendly, it is important to exercise caution when specifying recycled rubber flooring, especially if you have concerns about emissions. The rubber, binders, and additives used in the flooring may off-gas, contain heavy metals, or potentially compromise indoor air quality. Assessing the potential risks and considering alternative flooring options may be advisable in such cases.

Origins of Rubber flooring:

- Recycled rubber/latex flooring is primarily sourced from recycled tire chips rather than natural rubber or latex obtained from rubber trees. Tires themselves are predominantly made from synthetic rubber, which is derived from petroleum.
- It's worth noting that the recycled-rubber flooring may have a relatively low percentage of recycled tire rubber content, sometimes as little as 5 percent. The specific composition of rubber flooring can vary depending on the supply and manufacturing process.
- Due to its previous use on roads, rubber flooring may contain traces of heavy metals, chemicals, petroleum-based compounds, and other elements. However, quantifying the exact content is challenging as it can vary based on the source and supply of recycled materials.

Recycling the rubberlike compound used in recycled rubber flooring is indeed a possibility. However, it's important to note that if these materials end up in a landfill, they will take a significant amount of time to break down.

The incineration of tires, which are often the source of recycled rubber flooring, is a highly controversial practice. The process of incineration can release harmful pollutants into the air, posing a serious human health hazard. Therefore, proper disposal and recycling methods are crucial for minimizing the environmental impact of rubber flooring materials

Recycled tire "rubber" flooring may not be considered a healthy choice for a home due to its questionable content. While it does help prevent tires from ending up in landfills, the materials used in recycled tire rubber flooring can raise concerns about potential health risks. These concerns stem from the presence of various substances such as heavy metals, chemicals, and petroleum-based compounds that may be present in the recycled rubber material. It is important to carefully evaluate the potential health implications and consider alternative flooring options that prioritize indoor air quality and minimize exposure to potentially harmful compounds.

Carpet Flooring

The origins of conventional carpet can be traced back to the development of synthetic fibers derived from petroleum after World War II. These synthetic fibers revolutionized the carpet industry, making it more affordable and accessible to a wider population. However, concerns regarding the environmental impact and potential health hazards associated with conventional carpet have since emerged.

Conventional carpet is predominantly made from synthetic fibers that do not easily decompose or biodegrade at the end of their useful life. Unlike historical carpets made from natural animal and plant fibers, which were more expensive and reserved for the wealthy, modern carpet manufacturing relies heavily on synthetic materials.

One significant issue that arose with the widespread use of conventional carpet was the emergence of complaints related to multiple chemical sensitivities (MCS) or sick building syndrome (SBS). The carpet industry was implicated as a potential source of these problems. The outgassing of various chemical treatments used in carpet manufacturing, as well as the synthetic materials themselves, were identified as potential culprits. Laboratory tests on mice exposed to these chemicals have demonstrated adverse health effects, including sickness and death.

It is important to consider the environmental and health implications when choosing carpet for residential or commercial spaces. Alternative options such as natural fiber carpets, which are derived from renewable and biodegradable materials, may offer more sustainable and healthier alternatives to conventional synthetic carpets.

The Carpet and Rug Institute (CRI) has introduced a voluntary compliance Green Label program, which aims to test and verify the absence of potentially harmful substances in certain brands of carpet, padding, and adhesives. This program focuses particularly on indoor air quality and helps consumers identify carpet products that meet specific standards. While the majority of carpets on the market are still made from nonrenewable petroleum by-products and are not easily recyclable, there are more eco-friendly options available, especially in the form of natural fiber carpets. However, finding all-natural carpets without chemicals or synthetics can be challenging, as they are not common in the mainstream marketplace. Even carpets labeled as 100 percent wool, which is a natural fiber, are often chemically treated with mold and moth inhibitors. Similarly, natural backings and paddings are less commonly found.

In order to make a carpeted home more environmentally friendly, it is advisable to choose all-natural carpets that are free from chemicals and synthetics. Wool carpets, ideally with organic certifications, are a good choice as wool is naturally stain-repellent, fire-resistant, and highly durable without the need for additional treatments. Other natural fibers such as jute, coir, and plant materials are more commonly found in area rugs rather than wall-to-wall carpeting. It is worth noting that these fibers may not last as long as wool and can be more prone to staining, but they are fully biodegradable. Additionally, when selecting carpets, it is beneficial to opt for domestically made products to minimize transportation-related environmental impacts and to avoid potential pesticides that may be mandated for imported carpets.

Origins of Carpet materials:

- All-natural carpet is made from various natural fibers, including wool, silk, jute, coir, sisal, and sea grass. These fibers are derived from plants or animals and are considered more environmentally friendly compared to synthetic options.
- On the other hand, synthetic carpets or synthetic/natural blend carpets are made from artificial fibers such as nylon, olefin, and acrylic. These fibers are petroleum-based and are not biodegradable.
- Carpet backing, which provides stability and support to the carpet, is often made from synthetic latex, known as styrene-butadiene (SB latex) or styrene butadiene rubber (SBR). Natural-fiber backings, such as jute, are less common but offer a more sustainable alternative.
- Padding, used for cushioning and insulation beneath the carpet, can be made from various materials. It may include PVCs or vinyls, recycled carpet fibers, wool, jute, camel hair, or mohair. The choice of padding material can impact the environmental footprint of the carpet.
- It's important to note that carpets, padding, and backing can contain potentially toxic substances. These substances may include benzene, styrene, toluene, vinyl acetate, PVC, fungicides, mothproofing agents, stain-proofing agents, mildew inhibitors, and antistatic chemicals. Understanding the composition of the

carpet and its associated materials is essential for making informed choices about the potential environmental and health impacts.

Maintenance

1. To ensure the longevity and optimal performance of carpet, it's important to follow proper care and maintenance practices. Here are some recommendations: Avoid topical stain treatments: These treatments can release harmful contaminants into the air or flake off over time. It's best to avoid them, especially in the case of all-natural carpets.
2. Discourage DIY stain treatments: Advise clients against using do-it-yourself stain treatments that may contain harsh chemicals or solvents. Instead, recommend natural cleaning methods.
3. Regular vacuuming: Encourage clients to vacuum their carpets thoroughly at least once a week using a vacuum cleaner equipped with a high-efficiency particulate air (HEPA) filter. This helps remove dust, dirt, and allergens, maintaining a clean indoor environment.
4. Use natural stain removal methods: For stain removal, suggest using natural products such as club soda or a small amount of mildly soapy water. Blotting with cornstarch can help absorb stains, and sprinkling baking soda can help eliminate odors.
5. Avoid excessive moisture: Keep carpets dry to prevent mold and mildew growth, particularly for natural wool carpets. Avoid wet-extraction cleaning methods that involve excessive water or steam, as they can damage the carpet fibers and promote mold growth.

Nylon carpets can be recycled, and it's recommended to check with local authorities or carpet manufacturers for carpet recycling programs in your area. On the other hand, natural fibers like wool, jute, coir, sisal, sea grass, corn, cotton, and silk carpets are biodegradable and will naturally break down over time.

Some carpet manufacturers have committed to accepting returned carpets for recycling, ranging from small sections to entire housefuls. It's advised to retain the warranty and product information for future reference on recycling and disposal options.

Specification

- Carpets that meet multi-attribute, life-cycle assessment certifications, CA 01350, or CRI Green Label Plus.
- 100 percent wool carpet that is domestically produced, free of dyes, additives, and chemical treatments.
- Carpets made from 100 percent plant fibers such as jute, coir, sisal, and sea grass, without chemical additives and dyes.
- Carpet products that are recyclable and/or returnable to the manufacturer, particularly if they are made from natural fibers.
- Carpet tiles for easy cleaning and replacement.
- Jute backing for the carpets.
- FSC-certified wood underlayment or gypsum substrate.
- Tackless strip, tack strip, or Velcro-type fastening systems.
- Low-VOC adhesive backing.
- Limited use of water-based yellow or white glue, or low-VOC adhesives, applied only to perimeters.
- Formaldehyde-free materials.

- BHA-free materials.
- Brominated flame retardant (BFR)-free materials.
- Pesticide-free materials.
- Recycled-content carpet options.
- Recycling options for replaced carpets.

Avoid:

- Manufactured fibers like nylon.
- Stain repellents.
- Synthetic dyes.
- Chemicals such as benzene, styrene, toluene, vinyl acetate, and similar substances.
- PVC-vinyl, especially in the backing or padding.
- Treatments such as fungicides, mothproofing, stain-proofing, mildew inhibitors, antistatics, BFR, or other chemical treatments.

Wall Treatments

Wallcoverings

If a material is flat and can be hung vertically, it can be used as a wallcovering. While traditional paper is one eco-friendly option, there are several other alternatives available. These include sisal, bamboo, linen (made from flax), hemp, jute, wood, fabric, cork, and more. Using environmentally friendly wallcoverings is a great choice for covering old paint or imperfect walls, as well as for adding texture and color to a living space.

The practice of using rice paper to finish walls is believed to have originated in the Orient over 2,000 years ago. However, decorative wallpaper as we know it today made its debut in Europe during the fifteenth century. People with limited financial means used painted wallcoverings to imitate the opulent tapestries, paneling, moldings, and scrollwork found in the homes of the wealthy. By the late 1700s, fashionable wallpaper was being mass-produced on rolls.

In the mid-twentieth century, PVC-vinyl became the preferred wall "paper" material. Soft and flexible vinyl offered durability, could be easily cleaned and removed from walls, and came with practical and affordable features. However, it also had some concerning qualities:

- PVC-producing factories are responsible for releasing dioxins, which are highly toxic, into the air, water, and soil. This not only poses a threat to the environment but also endangers the health of the factory workers involved in the production process.
- Products made with vinyl, including PVC, emit hazardous volatile organic compounds (VOCs) during manufacturing, shortly after installation, in the event of fires, and if they are improperly incinerated. These VOCs can have detrimental effects on indoor air quality and contribute to various health issues.
- Both PVC itself and its softening agent, phthalate, have been linked to a range of illnesses. These health problems span from respiratory irritation to more severe conditions such as cancer. The presence of PVC and phthalates in wallcoverings raises concerns about their potential impact on human health and well-being.

Vinyl poses an additional drawback when it comes to indoor environments: it lacks breathability. This means that moisture trapped between the vinyl and the wall creates an ideal environment for mold growth and prevents proper drying within the home. On the other hand, open-weave wallcoverings allow for greater vapor permeability, while natural materials derived from plants and animals tend to be inherently more porous. Given these considerations, vinyl should be sparingly used in eco-friendly home design.

However, vinyl still remains prevalent in the composition of conventional wallcoverings, including their backings and coatings. The increasing public awareness of the toxicity and hazards associated with PVC has led to a significant decline in its popularity for wall applications, with a market share decrease of over 25 percent in recent years. As a way to mask the presence of PVC, the term "acrylic" is often substituted, but it typically refers to the same substance despite sounding less harmful.

Certain manufacturers have made the switch to alternative synthetic materials, which is a positive step for human health. However, these alternatives still rely on petrochemicals and nonrenewable resources. On the other hand, there are companies that offer new, greener options by using all-natural and recycled fibers in their wallcoverings.

Thorough research is necessary when considering wallcoverings for a client. Some companies may offer a specific line of wallcoverings with natural fibers but include vinyl in those products. Others may have an all-natural line but use synthetics and vinyl in their other offerings. It is important to specify wallcoverings that are completely free of vinyl, rather than just having a percentage of natural materials in their composition.

Consider the potential lifespan of the wallcovering. Will the treatment endure in the specific environment? Can it be easily cleaned? Is it possible to replace a single section if it becomes soiled? If the wallcovering is removed, will it biodegrade?

Once an eco-friendly wallcovering that meets the client's requirements and aesthetic preferences is found, attention should be given to any additives used on the paper or covering, as well as the methods and products used during installation. Water-based inks or dyes are preferable, and heavy metals should be avoided according to the manufacturer's specifications. Look for vinyl-free, low-VOC (volatile organic compounds), no-formaldehyde, and solvent-free products. These specifications should also be applied to strippers, lining papers, pastes, coatings, sizing, and backings. Avoid chemical additives such as stain repellents, biocides, fireproofing, and pesticides. However, mineral treatments like borate, which repels insects and resists fire, are acceptable.

It is worth exploring products that carry the multi-attribute, third-party certification from the National Sanitation Foundation (NSF-342). This certification evaluates the sustainability of wallcovering products throughout their entire life cycle. It utilizes a point system to compare products against established requirements, performance criteria, and quantifiable metrics related to product design, manufacturing, long-term value, end-of-life management, corporate governance, and innovation.

Paper and Nonwovens

Wallpaper offers an affordable and versatile option for enhancing interior spaces with a wide range of colors and patterns. It's important to note that the term "wallpaper" is used broadly to encompass various types of wall coverings, including those that do not contain paper. Vinyl sheeting without wood-fiber content is often referred to as wallpaper.

While conventional wallpaper is typically made from wood, there are alternative options that utilize natural, fiber-based materials such as rice, bark, cotton, linen (flax), straw, or parchment (animal skin). Although fully organic and pesticide-free wallpaper has yet to be developed, it is advisable to focus on specifying natural content with minimal processing or additives. Additionally, choosing wallpaper with a high percentage of postconsumer and postindustrial recycled content, such as recycled paper or sawdust, can align with the client's green objectives. When specifying, be specific about the desired paper content.

Some wallcoverings incorporate minerals like clay, sand, or powdered stone to add texture or color. Manufactured materials such as ceramic beads and glass fibers, which possess mineral-like qualities, can enhance durability and scrubability without emitting VOCs or causing harm to the environment when disposed of properly. These options are considered eco-friendly choices for wallcoverings.

Image courtesy Outwater Plastics - Anaglypta & Lincrusta Wallpaper & Borders

Embossed wallcoverings like Lincrusta or Anaglypta were invented by Frederick Walton, the creator of linoleum. These wallcoverings utilize many of the same ingredients as linoleum, including sawdust, linseed oil, plant resin, colored dye, and zinc oxide. This bio-based composition results in a durable wallcovering that becomes even tougher over time. In fact, many examples of these wallcoverings can still be found in buildings that are over a century old. However, it's important to note that a lining containing a fungicide is typically required.

In some cases, additional manufactured substances such as polyester, rayon, or polyvinyl alcohol (PVA) may be blended into the natural mix. While these additives may provide slightly enhanced durability, they are derived from nonrenewable petroleum sources and involve intensive manufacturing processes. Therefore, it is advisable to avoid synthetic materials in general when selecting wallcoverings. Lastly, specifying water-based inks or opting for ink-free options helps minimize the use of solvents and reduces VOC emissions, promoting a healthier indoor environment.

Woven

Eco-friendly woven wallcoverings offer a wide range of options in terms of fabrics, grasses, and fibers used. Materials such as sisal, silk, raffia, linen, hemp, and cotton are commonly utilized to create these sustainable wallcoverings. Grass cloth, a traditional woven wallcovering, is typically made from ramie, which belongs to the nettle family. However, it's important to verify the specifications as imitations and versions with vinyl backings are also prevalent in the market. All-natural fiber woven wallcoverings possess inherent breathability, although not all of them are suitable for high-humidity areas or near water sources where water stains can be a concern.

A recent innovation in wallcoverings involves the use of glass "yarns" made from sand and treated with a modified starch. These glass-based wallcoverings offer exceptional durability, can be easily wiped clean, and meet stringent low-VOC requirements. In case of heavy soiling, the surface can be painted over, eliminating the need for complete removal. While the fabric itself is not derived from natural materials, glass is an inert substance that eventually reverts back to silicon dioxide (sand) as it disintegrates at the end of the wallcovering's useful life cycle.

When considering woven wallcoverings, it's important to check the backing material. Look for products that do not contain PVCs or vinyl, added fire retardants, pesticide inhibitors (except borate), waterproofing agents, or other synthetic components. Opting for water-based dyes and inks, or choosing options without any added coloring, is preferable in terms of minimizing environmental impact.

Cork

Cork wallcovering offers excellent sound absorption properties, making it a desirable choice for any room. It possesses natural antimicrobial qualities, requiring only occasional dusting or light spot-cleaning for maintenance. Cork wallcovering is available in both unfinished and factory-finished options, with low-VOC waxes or polyurethane coatings.

In addition to its sound-absorbing capabilities, cork also exhibits impressive thermal qualities. It can effectively retain heat or provide a cooling effect as required. However, it's important to note that cork wallcovering may not be suitable for areas prone to frequent moisture or heavy soiling, such as kitchens. Cork cannot be scrubbed, and it tends to absorb oils and stains, making it less ideal for such environments.

Leather

Although not the most common choice for wallcoverings, leather offers exceptional durability and can be installed in the form of tiles or sheets. However, it's important to consider certain factors before opting for leather as a wallcovering material. Typically, leather undergoes processing with toxic chemicals in developing countries that often lack proper worker protections. Additionally, some clients may have ethical concerns regarding the use of animal products. When using leather wallcoverings, it's crucial to allow them to outgas the tanning substances outside the home. It's advisable to explore options such as recycled leather or locally sourced leather that has undergone minimal dyeing and chemical treatment. Third-party certifications like Greenguard, which address emissions, can provide additional assurance. To protect the finish and maintain the desired patina, it may be necessary to periodically apply natural oils, waxes, or sealants to the leather. Given that leather tends to stretch over time due to gravity, a combination of fasteners and low-VOC adhesives is recommended for proper installation on walls.

Wood, Bamboo, or Biocomposite Paneling

Wood paneling is a widely used and popular choice for wallcoverings, often seen in applications such as wainscoting and beadboard. In addition to traditional wood options, alternatives like bamboo and agricultural-waste biocomposites are gaining popularity. These alternatives offer several advantages, including faster renewal rates and similar qualities to wood. Bamboo, for example, is known for its rapid growth and sustainability, while agricultural-waste biocomposites utilize materials that would otherwise go to waste, making them environmentally friendly choices.

Maintenance

With proper care and maintenance, high-quality wallcoverings made from quality materials have the potential to last for decades. Regular gentle dusting and occasional spot-cleaning are usually sufficient to keep them in good condition. It's advisable to refer to the manufacturer's guidelines for specific care instructions. Certain materials like wood, leather, and cork are particularly durable and can outlast fabrics or papers. Wood paneling, in particular, has the potential to endure the entire lifespan of a house. While unsealed cork and leather may be susceptible to water spots, they can often be spot-cleaned using mild detergent and water if they have been properly sealed. Depending on the specific material, adhesive, and substrate used, some wallcoverings can be easily removed and replaced with a different wall finish if desired.

> **Wallpaper made from 100 percent natural fibers or materials has the advantage of easy decomposition. It can be shredded and used as garden mulch, providing a sustainable disposal option. Similarly, cork, leather, wood, and bamboo are materials that have potential for reuse or recycling. When these materials are disposed of, they will break down quickly, minimizing their impact on the environment. This aligns with the principles of sustainability and promotes a circular economy where materials are reused or returned to nature.**

Specification

When specifying eco-friendly wallcoverings, it is important to consider the following:

Preferred:

- Look for products that meet third-party, multi-attribute certifications, such as those certified by the National Sanitation Foundation (NSF-342) or other reputable organizations.
- Choose wallcoverings made from all-natural fibers, such as grasses, reeds, sisal, or other plant-based materials.
- Opt for wallpaper made from all-natural paper derived from sustainable sources, such as wood pulp or rice paper.
- Consider all-natural cork wallcoverings, which offer durability, sound absorption, and thermal qualities.
- Select leather wallcoverings that have been minimally processed with the use of natural tannins and consider those made from recycled or locally sourced leather.
- Look for wallpaper or wallcoverings with a high recycled-paper or fiber content, supporting a circular economy.
- Specify water-based inks or dyes for a more environmentally friendly option.

- Choose nontoxic, low-VOC wallpaper paste or adhesive to minimize indoor air pollutants.

Avoid:

- Avoid PVC-vinyl wallcoverings, as they are associated with environmental and health concerns.
- Ensure that inks or dyes used in the wallcoverings are free from heavy metals.
- Avoid wallcoverings that contain formaldehyde, a potentially harmful chemical.
- Specify strippers or removal products that are solvent-free to reduce harmful emissions.
- Steer clear of wallcoverings treated with stain repellents, biocides, fireproofing chemicals, or pesticides, as they can have negative environmental and health impacts.

Pigments and Sealants

Wall color is a commonly requested design change by homeowners, with many opting to paint shortly after moving into a new space. As designers, we understand that the choice of paint color goes beyond mere decoration and holds psychological significance. It is crucial to consider the psychological impact of well-selected hues while also prioritizing the health and performance of the occupants.

In order to support a healthy indoor air quality (IAQ) specifically for the Indian audience, it is essential to specify products that have zero- to low-VOC (Volatile Organic Compounds) content, with levels below 50 grams per liter. it is important to ensure that the paints and coatings comply with the relevant national standards and regulations for indoor air quality.

Paint serves the purpose of preserving and protecting the surfaces and structure of a home. It is an architectural coating that effectively seals out moisture, prevents mildew growth, resists abrasion, repels dust, and provides a washable surface. With minimal maintenance, paint can last for years, contributing to the longevity of a home.

However, evaluating paint from an environmental perspective is a complex task. While conventional paint contains chemical components that enhance its durability, they can also release volatile organic compounds (VOCs). These VOCs can be harmful, causing air pollution, unpleasant odors, and potential health issues for chemically sensitive individuals. Additionally, over time, conventional paint may chip or flake, releasing toxic substances. Considering that paint covers a significant surface area, its impact on both the health of clients and the environment should not be overlooked.

The growing emphasis on improving air quality, both indoors and outdoors, has compelled paint manufacturers to prioritize the safety and health aspects of their products, particularly with regard to the emission of volatile organic compounds (VOCs). When used indoors, VOCs in paint pose a particular risk due to limited ventilation and the potential for accumulation on soft surfaces such as furniture. Therefore, it is recommended to remove all furnishings during interior painting projects. Furthermore, VOCs can react with the atmosphere to form ozone, contributing to air pollution.

In response to these concerns, the market continually sees the introduction of new architectural coatings that have significantly reduced VOC levels and exhibit less odor. However, it is important to note that eliminating VOCs alone does not provide a comprehensive solution for improving paint ingredients.

In addition to VOCs, standard architectural coatings often contain a wide range of other chemicals, including preservatives, fungicides, biocides, drying agents, suspension agents, and more. Navigating the labels and MSDS (Material Safety Data Sheets) to understand the pros and cons of these chemicals can be challenging. Manufacturers are not always required to provide warnings on the label or MSDS unless certain hazardous compounds exceed a specified threshold. Furthermore, the potential risks that may arise from the combination of different chemicals are not always known in advance. Another issue is that while labels may provide warnings about known hazards, the specific formulation or "recipe" of the paint is often considered proprietary, keeping the exact contents a mystery to designers, contractors, and architects. This lack of transparency makes it difficult to fully assess the potential risks associated with a particular paint product.

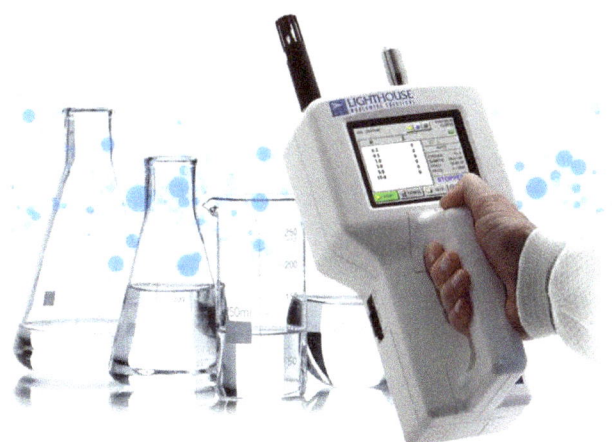

Measuring indoor emissions and toxic content from paints and coatings is a challenging task. The existing product certifications vary in their criteria, making it difficult to compare different products effectively. Some certifications consider the total volatile organic compound (TVOC) content and emissions during testing, while only a few address the VOCs specifically present in pigments and tints. To conduct a comprehensive assessment of sustainable products, it is necessary to consider various factors such as emissions testing, TVOC levels, toxic content, smog-based impacts, and the presence of chemicals of concern like SVOCs (semi--volatile organic compounds) and formaldehyde. These assessments should be conducted through third-party chamber testing protocols. Moving forward, a more holistic approach incorporating full life-cycle assessments is needed to ensure the sustainability and environmental impact of paints and coatings.

There are indeed alternatives to conventional paint that are made from naturally occurring substances. Some of these alternatives have excellent ecological characteristics and have been used for many years. However, it's important to note that paints marketed as "all-natural" or "organic" may not necessarily be environmentally friendly or benign in terms of their effects on human health. Unlike organic produce, there are no standardized labeling standards for coatings.

Natural-ingredient paints can contain just as many irritants and odors as conventional paints and may have their own potential health and environmental risks. Therefore, it is crucial to carefully evaluate any paint, including those marketed as natural or organic, before selecting it for use. It's advisable to try out the paint in a smaller area before committing to using it for an entire project.

It's also worth considering that painting may not always be necessary. The choice of materials used in wall construction or existing finishes can influence the environmental impact. If the walls have not yet been constructed, alternatives to conventional paint can be considered. For example, specifying no finish, opting for a natural finish over plaster or wallboard, or adding pigment to the plaster can be options with fewer volatile organic compounds (VOCs) and negative repercussions compared to conventional paint.

Faux Finishes

Faux finishes are decorative treatments that imitate the appearance of different materials, such as stone, metal, Venetian plaster, brick, or panoramic views, through the use of other materials. They can serve as alternatives to costly or rare materials, such as replicating marble tabletops or gilded trim. Faux finishes can also be used for purely whimsical purposes, like painting a landscape on the dining room walls.

In a green home, there can be benefits to using faux finishes if they replace the use of less environmentally friendly resources. For example, instead of using rare wood for trim, a skilled artisan can paint or stain sustainably grown wood to achieve the desired look. However, it's important to consider the environmental impact of the materials and techniques used in faux finishes. Some faux-finishing techniques may require the use of paints or compounds that are not eco-friendly. In such cases, it might be more sustainable to opt for non-toxic mineral-based plasters or other environmentally friendly alternatives instead of relying on layers of conventional paint.

It's essential to carefully weigh the options and consider the environmental implications before deciding on a faux finish for a green home. Evaluating the materials, techniques, and their ecological impact will help make a more informed and environmentally conscious choice.

However, there will be many situations where paint is the preferred finish due to factors such as cost-effectiveness, practicality (existing paint on the wall), or client preference (opting for low-irritant compounds in zero-VOC paints). Quality paint does offer some environmentally positive aspects. It provides an affordable wall treatment that can be easily refreshed or covered with additional layers of paint if the decor or homeowner's preferences change. No demolition or deconstruction is required, just a few gallons of paint and a brush. If the surface was properly prepped and the paint job is well-maintained, it can last for decades.

When evaluating conventional paint options, it is advisable to choose those with minimal amounts of harmful chemicals, especially VOCs that pose risks to homeowners, workers, and air quality. Whenever possible, specify zero- to low-VOC, water-based coatings that are free from preservatives, biocides, or solvents. It is important to avoid the chemicals identified as particularly hazardous in this chapter.

Thorough surface preparation is crucial to ensure the longest lifespan of the paint product. Thoughtful sampling and accurate estimation of the required quantities can help prevent waste, and any leftover paint can be reused or recycled to avoid sending it to the landfill.

This information serves as a starting point for evaluating the vast array of paint choices and combinations. As designers, it is our responsibility to continually educate ourselves about technological advancements and guide clients, contractors, architects, and crews in selecting and disposing of architectural coatings in an environmentally friendly manner.

Silicate Dispersion Paint

Silicate dispersion paint, also known as water glass or inorganic mineral paint, is made from liquefied potassium silicate. It reacts and binds with calcium salts, silica, ceramics, and certain metals to create a permanent coating on various surfaces. This type of paint is commonly used on exteriors due to its high durability, but it is also suitable for interior applications.

Silicate dispersion paint has been in use for over a century and has gained popularity in Europe, where lime plaster and rock walls are more prevalent. It forms an insoluble, rock-like finish on materials such as Portland cement, limestone, marble, mortars, concrete, brick, terra-cotta, and iron.

While silicate dispersion paint is not suitable for wood or plastic surfaces, it can be used over paper-faced drywall with the appropriate primer recommended by the paint manufacturer. It offers excellent permeability and durability, allowing air and moisture to pass through the surface without being damaged by water. The paint is noncombustible, odorless, VOC-free, and non-toxic. Its mineral-based colors are highly fade-resistant, and it possesses inherent antifungal properties, making it ideal for eco-friendly homes and clients with chemical sensitivities.

One major drawback of silicate paints is their energy-intensive manufacturing process. The primary ingredient, potassium carbonate (potash), is commercially prepared through electrolysis and carbonation applied to mineral compounds. The potassium carbonate is then fused with silica at high temperatures. The resulting potassium silicate compound, which is water-soluble, is blended with mineral pigments to create the paint.

Origins Silicate Dispersion Paint:

- Silicate dispersion paint is derived from various sources. The primary coloring agents in this paint are mineral pigments, which are derived from naturally occurring minerals.
- The main component, potassium silicate, is obtained through a complex manufacturing process. It involves electrolysis and carbonation techniques applied to mineral compounds. The potassium carbonate, historically known as potash, is subjected to electrolysis and carbonation to produce potassium silicate. This process requires high temperatures and specialized equipment.
- Water serves as the liquid carrier or solvent in silicate dispersion paint. It is mixed with the potassium silicate compound and mineral pigments to form the paint. The water content allows the paint to be applied smoothly and facilitates the bonding process when it reacts with various surfaces.
- Overall, the production of silicate dispersion paint involves a combination of mineral pigments, potassium silicate derived through electrolysis and carbonation, and water as the liquid carrier.

Maintenance

One of the notable properties of dried and hardened silicate dispersion paint is its reduced static charge compared to traditional paint. This characteristic helps repel dirt and dust particles, resulting in a surface that stays cleaner for longer periods. Additionally, silicate dispersion paint exhibits water resistance, making it suitable for areas that may come into contact with moisture.

The durability of the silicate surface is remarkable, often lasting for generations without significant maintenance. If touch-ups or additional coats are desired, they can be applied directly on top of the preexisting silicate paint without requiring extensive preparation. A simple cleaning of the surface is typically sufficient to ensure proper adhesion of the new layers of silicate dispersion paint.

Overall, the reduced static charge, water resistance, low upkeep requirements, and long-lasting nature of silicate dispersion paint make it a favorable choice for those seeking a durable and low-maintenance surface finish.

Silicate dispersion paints have the unique ability to chemically bond with the substrates they are applied to. For instance, if the underlying surface is made of limestone (calcium carbonate), the silicate paint and the limestone react together to form a harmless mineral compound that is also a carbonate. This chemical bond ensures a strong and durable adhesion between the paint and the substrate. In addition to the bonding with substrates, silicate dispersion paints have environmentally friendly characteristics. The minerals used as pigments in the paint, as well as any metals present in the substrate, will safely decompose at the end of their life cycles without posing known risks to the environment. This means that the paint and its components will naturally break down into benign substances over time.

The environmentally benign nature of silicate dispersion paints, along with their chemical bonding capabilities, makes them a sustainable and eco-friendly option for surface coatings.

Specification

When considering using silicate dispersion paint, it is important to ensure the following:

- Silicate dispersion paint: Look for high-quality silicate dispersion paints that are specifically designed for the intended surface. These paints are formulated with liquefied potassium silicate and mineral pigments. They provide excellent adhesion and durability while being water-resistant, noncombustible, odorless, and VOC-free.
- Low-VOC primer, if needed: If a primer is required based on the surface conditions, choose a low-VOC primer that is compatible with the silicate dispersion paint. This will help enhance the adhesion and performance of the paint while minimizing the release of volatile organic compounds (VOCs).
- Removal of furnishings: Before starting the painting process, it is advisable to remove all furnishings from the area to prevent them from being exposed to VOCs and odors. This will help maintain indoor air quality and prevent contamination of the furnishings.

Avoid the following:

- Primers or paint additives that outgas: To maintain a healthier indoor environment, avoid primers or paint additives that release harmful chemicals or VOCs. These can contribute to poor air quality and potential health risks.

Natural or Organic Paints

There is a wide range of paint products marketed as "natural" or "organic," but it's important to note that there are no standardized labeling requirements for paints using natural ingredients. These paints typically utilize natural oils, mineral or plant pigments, and plant resins. However, the extent to which these paints adhere to all-natural formulations can vary. Some companies have a strict policy of using only natural ingredients in their paints, while others may incorporate fossil-fuel solvents and chemicals in smaller quantities compared to conventional paints. Additionally, certain companies take a middle-ground approach by combining natural oils with traditional paint technology to create latex or oil-based paints with slightly more eco-friendly characteristics.

When opting for truly natural ingredients in paints, the manufacturer may include substances such as dammar resin, turpentine, natural-rubber latex, carnauba wax, tung oil, shellac (made from insect secretions), citrus extracts like d-limonene, vegetable oils, and beeswax. Heavy-metal pigments are typically excluded from these formulations, and calcium carbonate (chalk) or talc are often preferred as covering agents over titanium dioxide. However, it's important to recognize that not all natural paint ingredients are necessarily non-toxic or have lower VOC levels and less odor. Some natural compounds, like d-limonene and turpentine, have strong odors that can be irritating to individuals with sensitivities. Additionally, natural VOCs emitted by these organic compounds can still contribute to indoor air pollution, and the potential health risks associated with certain naturally derived oils and resins are being investigated.

It's advisable to carefully evaluate the ingredients of natural paints and understand any potential risks they may pose. Common vegetable oils like castor, soybean, canola, and safflower are considered safer choices as they have minimal odor and fewer associated concerns.

One advantage of specifying natural or organic paints is that manufacturers are typically more transparent about their ingredient lists, as these substances are a source of pride. In contrast, conventional paint companies often keep their paint compositions secret unless legally required to disclose certain risks.

When specifying an oil-based natural paint, conducting a "sniff test" on a painted patch within the home is a prudent step. It's important to note that different colors may have varying smells due to the chemical reactions between ingredients and the different color blends used to keep mineral pigments suspended.

Natural or organic paints offer several advantages over conventional paints. Firstly, their manufacturing process is typically less intensive, involving fewer chemicals and manufactured compounds. This results in a reduced environmental impact. The risks associated with natural paints are usually more straightforward and involve fewer hazardous substances, as indicated on Material Safety Data Sheets (MSDS). Additionally, natural paints have the advantage of better breakdown at the end of their life cycles, as they are derived directly from plant and mineral sources. It is important to evaluate specific products and their ingredients to ensure they meet desired environmental and health standards.

Origins Silicate Dispersion Paint:

- Plant-based oils, including turpentine, tung oil, d-limonene, safflower oil, and castor oil, serve as the primary carriers for natural paints.
- Resins and binders in natural paints are often derived from plants, such as dammar, shellac, carnauba wax, and beeswax.
- Natural paints utilize both mineral-based and plant-based pigments for color.
- Calcium carbonate is a commonly used covering agent in natural paints.
- Some natural paint manufacturers may combine natural ingredients with petrochemicals or synthetics in their formulations.

Maintenance

Natural paints generally require minimal maintenance, similar to conventional paints. However, their scrubbing capability may be limited compared to conventional options. It's worth noting that future touch-ups with natural paints can be challenging as some may not store well, and achieving precise color matching might be more difficult due to the limited color-matching technology available for natural paint formulations.

> The oils, pigments, and resins present in minimally processed natural paints have a tendency to break down more rapidly and in a safer manner compared to the complex chemicals found in conventional paints. It is important to handle leftover natural paint responsibly and avoid disposing of it down the drain or with regular trash. Due to the flammable nature of solvents and oils, they should be treated as hazardous materials. Proper disposal methods should be followed to ensure safety and environmental protection.

Specification

- Specify all-natural plant-based or mineral-based oils and pigments, preferably food-grade.
- Use zero- to low-VOC additives in the paint formulation.
- Ensure all furnishings are removed from the area before painting to prevent contamination with VOCs and odors.
- Dispose of leftover paint as hazardous waste following proper disposal procedures at the end of the project.

Avoid:

- Avoid using d-limonene or paints with strong odors if the client is sensitive to them.

Conventional Paint

When assessing conventional paints, there are several factors to consider regarding their composition. These include the presence of volatile organic compounds (VOCs), the types of chemical additives used, and the choice between latex and oil-based formulations. To ensure a healthy indoor air quality (IAQ), it is recommended to select paints with low or zero VOC content (below 50 grams per liter) that comply with emission standards. Additionally, you can look for paints that meet the higher standards of the MPI X-Green standard, which incorporates both environmental criteria and performance metrics.

Initially, it may appear that using water as a liquid vehicle for paint is the obvious choice. Water is considered better than oil in terms of environmental impact, as it is a natural and renewable resource, and water-based paints can be easily cleaned up with water. While it is important not to dispose of large quantities of paint down the drain, the small residue left on brushes can typically be rinsed away at the sink. Another reason for the preference for latex paints, which are primarily water-based, is their lower level of off-gassing compared to solvent-based paints. Latex paints allow the water carrier to naturally evaporate without releasing volatile organic compounds (VOCs). In contrast, solvent-borne paints, often referred to as oil-based paints, contain solvents that can be either naturally derived or manufactured. These paints dry by exposure to air but emit VOCs in the process.

Furthermore, oil-based paints require the use of additional solvents for cleanup, which adds to their outgassing properties. As a result, latex paints have become the preferred choice over oil-based paints due to their easier cleanup and less unpleasant odor. However, latex paints have their drawbacks as well. In order to ensure effective drying and prevent spoilage and mildew, manufacturers incorporate drying agents, preservatives, fungicides, suspension agents, and various other chemicals into water-based paints. Therefore, while oil-based paints release VOCs due to their solvents, latex paints introduce different chemical concerns. Both types of paints initially emit the highest levels of VOCs after application, which gradually decrease over time. Nonetheless, VOCs can linger in fabrics and carpets, potentially causing longer-term effects. If a client has sensitivities to specific chemicals, it is important to carefully examine labels, even for water-based and low-VOC paints.

Other Considerations

Regardless of whether it's oil-based or latex, there are other important considerations when choosing paint. Typically, higher-gloss paints contain components that contribute to higher VOC levels, while dead flat paints tend to have the lowest VOC levels. Deep colors, especially when the colorant is solvent-based, may slightly increase VOC emissions. It is advisable to specify natural food-grade or mineral-based pigments.

Conventional paint commonly utilizes petroleum-based acrylic binders, such as polyvinyl acetate (PVA). Acrylics are derived from non-renewable resources and have a complex chemical composition that makes them difficult to break down properly during disposal. The production of acrylics generates a significant amount of waste and by-products.

Another environmental concern associated with conventional paint is the production of titanium dioxide. While titanium dioxide has replaced lead as a whitening pigment, its manufacturing process is environmentally unfriendly. Synthetic and natural rutile, combined with titanium-rich slag, are used in the complex production process involving high temperatures, chemical washes, and reductions. This manufacturing process contributes to pollution and

VOC Conscious Paint Label

The labeling of paint based on VOC content is influenced by the desire for cleaner air indoors and outdoors, as well as the convenience of using latex paints. Various governing bodies, such as those in California and the European Union, have implemented restrictions on VOC levels in paint and have established strict labeling requirements.

The criteria for labeling paint as "low-VOC" differ depending on the region and the type of paint. Although "low-VOC" and "low-odor" are often used interchangeably, they are not synonymous. While low-VOC paints emit fewer VOCs, there may still be components in the paint that produce unpleasant odors. It is important to note that a paint labeled as "low-odor" does not necessarily indicate low VOC content; it simply implies that it has a milder odor compared to other types or product lines.

The term "zero-VOC" is commonly used by paint manufacturers, but its true meaning may be deceptive. The testing method (EPA Reference Test Method 24) used to measure VOCs accurately applies only to concentrations above 5 grams per liter. Below this threshold, the compounds cannot be reliably assessed. Consequently, paint labeled as zero-VOC or no-VOC may still release trace amounts of VOCs. Furthermore, it should be noted that these standards primarily focus on the impact of VOCs on ozone and low-level smog, and they may not account for other toxic chemicals that can emit odors or vapors in low-VOC paints. Regardless of the product used, adequate ventilation is crucial.

poses hazards to workers. Additionally, other pigments like chalk and clay, though occasionally used as primary pigments, have their own drawbacks and health risks for workers involved in their mining.

Heavy metals are also a concern in paint, often present as pigments or colorants. Lead was banned from architectural coatings in 1978, and mercury was banned from interior paints in 1992. Cadmium and chromium hexavalent (chromium VI) can be found in artist paints and colorants. It is important to specify paints that are free of these hazardous heavy metals, and caution should be exercised when removing old paint that may be contaminated with lead or other toxins.

Formaldehyde-based resin is still found in some paints and should be avoided. Biocides, such as copper, arsenic, phenol, and ammonium compounds, are used to prevent mold, mildew, and spoilage but are associated with various health risks and can trigger reactions in individuals with chemical sensitivities. It is recommended to specify paint that is mixed "fresh" and free of biocides.

Artist Paints

When it comes to artist paints, lacquers, and thinners used for faux finishes and murals, it's important to note that these products often contain concentrated amounts of toxins such as petrochemicals, VOC-emitting solvents, and heavy metal pigments. As a result, their compatibility with green homes is limited. While there may be instances where a faux finish is a more practical choice compared to rare or nonrenewable natural materials desired by the client, it is crucial to minimize the negative impact. One approach is to encourage the use of eco-friendly alternatives like non-toxic paints or finishes such as plaster, mineral pigments, lime washes, or milk paints. Opting for water-based products whenever possible is recommended, while avoiding spray applications that can introduce harmful airborne particles and compromise indoor air quality. For clients sensitive to odors, an alternative solution could involve having the artist create the mural on canvas at a separate location, allowing it to dry and air out before transferring it to the home. This approach helps mitigate potential exposure to odors and volatile compounds.

Reengineered Paints

Instead of being disposed of as hazardous waste, leftover paint is now being collected by manufacturers and recycled into usable new products, which is a commendable effort for the environment. The process involves sorting the used paint by its type (oil or latex, interior or exterior), conducting tests to determine its specific properties, and combining it with compatible materials. In some cases, the recycled paint is mixed with fresh paint to create high-quality remanufactured blends.

The recycled paint is then tested for VOCs and can be used for various purposes, although the color options are typically limited to muted tones like gray or beige. To minimize potential effects on individuals with chemical sensitivities, it is recommended to use remanufactured paint in storage areas, garages, or exteriors. As remanufacturing technology continues to advance, we can anticipate the availability of more low-VOC and specialized paints.

Recycled Paint

Many communities provide drop-off points where excess paint is diverted away from landfills and made accessible to the public through exchange programs. The collected paint is sorted based on its properties, such as whether it's suitable for interior or exterior use and if it's water or oil-based. Similar types of paint are mixed together, resulting in various shades of gray. This recycled paint is commonly utilized for tasks like graffiti removal, community restoration projects, or applying finishes to park shelters. In some locations, the remixed paint is offered to consumers at a nominal fee. However, unlike remanufactured paint that undergoes testing, adheres to safety standards, and discloses VOC emissions and chemical content on its labels, there is limited information available about VOC emissions and other details of these recycled paints. While community recycling initiatives effectively reduce waste, the remixed paint is not recommended for interior projects focused on maintaining a healthy environment and is more suitable for less critical exterior applications.

Defining Paint Terminology

To avoid confusion, let's clarify a few terms commonly used in the paint industry:

- Latex: In the past, "latex" referred exclusively to the material derived from the rubber tree. However, it is now used to describe various synthetic resins that retain elasticity. It's important to note that "latex" paint does not contain rubber.
- Enamel: Initially, "enamel" paint denoted the glossy, oil-based variety known for its durability. Over time, manufacturers began using the term more broadly to describe almost any type of paint, including water-based, oil-based, glossy, or flat finishes. Essentially, "enamel" has become synonymous with "paint."
- PVC: While "PVC" typically refers to PVC-vinyl, this material is rarely used in architectural coatings. Instead, vinyl-acrylics are more commonly employed. It's worth noting that within the paint industry, PVC stands for "pigment-volume concentration," representing the relative volume of pigment compared to binder. A higher PVC ratio usually corresponds to lower VOC levels, particularly in conventional paint formulations.

Origins of Paint

- Conventional paint, with few exceptions, is primarily composed of numerous petrochemicals, synthetic oils, resins, and binders. The specific formulation is typically proprietary and not fully disclosed on the product label.
- The manufacturing process for conventional paint is energy-intensive.
- Water-based paint relies on water as its carrier, while oil-based paint utilizes manufactured solvents.
- Water-based paint, commonly referred to as latex, does not contain natural rubber. Instead, it is made from flexible synthetic latex compounds produced through manufacturing processes.
- Colorants used in paint consist of a combination of mineral pigments and solvents.
- Additional chemical additives may be included in paint formulations, serving various purposes such as enhancing drying time, improving flow characteristics, acting as suspension agents, and providing preservation and biocidal properties.

Maintenance

Water-based paint can be easily cleaned up with water. Any remaining paint should be poured back into the original cans or containers and kept for future touch-ups. It is important to store the containers in a constant, cool temperature area away from living spaces. To keep track of the paint, remember to record the date and location on the lid. If there is leftover paint that will not be used, it is highly recommended to consider donating it to a graffiti-abatement program, a community restoration project, a local nonprofit organization, or a theater program. Additionally, check for recycling or remanufacturing options available in your area.

When dealing with nearly empty paint containers, allow the residue to air-dry completely outdoors, ensuring it is kept away from pets and children. Depending on local regulations, steel paint cans may be recyclable, while in other places they may need to be disposed of as hazardous waste.

Conventional paint is a sophisticated product formulated to withstand the challenges of everyday life in homes. While its durability is beneficial, it also prevents biodegradation, making it a potential hazard when disposed of. Due to its chemical composition, conventional paint is typically classified as hazardous waste.

When conventional paint is applied, the water and solvents it contains will gradually evaporate, releasing volatile organic compounds (VOCs) that contribute to the formation of ground-level ozone, a harmful air pollutant. The remaining components of the paint, including various additives and pigments, can persist in landfills or on painted surfaces for extended periods—ranging from years to decades, or even centuries. The long-term implications of these residual chemicals are not yet fully understood, posing potential future hazards. It is important to consider these factors when selecting and using paint, and to explore alternative options that prioritize environmental sustainability and human health.

Specification

- Prioritize products that comply with California Section 01350 standards and have low VOC levels of 50 grams per liter or less.
- Look for products that meet the MPI X-Green standard, which includes performance metrics and ensures environmental friendliness.
- Give preference to paints with third-party certifications that verify their sustainability and low VOC content. Consider conventional paint only if no other paint or finish options are feasible.
- Opt for water-based paints or those made from natural plant-based oils as the base.
- Explore zero-VOC or no-VOC paint options that minimize harmful emissions.
- Choose low-VOC paints that have reduced levels of volatile organic compounds.
- Select paints that are free of formaldehyde, a harmful chemical commonly found in paints.
- Specify paints that are mixed fresh, if possible, to avoid the use of preservatives, biocides, and fungicides.
- Use a low-VOC, formaldehyde-free, water-based primer with minimal additives for addressing surface problems, preparation, deep colors, or color changes.
- Take a conservative approach when sampling paints to minimize waste.
- Encourage the recycling of leftover paint or proper storage for potential touch-ups.

Avoid:

- Paints that contain preservatives, as they can be harmful to human health and the environment.
- Products that include biocides, fungicides, or mildew preventatives, as these chemicals pose potential risks. Paints that contain formaldehyde, a hazardous substance.
- Avoid paints that utilize lead and other heavy metal pigments or drying agents, especially those containing chromium hexavalent, cobalt, cadmium, and mercury.
- Be cautious about using recycled or remanufactured paint for indoor projects, as their chemical composition and VOC levels may be uncertain.

Understanding Stains, Finishes, and Adhesives

As environmentally conscious designers, our responsibility is to choose the best products for our projects while minimizing harm to clients, construction teams, and the planet. It's impossible to cover every substance used in residential interiors, but we strive to make informed choices that prioritize sustainability and human well-being.

The world of chemicals used in design and construction is vast and complex. While it's easy to place blame on manufacturers, as consumers, we often demand products that offer exceptional performance, color consistency, and durability, which can come at the expense of our health and the environment. However, it's not all negative. Many companies are dedicated to providing high-quality products that balance consumer needs with environmental considerations. Additionally, there are still simple and eco-friendly options available for many applications.

When selecting stains, colorants, finishes, adhesives, or stripping agents, thorough research into the product's composition is essential. Request the Material Safety Data Sheet (MSDS) from the manufacturer, distributor, or retailer, or access it on the company's website. Look for products with minimal ingredients, as complex chemical interactions can lead to unforeseen hazards. Choose products with low health risks and no phthalates, heavy metals, or aromatic solvents. If a product contains carcinogenic or reproductive toxins, or poses significant health risks, opt for a safer alternative. Aim to stay well below the VOC standards set by the South Coast Air Quality Management District (SCAQMD). Remember, risks to human health often correspond to risks to environmental health. Apply the precautionary principle by specifying natural products that have a minimal environmental impact and low health burdens.

If the client is sensitive to chemicals or odors, request a sample for testing. After product selection, ensure that workers follow all recommended precautions and disposal guidelines. Finally, provide the client with maintenance instructions to help them care for the finished surfaces appropriately.

Here is a general overview and a list of specifications to help you select the suitable stains, finishes, and adhesives. To obtain more detailed information regarding the recommended products for specific materials such as wood, metal, or concrete, please refer to the relevant chapter within this book.

Stains, Colorants, and Tints

Most synthetic colorants are solvent-based and derived from petroleum compounds. These compounds evaporate during the drying process. Despite using small amounts of colorant, stains, or dyes, the solvents and other chemicals present can contribute to outgassing, volatile organic compounds (VOCs), toxicity levels, and odors. Even if a product claims to be zero-VOC, the addition of colorants or other additives can alter the VOC levels, often for the worse. Darker shades, particularly those created with solvent-based colorants, may have higher outgassing tendencies compared to lighter hues.

The most environmentally friendly choice is to specify that the material remains in its natural state without any added color. The next best option is to specify natural mineral pigments, natural penetrating oils, or water-based vegetable dyes. Food-grade or mineral-based colorants are safe at any concentration level.

It is important to avoid heavy metals like chromium, lead, and uranium (which were once commonly used in yellowish colorants). Due to varying regulations in different countries regarding the use of harmful substances in dyes, paints, and glazes, it is advisable to steer clear of painted objects such as souvenir tiles that have not been imported through regulated channels.

Finishes, Sealants, and Topcoats

Opting for no finishes, sealants, or topcoats is the most environmentally conscious choice, particularly for natural materials that possess inherent durability and beauty. While some materials require no assistance to maintain their condition, others are prone to rapid deterioration if not protected from moisture, dirt, stains, mold, or insects. For instance, sealing grout is a prudent ecological decision to avoid the need for extensive tile replacement. Additionally, finishes can serve the dual purpose of safeguarding clients from mold, volatile organic compounds (VOCs), and unpleasant odors by applying effective nonporous sealants. Factory-finished products offer the advantage of allowing materials to outgas prior to installation, minimizing potential harm to occupants of a home (although it still contributes to environmental impact). However, specifying on-site finishing or sealing provides greater control over the application method and the substances used, potentially leading to an improved ecological balance and healthier home environment.

Porous and breathable protection for various surfaces can be achieved with all-natural waxes and oils. It's important to note that these may require regular reapplication. Certain finishes, such as silicate dispersion paint, chemically bond with the substrate (typically mineral-based products) and become completely inert and safe once they are dry. In addition, borate, a mineral, can be incorporated into a finish or treatment to enhance resistance against pests and fire hazards.

If you require a nonporous or hard finish, it is advisable to specify a product that is least toxic and meets the following criteria: it should be free of formaldehyde, contain low levels of solvents and volatile organic compounds (VOCs), and be water-based. It is important to avoid the use of chemical biocides. While zinc was once commonly used as a hardening agent in floor finishes, it has been found to be toxic to aquatic life, so it should be avoided as well.

The method of application is also crucial, and not just the ingredients in the finish. Spray-on sealants should be avoided unless they can be applied within a manufacturer-approved spray booth. Instead, consider alternative application methods such as wiping, brushing, rolling, or pouring. The use of sprays directly impacts air quality and can be particularly irritating to clients with chemical sensitivities.

Glues and Adhesives

Manufacturers categorize adhesives differently, providing guidelines to specify more environmentally friendly options:

- Paste is typically composed of flour and water.
- Glue is commonly derived from animal products (such as casein and hide) and plant sources (like natural rubber, cellulose, paste).
- Adhesives can be made from various synthetics, including epoxy, cyanoacrylate, contact cement, hot melt, polyurethane, polyvinyl acetate (PVA), resin, resorcinol, silicone, or urea formaldehyde.

While these terms may be used interchangeably, understanding their distinctions can help when seeking environmentally friendly alternatives. Paste and glue are generally considered milder options that can be used with many porous natural materials, such as unfinished wood, wallpaper, or cork. Adhesives are more suitable for nonporous surfaces or challenging applications like stone, tile, or finished bamboo. It is important to review product information and safety data sheets to ascertain the content of pastes, glues, and adhesives.

When selecting adhesives, look for those with low VOC levels and minimal odors. Seek out companies that specialize in manufacturing low-toxic, environmentally safe compounds, which may align with stringent air quality standards and certifications relevant to Asian countries. Additionally, considering alternative methods such as tack strips, staples, decorative studs, nails, trim pieces, or screws can help reduce the amount of adhesive required for certain applications. By being mindful of the distinctions and choosing eco-friendly options, individuals in Asia can make informed decisions when it comes to selecting adhesives that are both effective and environmentally conscious.

Specification

- Products compliant with local regulations and standards for emissions and environmental impact.
- Low levels of volatile organic compounds (VOCs) to minimize air pollution.
- Third-party certifications indicating rigorous emissions testing and adherence to environmental standards.
- Avoidance of colorants, tints, or dyes in the product.
- Light colors if synthetic colorants are necessary.
- No finish if it doesn't compromise material integrity or durability.
- Low- or zero-VOC options to minimize environmental impact.
- Low-odor formulations to reduce discomfort.
- Consider factory-finished materials if client sensitivity to odors or on-site outgassing is a concern.
- Utilize nails, staples, tacks, trim pieces, or alternative fasteners to reduce reliance on adhesives.
- Preference for solvent-free, water-based, or natural-oil-based products.
- Choose natural plant-based, animal-based, or mineral-based dyes, oils, waxes, and finishes.
- Opt for animal- or plant-based pastes or glues instead of chemical adhesives.
- Specify formaldehyde-free options.
- Explore natural borate preservatives or pest controls for added sustainability.
- Consider brush-on, wipe-on, or pour-on application methods for ease of use and reduced waste.

Avoid:

- Heavy metals such as chromium, lead, cadmium, or mercury due to their environmental and health risks.
- Metallic hardening or drying agents like zinc.
- Sprays, as they can negatively impact air quality.
- Solvent-based formulas that contribute to air pollution and health hazards.
- Biocides, which can be harmful to the environment.
- Compounds that require chemical solvents or thinners to minimize exposure to harmful chemicals. Factory finishes of unknown content to ensure transparency and environmental safety.

FURNISHINGS

The residential furnishings market is increasingly embracing sustainability, health, and eco-friendliness, taking cues from the successful efforts of the commercial industry. While it is relatively easier to find and specify green architectural materials due to regulations like Occupational Safety and Health Administration (OSHA) and Leadership in Energy and Environmental Design (LEED), the same level of rigor has not been established for interior furnishings.

However, there is positive progress in the industry. Many manufacturers operate in both the commercial and residential sectors, recognizing the advantages of adopting sustainable practices and making green residential building materials more readily available. Although a comprehensive system for interior furnishings is yet to be established, this chapter will guide designers in the order they would typically research and specify residential furnishings.

Cabinetry - Modulars

Wood is a prominent material used in residential cabinetry, with solid wood being the preferred choice for door and drawer fronts due to its attractive grain. However, to make drawer boxes, bodies, and frames where visibility is less of a concern, less expensive options like particleboard and medium-density fiberboard (MDF) are commonly used. Additionally, materials such as bamboo, agricultural biocomposites, metal, particleboard, and glass shelves and doors are also used in cabinetry, often in combination.

Wood remains the most popular choice for cabinetry due to its natural beauty, durability, biodegradability, and renewable nature, albeit at a slow pace. However, the use of forest products is a topic of concern for environmentalists due to the loss of large stands of old-growth trees and extensive rainforests. The demand for construction materials and specialty or rare woods for carpentry and furnishings has led to deforestation and the disturbance of ecosystems, soil erosion, and a disruption in the natural balance of life. Furthermore, these practices contribute to the loss of species, increased greenhouse gas emissions, and exacerbation of global warming.

To address these environmental concerns, it is important to specify wood for cabinetry that has been grown and harvested with minimal impact on the environment. Third-party certifications that ensure a responsible chain of custody, where eco-friendly standards are adhered to and documented throughout the forestry, milling, and distribution processes, are crucial for maintaining healthy forests for future generations. The Forest Stewardship Council (FSC) sets the standards for third-party certification that is recognized worldwide.

To ensure the sustainability of wood used in cabinetry, it is important to avoid selecting wood species that are endangered or come from unknown or uncertified sources. Tropical woods should be avoided unless they have been certified as sustainable through the Forest Stewardship Council (FSC) certification. Encourage the client to choose locally available or domestic wood species whenever possible to minimize the environmental impact of long-distance transportation.

Consider the client's sensitivities or allergies when selecting tree species for cabinetry, as some species may have inherent odors. Even with finishing or sealing, certain odors may still be present in the home after installation. For a greener approach, consider using reclaimed or salvaged cabinets instead of purchasing new ones. In remodeling projects, explore the possibility of updating the cabinet faces or opting for open shelving to minimize resource consumption. Simple changes like replacing drawer pulls, handles, or applying an eco-friendly paint coat to the existing cabinetry can transform its appearance without the need for complete replacement. Specifying reclaimed wood for cabinetry is another environmentally conscious choice. Look for local sources of reclaimed wood and work with local cabinetmakers to minimize the energy expended on transportation. Ensure that reclaimed wood used for kitchen applications is free from peeling paint, chemically treated wood, or any potential contaminants from previous industrial use. It is crucial to avoid using reclaimed wood that may come into contact with food, cutlery, or dishes, to maintain health and safety standards.

While third-party certification programs are valuable for verifying the sustainability of wood sources, it's important to recognize that some small local businesses involved in reclaimed wood operations may not participate in such programs. However, these businesses often have a deep understanding of the wood's source, engage in local recovery and sales, and may have deconstructed the materials themselves. If these businesses adhere to strict internal environmental policies, they can be reliable sources of reclaimed wood. The Rainforest Alliance offers certification for rediscovered wood and underwater salvage wood products, ensuring that the wood is obtained through procedures that preserve the environment and prioritize the well-being of workers and the community. Choosing products with rediscovered wood and underwater salvage certification is a responsible way to contribute to forest preservation. In cabinetry, solid wood is not the only option. The boxes, frames, and shelving are frequently made using cost-effective wood-based sheet goods like particleboard, engineered wood products, fiberboard, MDF, or plywood. These sheet goods are often manufactured from mill by-products, wood chips, and other waste materials, making them both economical and environmentally friendly alternatives that reduce the need for wide planks of solid wood sourced from old-growth trees.

When specifying engineered wood products, prioritize those with FSC or third-party certification. This ensures that the wood used in these products has been sustainably grown and is not sourced from endangered tropical rainforests or poorly managed tree farms. Additionally, look for sheet goods that contain a high percentage of recycled wood, further contributing to resource conservation.

The drawback of using sheet goods in cabinetry is that standard cores and veneers often contain formaldehyde-based binders or solvent-based finishes that release harmful gases. These gases can impact indoor air quality and pose health risks. It is important to note that methylenediphenyl isocyanate (MDI), an alternative binder with lower outgassing potential, is still considered a concern and should be avoided.

To address this issue, when specifying cabinetry, look for custom cabinetmakers who prioritize using formaldehyde-free and low-VOC adhesives, binders, and finishes. These alternatives have reduced emissions and contribute to better indoor air quality. By working with cabinetmakers who are committed to using eco-friendly materials, you can ensure that your cabinetry is free from harmful chemicals and promotes a healthier living environment.

Biocomposite boards offer an alternative solution for cabinetry, particularly as substitutes for wood-based sheet goods. These boards are made from rapidly renewable agricultural by-products, making them a sustainable choice. Some biocomposite boards are not only durable but also visually appealing, making them suitable for cabinet faces. One of the advantages of biocomposite boards is that many manufacturers prioritize ecological considerations and avoid the use of harmful chemicals in their production processes. When specifying biocomposite boards for cabinetry, it is important to give preference to products with low-VOC and formaldehyde-free binders. Additionally, look for boards that incorporate low-toxic borate preservatives or pest repellants for added eco-friendliness. It is worth noting that establishing consistent standards and performance for biocomposite boards can be challenging due to variations in manufacturing processes. Furthermore, organic farming practices are not yet mandatory for biocomposite suppliers, so it is advisable to inquire about the farming standards followed by the manufacturers.

In the search for eco-friendly cabinetry options, it's essential to consider sustainable alternatives to traditional wood. One such alternative is the use of rapidly renewable plants like bamboo and palmwood, which are commonly found in Asia. These plants grow at a faster rate compared to trees and can be transformed into durable and visually appealing sheet goods, cabinet faces, and frames. While third-party certifications for bamboo may be less prevalent in Asian markets, it's important to prioritize companies that uphold high environmental standards and can provide information on sustainable sourcing and responsible manufacturing practices. Another unconventional choice for cabinetry is the use of metal or glass materials. Metal cabinets and shelving are known for their durability; however, it's important to consider the environmental impact of the mining process, ore extraction, and transportation. To minimize the ecological footprint, explore opportunities for salvaging metal cabinets and shelves from commercial settings or older homes. Glass, on the other hand, offers a sleek and modern aesthetic. It can be crafted from recycled glass or manufactured using abundant sand. Both metal and glass are inert materials that can be recycled or repurposed, making them

When selecting cabinetry, it's crucial to pay attention to the adhesives, paints, stains, and finishes used, especially for individuals with sensitivities or concerns about chemicals. Opt for low-VOC adhesives, water-based wood glues, and finishes that minimize off-gassing. Inquire about certifications or eco-labels that ensure the products meet environmental standards. Additionally, explore the option of unfinished cabinets, allowing for on-site finishing with low-VOC, water-based products or natural oils and waxes.

Melamine

Melamine is a crystalline substance commonly used as a resinous laminating agent in various industries, including wood products, paper and textile production, and leather tanning. In the past, it was popularly used to make dishes, such as vintage Melmac. Melamine-coated particleboard, often referred to as "melamine," is frequently used for countertops. When hardened, most types of melamine are inert and insoluble, providing a shiny surface that is easy to clean and serving as a cost-effective way to enhance the appearance of particleboard. However, there are concerns about the manufacturing process of melamine, which involves a chemical reaction with formaldehyde. This process is believed to be harmful to workers and the environment. At the very least, melamine can cause skin, eye, and throat irritation, but it is also suspected to cause kidney damage and other serious health issues. Furthermore, melamine is not biodegradable or recyclable. Although formalized studies on the risks of melamine to humans and the environment are limited, it is advisable to avoid using melamine in an eco-friendly home. Instead, consider using particleboard without melamine coating for closet shelving, particularly in areas without moisture. This type of particleboard can be stained or painted with non-toxic products, and it offers an attractive and often affordable alternative. By opting for melamine-free particleboard, you can reduce potential health and environmental risks associated with melamine usage.

Origins

- Solid wood cabinetry is derived from trees, typically hardwood or softwood species.
- Some wood products are made from recycled wood scraps or sawdust, combined with acrylics or resins for binding.
- Sheet goods, such as particleboard or plywood, may incorporate different binders, including low-VOC glues, outgassing solvents, formaldehyde, soy-based products, or natural and synthetic resins.
- Reclaimed wood is obtained from salvaging residential, commercial, and agricultural structures, such as floors, walls, or complete units. This reclaimed wood can be used to make cabinets.
- Wood finishes or stains may contain a variety of ingredients, including natural oils and resins, pigments, solvents, chemical compounds, petroleum distillates, metal drying agents, formaldehyde, or water.
- Biocomposite boards are made from agricultural by-products such as wheat, rice, barley or oat straw, sunflower hulls, bluegrass or rye grass stubble, cornhusks and sorghum stalks, hemp, soybean plants, and bagasse (sugar cane pulp).
- Biocomposites may contain residual pesticides or chemicals from the crops used, although the specific amounts or frequency of use are unknown.
- Bamboo, which is technically a grass, is grown for approximately ten years before it is harvested and can be used for cabinetry.
- Metal cabinetry can be manufactured using all-new metal materials or recycled metal.
- Glass shelves and cabinet fronts are typically made from common sand or recycled glass.
- Cabinet hardware is primarily made from metals like steel or brass, but it can also include components made from glass, ceramic, or wood.

Maintenance

In general, casework requires minimal maintenance, usually limited to occasional dusting and cleaning with a damp cloth. However, when it comes to specific finishes, here are some considerations:

- Wood with natural oil or wax finishes: These finishes require regular reapplications to maintain their appearance and protection. Over time, the wood may need to be reoiled or rewaxed to keep it nourished and enhance its natural beauty.
- Biocomposite materials with natural oil or wax finishes: Similar to wood, biocomposite materials with natural oil or wax finishes may need periodic reapplications to preserve their finish and keep them looking their best.

It's important to follow the manufacturer's instructions or consult with professionals to determine the specific maintenance requirements for your chosen materials. By properly maintaining your casework, you can ensure its longevity and preserve its aesthetic appeal.

When cabinets are in good condition, there are several eco-friendly options for their disposal. One option is salvaging and reusing the cabinets in other locations or repurposing them for different uses, extending their lifespan and reducing waste. Alternatively, cabinets can be downcycled by breaking them down into their constituent parts and using the materials to create new wood-based products. Wood or biocomposite boards can be recycled or repurposed into other items.

It's important to note that while wood and biocomposite boards can easily decompose, the binders, resins, stains, adhesives, and finishes used on the cabinets may break down more slowly and require proper disposal methods. Metal components, such as hinges and knobs, as well as glass components, can usually be recycled. By sending these materials to recycling facilities, they can be processed and used in the production of new products. To minimize waste further, usable cabinet hardware like pulls, hinges, and knobs can be taken to construction exchanges or salvage yards. These organizations can repurpose the hardware or make it available for others to use, promoting reuse and reducing waste.

Specification

- Use locally or domestically sourced wood species that are certified by the FSC and not endangered.
- Consider salvaging existing cabinetry or renovating it instead of purchasing new.
- Opt for glass shelving or cabinet door accents made from recycled glass.
- Choose biocomposite boards, third-party certified particleboard, or plywood with a high percentage of recycled wood.
- Select metal components that contain a high proportion of recycled material.
- Prioritize salvaged hardware or hardware made with a significant amount of recycled material.
- Remove oil finishes before installation.
- Ensure the use of formaldehyde-free, low-VOC, water-based binders, sealants, adhesives, glues, and stains.
- Minimize shipping and handling with all-recyclable and recycled-content paper, cloth, and cardboard.

Specify finishes and stains that are:

- Water-based and low-VOC.
- Made with natural oils, resins, pigments, and waxes (food-grade).
- Formaldehyde-free and free of metallic drying agents. Solvent-free.

Avoid:

- Using reclaimed wood of unknown origin, especially in kitchen applications or where safety is a concern.
- Choosing uncertified wood.
- Selecting rare or threatened tree species.
- Applying solvent-based finishes. Using melamine.
- Including formaldehyde or other preservatives in wood products or finishes.
- Utilizing finishes with metal-based drying agents.
- Opting for uncertified engineered wood.
- Incorporating formaldehyde in binders or finishes.
- Using preservatives or pesticides, except for borate.
- Using foam, "peanuts," or plastic shipping materials.

Textiles

Textiles play various roles in residential design, serving both utilitarian and aesthetic purposes. They offer protection, softness, light filtration, and warmth. However, their greatest function for clients is adding beauty, color, texture, and pattern to their homes. Residential fabrics, including bedding, upholstery, rugs, window treatments, accessories, and art, personalize the living space and enhance comfort. The term "textiles" encompasses a wide range of fabrics, from natural knits and woven materials to synthetic fibers derived from petroleum or fiberglass. When prioritizing a healthy and environmentally conscious home, it is advisable to emphasize natural materials. Fibers sourced from plants and animals are renewable resources that can be harvested regularly, ensuring a continuous supply. Additionally, natural fibers will biodegrade when they reach the end of their lifespan.

On the other hand, most synthetic fibers are derived from nonrenewable petroleum resources, which are liquefied and extruded into filaments or yarns. Chemical dyes are commonly added during the blending process since synthetic fabrics do not readily accept dyes once they are formed. As a result, these synthetic residential textiles do not easily biodegrade and are rarely recycled. Newer synthetic materials are being developed from renewable sources such as soy or perpetually recyclable polyester. Some of these alternatives are biodegradable or can be easily recycled or down-cycled, but it is important to verify specific information from the manufacturer or supplier.

It is worth noting that the production of synthetic fabrics requires more energy compared to natural fiber spinning or handmade textiles. To fully embrace eco-friendly residential textiles, it is necessary to go beyond considering the fiber type alone. While it is relatively easy to find fabrics made from natural materials like cotton, silk, hemp, flax, or wool, it is more challenging to find fibers that haven't been dyed with synthetic colorants, treated with performance-enhancing chemicals, or produced with the use of pesticides. Textiles made from organically grown or sustainably raised raw materials represent only a small portion of the market. For instance, organic cotton comprises a mere 0.03 percent of the overall cotton supply. Finding all-organic textile sources may require some effort and research.

Textile factories, much like other large industries, face various challenges related to environmental impact and working conditions. These include issues such as wastewater pollution, hazardous by-products, questionable labor practices, and concerns regarding air quality. Within the textile production process, a range of chemicals may be used for washing, dyeing, weaving, and finishing fabrics. Unfortunately, these chemicals often remain on the fabric without being disclosed on labels. Some common chemicals used in textile production include chlorine compounds, heavy metals, azo dyes, halogenated solvents, and flame retardants like polybrominated diphenyl ethers (PBDEs) and decabrominated flame retardants.

To mitigate these issues, it is important to prioritize textiles that embrace natural dyes, fibers, processes, and fabric treatments. Collaborating with companies that uphold the highest environmental standards across all stages of fabric production, from agricultural practices to mill processes and labor conditions, is crucial. It is worth seeking out production processes that utilize biodegradable surfactants, detergents, and degreasers.

An exemplary textile manufacturer would operate a fabric mill powered by renewable energy sources and employ on-site wastewater treatment to minimize pollution. They would also commit to avoiding the use of harmful and hazardous chemicals throughout the production process. Ideally, such manufacturers would pursue third-party certifications to validate their sustainability efforts. Fabrics would be sourced from bio-based and sustainably harvested resources, and bleaching methods would utilize ozone instead of chlorine. Dyes and colorants would undergo rigorous testing to meet third-party standards. Furthermore, the manufacturer would prioritize fair trade practices and uphold socially responsible labor conditions. These comprehensive measures collectively embody intelligent style that harmonizes aesthetics with sustainability and environmental consciousness.

Natural Fibers: From Plants and Animals to Leather

Indulging in natural fibers is akin to savoring comfort food, providing a sense of warmth and satisfaction. Natural fibers such as cotton, wool, soy silk, flax/linen, ramie, bamboo, lyocell, corn, jute, and hemp, among others, offer a lower embodied energy compared to their petroleum-based counterparts. Derived from renewable sources, these fibers replenish themselves within months or years, far shorter than the typical lifespan of fabric. Additionally, natural fibers possess breathability, a quality often lacking in synthetic alternatives, and they readily biodegrade.

The production of natural fibers requires minimal processing prior to manufacturing, resulting in reduced environmental impact. These fibers boast eco-friendly characteristics such as minimal chemical and pesticide usage, responsible land management, sustainable ranching and farming practices, certifications, and fair trade practices. Nevertheless, it is crucial to delve into the details of raw material selection, production methods, dye processes, usage, and disposal, as well as the consumption of energy, water, and chemicals. It is important to note that not all fiber farming, harvesting, and acquisition methods are created equal. Some approaches prioritize the Earth and its inhabitants more than others. Traditional cotton crops, for instance, are notorious for heavy pesticide and fertilizer use, while many animal farms rely on chemical pest control methods. Although it is unlikely that pesticide residues will directly harm consumers after extensive washing and processing of fibers and fabrics in mills, these chemicals pose significant environmental risks and are highly toxic to water, air, and soil ecosystems.

Textile products like wool and silk, which are commonly imported from overseas, often undergo chemical treatments to protect against moth infestation and microbial growth. In contrast, materials like hemp and jute, also sourced primarily from overseas, exhibit natural resistance to pests, both in their plant form and as fabrics.

Organic and sustainable farming practices offer an alternative approach by using natural methods to enrich the soil and prevent damage from pests and diseases. Instead of relying on chemicals, these practices employ techniques such as beneficial insects, compost as fertilizer, and crop rotation to maintain soil productivity. Sustainable agriculture also emphasizes providing animals with open grazing ranges, natural food sources, and humane treatment. Although initially more expensive for farmers and consumers, sustainable agriculture yields long-term benefits such as reduced erosion, improved soil fertility, healthier ecosystems, and environmentally-friendly products.

Certification under the Global Organic Textile Standard (GOTS) ensures that finished textile products meet stringent criteria for organic processing. GOTS covers various stages of post-harvest processing, including spinning, knitting, weaving, dyeing, and manufacturing. It includes environmental and social provisions, such as the prohibition of child labor, genetically modified engineering, heavy metals, and hazardous chemicals like formaldehyde. Additionally, GOTS requires fair wages and strict wastewater treatment practices. It is advisable to choose natural-fiber textiles from companies that adhere to this global certification process or follow eco-friendly farming practices.

Artisans are valuable sources for all-natural textiles, as many of them prioritize traditional techniques such as hand-weaving, hand-spinning, and dyeing with locally sourced plants. Some artisans even cultivate their own crops or raise animals for fiber production. Opting for textiles created by local artisans not only supports the reduction of energy consumption but also minimizes shipping requirements. Cooperatives can be excellent resources for locating artisans, and suggestions can be obtained from local indigenous tribes, county extension offices, or artist guilds.

When dealing with textiles sourced from abroad, it is important to investigate whether they adhere to environmental and fair trade standards. Although reasonable pay and good working conditions may not directly appear to impact the environment, they often reflect a company's commitment to the well-being of workers, environmental health, and the avoidance of highly toxic chemicals or ecosystem destruction for profit. Opting for fair trade or cooperative-made textiles when purchasing from developing regions helps maximize the region's existing assets, both human and environmental.

In addition to considering the origin of textiles, their suitability for specific applications or environments is crucial. It is essential to choose fibers that can withstand typical use, water washing, and sunlight exposure without deteriorating quickly. Textiles should be durable enough for their intended purpose, requiring minimal maintenance. Easy washability or cleanability is also important, as chemical dry cleaning and stain repellents can compromise the eco-friendly attributes of natural fabrics.

Here are some popular eco-friendly choices to consider when specifying natural fibers for textiles. While this list is not exhaustive and various combinations and blends are available, these options are commonly preferred for their sustainable qualities.

Organic Cotton

Organic cotton is a type of cotton that is cultivated without the use of pesticides, herbicides, insecticides, or chemical fertilizers. Instead, sustainable agricultural methods are employed, reducing or eliminating pests, promoting healthy growth, maintaining soil quality, and protecting the well-being of cotton harvesters. Notably, organic cotton fibers are stronger because they are not subjected to chemical processing.

However, it's important to consider that organic cotton cultivation requires significant amounts of water. Whenever possible, it is advisable to seek out crops that rely on rainfall for irrigation, reducing the strain on water resources. Organic cotton naturally grows in shades of green, brown, and natural hues, and it possesses several desirable characteristics. It is fade-resistant, rapidly renewable, minimally processed, moisture absorbent, reusable, recyclable, and biodegradable.

When specifying organic cotton, it is recommended to look for certifications that address both the growing and processing aspects, such as the Global Organic Textile Standard (GOTS) or the Oeko-Tex Standard 1000. These certifications ensure that the organic cotton meets strict criteria regarding its cultivation and processing methods, assuring its eco-friendly and sustainable attributes.

Conventional Cotton

Cotton is renowned for its comfort against the skin and its remarkable ability to absorb moisture, capable of holding up to twenty times its weight in water. The cotton fiber is obtained from the cottonseed pod. While cotton fibers typically have a white or cream color, they can also be grown in various natural color variations, including rust, tan, gray, and even with a bluish tint. Cotton readily accepts dyes and can withstand hot water and sanitization processes, making it an excellent choice for individuals with allergies or health concerns. However, it's important to note that conventional cotton farming practices involve the extensive use of water, as well as the application of chemical pesticides and fertilizers. Additionally, the majority of cotton crops have been genetically engineered. To prioritize sustainability and eco-friendliness, it is advisable to seek out unbleached or naturally dyed cotton fibers. It's also recommended to avoid fabrics treated with wrinkle-resistance or sizing treatments, as well as those containing flame retardants, in order to minimize exposure to potentially harmful chemicals.

Organic Wool

Organic wool offers a range of beneficial characteristics, making it a desirable choice for environmentally conscious consumers. It is a rapidly renewable resource that undergoes minimal processing, making it more sustainable. Wool is naturally moisture absorbent, inherently fire retardant, and resistant to stains. It is also highly durable and long-lasting, allowing for extended use and reducing the need for frequent replacements. Furthermore, wool is both reusable and recyclable, ultimately biodegrading without causing harm to the environment.

When selecting organic wool, it is important to ensure that the fiber is unbleached or bleached using ozone-based products, as well as dyed using responsible and eco-friendly methods that do not involve heavy metals. By adhering to these practices, the environmental impact of wool production can be minimized. It is worth noting that concerns have been raised about the carbon dioxide emissions associated with sheep farming and its potential impact on land. However, when sourced from sustainable ranchers who follow organic or holistic management principles, wool can be a strong and beautiful fiber with fewer limitations.

One aspect to consider is that wool requires scouring, a process that involves significant water usage and can result in polluted wastewater. To address this, it is recommended to specify organic wool that is woven according to the Global Organic Textile Standard (GOTS), which includes guidelines for responsible production practices. In addition to GOTS certification, it is beneficial to look for sustainable farming practices that prioritize the well-being of animals and adhere to organic or holistic management principles. This ensures that raw wool processing avoids the use of typical scouring and descaling chemicals. If dyes are necessary, opt for natural dyeing processes that align with eco-friendly standards.

Wool

Wool is renowned for its warmth, durability, and longevity, making it a preferred choice for many. It has the remarkable ability to last for centuries with proper care. Various animals, such as sheep, goats, vicuñas, alpacas, llamas, angoras, and camels, produce distinct types of wool. The process of shearing these animals for their wool can be beneficial for their well-being. Additionally, some animals are selectively bred for their coat colorations, resulting in a wide range of subtle, natural hues. When choosing wool products, it is important to support firms that practice good animal husbandry. These practices not only ensure the welfare of the animals but also contribute to carbon sequestration, reduce greenhouse gas levels in the atmosphere, and promote the replenishment and renewal of grassland soils.

Wool possesses excellent moisture-absorbing properties, able to absorb approximately thirty times its weight in moisture before feeling wet. Furthermore, the natural lanolin and oils present in wool help it repel water. Wool can even contribute to improved air quality by absorbing and retaining volatile organic compounds (VOCs). It also breathes well and helps regulate humidity, making it a versatile and sustainable resource.

While some individuals may find wool fibers itchy, true allergies to wool are very rare. Certain species, such as merino, are less likely to cause discomfort for those with sensitivities. The unique structure of wool fibers, with their characteristic scales, allows them to interlock when abraded, creating dense felts that are often used in the production of rugs, blankets, and clothing.

It is important to note that the washing and processing of wool often involve the use of chemicals and significant amounts of water. While wool itself is naturally flame-resistant and does not require fire-retardant chemicals, other treatments like moth repellents are common. Additionally, sheep emit methane, a potent greenhouse gas that can contribute to climate change. However, the inherent durability and longevity of wool provide it with an environmental advantage.

Silk

Silk, a luxurious fabric, is derived from the natural protein fibers found in the cocoon of the silkworm. These fibers are spun into filaments to create silk fabric. Despite its delicate appearance, silk is incredibly durable. In fact, a strand of silk of the same diameter is stronger than a strand of steel. However, it should be noted that silk is not highly abrasion-resistant and may not withstand heavy wear. Silk has a lustrous sheen and accepts dye exceptionally well. It offers excellent thermal properties, providing warmth in winter and keeping cool in summer. Silk is also absorbent and resistant to shrinkage. However, it is important to protect silk from prolonged exposure to bright sunlight or high heat, as it can damage the fabric.

In conventional textile manufacturing, chemicals play a significant role, and silk is no exception. Chemical treatments are often applied to silk fabrics to control static, repel water and oil, impart flame-retardant properties, and enhance stability. It is essential to inquire about the specific chemical treatments used on silk to understand any potential health hazards they may pose. Organic methods of silk cultivation are increasingly practiced, which involves harvesting the cocoons after the butterfly has naturally emerged rather than boiling them to remove the larvae. This approach promotes more sustainable and humane silk production. Child labor has been a concern in certain Asian countries where silk is produced. It is important to support silk producers that have strict policies against child labor and prioritize sustainable and organic production methods.

Linen (Flax)

Linen, considered one of the oldest textiles, is made from the fibers of the flax plant. It derives its unique luster from the natural waxes present in the plant. The production of linen involves extracting the fibers from the flax stalk through a process called "retting." This process involves rotting the woody bark of the plant to expose the resin that holds the fibers together. Chemicals are used in the retting process, and it is crucial to neutralize these chemicals to minimize their environmental impact when they enter water supplies. While linen lacks elasticity and can fray along creases, the individual linen fibers are remarkably strong, surpassing cotton in strength. Linen can withstand hot water sanitation. Its natural color is a light tan or cream, but linen readily accepts dye and retains its color well. Linen is nonallergenic, rapidly renewable, absorbent, reusable, recyclable, and biodegradable. It is also an eco-friendly choice as it requires minimal water and fertilizers during cultivation.

Hemp

Hemp, a type of cannabis cultivated for its fiber rather than as a drug, possesses exceptional qualities that make it a versatile and environmentally friendly natural fiber. Its long fibers require minimal processing and result in a highly durable and absorbent material. With its rapid growth and dense cultivation, hemp eliminates the need for herbicides, pesticides, and artificial fertilizers. It is also resilient to drought and can often thrive without irrigation. Additionally, hemp is biodegradable, recyclable, and resistant to fading, rot, mildew, and mold. These qualities have made it a preferred choice for centuries in applications such as twine, rope, and ship riggings. Hemp is a rapidly renewable resource that undergoes minimal processing, making it highly absorbent and reusable.

It is important to note that hemp, although derived from the same plant species as marijuana, is cultivated specifically from the stems and not the narcotic flowers, seeds, or leaves. Hemp offers a range of textures and weights, making it suitable for various products such as woven or knit fabrics, ropes, belts, area rugs, and carpets. As a closed-loop product, hemp farming maximizes yield while minimizing land usage. Its waste and byproducts can be recycled repeatedly, further enhancing its environmental sustainability.

Ramie, Jute, Coir, and Sisal

China grass, also known as ramie, is a flowering plant belonging to the nettle family. It is highly renowned for its strength, excellent absorbency, and natural resistance to stains. Ramie fibers are often blended with other materials like cotton and hemp to create fabrics that are incredibly durable. Although similar to linen, ramie may have a tendency to shrink or become rough when washed. Ramie is a rapidly renewable resource that undergoes minimal processing. It is absorbent, reusable, recyclable, and biodegradable. Additionally, ramie requires little water and fertilizer for growth.

Jute is derived from the stalk of a tall flowering vegetable plant and has a long history of being used to make rope, twine, carpets, and rugs. It is known for its inherent strength and affordability, making it one of the most cost-effective natural fibers available. Jute has also been utilized in the production of paper, geotextiles, and particleboard. It contributes to improving soil quality and requires minimal water and fertilizers for growth. Jute is a rapidly renewable resource that is carbon-neutral, minimally processed, absorbent, reusable, recyclable, and biodegradable.

Coir and sisal are similar fibers, both known for their durability but having a rough texture. They are commonly used in the production of ropes, twines, rugs, and backings. Sisal is obtained from plant stalks, while coir is derived from coconut husks.

Bamboo

Bamboo, a renewable grass, possesses several notable characteristics. It is naturally antibacterial, hypoallergenic, and exhibits silk-like draping qualities with enhanced durability and affordability. Bamboo is rapidly renewable, requiring minimal water and fertilizers for growth. It is absorbent, reusable, recyclable, and biodegradable. However, caution should be exercised as bamboo can become invasive when planted in nonindigenous areas.

To ensure the sustainability of China's endangered panda species, it is crucial to prioritize "panda-friendly" bamboo cultivation practices. Bamboo plants grow rapidly without the need for fertilizers or pesticides and have low water requirements. Moreover, bamboo grasses release 35 percent more oxygen into the atmosphere compared to an equivalent stand of trees. Bamboo fabric is derived from the pulp of the bamboo stalk, which readily accepts dyes and does not require chlorine bleach.

One drawback of bamboo processing involves the use of sulfuric acid, which contributes minimally to air pollution. Additionally, the wastewater generated during processing needs to be neutralized with bacteria before being reintroduced into the ecosystem.

Tencel

Tencel, a branded lyocell fiber, is a relatively new fabric derived from wood pulp cellulose, specifically from eucalyptus trees. This fiber is known for its high quality and requires less water compared to fast-growing trees. For a more environmentally friendly option, it is advisable to seek eucalyptus trees certified by the Forest Stewardship Council. Tencel is rapidly renewable, requiring minimal water and fertilizers. It is also reusable, recyclable, and biodegradable.

Tencel, a branded lyocell fiber, is a relatively new fabric derived from wood pulp cellulose, specifically from eucalyptus trees. This fiber is known for its high quality and requires less water compared to fast-growing trees. For a more environmentally friendly option, it is advisable to seek eucalyptus trees certified by the Forest Stewardship Council. Tencel is rapidly renewable, requiring minimal water and fertilizers. It is also reusable, recyclable, and biodegradable. The production of Tencel involves the creation of a nontoxic organic solvent from wood pulp, which is then reclaimed and recycled in a closed-loop spinning process to conserve energy and water. It has been reported that up to 95 percent of the solvent can be recovered and reused.

When selecting Tencel products, it is important to choose those that do not employ harmful chemicals, such as formaldehyde, in the treatment of fiber fibrillation.

One limitation of Tencel and other lyocell-based fabrics is that they may not readily absorb dyes. As a result, chemical-based dyes or other treatments that are not environmentally friendly may sometimes be used in the dyeing process.

Ingeo™ Corn Fiber

Ingeo is an innovative, eco-friendly fabric made from a man-made fiber derived from corn. The process involves extracting starch and sugars from corn, which are then transformed into a fiber that can be spun into yarn or woven into fabric. Ingeo is known for its stain and fade resistance, odor absorption properties, and hypoallergenic nature. Additionally, it does not retain moisture.

Ingeo is a trademark of NatureWorks, and it is claimed to be the world's first man-made fiber derived entirely from renewable resources. According to NatureWorks, Ingeo fiber combines the desirable qualities of both natural and synthetic fibers. It offers strength and resilience while maintaining comfort, softness, and drape in textiles. Moreover, Ingeo fiber has good moisture management characteristics, making it suitable for a wide range of applications, from fashion to furnishings.

Leather and Skins

Leather and skins have long been used for various purposes such as upholstery, accessories, and rugs. Known for their breathability, softness, and durability, these materials offer versatility in design. When considering the use of animal skins, it is important to acknowledge the cultural and symbolic significance attached to them in many societies. While some embrace the holistic use of animals and waste no part after slaughter, others have ethical or religious objections. Consulting with clients becomes crucial in making informed decisions about incorporating animal products.

One of the key factors to evaluate when it comes to leather and skins in a green home is the processing method employed. Traditional leather tanning often involves toxic chemicals like chromium and substantial water usage, posing risks to workers and the environment. However, there are alternatives, such as vegetable-based tanning processes that utilize natural tannins from sources like rhubarb, tree bark, tare, and valonea.

While some companies strive to reduce the environmental impact of leather production by using natural vegetable and mineral dyes, it is important to note that achieving a completely sustainable leather industry is challenging. However, by sourcing responsibly processed leather and skins and supporting sustainable practices, it is possible to minimize the environmental footprint associated with these materials.

When it comes to vegetable tanning, the use of bark or plant tannins replaces chromium, but unfortunately, other steps in the tanning process remain unchanged. Tanning hides involves the use of approximately 250 different chemicals, including alcohol, coal tar, sodium sulfate, sulfuric acid, chlorinated phenols, azo dyes, heavy metals like cadmium, cobalt, copper, and more. These chemicals, along with pesticide residues, contribute to the environmental impact of leather production.

To assess the eco-friendliness of leather, it's essential to consider the environmental stewardship practices of tanners and the chemicals they use. Several areas of leather manufacturing have a significant potential impact, such as managing restricted substances, reducing energy and water consumption, controlling air emissions, implementing effective waste management systems, including hazardous and nonhazardous waste, and ensuring traceability of materials back to their source.

Improving the eco-profile of leather involves using biodegradable wetting agents, minimizing sulfide processing, employing non-synthetic or polymeric re-tannage systems, optimizing dyestuffs, utilizing vegetable oil-based fat liquors, implementing waste-reducing finishing systems, and focusing on materials that biodegrade within a year. These factors contribute to the concept of "eco-leather."

Key determinants of eco-leather include the control of manufacturing processes, the use of clean technology and transparent chemical selection, effective management of restricted substances, and an assessment of the end-of-life impact. Leather and skins often stem from the meat industry as a secondary product. Tanneries committed to sustainability may source their materials from organic ranches that provide a pesticide-free, natural environment for the animals. It's important to inquire about the source and consider partnering with natural tanneries or organic ranches.

While leather is naturally durable and resilient to the elements, it eventually decomposes. However, the chemicals used in tanning and synthetic fabric treatments, when improperly disposed of in landfills, pose significant risks to water and soil, as they are considered hazardous waste.

BIO-BASED SYNTHETICS

Rayon, the initial synthetic textile, is created by subjecting wood pulp (cellulose) to chemical treatment, transforming it into a liquefied form, and subsequently extruding it as a filament. While it does not qualify as a fully natural fiber, incorporating renewable materials into its production carries ecological merits. In an effort to diminish reliance on nonrenewable resources like petroleum, manufacturers have been exploring alternative bio-based synthetic textiles derived from sustainable sources such as corn, soybeans, sugar beets, rice, and wood pulp. Some of these textiles are designed to enhance specific characteristics that are typically challenging to find in all-natural materials, making them suitable for surgical applications or institutional settings.

The commendable development of novel textile fibers, particularly when derived from renewable resources and capable of biodegradation or recycling, should be acknowledged. However, the intensive manufacturing process results in a substantial amount of embodied energy compared to the spinning or weaving of plant or animal fibers. For most residential purposes, the benefits of bio-based synthetics are negligible.

SYNTHETICS

Accounting for 65 percent of global fiber production, synthetic fibers dominate the industry, with the remaining 35 percent comprising natural fibers. Prominent synthetic fabrics and fibers include acetate, acrylic, nylon, and polyester, with polyester being the most widely manufactured synthetic fiber, representing 70 percent of the total. Polyester is primarily composed of polyethylene terephthalate (PET). Polyester fabrics are commonly preferred for commercial projects due to their cost-effectiveness and flame-resistant properties. Traditionally, synthetic fabrics are produced from virgin polymers using toxic substances or additives, making them non-recyclable. Furthermore, the majority of synthetic fibers are derived from chemicals or petroleum.

Synthetic fibers, such as nylon, possess unique characteristics that are challenging to replicate naturally, notably nylon's elasticity. However, in general, synthetic fibers are less breathable and have poor moisture absorption, which can be either advantageous or disadvantageous depending on the intended application. Conventional synthetic textiles are often dyed using artificial colorants and treated with additional chemical finishes. It is advisable to limit the use of these conventional synthetic textiles and seek alternatives that reduce their environmental impact, such as low-emitting options, reduced chemical toxins, recycled content, absence of hazardous ingredients, recyclability, bio-based materials, compostability, sustainably sourced materials, and third-party certifications.

Textile manufacturers have made concerted efforts to develop synthetic fibers that are safe for consumers and biodegradable or recyclable. These new synthetics may even surpass the properties of natural materials, offering extended lifespan, enhanced durability, or specialized applications like medical settings. Some synthetic textiles are made from consumer and commercial waste, diverting materials from landfills, while others are hybrids created through synthetic processes using natural materials. Certain manufacturers facilitate the recycling of their synthetic textiles, transforming them into new fibers or fabrics and establishing closed-loop systems.

While the majority of these new synthetic textiles are currently tailored for commercial use, a few have made their way into the residential market. Natural materials still reign supreme in most applications of green residential design. However, it is anticipated that there will be a growing availability of environmentally friendly synthetic textiles in the future.

RECYCLED TEXTILES

Prior to the industrialization era, fabric scraps were rarely wasted due to the labor-intensive nature of textile production, which involved fiber preparation, spinning, knitting, and weaving. The practice of using fabric remnants in creative ways is exemplified by patchwork quilts. In a sustainable approach, repurposing what the client already possesses can be a highly innovative eco-strategy. Antique or vintage quilts, tea towels, and other linens that have been stored away can find new life as pillowcases, window coverings, tablecloths, or slipcovers.

In response to environmental concerns, both large manufacturers and individual artisans are now utilizing textile waste to create new products. Various sources of waste, such as scraps from mill floors, yarn ends, and even recycled denim jeans, are transformed into new fabrics or repurposed for insulation. Some processes require minimal additional energy, such as hand-sewing rags into patchworks or hand-weaving them into rugs. Others involve more energy-intensive methods carried out in factories, such as converting fibers into pulp, respinning them, and then weaving or pressing them into new textiles. To prevent materials from ending up in landfills, polyester, carpet fibers, and other synthetics are recycled by mills into new textiles. Certain synthetic or natural-fiber textiles can be continuously recycled, and some manufacturers offer take-back programs for their textiles at the end of their life cycle.

When considering recycled materials, it is important to consult the manufacturer or artisan for specific details about the content, processing methods, and the health and environmental impacts associated with the recycled textiles. This information will help the client make informed decisions regarding their choice of recycled materials.

DYES

While using natural, undyed fabrics is considered a best practice, the desire for a colorful world is understandable. To incorporate color in a more sustainable manner, it is recommended to look for natural dyes derived from plants, animals, minerals, or low-impact reactive dyes that are free from heavy metals. A wide range of materials such as berries, bark, insects, spices, and common plants can be used to create natural dyes, and vinegar or pickling alum is often employed to set the dye. Generally, natural dyes are unlikely to cause issues for sensitive individuals, but if chronic allergies are a concern, it may be advisable to specify no dye.

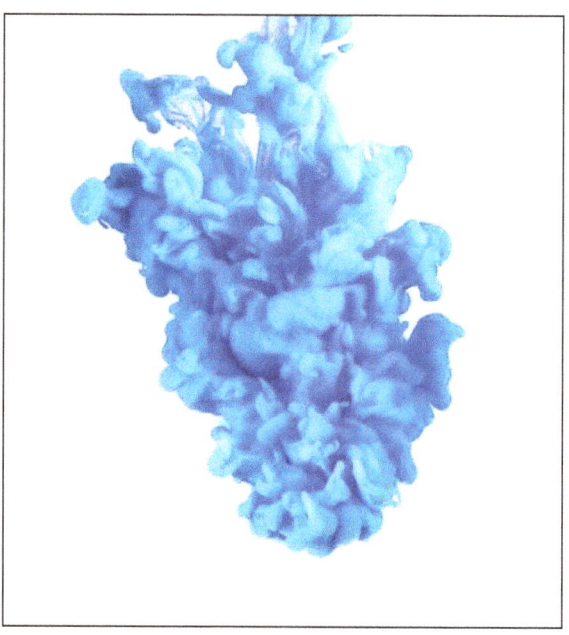

Natural dyes offer a full spectrum of colors, although they tend to have a more subdued appearance compared to vibrant chemical dyes. It is important to handle naturally dyed textiles with care during washing to preserve their vivid hues—gentle washing in cold water with minimal agitation and mild soap is recommended. Chlorine bleach, commonly used to whiten cotton and other fibers, is highly caustic and toxic. It not only poses environmental risks but also affects the natural finish of cotton, making the texture rougher. Instead of chlorine bleach, opt for oxidizing chemicals such as ozone and hydrogen peroxide, which break down into harmless oxygen and water, providing "next-to-skin" comfort.

FABRIC TREATMENTS

Textile mills utilize a wide range of chemicals for various purposes such as stiffening, softening, wrinkle-proofing, stain and water resistance, and enhancing colorfastness and shine. Although certain treatments like special stain resistors may be listed on the label, there is no requirement to disclose all chemical agents used. Some of these chemicals are being scrutinized for their potential health hazards, and individuals with chemical sensitivities may find them problematic. To completely avoid chemical treatments, it is advisable to seek out specialty textile producers such as artisans or small mills that specialize in creating all-natural fabrics. Working with companies that have restrictions on the use of flame retardants is also important. Flame retardants, often made from polybrominated diphenyl ethers (PBDEs) and other brominated chemicals, are commonly added to foam padding, plastics, and fabrics to reduce flammability. However, these chemicals break down slowly and persist in the environment for extended periods. If flame retardants are necessary, it is recommended to specify that they be free of hazardous chemicals. Certain fibers have inherent properties that make them naturally stain and water-resistant. For example, wool contains lanolin, an oily substance known for its waterproofing abilities. It is so effective that it is used in furniture polish and hand creams. Selecting the most appropriate fabric for the intended purpose is crucial in preventing textile damage and ensuring longevity. Some specialty retailers and distributors catering to environmentally friendly interiors offer prewashed textiles that have been thoroughly cleansed of all finishes and fabric treatments. These companies may provide this service even for textiles they haven't manufactured themselves. This can be particularly valuable for clients with chemical sensitivities, as it reduces the exposure to potentially harmful substances.

Origins

- Textiles are derived from a variety of sources, including all-natural plant or animal fibers, recycled fabrics and yarns, petroleum-based or chemical synthetics, as well as bio-based synthetics.
- Bio-synthetic fabrics are created using renewable raw materials like paper or wood pulp, soy, corn, or bamboo. These materials offer a more sustainable alternative to traditional synthetic fabrics.
- Plant-based fibers, such as cotton, jute, hemp, and ramie, can be cultivated using organic or conventional farming methods, depending on the desired level of environmental impact.
- Animal products like wool and leather can be sourced from sustainably managed or "humane" ranches, or from conventional ranch facilities. It is important to consider the ethical and environmental aspects when choosing animal-based textiles.
- Dyes used in textiles can be derived from natural sources such as plants and minerals, or they can be chemically synthesized. Natural dyes offer a more eco-friendly option compared to their chemical counterparts.
- Fabric treatments are typically chemical-based, but there are also all-natural alternatives made from plants and minerals. These natural treatments provide a more environmentally conscious choice for those seeking sustainable textiles.
- In the case of leather, it can be tanned using chromium and various other chemicals. Alternatively, there is the less common method of using natural bark and vegetable agents as substitutes for chromium. The choice of tanning process can significantly impact the environmental footprint of leather production.

Maintenance

To maintain textiles effectively, it is crucial to choose materials that are suitable for the specific setting and intended use. Factors such as the presence of children or animals, daily use, regular washing, and exposure to sunlight should be taken into consideration. Delicate fabrics with special care requirements may not be suitable for environments with high activity or frequent cleaning, as they can wear out, fade, or require specialized chemical cleaning methods to maintain their appearance.

For residential textiles, simple cleaning methods like soap and water, dusting, or vacuuming are generally preferred. Whitening agents such as borax or borate, which are natural minerals, can be added to the wash cycle. Baking soda is an effective and natural deodorizer, either dissolved in water or sprinkled on textiles like rugs and then vacuumed. Natural stain removal techniques often outperform commercial solvents, and there are numerous resources available on the internet or through books that provide healthy cleaning tips. Local county extension offices can also offer valuable advice on textile care.

Fabrics that require dry cleaning are generally less desirable due to the need for transportation to a dry cleaner and the use of chemicals and solvents in the process. However, there are healthier dry cleaning methods available, such as carbon dioxide (CO_2) cleaning, which uses the "fizzy" gas found in soda pop. If dry cleaning is necessary, it is advisable to choose businesses that utilize CO_2 cleaning methods for a more environmentally friendly approach.

Textiles made from natural plant fibers can be broken down and used for composting. On the other hand, specific types of synthetic fabrics can undergo recycling or down-cycling processes to create new textiles or alternative polymers. However, the majority of synthetic fabrics typically end up in landfills, where they decompose at a slow rate, if at all.

Specification

- Seek out textiles made from certified organic natural fibers.
- Look for third-party certifications for textiles to ensure their environmental and social sustainability.
- Choose fabrics derived from natural plant- or animal-based fibers.
- Opt for textiles sourced from rapidly renewable and sustainable sources.
- Select textiles made from sustainably farmed products with minimal ecological footprint on the land, energy, water, resources, and waste.
- Consider textiles made in a closed-loop cycle, promoting a circular economy.
- Prioritize reusable, recyclable, and biodegradable fabrics.
- Look for textiles that undergo minimal processing without added chemicals or dyes.
- Explore natural dyes derived from plant, animal, or mineral sources.
- Consider textiles produced using environmentally sound mill practices, such as proper water treatment for pH balance.
- Look for textiles with benign chemical and biological impacts on the environment.
- Give preference to textiles produced in fair-trade and socially responsible mills.
- Choose textiles that can be cleaned using natural or benign methods such as dusting, soap and water, or vacuuming.
- Consider the use of ozone or hydrogen peroxide oxidization for textile cleaning.
- Look for textiles with natural stain and water repellants, such as those with a tight weave or lanolin in wool.
- Explore biosynthetic fabrics that are preferably recyclable or biodegradable, made from renewable and natural products like paper, wood pulp, soy, corn, or bamboo.
- Consider vegetable tanning and dyeing processes for leather, utilizing natural elements such as tare, rhubarb, valonea, and tree bark instead of chromium.
- Prioritize locally tanned leather with minimal chemical processing or dyes.
- Seek out locally made artisanal textiles, especially those crafted through nonmechanized methods.
- Consider textiles with recycled content, promoting the reuse of materials.

Avoid:

- Steer clear of synthetic fibers made from petroleum products or hazardous chemicals. Avoid textiles made from acrylic and polyvinyl chloride (PVC) yarns and backings. Refrain from purchasing fibers sourced from farms or suppliers that use pesticides, biocides, or herbicides. Avoid the use of chlorine bleach for textile cleaning. Stay away from chemical deodorizers, detergents, and dry cleaning agents. Avoid textiles treated with fireproofing treatments. Refrain from purchasing textiles with chemical dyes. Avoid textiles treated with synthetic waterproofing and stain-proofing treatments. Opt for leather that is not tanned with chromium. Avoid chemically dyed or treated leather.

Area Rugs

Area rugs offer a variety of eco-friendly options compared to wall-to-wall carpets. They come in various sizes, from small rugs made of delicate fibers like cotton rags, chenille, or even paper, to larger rugs. Cleaning smaller rugs is convenient as they can be laundered at home using detergent and water. For larger rugs, they can be taken to an eco-friendly cleaner, which is advantageous for individuals with allergies or sensitivities.

Moreover, rugs often have lower embodied energy compared to carpets. While carpets are typically manufactured on large looms in factories, many types of rugs are woven on small hand-looms. These rugs often utilize local specialty fibers sourced from indigenous sheep or native grasses. In some cases, rug-makers and weavers may even handle the dyeing process themselves. When working with an artisan, it is often possible to specify the use of all-natural colorants for the rug.

Rugs offer a wide range of options when it comes to the materials used, and natural fibers are a preferred choice. Unlike wall-to-wall carpets that are typically made from synthetics, area rugs can be woven, knotted, or knit using various plant and animal fibers. Some common natural fibers used for rugs include wool, cotton, silk, jute, hemp, coir, sisal, and sea grass. The selection of fiber or blend should be based on the intended purpose and durability requirements.

Whenever possible, it is advisable to choose fibers that are organically grown or farmed using sustainable methods. While wool and cotton growers may have third-party certifications, it is less common for other fiber producers. Look for manufacturers that adhere to strict environmental production standards, efficient waste management and recycling practices, and prioritize worker safety. Alternatively, consider purchasing rugs from local artisans who specialize in working with all-natural materials, which reduces the energy consumption associated with long-distance transportation. Specify the use of all-natural dyes or no dyes at all. Avoid chlorine bleaching and chemical colorants. Synthetic materials derived from petroleum, such as polyester, olefin, nylon, acrylic, or acetate, should be avoided. Some synthetic rug fibers may emit odors or volatile organic compounds (VOCs) that can be irritating.

It is recommended to avoid stain repellants, waterproofing treatments, and other chemical applications on rugs. While these treatments may not be listed on the label, request detailed information from the manufacturer. When working with local artisans or specialty rug-makers, request the use of only natural dyes. If the client has sensitivities or allergies that might be triggered by dyes, specify no dye. Additionally, area rugs can be made from a variety of recycled materials. Old denim jeans, T-shirts, fabrics, and even paper can be torn into rags and woven, braided, or sewn into rugs. This option is both cost-effective and eco-friendly as it eliminates the need for new materials and minimizes the use of natural resources. However, for clients with chemical sensitivities, recycled materials may not be the best choice due to the varied fabric content and unknown origins.

RUG PADS

When considering the padding for a rug, it's important to choose options that not only provide comfort and safety but also align with eco-friendly practices. The padding serves as a protective layer, preventing abrasion between the rug and the floor while also extending the rug's lifespan.

There are two primary types of rug pads to consider. Cushioning pads offer a soft and comfortable feel underfoot and can be made from natural materials such as wool, which is both eco-friendly and sustainable. Synthetic pads are more commonly available but are not ideal for green rooms due to their environmental impact.

For those concerned with slipping rugs, gripping pads are an excellent choice. These pads are typically made from latex, and it's essential to specify all-natural rubber latex to ensure an eco-friendly option. It's worth noting that the term "latex" can refer to both natural and synthetic types, so it's crucial to inquire specifically about all-natural options to maintain a green approach.

Avoid using pads made from PVC or vinyl, as they emit a noticeable odor and release harmful substances through a process called outgassing. By opting for environmentally friendly padding materials, you can create a healthier indoor environment while still enjoying the benefits of a well-padded rug.

Origins

- Rugs offer a wide range of options when it comes to the materials they are made from. Natural fibers like wool, silk, jute, coir, sisal, sea grass, and cotton are popular choices for eco-friendly rugs. These fibers are derived from renewable resources and have minimal environmental impact.
- Alternatively, there are also rugs made from artificial fibers such as nylon, olefin, and acrylic. While these synthetic options may offer certain advantages like durability or affordability, they are derived from petroleum-based products and can have a higher environmental impact compared to natural fiber rugs.
- When it comes to rug pads, there is a variety of materials available, each with its own characteristics. Some common options include PVC or vinyls, synthetic or natural latex, recycled carpet fibers, wool, jute, camel hair, or mohair. It's important to consider the environmental implications of each material and choose pads made from eco-friendly and sustainable sources.
- Opting for natural fiber rugs and environmentally friendly rug pads can contribute to creating a more sustainable and eco-conscious living environment.

Maintenance

Maintaining proper care for rugs is essential to prolong their lifespan and keep them looking their best. Here are some recommended practices: Regular vacuuming:

1. Vacuum both sides of the rug to remove dirt, dust, and debris. This helps prevent particles from scratching the floor and keeps the fibers clean.
2. Laundering small rugs: If the fiber content allows, small rugs can be laundered regularly using mild detergent and water. Follow the care instructions provided by the manufacturer.
3. Professional cleaning: For larger rugs, consider professional cleaning services that use environmentally friendly methods. Look for cleaners that use water-based processes or carbon dioxide (CO_2) processes instead of harsh chemicals.
4. Avoid solvent-based treatments: Advise the client to avoid solvent-based stain treatments and chemical dry cleaners, as these may contain harmful chemicals and pollutants.
5. Stain repellents: It is recommended to avoid using stain repellents that contain synthetic chemicals. Instead, opt for natural or eco-friendly alternatives, or rely on proper maintenance and prompt spot cleaning to address stains.

Specification

- Choose carpets that are made from 100% natural fibers such as wool, cotton, silk, jute, coir, sisal, sea grass, or paper.
- Opt for rugs with all-natural dyes or no dye at all to minimize chemical exposure.
- Consider recycled-content rag rugs, which utilize reclaimed materials and reduce waste.
- Support local artisans and look for rugs that are locally made or artisan-produced, promoting sustainable and ethical practices.
- Look for rugs with Green certification, ensuring they are produced without child labor and adhere to fair labor practices.
- Select rug pads made from all-natural rubber latex, wool, or other natural materials to avoid synthetic options.

Avoid:

- Avoid carpets made from manufactured fibers such as nylon, polyester, olefin, and acetate, as these are derived from petroleum and have a higher environmental impact.
- Steer clear of stain repellents, waterproofing treatments, or other chemical treatments that can be harmful to the environment and human health.
- Avoid rugs with synthetic dyes, which can contain hazardous chemicals and contribute to pollution.
- Refrain from using synthetic rug pads, especially those made with PVC-vinyl, as they can release harmful substances and have negative environmental implications.

Window Treatments

Before selecting window treatments for an eco-friendly home, it's important to consult with the client to understand their specific needs and preferences. Window treatments can serve various purposes, such as functionality, decoration, and necessity. They play a crucial role in regulating sunlight, managing weather conditions, conserving energy, providing privacy, and enhancing the overall ambiance of a room.

In the case of new construction, the positioning of windows should be optimized to maximize solar gain and minimize heat loss. However, once the house is built, changing the window orientation is usually impractical. For homes located in climates with significant temperature variations, appropriate window coverings are essential for improving energy efficiency. They help keep the house warm during winter, block excessive sunlight in summer, and prevent drafts. Insulating, reflective, or blackout window treatments can have a noticeable impact on both comfort levels and utility bills. By reducing the need for nonrenewable fuel consumption for heating and air conditioning, they contribute to a more sustainable living environment.

Most homes require additional window insulation and light regulation to enhance energy efficiency. If the windows are not only highly functional but also serve as focal points in a room, the client may desire window treatments that showcase the view or enhance the overall ambiance.

DRAPERIES AND WINDOW TEXTILES

When selecting window coverings for an eco-friendly home, prioritize long-lasting textiles and materials that require minimal maintenance and have a low environmental impact. Opt for fabrics made from organically grown cotton, hemp, flax (linen), ramie, wool, or silk sourced from sustainably managed operations. Additionally, consider window coverings crafted from grasses, bamboo, or wood for a natural and sustainable touch. Look for products that have obtained third-party certifications for sustainability or organic production. If the client prefers no additional dyes, ensure that the window coverings remain undyed. However, if color is desired, specify the use of natural dyes instead of chemical-based alternatives. Furthermore, prioritize low-impact finishes and avoid fabric treatments such as stain repellents or flame retardants that can harm the environment.

It's important to avoid specialty coatings on textiles that contain vinyl, plastic, synthetic rubber, or other manufactured polymers, as they have negative environmental implications. Instead, choose fabrics with a tight weave that are both washable and naturally stain-resistant. Synthetic waterproofing treatments may lead to condensation on the window or fabric, defeating their intended purpose. For moisture control, opt for highly breathable textiles with natural resistance to mold, such as wool.

SHUTTERS

Shutters installed on the inside of windows offer effective control over light, privacy, and to some extent, temperature regulation, especially when they completely cover the window and fit tightly. When selecting shutters, consider wood as a durable and environmentally-friendly option. Wood shutters can be ordered unfinished and left as is, or they can be finished on-site using low-VOC (volatile organic compound), low-odor paint, all-natural waxes, or oils. Over time, wood shutters can be salvaged, reused, or naturally decomposed. To ensure sustainable sourcing, specify shutters made from FSC (Forest Stewardship Council) or other third-party certified wood.

For clients with sensitivities, factory-finished wood shutters are a suitable choice as they undergo off-site outgassing. However, it's important to note that the outgassing still impacts the environment and indoor air quality. Specify low-VOC, formaldehyde-free finishes and look for Green certifications, which address indoor air quality standards.

While wood shutters may be more expensive, they are a preferable alternative to vinyl shutters that emit potentially hazardous substances. Vinyl and polymer shutters, sometimes marketed as "satinwood," "faux wood," or "composite," are essentially made from petroleum and various chemicals. To ensure a sustainable and environmentally-friendly home, avoid these plastic-based composites, unless they are explicitly manufactured from certified recycled wood products. It's important to prioritize the well-being of individuals who may be chemically sensitive and opt for materials that promote a healthy indoor environment.

BLINDS

Blinds serve the purpose of blocking sunlight and providing privacy, and it's important to choose materials that align with eco-friendly principles. Conventional venetian blinds are typically made from PVC-vinyl or metal, both of which have drawbacks. PVC-vinyl blinds release harmful substances through outgassing, posing risks to workers and consumers. It is recommended to opt for PVC-free alternatives that have obtained third-party certifications such as Greenguard Gold and Cradle to Cradle (C2C). Metal blinds, on the other hand, can accumulate static charge and attract dust, which can be troublesome for individuals with allergies. Additionally, metal blinds are not energy-efficient as they conduct heat, cold, and moisture.

To promote sustainability, consider blinds made from bamboo, wood, or natural textiles. Look for blinds with unfinished slats or those with low-VOC, odor-free finishes. While it may require some extra effort, search for blinds made from natural materials that are certified by the Forest Stewardship Council (FSC) or other reputable third-party organizations. Although it is not as common to find such materials in window blinds, the benefits they offer make the search worthwhile in order to align with eco-friendly goals.

ENHANCING PRIVACY, ENERGY EFFICIENCY, AND LIGHT CONTROL

In hot climates or areas with limited shade, it's beneficial to use reflective textiles or backings to regulate the amount of heat and sunlight entering the house. The most environmentally friendly options are natural textiles that are light-colored or have a reflective sheen. These textiles provide effective heat reduction while maintaining a healthier indoor environment. On the other hand, reflective synthetics like Mylar, which are sometimes used as backings or liners, are less eco-friendly. They are made from petroleum and other chemicals, counteracting some of the overall energy-saving benefits. Additionally, they are not breathable and can trap moisture.

When using reflective textiles, they can be incorporated between insulating layers in blinds or heavy draperies. However, depending on the fabric choices and specifications, the need for reflective materials may be minimized. Using batting or heavy textiles, along with magnetic seals, weights, or fasteners to secure the window treatment to the frame, can be highly effective in regulating home temperature. Natural materials like cotton, wool felt, and suede provide breathability and moisture control while still offering insulation against drafts, light, and harsh weather.

It's important to consider the environmental pros and cons when evaluating other options that aim to improve energy efficiency. Many of these offerings are made with synthetic textiles, and their impact should be weighed against the need for comfort and privacy. For instance, cellular or honeycomb shades are designed to trap air within the cells, effectively controlling heat loss during winter and solar gain during summer. Triple-cell shades offer the highest level of heat and light insulation, but double- and single-cell varieties are also available. Solar screens, another specialized window textile, allow for maximum visibility while diffusing harsh sunlight. When specifying solar screens, opt for PVC-free products to maintain environmental friendliness.

CONTROLS

Manual controls are the most environmentally friendly way to regulate light, darkness, privacy, and heating and cooling in a sustainable manner. Window treatments should be designed to be easily adjustable, allowing for effortless opening and closing and allowing for subtle changes in light and glare control.

his can be achieved through a multiple-layer system of sheer curtains, shades, and heavy draperies, or by using horizontal blinds that can be manually adjusted. Mechanical pulleys, levers, drawstrings, or sashes can also be employed to provide manual control over the window coverings.

By opting for manual controls, clients can enjoy eco-friendly, energy-efficient, and all-natural window coverings that not only lower utility bills but also help maintain a comfortable temperature and desired light levels. It's important to consider the overall impact of manufacturing these specialty controls, built-in window shades, and electrical systems, as well as the energy required for their transportation and operation. In many cases, a simple manual curtain pull or control rod can offer a more sustainable and practical solution.

HARDWARE

When specifying hardware for window treatments, it's important to consider the ease of removing the treatments for cleaning purposes. Some rods, rings, blind mechanisms, and drawstrings can be challenging or even impossible to detach and reattach, which can make maintenance difficult.

In terms of material selection, hardware for window treatments is typically made of metal, but it can also incorporate glass, ceramic, bamboo, wood, or other materials for structural or decorative accents. Whenever possible, it is recommended to specify hardware made from all-natural materials such as wood or bamboo, or materials with a high percentage of recycled content such as metal or glass. This promotes sustainability and reduces the environmental impact of the window treatment hardware.

Local fabricators or metalworkers may offer the option to custom-make hardware to specific requirements while incorporating recycled steel from minimills or other recycled metals. Additionally, specialty artisans may create unique finials using salvaged items, recycled glass, or hand-thrown pottery, adding a touch of individuality and eco-friendliness to the window treatments.

When specifying finishes for window treatment hardware, it is advisable to avoid platings on metal and instead opt for low-toxic, durable alternatives such as powder-coating on steel or natural beeswax on wood. Additionally, PVD (Physical Vapor Deposition) coatings can be considered as a low-toxic option for metal finishes, offering durability and decorative possibilities without significant environmental impact.

Origins

- Window treatments and hardware can be made from a wide range of materials including wood, bamboo, grasses, and reeds, which provide a natural and eco-friendly option.
- Natural textiles such as cotton, linen, and silk offer a soft and sustainable choice. Alternatively, synthetic textiles may be used, but it's important to consider their environmental impact.
- Metal is commonly used for hardware, but it's crucial to choose options with low-toxic finishes. Vinyl, although commonly used, is not environmentally friendly and should be avoided in favor of more sustainable alternatives.

Maintenance

To ensure a healthy and clean indoor environment, it is important to consider the maintenance and cleaning requirements of window coverings made from porous textiles. These textiles have the potential to collect allergens, dust, and toxins over time. Ideally, the window coverings should be easy to dust, vacuum, wipe clean, or launder with soap and water to remove any accumulated dirt or pollutants.

However, it's worth noting that reflective and specialty textiles used in thermal systems or blinds may not be washable, as they are designed to serve specific functions. In such cases, it's important to consider the compatibility of the textiles with cleaning methods. If dry cleaning is necessary, it is advisable to choose eco-friendly dry cleaning outlets that use carbon dioxide methods, which are gentle on the environment and minimize the use of harsh chemicals.

Specification

- Look for third-party certifications for wood products, organic content, and indoor air quality.
- Choose window treatments that help minimize heating and cooling needs, promoting energy efficiency.
- Opt for window treatments that can be manually opened, closed, and adjusted to meet the needs for privacy, lighting, and thermal comfort.
- Prioritize all-natural materials and textiles such as wool, cotton, wood, bamboo, and grasses, preferably from sustainable or organic sources.
- Select window treatments that are easy to clean or launder to maintain a clean and healthy indoor environment.
- Specify no dye or natural dyes for all textiles used in the window treatments.
- Use inert, low-VOC metal finishes such as powder coating for hardware and avoid finishes that emit VOCs or odors.
- Choose window treatments with no finish or low-VOC, all-natural finishes on wood, bamboo, and reeds.

To ensure environmental friendliness, it is important to avoid synthetic materials, metal blinds, PVC-vinyl, electronic controls (unless necessary), textile finishes such as stain repellents, waterproofing, and sizing, as well as finishes on rods or blinds that emit VOCs or odors. By following these guidelines, you can create eco-friendly window treatments that align with sustainability and health-conscious principles.

Décor and Accessories

When it comes to art and accessories in an eco-friendly home, it is important to guide the client in making wise decisions that enrich their life while minimizing harm to the environment. Artwork and accessories can be highly personal, ranging from traditional paintings and sculptures to blankets, pottery, photographs, or even unique collages. As designers, we can help clients make environmentally friendly choices by focusing on their values and providing guidelines rather than strict specifications. By understanding what is most important to the client and encouraging them to reconsider frivolous or environmentally harmful purchases, we can enhance their life and improve the living space while also being mindful of the Earth's well-being. It's about striking a balance between personal expression and sustainability, ensuring that the chosen art and accessories align with the client's values and contribute positively to the overall environmental impact of the home.

NEW ACCESSORIES AND ART

When selecting accessories and artworks for an eco-friendly home, it is ideal to choose items made from all-natural materials such as wood, clay, bone, rock, or other readily available resources. Renewable resources are preferable, but if not possible, consider whether the item can be recycled or reused at the end of its useful life. It is important that the piece does not emit VOCs or odors that may be harmful to the occupants. Opting for locally or domestically made objects helps reduce embodied energy by minimizing shipping distances.

Caution should be exercised when considering foreign-made objects. Some companies in developing countries may engage in exploitative labor practices and disregard environmental stewardship. Supporting fair trade organizations can help ensure that artisans and workers are provided with decent working conditions and fair wages, particularly in underdeveloped areas.

Evaluate the eco-friendliness and safety of materials, their responsible extraction or harvest, their longevity, and their potential to enhance the client's home and lifestyle. Instead of selecting pieces solely based on their decorative match, discuss their value with the client. Consider their necessity, everyday usability, long-term beauty and functionality, use of all-natural materials, recyclability, fair treatment of workers, and their overall impact on the environment.

Highlight artists who are dedicated to the well-being of the environment and create artwork using all-natural and least toxic materials, or who work with salvaged materials. By focusing on enduring value rather than fleeting trends, and by understanding what truly inspires and resonates with the client, you can ensure their lasting satisfaction with beautiful and eco-friendly art and accessories.

SHOWCASING EXITING ACCESSORIES AND ART

When assessing a client's existing accessories and artwork, it's important to consider both their ecological impact and their value and function. While the origin and environmental footprint are important factors, the functionality and lasting value of a piece should also be taken into account. Antiques, collectibles, useful accessories, and cherished artwork that serve a purpose and bring enjoyment to the client can be retained without compromising ecological sensibilities.

However, if the client possesses items that have surpassed their usefulness or no longer fit their aesthetic preferences, it is advisable to discuss options for donation, sale, or responsible disposal. Charitable organizations, thrift stores, and online auctions can be excellent avenues for finding new homes for still-usable household items. It is an environmentally conscious practice to repurpose and rehome items where they will be appreciated. In cases where items are beyond repair, encourage the client to disassemble them and recycle as many components as possible, minimizing waste.

Origins

- Art and accessories have the flexibility to be crafted from a wide range of materials. In the context of a green home, it is preferable to prioritize art and accessories that align with principles of naturalness, healthiness, environmental sustainability, and biodegradability. Choosing items made from natural materials that are free from harmful chemicals and can safely return to the earth is ideal. Alternatively, if an item possesses exceptional value and beauty, ensuring its longevity and avoiding disposal becomes a priority.
- When considering art and accessories sourced from other countries, it is important to look for products produced under fair trade guidelines. Fair trade organizations promote ethical practices, ensuring that artisans and workers are treated fairly and work in humane conditions. By supporting fair trade, one can contribute to the well-being of individuals in underdeveloped areas while fostering sustainable and responsible production practices.

In summary, prioritizing natural, healthy, environmentally sustainable, and biodegradable materials for art and accessories, as well as supporting fair trade initiatives, can help create a greener and more socially responsible approach to decorating a home.

…ity and lasting
…, can lead to
…ns that possess enduring value

…e relevant and functional in the coming years,
…eauty and usefulness? Choosing timeless designs and
…can ensure that the item remains a cherished part of the home for

…of enduring value, we can reduce the need for frequent replacements and minimize the
…ntal footprint associated with the production and disposal of short-lived items. This approach
…ns with sustainable principles and promotes a more thoughtful and responsible consumption pattern.

Specification

When evaluating existing accessories and art in a green home, it is important to consider their relevance and value. Here are some guidelines to follow:

- Accessories that are regularly appreciated and used: Focus on items that serve a purpose and are actively enjoyed or utilized by the client in their daily lives.
- Collectibles, heirlooms, memorabilia, and art that are appreciated or cherished: Give importance to items that hold sentimental or historical value, as they contribute to the client's personal connection and appreciation.

Avoid:

- Accessories that are never used: Discourage the retention of items that serve no practical function and remain unused, as they can create unnecessary clutter and waste.
- Accessories or art that are not appreciated or cherished: Encourage the client to let go of items that hold no personal significance or are not valued, as they may be better appreciated by someone else.
- Items that take up valuable space in the home that is needed for another purpose: Prioritize the efficient use of space and encourage the client to assess whether certain items are worth occupying valuable storage or living areas.
- Objects that require maintenance or cleaning beyond their value to the client: Discourage the retention of items that demand excessive resources or effort to maintain, especially if their value or importance to the client is minimal.

When selecting new accessories and art for a green home, it's important to prioritize sustainable and environmentally friendly choices. Here are some guidelines to follow:

- All-natural materials: Opt for accessories and art made from natural materials such as wood, stone, clay, bamboo, or organic textiles like cotton or wool.
- Recycled materials: Encourage the use of accessories and art made from recycled or upcycled materials, reducing the demand for new resources.
- Safe and non-harmful materials: Ensure that the materials used are non-toxic, free from VOCs (volatile organic compounds), and do not emit odors or harmful substances into the home environment.
- Environmentally friendly materials: Choose accessories and art that have minimal negative impact on the environment, both in terms of their manufacturing process and their eventual disposal.
- Long-lasting and durable accessories: Prioritize items that are well-crafted and designed to be durable, ensuring they have a longer lifespan and reduce the need for frequent replacements.
- Valuable and timeless pieces: Encourage the selection of art and accessories that hold long-term value and will continue to be cherished and appreciated by the client for many years to come.

Avoid:

- Manufactured, synthetic, or chemically derived materials: Discourage the use of accessories and art made from synthetic materials, plastics, or chemically derived substances that have a significant environmental footprint.
- Materials that emit VOCs or are unsafe for home use: Avoid materials that release volatile organic compounds or pose health risks to the occupants.
- Environmentally harmful materials: Steer clear of materials that are known to cause harm to the environment during their production or disposal.
- Trends, fashions, and impulses: Discourage the selection of accessories and art based solely on current trends or temporary impulses, as these can lead to shorter lifespans and contribute to wasteful consumerism.

COMMERCIAL INTERIOR DESIGN.

Every day, you engage with Commercial Interiors. Perhaps you go to a textile showroom to get samples for a project, or you go to an athletic club with a friend to work out. You could have a client meeting in a restaurant or a doctor's appointment for a checkup. Perhaps you pick up your child from a creche. All of these facilities, as well as many more, are examples of the types of interior spaces developed by the part of the interior design industry known as commercial interior design. Commercial interiors are those of any facility that is used for business. Businesses that engage the public, such as those described above, fall under the category of commercial interior design. Others, however, are business businesses that limit public access, such as corporate offices or industrial sites. Commercial interiors may also be seen in public buildings such as libraries, courthouses, government offices, and airport terminals, to mention a few.

These interiors may be as thrilling as a restaurant in a resort hotel, as exquisite as a jewelry store, or as lavish as a casino in a luxury hotel abroad. An office for a large business or a travel agency in a small town are examples of commercial interiors that are solely practical. As at a medical facility, it could be necessary to comfort and care for the sick. In a spa, it can also serve as a space to unwind. In the field of interior design and the built environment, there are several specialization options. The professionals involved in the development, design, construction, and completion of any sort of structure are, of course, a part of the built environment industry. Specializing can be very sensible, as the expertise one gains in a specialty can provide added value to clients. Be careful not to create a specialty that is too narrow, as there may not be sufficient business to support the firm.

CLIENT BUSINESS INSIGHT

Imagine if your doctor diagnosed your illness or pain without asking you any questions about your symptoms. It would be unacceptable, right? While this example may be extreme, the same principle applies to designing commercial interiors. Failure to ask the right questions and understand the core aspects of a business can result in project failure. Understanding "the business of the business" entails comprehending the goals and purposes of a business. It is crucial to have this understanding even before pursuing projects within a specific industry. The interior designer and their team must have a general understanding of the client's business and their project goals from a business perspective. By doing so, the design solutions and outcomes will be more practical and foster more innovative design concepts.

The requirements of each client will differ depending on their business focus. For instance, the space planning and product specifications for a pediatrician's suite will be distinct from those of a cardiologist's office. Similarly, planning decisions for a small gift shop in a strip shopping center will vary from those for a shop in a resort hotel. Recognizing these differences from the beginning is crucial for the design firm.

One evident advantage of understanding the client's business is that the interior design will be more than just aesthetically pleasing; it will also be highly functional. Clients seek interior design firms that are experienced and knowledgeable in their specific projects, rather than those who are learning on the job. While creative and visually appealing solutions are important, an office that lacks functionality or safety is of no benefit to the client. Success in commercial interior design requires more than just creativity; it necessitates a comprehensive understanding of the client's business needs.

There are five crucial factors that significantly influence the design approach and final solutions for commercial projects:

1. Type of Facility: Each facility type comes with its own set of requirements. Factors such as space planning, furniture specifications, materials usage, compliance with codes and regulations, and the functions and goals of the business all play a role in shaping the interior design based on the facility type.

2. Location: The location of a business is directly related to the desired client base it aims to attract. The amount of investment allocated to the interior design may vary depending on the project's location. Customer expectations are generally higher for businesses situated in upscale areas compared to those in strip malls.

3. Target Customer: When a business plans its operations, it identifies a target client base. Design decisions will differ based on the specific target clientele. For instance, a hotel situated along an interstate will have a different target customer compared to a mountain resort.

4. Nature of the Business's Product: Design specifications for a coffee shop will differ significantly from those for a high-end, full-service restaurant. The design of an advertising agency's office will also vary greatly from that of a law firm.

5. The Client: Clients can range from sole proprietors of various commercial facilities to branches of multi-location businesses, developers, or the board of directors of nonprofit organizations. The client may be an individual facility manager or the board representing a major corporation, or even the governing body of a school district.

Each client has distinct business goals, and the interior designer faces the challenge of meeting their unique requirements. Therefore, comprehending the business's nature and characteristics is crucial for understanding how to approach the interior design process. The more knowledge one possesses about a specific industry, such as the hospitality sector, the more effective the solutions will be for lodging or food service establishments. Similarly, familiarity with retail practices will be advantageous when designing retail spaces. In essence, the more expertise one has in various specialty areas of commercial interior design, the higher the chances of success when working with clients in those fields.

Subsequent chapters in this context provide an overview of the business aspects related to various specialties within commercial interior design. They aim to help you gain an understanding of the critical issues that clients in each industry expect you to comprehend as you engage in a project. Additionally, these chapters serve as references for design-related matters in planning and designing commercial interiors, and they also indicate areas that may require further research.

THE DYNAMICS OF COMMERCIAL INTERIOR DESIGN

Designing commercial interiors presents a dynamic and demanding task, characterized by a multitude of project intricacies. The effective organization of these details stands as a paramount concern for designers. Within the realm of commercial interior design, keen attention to detail, adept teamwork skills, and the ability to collaborate with diverse stakeholders are essential. Moreover, a comprehensive understanding of the client's specific business type is crucial prior to accepting any contracts.

While the interior designer often interacts with employees of the business rather than the owner, it is essential to ensure that design decisions align with the owner's preferences. The involvement of an architect is typically indispensable in most commercial design projects. Seamless collaboration with the architect is critical as the team strives to fulfill both the functional and aesthetic aspirations of the client.

The significance of teamwork and collaboration cannot be overstated in commercial design. Given the scale of such projects, it becomes impractical for only one or two individuals to handle all the work. The willingness to actively contribute to the team, effectively execute assigned responsibilities, and actively engage with others not only facilitates project completion but also enhances prospects for professional growth within the firm. As experience grows, it is not uncommon for project managers and senior design staff to assume leadership roles, surpassing the responsibilities traditionally assigned to entry-level designers.

Effective communication is inherently intertwined with successful teamwork. Project-related communication takes various forms, including email, text messaging, phone calls, written documents, design graphics, and other electronic means. Designers rely on tablets, smartphones, and laptops both on-site and in the office to document meetings, capture ideas, and archive site-related photographs showcasing notable issues or concepts. Marketing and progress presentations are often conducted using computer-based tools like PowerPoint or Pinterest. Proficiency in computer-aided drafting (CAD), SketchUp, or similar software is a mandatory requirement in the field of commercial interior design.

It is crucial to maintain professionalism in all forms of communication. Whether engaging in face-to-face discussions with clients, sending emails, or texting vendors (avoiding such activities while driving), one must exercise professionalism in both content and tone. It is important to recognize that older clients may not readily interpret the shorthand commonly used by younger designers in wireless communication. Additionally, it is essential to bear in mind that electronic messages are typically archived by clients. Therefore, it is crucial to ensure that statements made in emails align with what can be feasibly delivered, in order to avoid potential legal and ethical complications.

In commercial projects, it is vital to identify and address the diverse stakeholders with whom the designer will collaborate. While residential design primarily focuses on satisfying the homeowner and family members, commercial projects involve meeting the requirements of several users in addition to the property owner themselves.

Design decisions in commercial projects are influenced by various stakeholders, including the property owner, employees, and indirectly, the customers of the business. Property owners can take different forms, such as single business owners seeking tenant improvements, developers constructing office or retail structures, corporations establishing branch facilities, chains renovating properties, or government entities building agency offices or schools.

The input of employees is significant as they directly impact the design and can offer valuable insights. Research indicates that a well-designed facility, offering a pleasant and safe environment, enhances employee productivity. For instance, an appealing interior in a restaurant attracts customers and encourages high-quality waitstaff to provide exceptional service. Although employees may not have a formal vote in design decisions, their commitment to the company and effective service delivery indirectly reflects their satisfaction with the design.

Customers, the third influencer, can be swayed by the ambiance or aesthetics of a facility. In certain cases, the atmosphere and beauty of a restaurant or setting can determine whether a customer returns. However, there are instances where ambiance plays a minimal role in the decision-making process. For example, the doctor-patient relationship holds greater importance than the design of a doctor's office. Designing for these diverse users presents a challenging task, requiring careful consideration. Regarding project execution, commercial interior design projects encompass all phases of the design process. The responsibilities of the interior designer within each phase vary based on the project, licensing requirements, and the designer's experience. It is crucial to avoid skipping steps or approaching tasks halfheartedly, as errors can have disastrous consequences. Many projects are fast-tracked, with design plans created for one phase while construction proceeds on another to facilitate early occupancy. Attention to detail and organizational skills are vital qualities for a successful commercial interior designer.

Commercial interior designers must possess project management skills in addition to design expertise. Project management involves a systematic approach to coordinating and controlling a design project from start to finish. It requires leadership, planning, coordination, and control of various activities, individuals, finances, and timelines to achieve project goals. Experienced designers typically oversee project management, leading a team of designers and other professionals involved in the project.

Over time, project delivery methods have evolved and now encompass four distinct approaches, each with its own characteristics and implications. Here are brief definitions to provide context for this chapter's scope:

1. **Design-bid-build**: This method follows the traditional approach where a client hires a firm to design the project. Subsequently, the design is put out for competitive bidding to multiple suppliers, and the contract is awarded to the firm selected by the client. It involves separate contracts for design and construction.
2. **Construction management**: In this approach, the client hires a firm to oversee and manage all aspects of the project, starting from feasibility studies and design to construction and installation. The construction management firm assumes responsibility for coordinating and supervising the work of all project stakeholders.
3. **Design-build**: The design-build method involves a collaborative process where multiple stakeholders are typically brought together under a single contract for both the design and construction of the facility. This integrated approach encourages close collaboration and communication among all parties involved.
4. **Integrated process**: The integrated process is a team-oriented approach that places greater emphasis on the people involved in the project. It aims to foster a collaborative environment where all stakeholders work closely together, pooling their expertise and perspectives to achieve a better outcome.

These four project delivery methods offer different approaches to managing the design and construction processes, each with its own advantages and considerations. Understanding these methods can help designers navigate the complexities of commercial interior projects more effectively. The design process for nearly all project types covered in this book typically follows a sequence of programming, schematic design, design development, contract documents, and contract administration. Even if designers are not directly responsible for all tasks in each phase, it is important for them to have a comprehensive understanding of the tasks involved.

Programming holds particular significance as it sets the foundation for the project. Gathering information at the project's outset goes beyond understanding the client's spatial and aesthetic preferences. It is crucial to identify applicable codes and standards. Moreover, comprehending the client's business goals and future plans is vital for successful functional interior design. Design firms often offer strategic planning assistance for businesses lacking such expertise.

Strict adherence to building, life safety, and accessibility codes is paramount in commercial projects. The health, safety, and well-being of clients and facility users significantly impact design decisions, including space planning, materials, lighting, furniture, fabric specifications, and even color palettes. Clients trust that the facility's design and specifications align with jurisdictional requirements, making regulatory comprehension and application an essential requirement.

Lastly, prior knowledge of the client's business, as emphasized earlier, is crucial for designers pursuing commercial interior projects. Understanding the intricacies of the client's business is instrumental in problem-solving and achieving the client's functional and aesthetic goals. Deep comprehension of the client's challenges is indispensable for designers in effectively addressing and resolving them.

The following offers a diverse compilation of specialties found within the field of commercial interior design. It's important to acknowledge that this list is not exhaustive and there may be additional areas of specialization beyond those mentioned.

Designing of corporate and executive offices

- Creation of functional and aesthetic spaces for professional offices
- Tailored interior design for financial institutions
- Optimizing workspace for law firms
- Design solutions for stockbrokerage and investment brokerage companies
- Creating efficient and organized environments for accounting firms
- Enhancing workspaces for real estate firms
- Designing inviting and functional spaces for travel agencies
- Restoration and renovation of various types of business offices

Designing healthcare facilities

- Creating efficient and comforting spaces for surgery centers
- Designing therapeutic environments for psychiatric facilities
- Specializing in the design of care facilities for individuals with specific needs
- Creating functional and welcoming medical and dental office suites
- Designing senior living facilities that promote well-being and comfort
- Creating rehabilitative spaces for rehabilitation facilities
- Designing efficient and hygienic medical labs
- Creating optimal environments for veterinary clinics

Entertainment Retreats and Hospitality facilities

- Crafting welcoming and enchanting spaces for hotels, motels, and resorts
- Designing captivating and inviting environments for restaurants
- Creating enjoyable recreational facilities for leisure and entertainment
- Designing rejuvenating health clubs and serene spas
- Crafting dynamic and functional sports complexes
- Designing exquisite golf clubs with stunning landscapes
- Creating versatile convention centers for various events
- Crafting immersive experiences in amusement parks and other parks
- Designing captivating theaters for live performances
- Creating engaging and educational environments in museums
- Restoring the charm and historical significance of historic sites

Department stores - Retail/Merchandising Facilities

- Creating engaging and enticing environments for malls and shopping centers
- Specializing in the design of specialized retail stores to showcase specific products
- Designing showrooms that effectively display and highlight merchandise
- Creating aesthetically pleasing spaces for art galleries to showcase artwork

Production Hubs

- Designing effective and optimized manufacturing areas in industrial facilities
- Creating functional and safe training areas within industrial buildings
- Designing research and development laboratories that facilitate innovation and experimentation

Service Centers

- Designing functional and efficient government offices and facilities
- Creating inspiring and conducive learning environments for schools at all levels
- Designing safe and nurturing spaces for daycare centers
- Creating serene and sacred spaces for religious facilities
- Designing secure and controlled environments for prisons

Transit Hubs

- Designing efficient and aesthetically pleasing airports
- Creating comfortable and functional bus and train terminals
- Crafting luxurious and captivating interiors for tour ships and yachts
- Designing custom interiors for airplanes and corporate vehicles
- Creating innovative and practical spaces in recreational vehicles

FACTORS SHAPING COMMERCIAL INTERIOR SPACES

The field of interior design has undergone significant transformations in recent times, reflecting the rapid advancements in technology and global interconnectedness. Consider how the widespread adoption of sleek, wireless smartphones has revolutionized communication compared to the clunky cordless phones of the past. Environmental consciousness now extends beyond basic paper recycling, with a broader understanding of sustainability practices shaping the industry. The advent of email and the subsequent rise of the World Wide Web have connected designers with clients and collaborators worldwide, transforming the way projects are managed and executed. Moreover, the proliferation of social media platforms in the early 2000s has further influenced design trends and allowed designers to showcase their work to a broader audience.

These advancements have profoundly impacted the interior design profession, a fact that becomes evident when contrasting the practices of today with those of the 90s. Interior design is no longer a static discipline; it is constantly evolving and presenting new challenges to designers of all scales. The emergence of computer modeling has replaced the sketch-on-napkin approach, facilitating the creation of precise and immersive design representations. The evolution of graphic presentation techniques is equally remarkable, enabling designers to produce stunning visualizations that were unimaginable just a few decades ago. The interplay of global influences has also sparked creativity and expanded the realm of design possibilities by exposing practitioners to diverse aesthetics and innovative product options.

Multiple forces continue to shape the field of commercial interior design, necessitating ongoing learning and skills development for professionals in this arena. Staying up-to-date with the factors mentioned above is crucial for designers seeking success in this dynamic industry. This chapter serves as an overview of the many significant issues impacting commercial interior design practice and the profession as a whole. While each of these topics could warrant its own in-depth exploration, space limitations confine our discussion. For further study, extensive resources are provided in the references section.

This chapter provides insights into several important factors that individuals pursuing a career in commercial interior design should be mindful of. It starts by emphasizing the significance of cultural sensitivity in the present-day practice. Subsequently, it touches upon the impact of the global marketplace and briefly mentions a few related aspects.

Cultural Sensitivity

In the dynamic field of commercial interior design, it is essential for professionals to be aware of the latest trends and market demands, including the importance of cultural sensitivity. As designers cater to clients from diverse backgrounds and tap into the global marketplace, understanding and appreciating cultural differences have become key considerations in delivering successful projects.

Regardless of our varying backgrounds—religious, ethnic, racial, or geographic—we all share common desires for safe, secure, enjoyable, comfortable, and caring spaces. It is the responsibility of commercial interior designers to strive towards fulfilling these needs, irrespective of the facility type. Cultural sensitivity involves not only comprehending influences from clients of different nationalities but also acknowledging cultural nuances within a single country. By focusing on the unique cultural characteristics of clients, their employees, and target markets, designers can better plan and execute projects that resonate with their cultural identity.

To achieve cultural sensitivity, designers must set aside personal biases and embrace a client-centered approach. Understanding the culture, symbolism of cultural icons, colors, and even language nuances is crucial before embarking on any project. It's worth noting that some international clients specifically hire U.S. designers for their Western design expertise, which holds high regard in foreign countries. As a result, many prominent design firms have established global offices to undertake international projects.

Unlike personal expressions of art, interior design is a collaborative process centered around serving the client's needs rather than the designer's preferences. Most clients come from backgrounds distinct from the designer's own, expecting cultural and aesthetic differences to be acknowledged. Failing to comprehend and respect a client's cultural preferences can lead to frustration and communication gaps. Therefore, it is vital for designers to invest time in learning about their clients' cultural backgrounds and design aesthetics. Cultural sensitivity not only enhances the effectiveness of designers in serving their clients but also makes them more appealing in the market. Designers can acquire cultural knowledge through various sources, such as formal education in art, architecture, interior design history, and interdisciplinary classes. Staying informed about world events and learning additional languages can further broaden cultural understanding and facilitate communication with a diverse clientele.

Cultural sensitivity extends beyond clients to employees working in the environments created by designers. Designers must strike a balance between personalization and adherence to company design standards, ensuring that office spaces accommodate individual preferences within established guidelines. Additionally, recognizing generational differences in design preferences is crucial, as what may appeal to older generations may differ from the tastes of millennials. Valuing cultural diversity not only makes individual designers more marketable but also enhances the appeal of design firms to potential clients. Understanding the significance of color in different cultures is another aspect of cultural sensitivity. Colors can hold various meanings and implications, and designers need to be aware of these cultural associations. Researching online resources and engaging with diverse cultural groups can provide valuable insights into cultural markers and color symbolism.

By embracing the opportunities to learn about other cultures and incorporating cultural elements into their designs, interior designers can deliver more effective solutions and address the challenges presented by diverse clientele. Creating commercial facilities that reflect clients' visions for their customers, employees, and users requires a deep understanding of different cultures. Today's interior designers must appreciate and respect the cultural differences inherent in their clients' backgrounds, ensuring that their designs resonate with their target audience in a globalized industry.

Global Marketplace

Advancements in technology have made the world more accessible for designers to connect with clients from different countries, and vice versa. Through internet searches, social media, international publications, professional associations, and conferences, designers can easily learn about firms and clients worldwide. In the past, obtaining such information would have taken much longer. Moreover, technological progress enables rapid communication, allowing designers and clients from different countries to exchange drawings, specifications, and 3D images instantly. However, working in the global marketplace requires effort and preparation. Design firms must be willing to learn about other cultures, as designing a project solely based on their own country's standards may not satisfy clients from other countries. Cultural differences impact various aspects, such as communication methods, expectations, language skills, and project management approaches. To succeed globally, design firms and their staff need to be open-minded and receptive to ideas from other cultures and regions.

To engage with offshore clients, design firms must be prepared and decide if they want to pursue such opportunities. Successfully completing projects for offshore clients in the home country can open doors for international work. Establishing specializations, developing strong marketing programs, and leveraging the internet and trade publications can also help design firms gain recognition in other countries. Developing a business plan with a global focus is essential. This includes strategies to understand the culture and business practices of the target market. Cultivating joint ventures with established global design firms can provide valuable learning experiences. Additionally, participating in local professional association chapters and leveraging internet searches can help find potential projects and partnerships.

Financial considerations, such as evaluating the return on investment and understanding tax regulations and business practices in foreign countries, are crucial. Building a quality website, assessing the firm's brand, and utilizing social media can enhance marketing efforts for global work. Thorough research on how international companies conduct business, social customs, language, and client background is necessary.

Understanding and adapting to the approval processes, regulations, and standards of foreign countries is vital. Collaboration with local professionals who have knowledge of the foreign jurisdiction can provide valuable insights and ensure compliance. Researching business partners and local sources is also important, as the project may require local products and workers. Ensuring payment for global projects requires clear agreements that outline the scope of work, deliverables, billing terms, and currency preferences. Consulting with an attorney experienced in international contract law is advisable. Understanding payment practices and currency fluctuations is crucial for financial stability.

10 In a Nutshell

1. **Functionality and Space Optimization**: Commercial interior design focuses on creating spaces that are practical and efficient for businesses. It involves understanding the specific requirements and operations of the organization to design layouts, workflows, and storage solutions that maximize productivity and functionality.

2. **Branding and Identity**: A company's brand image and identity heavily influence the design of commercial spaces. The interior design elements, color schemes, materials, and furnishings are selected to reflect the brand's values, personality, and desired perception among customers. Consistency with the brand's visual identity is crucial to reinforce brand recognition.

3. **User Experience and Customer Journey**: Commercial spaces are designed to enhance the overall experience for customers. The layout, lighting, signage, and ambiance are carefully considered to guide customers through the space, create a positive impression, and encourage desired behaviors. A well-designed customer journey can lead to increased engagement, loyalty, and sales.

4. **Ergonomics and Well-being**: The well-being and comfort of employees, customers, and visitors are essential considerations in commercial interior design. Ergonomic furniture, proper lighting, good air quality, noise reduction measures, and comfortable temperature control contribute to creating a healthy and productive environment. Prioritizing well-being can improve employee satisfaction, productivity, and customer satisfaction.

5. **Technology Integration**: Technology plays a significant role in commercial interior design. Smart systems, automation, digital displays, interactive elements, and integrated audiovisual solutions are integrated into the design to enhance functionality and provide an immersive experience. Technology can streamline operations, enable personalized interactions, and create memorable experiences for customers.

6. **Sustainability and Environmental Considerations**: There is an increasing emphasis on sustainable design practices in commercial interior design. Designers aim to minimize the environmental impact by incorporating eco-friendly materials, utilizing energy-efficient systems, promoting recycling and waste reduction, and integrating renewable energy sources. Sustainable design not only benefits the environment but also enhances the reputation and image of businesses.

7. **Regulatory Compliance and Safety**: Commercial interior design must comply with building codes, accessibility standards, fire safety regulations, and other legal requirements. Designers ensure that the space is safe, accessible, and meets the necessary standards to protect the well-being of occupants. Compliance with regulations is crucial for the smooth operation of businesses and the safety of employees and customers.

8. **Cultural and Social Influences**: Commercial interior design takes into account cultural preferences, local norms, social trends, and demographic factors. Designers consider the target audience and the community in which the business operates to create spaces that resonate with them. Adapting the design to cultural and social influences helps businesses connect with customers and create a sense of belonging.

9. Budget and Cost Constraints: Commercial interior design projects must often operate within budget constraints. Designers work closely with clients to understand their financial limitations and find cost-effective solutions. This involves optimizing resources, prioritizing design elements, exploring affordable materials, and seeking creative alternatives to achieve the desired aesthetic and functionality without exceeding the budget.

10. Industry Trends and Innovation: Commercial interior design professionals stay up to date with industry trends, emerging materials, technologies, and innovative approaches. They continually explore new design concepts, techniques, and products to deliver cutting-edge and competitive interior spaces. Keeping pace with industry trends allows designers to offer fresh perspectives and create unique, contemporary environments for businesses. These detailed explanations highlight the multifaceted considerations that shape commercial interior design, ensuring that the spaces meet functional, aesthetic, cultural, and regulatory requirements while providing optimal experiences for users.

These points highlight the multifaceted considerations that shape commercial interior design, ensuring that the spaces meet functional, aesthetic, cultural, and regulatory requirements while providing optimal experiences for users.

SUSTAINABLE DESIGN

Sustainable design, also known as green and environmental design, has been a significant influence in the commercial interiors design/build industry long before the establishment of the U.S. Green Building Council (USGBC) in 1993. The concept of sustainable design gained prominence in the 1970s, coinciding with the creation of the Department of Energy in 1977 to address energy conservation in the United States. This era also witnessed the rise of recycling initiatives as a response to overflowing landfills. The importance of sustainable design and the conservation of energy and resources gained further attention through Earth Day programs in the early 1990s.

Throughout the 1980s and 1990s, extensive research and conferences on environmental issues continued to drive the sustainable design movement. In 1987, the World Commission on Environment and Development formulated a widely accepted definition of sustainable design, emphasizing its aim to fulfill present needs without compromising the ability of future generations to meet their own needs. This definition played a significant role in fueling the concern for sustainable buildings and green design. The Energy Policy Act of 2005 established sustainable standards for federal buildings, further reinforcing the commitment to sustainability.

The efforts to promote sustainable building and design, along with education for professionals and consumers, have been led by architecture and interior design professional associations, as well as government and business entities. Notably, the U.S. Green Building Council (USGBC) has emerged as a prominent nonprofit organization dedicated to sustainable design. It brings together professionals in architecture, construction, interior design, product manufacturing, and other stakeholders in the design-build industry. The USGBC's mission is to transform the approach to building and community design, construction, and operation to create environmentally and socially responsible, healthy, and prosperous environments that enhance quality of life. With each energy crisis, more individuals and companies are motivated to learn and implement sustainable concepts in their projects.

Overview

Sustainable design aims to strike a balance between meeting immediate user needs in constructing and finishing a building's interior while minimizing harm to the environment. It involves adopting design methods and processes that consume fewer nonrenewable resources and are more energy-efficient. Numerous sustainable design considerations revolve around the design and construction of buildings. Interior designers contribute to sustainable design by selecting materials and products for the interior that have minimal environmental impact, both in their manufacturing and as finished products. For instance, choosing veneer from certified sustainable sources for furniture demonstrates a commitment to green design.

The terminology associated with sustainable design is extensive. Some key terms relevant to this discussion and other parts of the text include:

- Brownfield: Abandoned or underutilized commercial or industrial properties with environmental contamination.

- "Cradle-to-cradle": Products that can be reused, recycled, or decomposed in landfills.

- "Cradle-to-grave": Products that are not reused or recycled and are discarded before their useful life ends.

- "Energy efficient": Products that consume less energy.

- "Graywater": Water from sinks, showers, and laundry that is collected and lightly treated for non-potable uses like watering lawns.

- "Life cycle assessment (LCA)": Evaluation of the environmental and health impacts of materials, products, and buildings over their lifespan.

- "Life cycle costing (LCC)": Methodology that combines the initial cost of products with maintenance, replacement, and residual value costs.

- "Potable": Water suitable for drinking and cooking.

- "Renewable energy": Energy sources that are not depleted when utilized, such as solar energy.

- "Sick building syndrome": Health issues experienced by users of interior spaces due to factors like poor indoor air quality, inadequate lighting, and unfavorable acoustics.

- "Volatile organic compounds (VOCs)": Toxic fumes emitted by carpeting, paints, glues in composite woods, and other common materials or products.

Despite the growing interest in sustainable design, the design/build industry continues to rely on products and methods that deplete natural resources. Landfills receive significant amounts of waste construction materials, including out-of-fashion carpeting and other interior finish materials discarded during remodeling projects. Toxic pollutants are still emitted by certain specified products, and exotic woods from uncertified forests are used in design. One reason for this is the difficulty in convincing clients that using sustainable materials will benefit their business in the long run. The section "Does Going Green Cost More?" addresses this issue later in the text.

Environmental concerns, including sustainable design, remain controversial in the United States and other countries. Climate change has had wide-ranging effects on our lives, with extreme rainfall and snowstorms forcing individuals to allocate more financial resources to stay warm and safe, leaving little room for replacing off-gassing carpeting. Some individuals view these climate changes and resource depletion as natural processes rather than indicators of an environmental problem.

Specifying green and sustainable products is an admirable goal that may not always be achievable. While many designers aspire to use these products, some may step back if clients object due to perceived higher costs or other reasons. This can sometimes be attributed to designers' limited knowledge about green products. By incorporating thoughtful space planning and careful product selection, designers can integrate sustainable design into various commercial projects. Nevertheless, environmental issues, including sustainable design, should be considered to some extent by those involved in the interior design and construction industry at both local and global levels.

Environmental Stewardship

Environmental stewardship refers to the collective responsibility for maintaining the quality of the environment, shared by all individuals and entities whose actions impact the environment. It encompasses various actions and concerns aimed at protecting the environment. These include:

- Personal activities: Engaging in actions such as volunteering to clean up trash along highways or participating in community cleanup initiatives.

- Professional endeavors: Professionals in the design/build industry can contribute to environmental stewardship by incorporating green design principles and sustainable methods in their projects.

- Business practices: Businesses can demonstrate environmental stewardship by adopting green design and sustainable practices in their day-to-day operations.

- Waste reduction: Reducing landfill waste through recycling efforts and implementing improved practices for the efficient use of goods and materials, rather than disposing of items prematurely.

Even if a designer is not fully committed to embracing sustainable design, there are still ways they can practice environmental stewardship. The choices made in the design process can have either a positive or negative impact on the environment. For example, specifying exotic wood products sourced from unregulated forests has a negative impact, while finding ways to reuse or refurbish products instead of sending them to the landfill has a positive impact. Even simple actions like using washable coffee cups instead of disposable ones in the design office can make a difference

By increasing their knowledge about sustainable design through attending continuing education classes or webinars, designers can better communicate the benefits to clients. They can educate clients about the advantages of using furniture products without toxic binders and finishes during production, which off-gas harmful chemicals in facilities. Interior designers can take a proactive role in environmental stewardship by:

- Acquiring knowledge of sustainable design concepts
- Specifying products that do not emit volatile organic compounds (VOCs) whenever possible
- Avoiding the specification of products that are not sustainably produced

- Educating clients about the health and long-term cost benefits of sustainable products over non-sustainable alternatives
- Exploring opportunities to reuse or refurbish products
- Operating their design businesses in an environmentally responsible manner.

These suggestions serve as a foundation for interior designers to embark on their journey towards environmental stewardship. To deepen their commitment and expand their impact, designers can explore additional resources available online and in their local communities. These resources provide opportunities for further education, active involvement, and the practical implementation of environmental stewardship practices.

By seeking out activities and initiatives that resonate with their interests and values, designers can actively contribute to the well-being of the global environment. Whether it's participating in local sustainability projects, engaging in community outreach, or collaborating with like-minded professionals, designers have the power to make a meaningful difference. Through their dedication and actions, they can help create a more sustainable and environmentally conscious future.

LEED Certification

LEED certification is a voluntary and environmentally friendly rating system that defines buildings designed to be sustainable, profitable, and conducive to health. This certification can be obtained for various types of construction projects, including new buildings, existing structures, commercial interiors, and residential homes. The LEED rating system encompasses different categories, which are as follows:

1. BD+C Building Design and Construction: Pertains to new buildings or those undergoing significant renovations.
2. ID+C Interior Design and Construction: Focuses on the interior specification and installation of a facility.
3. O+M Building Operations and Maintenance: Applicable to buildings undergoing renovations with minimal construction involved.
4. ND Neighborhood Development: Applies to land-use design projects.
5. Homes: Pertains to single-family and multi-family residences with multiple stories.

Regarding commercial interiors, this book primarily focuses on the LEED ID+C Interior Design and Construction rating category. While other categories may also apply, ID+C is the primary certification category for interior design.

There are four levels of certification that building owners or project leaders can apply for:
1. LEED Platinum
2. LEED Gold
3. LEED Silver
4. LEED Certified

LEED Platinum represents the highest certification level, requiring a minimum of 80 points. On the other hand, the LEED Certified designation is the lowest level, requiring a minimum of 40 points. Achieving the Platinum level provides significant public relations and marketing benefits, although it is a challenging feat to accomplish.

To determine the certification level, various categories of design impact are evaluated, and points are earned based on different evaluation sets. The evaluation criteria vary depending on the building category and the specific certification being sought. The five main categories of achievement that a project must meet are:

1. Sustainable Sites
2. Water Efficiency
3. Energy and Atmosphere
4. Materials and Resources
5. Indoor Environmental Quality

Additionally, points can be awarded for innovative efforts in design. Let's explore these categories in relation to a generic commercial structure, with a focus on the interior. For detailed information on how to earn points within these categories, please refer to the USGBC online resources. While categories like Sustainable Sites, Water Efficiency, and Energy and Atmosphere are typically outside the scope of responsibility for most interior design firms, it is still important to mention them briefly. Sustainable Sites consider the location of the building, awarding points for selecting developed areas with existing infrastructure over undeveloped greenfields or farmland. Points can also be earned by providing priority parking for carpooling, van pools, or alternative fuel vehicles, as well as opting for underground parking instead of on-grade parking lots. Water Efficiency awards points for using highly efficient fixtures and equipment, such as low-flow faucets and toilets. Energy and Atmosphere category requires compliance with specific and stringent code requirements related to refrigerants for HVAC systems.

For interior designers, the Materials and Resources category is of primary concern. Examples of earning points in this category include using salvaged, refurbished, recycled, or reused materials (e.g., repurposing wood from demolished buildings for flooring), reusing existing furniture from previous locations, diverting construction waste through recycling, specifying low-toxicity or non-toxic materials for carpets, wall finishes, and ceiling treatments, and using materials made from recycled content such as recycled plastic bottles.

Indoor Environmental Quality is another important category influenced by interior designers. It involves specifying low-VOC (Volatile Organic Compound) materials, such as paint, carpets, wall coverings, and low-toxicity upholstered goods. Choosing adhesives for carpeting and architectural materials that are low-VOC is also crucial. Effective planning, including full-height partitions and high divider panels, can improve indoor environmental quality, while maximizing occupants' access to daylight can earn additional points.

LEED Professional Certification

The initial credential offered is the LEED Green Associate, which is suitable for individuals who have a grasp of green building principles and practices. However, it is more geared towards individuals in non-technical fields and may not be as relevant for interior designers who are involved in producing drawings and specifications.

For designers and specifiers, there are specific LEED credential designations aligned with the building certification program designations. These credentials require a deeper understanding of green design and sustainable building practices. It is not mandatory to take the LEED Green Associate exam before taking the LEED AP exam. LEED AP stands for LEED Accredited Professional. The LEED credentials defined by the USGBC are as follows:

1. LEED AP Building Design + Construction (LEED AP BD+C)
2. LEED AP Operations + Maintenance (LEED AP O+M)

3. LEED AP Interior Design + Construction (LEED AP +C)
4. LEED AP Neighborhood Development (LEED AP ND) LEED AP Home

Among these designations, the most commonly sought after by commercial interior designers is LEED AP+C. It requires passing a multiple-choice examination. The USGBC provides study guides, and there are numerous third-party study materials and tutorials available as well. Once a professional obtains a LEED credential, they must earn continuing education credits, many of which are available online.

Interior designers who wish to learn more about the qualifications and the process of obtaining a LEED credential should refer to the USGBC website. It provides detailed content information, study references, and sample questions for each credential category.

The Triple Bottom Line

The phrase "triple bottom line" (TBL) has been widely discussed and utilized in the commercial interior design field for approximately the past 20 years. It was coined by John Elkington in 1994 and further clarified in his book "Cannibals with Forks: The Triple Bottom Line of 21st Century Business" in 1997.

Traditionally, the bottom line in business refers to the difference between revenue and expenses, focusing solely on financial profit. However, Elkington and others have expanded this concept to include the triple bottom line, which considers three dimensions: profit, planet, and people. These terms are often used interchangeably. The triple bottom line has played a significant role in driving the growth of sustainable design within the business community.

While profitability remains a crucial aspect of today's business world, interior designers recognize that creating functional and effective interiors for their clients can positively impact profitability. Businesses have also come to realize that their environmental stewardship and concern for the well-being of people, including employees and consumers, also affect their bottom line.

Interior designers understand that their responsibility in the twenty-first century includes producing designs that contribute to environmental sustainability and consider the well-being of those affected by the business. Product specification plays a significant role in this responsibility. By recommending green or sustainable products over non-sustainable options, designers not only impact the environment but also the health of the users of those interiors. For example, selecting low-VOC paint addresses both the people and planet aspects of the triple bottom line. While profitability remains the primary concern for commercial interior designers' clients, designers can also influence and assist clients who aim to be regarded as environmentally conscious in the community, going beyond simple recycling efforts. This environmental consciousness can also attract employees who seek a healthy work environment.

Designers can help clients understand that providing sustainable interiors improves employee productivity, reduces utility costs, promotes healthy air quality, and even leads to long-term cost savings. Thus, by considering the planet and people alongside profitability, the elusive bottom line of profitability can be achieved.

It is recommended to explore the websites of professional organizations such as ASID, IIDA, AIA, and IDC for articles directly related to the discussion of the triple bottom line and its application in interior design practice. Additionally, publications by John Elkington and other authors listed in the references can provide further insight into this topic.

The Economic Implications of Sustainable Practices

Despite the perception that going green will incur additional costs, recent projects have demonstrated that green design and sustainable building practices do not have to be more expensive. While there may be some upfront cost increases in certain projects, green buildings offer significant long-term cost savings due to factors such as improved energy and water efficiency, better long-range cost management, and enhanced employee performance

Although initial costs for green products may be higher compared to non-green alternatives, a comprehensive analysis of the long-term costs reveals that the overall cost difference is minimal. However, convincing clients of this requires effective methods of demonstration.

One economic technique that can be employed in planning for green or sustainable projects is life cycle assessment (LCA). LCA evaluates the environmental and health impacts of materials, finished products, and buildings throughout their entire life cycle, from raw material extraction to disposal. This assessment helps clients committed to green facilities make informed choices regarding products and materials.

Another economic technique used in sustainable design is life cycle costing (LCC). LCC involves quantifying costs over the life cycle of a product, including initial purchase and installation costs, day-to-day maintenance, replacement costs, insurance, operational costs, potential disposal costs, and recyclability.

The extent to which clients prioritize sustainability goals will influence costs. Clients aiming for a high degree of sustainable design should expect higher costs, while those seeking minimal green design or engaging in greenwashing for marketing purposes may not invest as heavily. Various factors impact the economic impact of sustainable projects, including the type of facility or business, the interior designer's expertise in product specification, the stage at which the designer is involved in the project, the experience of installers and fabricators, and location and climate considerations. To make fair comparisons, products must be evaluated on equal grounds. Tools like the Athena Environmental Impact Estimator from the Athena Sustainable Materials Institute can assist in this process. However, simple cost comparisons based solely on price often overlook sustainable criteria and fail to consider other cost factors mentioned above. To determine the potential cost differential of a green project, designers need to understand their client's goals, practice effective budgeting, and identify necessary trade-offs. For example, in a healthcare environment, designing a healthy and green interior may be considered more critical than in a small professional office unless environmental sensitivities are a concern for the accounting office owner and employees.

Overall, demonstrating the economic viability of sustainable projects involves thorough analysis, clear communication, and aligning clients' goals with appropriate budgeting and trade-offs

The Influence of Indoor Environment on Interior Design

We spend the majority of our day indoors, whether it's in our homes, workplaces, or places we visit for various purposes. The indoor environment has a significant impact on our health, and interior designers play a crucial role in improving it through careful product specification. Pollutants from various sources can make the indoor environment hazardous, including off-gassing from furniture and architectural finishes, as well as cleaning products used by occupants.

Air quality is a challenging issue for interior designers to control. There are no federal standards for indoor air quality, and state standards, if they exist, vary across jurisdictions, making it difficult to determine appropriate specifications for each project.

Thermal comfort is another important environmental factor influenced by interior designers. Lighting fixtures and lamps play a significant role in this regard. For example, extensive use of incandescent lighting can contribute to heat buildup in the environment. While LED lighting is environmentally desirable, clients may be hesitant due to the initial cost compared to other lighting options. It's essential for designers to be knowledgeable about both the cost differentials and the environmental impact of lighting.

Window treatments/coverings also impact thermal comfort. Commercial buildings often include shades or blinds as standard features, although some designers may find them aesthetically limiting. However, shades and window films can help regulate temperature and protect furniture and textiles from fading.

Noise pollution is another significant environmental factor in commercial facilities. Offices are filled with noise from computers, copiers, phones, and human activity. Open ceilings and collaborative workstations, popular in modern designs, can exacerbate noise problems. Sound-masking systems can be employed to address this issue. On the other hand, some food service establishments intentionally utilize noise to encourage quick customer turnover, while high-end dining rooms prioritize peace and quiet. In healthcare facilities, various noises can cause additional stress for patients and families.

These environmental factors have a significant impact on occupants' well-being. A noisy doctor's office can be stressful for patients, which is why waiting areas are often separated from exam rooms. Office spaces designed for collaboration need to consider different strategies for maintaining individual focus.

To make positive improvements, interior designers should be involved early in the design process. Careful research with clients to understand their needs and thorough product research to address environmental issues are essential for making a positive impact on the interior environment.

This overview highlights the many ways interior designers influence the overall indoor environment. Their role extends far beyond selecting colors and fabrics, emphasizing the importance of considering environmental factors for occupant health and well-being.

Principles of Product Specifications

The selection and specification of sustainable or green products are indeed important aspects of the discussion. The involvement of the interior designer in the project at an early stage allows for a better selection process of sustainable products. The designer can provide expertise in coordinating design decisions with the architect as the structure is being designed, ensuring a cohesive and sustainable approach.

It is crucial for commercial interior designers who aim to be environmentally responsible and sustainable to educate themselves about the issues surrounding sustainable product specification. The market is filled with products claiming to be sustainable or green, but not all of them live up to their claims. Some products may engage in greenwashing, intentionally providing misleading information to appear more environmentally responsible than they truly are. Environmentally responsible design and products are those that have the least environmental impact on people (occupants, workers, and nearby communities) and on the sustainability of the global environment.

Before product selection begins, several factors need to be thoroughly researched. Understanding the client's specific needs is paramount. Requirements for a senior living facility will differ from those of an office space. Another important question is the desired level of greenness the client wants to achieve. Not all clients aiming for sustainable products necessarily seek LEED Platinum certification. Additionally, product performance is a crucial criterion for most commercial facilities. Some products may require more frequent replacement, and the cost of replacement must be factored into the initial specification. The project location can also impact the specification process. For example, using natural wool for upholstery or floor coverings may be desirable, but if the area is prone to moth damage, the treatments on the fabric may offset the positive aspects of using wool over a synthetic alternative.

There are numerous considerations in the specification of sustainable products. Some common ones include:

1. Minimal off-gassing: Selecting products that emit minimal harmful substances into the indoor environment.
2. Wood products obtained from sustainable sources: Ensuring that wood materials are sourced from responsibly managed forests or certified sustainable sources.
3. Verifiable green manufacturing processes: Assessing whether the manufacturing processes of the products align with sustainable and environmentally conscious practices.
4. Compliance with applicable codes: Ensuring that the specified products meet relevant codes and regulations.
5. Life cycle cost factors: Considering the life cycle cost of the products, including their performance over time and potential future replacement needs.
6. Supplier documentation: Including supplier-provided documentation that confirms the green characteristics of the product within the specifications.
7. Impact on performance needs: Assessing how the product will meet performance requirements and considering any potential implications for future replacements (life cycle cost considerations).

This overview provides a glimpse into key considerations for the specification of sustainable products. Due to space limitations, only a few product types are highlighted. For more detailed information on sustainable products, further research can be conducted using the sources provided in the chapter references.

Wood Products

When it comes to wood products, there are several considerations for sustainable specification:

- Forest Stewardship Council (FSC) Certification: New wood products should include documentation certifying that they are sourced from Forest Stewardship Council (FSC) certified forests. The FSC offers different options and certifications. Detailed information can be found on the FSC website.
- Sustainable Species: New wood products should come from sustainable species. It's important to select wood species that are responsibly harvested and have a lower impact on the environment.
- Reclaimed Wood: In some projects, there may be opportunities to incorporate reclaimed wood products for various interior details. Reclaimed wood reduces the demand for new wood and gives a new life to

salvaged materials.
- **Engineered Wood and Formaldehyde:** Products utilizing engineered wood should be free of urea-formaldehyde, a compound known to emit harmful volatile organic compounds (VOCs). Look for products that meet formaldehyde emission standards to ensure healthier indoor air quality.
- **Low- or No-VOC Finishes:** Finishing materials used on furniture should be low- or no-VOC treatments and stains. This helps minimize the emission of harmful chemicals into the indoor environment.
- **Solid Materials:** Whenever possible, opt for solid materials like solid wood and stone for furniture and cabinet tops. Solid materials tend to have a longer lifespan, reducing the need for frequent replacements.
- **Refurbishing and Reupholstering:** Consider refurbishing, refinishing, and reupholstering options for existing furniture instead of purchasing new goods. This extends the lifespan of furniture and reduces waste.

Upholstered Goods

When it comes to cushion fillings and fabric finishes, here are some considerations for sustainable product specification:

- **Ozone-Free Cushion Foams:** Cushion foams should be made using ozone-free processes. Ozone-free manufacturing helps reduce harmful emissions and promotes a healthier indoor environment.
- **Allergy-Friendly Fillings:** Investigate how cushion fillings, such as down, have been processed to reduce allergy issues for the client. Some fillings may undergo treatments or have specific certifications that indicate their hypoallergenic properties.
- **Natural Fabrics:** Finishing fabrics made from natural materials rather than synthetic ones is generally more environmentally friendly. However, it's worth noting that advancements have been made in the sustainability of some synthetic fabrics compared to earlier versions.
- **Flame Retardant Treatment:** Many commercial-grade fabrics are treated with flame retardants, which can have adverse health effects. Care must be taken when specifying flame-retardant-treated textiles. Safety considerations should take precedence over meeting green demands. However, it's worth exploring alternatives or selecting fabrics that meet strict safety standards without harmful flame retardant additives.
- **Recycled Polyester Textiles:** If feasible for the project, look for recycled polyester textiles. These fabrics are made from recycled plastic bottles and help reduce waste and resource consumption.
- **Manufacturer Specifications:** Obtain specifications from manufacturers to ensure that upholstered goods are manufactured and finished using environmentally friendly practices. This includes verifying green manufacturing processes and the use of sustainable materials.

Wall Finishes

When it comes to wall finishes, here are some considerations for sustainable product specification:

- **Low-VOC and Water-Based Paints:** Opt for low-VOC (volatile organic compounds) paints, which release fewer harmful chemicals into the air. Water-based paints are generally lower in VOC content compared to oil-based paints. Choosing environmentally friendly paint options contributes to better indoor air quality.
- **Paint Pigments and Heavy Metals:** Be aware that certain paint pigments can contain carcinogenic heavy metals. Consider paints that are free from toxic heavy metals such as lead, mercury, and cadmium.
- **Natural Wall Coverings:** Select wall coverings made from natural materials like sisal and cork. These materials are renewable and have a lower environmental impact compared to synthetic options. Fabrics may also be used as wall coverings, but it's important to consider applicable codes and regulations.
- **Avoid Vinyl (PVC) Coverings:** Vinyl or PVC (polyvinyl chloride) wall coverings should be avoided. PVC is associated with environmental concerns and potential health hazards. Ensure that specified wall coverings do not contain any PVC or PVC coatings.

- Green Adhesives: Specify adhesives that are considered green or environmentally friendly. Look for low-VOC adhesives that are free from harmful chemicals. Choosing sustainable adhesives reduces indoor air pollution and contributes to a healthier environment.

Flooring

When it comes to flooring, here are some considerations for sustainable product specification:

- Subfloor Construction: Keep in mind that flooring also includes the subfloor construction materials. Consider sustainable options for subfloor materials, such as using recycled or reclaimed materials. Low-
- VOC Off-Gassing: Research carpeting and other flooring underlayment materials for potential low-VOC off-gassing. Opt for products that have been tested and certified for low emissions of volatile organic compounds, which can contribute to better indoor air quality.
- Reclaimed Wood: Reclaimed wood can be a suitable option for certain projects. It provides a sustainable choice by giving new life to salvaged materials.
- Carpet Composition: Carefully research the composition of face and backing materials for carpets and rugs. In commercial interiors, where carpet is often glued down rather than installed over underlayment, use low-VOC glues to minimize emissions.
- Carpet Recycling: Investigate the possibility of recycling carpeting rather than sending it to a landfill at the end of its life cycle. Many manufacturers and organizations offer carpet recycling programs, promoting a more sustainable approach to disposal.
- Linoleum Flooring: Consider linoleum as a durable and sustainable alternative to vinyl (PVC) flooring materials. Linoleum is made from natural materials and offers a low environmental impact. However, be aware that "linoleum" can refer to both a brand name and an industry term.
- Tile Flooring: Tiles are known for their durability and low maintenance. When using tiles, opt for low-VOC adhesives and grout to ensure a healthier indoor environment. However, keep in mind that tiles can be noisy and may not be suitable for all projects.

These tips and points serve as a starting point for incorporating sustainable materials into your projects. However, it's important to note that this is not an exhaustive guide, and further research is necessary to delve deeper into sustainable design practices.

To expand your knowledge on the subject, consider seeking information from manufacturers' representatives who can provide specific details about their sustainable products. Online sources and resources can also offer valuable insights into sustainable materials and practices. Additionally, exploring books written by various authors can provide more in-depth explanations and guidance on incorporating sustainability into the indoor environment. Chapter 10 of the book mentioned provides a more detailed explanation of sustainable practices in the indoor environment. This chapter could serve as a valuable resource to further your understanding of creating healthy and sustainable interiors.

Remember that sustainable design is an evolving field, and staying up-to-date with current research, industry standards, and emerging trends is essential for incorporating the most effective and environmentally conscious practices into your projects.

Security and Safety

In the modern landscape, the safety and security of customers and employees in commercial environments have become paramount concerns. With the rise of workplace violence, cyber threats, and identity theft, businesses must prioritize robust security measures to protect their stakeholders and ensure the continuity of their operations.

The expectations of clients have evolved, with an increasing emphasis on comprehensive security planning and implementation across all types of commercial facilities. The goal is to create an environment where people feel safe and protected.

Business owners face a wide range of security challenges, including physical harm, theft, vandalism, and safeguarding sensitive information. These risks can vary based on the industry and the specific nature of the business. Developing tailored security solutions is crucial to effectively address these issues. Design teams play a crucial role in integrating security measures into the fabric of commercial spaces. Adherence to relevant building codes and industry standards is essential. These codes provide guidelines and requirements for creating secure environments, ensuring that the design aligns with the latest safety regulations. Collaboration between interior designers, architects, and security consultants is necessary to develop holistic security strategies. This collaboration ensures that security considerations are seamlessly integrated into the design process, leading to the creation of safe and functional spaces.

Transparency and integration are key principles in security design. Balancing the need for safety with the aesthetic and functional requirements of the space is crucial. Designers must carefully plan sight lines, incorporate discreet security features, and leverage appropriate lighting techniques to enhance visibility and foster a sense of security. Effective security solutions require thorough programming and a deep understanding of the specific needs and vulnerabilities of each business. Customized measures, such as access control systems, surveillance cameras, alarm systems, and advanced technology solutions, should be carefully considered in collaboration with security experts and vendors.

By prioritizing security in commercial design, businesses can establish trust, protect their assets, and create a secure environment for customers and employees alike. It is essential to continuously assess and update security measures to stay ahead of evolving threats and ensure the ongoing safety of all stakeholders. While this book may not delve into the intricate details of security design, it emphasizes the critical importance of addressing security concerns in today's commercial facilities. By implementing comprehensive security strategies, businesses can mitigate risks, enhance their reputation, and provide peace of mind to all who enter their premises.

Permitting Process and Officials

Commercial interior designers should have a global understanding of the building permitting process and the officials involved. The interior design layout, egress, and safety considerations often fall under the designer's responsibilities. However, it's important to note that local laws may restrict the extent to which the interior designer can prepare certain drawings.

Obtaining a building permit is typically required for new construction, as well as major interior renovations or changes in occupancy type or use. The issuance of a building permit is based on working drawings and specifications provided by the architect or property owner, and whether an interior designer can prepare these materials depends on local regulations.

Designing the interior requires compliance with the codes, regulations, and standards applicable to the project's location, rather than the location of the design firm. It is essential to clarify which jurisdiction has code authority for the project when initiating a new contract.

Jurisdictional authority refers to the governmental department, group, or individual responsible for overseeing the project's development. This authority is typically held by the local municipality but may also involve county, state, or even federal agencies. The jurisdictional authority reviews the submitted drawings and documents to ensure compliance with the relevant codes and regulations. They are responsible for approving building permits, monitoring the construction process, and issuing occupancy documents to the project owners. In many jurisdictions, the permitting process has been streamlined through online platforms, allowing for electronic permit applications, digital document transfers, and other related tasks. Throughout the process, the interior designer may encounter various building officials, including the code official, plans examiner, and building inspector. Additional officials, such as fire marshals and health department representatives, may also be involved depending on the jurisdiction and the project's nature.

The code review and approval process involves several steps, including determining which codes and regulations apply to the project, verifying the permitted scope of the interior designer's drawings, submitting the required documents to the jurisdiction's building office, and making any necessary modifications based on their feedback. Building officials conduct periodic inspections to ensure compliance with the approved plans. The final inspection by a building official precedes the issuance of a certificate of occupancy, indicating that the building has been constructed according to the approved drawings and documents.

It is crucial for designers to recognize that this process, including inspections, approvals, and the potential for appeals, is essential for the protection of the client, designer, and users of the property. Even if certain requirements may seem inconsequential, they must be incorporated into the design. Meeting scheduled dates and appointments with building officials is important, as the preparer of the documents and applications holds legal responsibility.

THE STEPS OF RESEARCH AND PROJECT IMPLEMENTATION

Interior designers engage in research as an integral part of their project development process. While research is commonly associated with project programming to determine the needs and requirements of a project, it encompasses various other forms as well. Research involves a systematic investigation and study of materials and sources to establish facts, reach conclusions, and acquire necessary information. Designers actively seek out information to inform their design process, write articles, or prepare reports. Additionally, research can lead to new evidence and conclusions, contributing to the expansion of knowledge in academia and the profession.

The first form of research, focused on gathering information for design projects, has long been a fundamental task for interior designers. The second form, involving academic research, has gained prominence as professionals recognize the importance of contributing to the knowledge base of the profession. Having an understanding of research methodologies beyond programming is essential for professional interior designers. While designers may not seek evidence in the same way as researchers investigating provable outcomes, they still strive to find information that supports and convinces clients of the decisions and specifications proposed to them. Research skills enhance their ability to effectively communicate and justify their design choices.

Problem Solving in the Design Process

All interior design projects involve the process of problem-solving. While clients may initially seek out interior designers for their creativity and aesthetic expertise, they ultimately hire them to address and resolve specific problems. These problems can range from large-scale challenges like designing a dynamic hotel interior or functional office space, to smaller tasks such as changing the color scheme of a restaurant while retaining existing furniture.

The process of problem-solving follows a general framework:

1. Clearly identify the problem at hand.
2. Explore potential alternatives that could solve the problem.
3. Conduct a detailed analysis of each alternative.
4. Make a decision on the best solution for solving the problem.
5. Take action based on the chosen solution, whether it's informing the client or implementing the decision.
6. Evaluate the effectiveness of the decision, which can be done through questionnaires, interviews, or assessing the outcomes.

Clients play a crucial role in the problem-solving process by articulating the difficulties they face and seeking the expertise of interior designers. The designer, in turn, utilizes the design process as a means to address and resolve these problems. Through thorough analysis and understanding of the problem, designers generate potential solutions during the programming and schematic design stages. Programming involves gathering information and comprehending the underlying issues, while schematic design allows for the creation of alternative solutions presented to the client for approval.

These alternatives are evaluated to determine the most suitable solution to recommend to the client. During the early stages of schematic design, the designer typically presents multiple options, whether it's different fabric choices for upholstery or various floor plan configurations. The decision-making step is crucial, as the designer must select the most appropriate options based on specific criteria and logical reasoning. It's important to go into client presentations equipped with not just drawings and samples but also well-founded justifications for the choices made.

Clients may have questions or concerns about the proposed solution, and it's essential to address these with patience and professionalism. The client's satisfaction and agreement with the recommended solution are paramount. If there is disagreement, it may indicate a need for further research and alignment with the client's objectives.

Assuming the client approves the recommended solutions, the final step involves preparing the necessary drawings or specification documents for purchasing goods and materials. In most cases, another presentation is required to review these documents with the client before proceeding to permits, construction bids, or ordering from suppliers. This process combines problem-solving, decision-making, and the design process itself.

It's worth noting that the final step of evaluating the decision is often overlooked by many designers who are occupied with new projects. However, conducting post-occupancy evaluations and engaging in internal discussions within the design team can provide valuable insights and help assess client satisfaction. This evaluation step is crucial for the continuous improvement of the design firm's processes and outcomes.

Design Thinking

Design thinking is a mindset and approach that encourages businesses to embrace the principles of design to foster innovation and solve complex problems. It recognizes that traditional business practices may not always lead to breakthrough ideas or transformative solutions. By adopting design thinking, organizations can uncover new opportunities, improve processes, and create innovative products and services. Designers are accustomed to following a systematic and iterative process to address design challenges. Design thinking follows a similar structured approach, incorporating key stages such as empathy, ideation, prototyping, and testing. It promotes interdisciplinary collaboration, user-centered design, and a willingness to learn from failures.

At the core of design thinking is a deep understanding of user needs and perspectives. It emphasizes empathy, encouraging businesses to truly grasp the desires, motivations, and pain points of customers or end-users. This empathetic understanding serves as the foundation for generating creative solutions and innovative concepts.

The iterative nature of design thinking allows for multiple rounds of prototyping and testing. This enables organizations to gather feedback, refine ideas, and ensure that solutions align with the desired goals. By embracing an iterative process, businesses can mitigate risks and increase the likelihood of success by making adjustments and improvements along the way.

Although design thinking originated in the business world, its principles and methodologies can be applied across various fields, including commercial interior design. Incorporating design thinking into their practice empowers interior designers to gain a deeper understanding of their clients' needs, generate more innovative design solutions, and create spaces that truly meet the requirements and aspirations of the end-users.

Lighting design plays a crucial role in enhancing occupants' sense of security and safety. Thoughtfully designed lighting eliminates dark or hazardous areas, ensuring clear visibility and enabling individuals to feel secure and aware of their surroundings.

While this book cannot delve into the complexities of security design, it aims to emphasize the importance of considering security factors in commercial facilities. Each facility type presents unique safety and security challenges, and the relevant chapters within this book provide valuable insights into security-related topics. In our contemporary society, security systems have become essential requirements to safeguard businesses, employees, and customers.

In 2003, David Kelley introduced the concept of "design thinking" and its application to the business world. He emphasized the importance of integrating the principles of design into business operations, recognizing that conventional approaches often hinder innovation and the exploration of new ways of conducting business. Kelley's premise was that adhering to traditional business practices, or "business as usual," restricts the ability to generate innovative ideas and find effective solutions. To address this, he advocated for the adoption of design thinking, which brings a fresh perspective and encourages a more creative and customer-centered approach to problem-solving. Tim Brown, the founder of IDEO, further refined and developed the concept of design thinking through his work and publications, including the influential book "Change by Design" (2009). Brown's insights and contributions have solidified design thinking as a valuable resource for businesses seeking to drive innovation and reimagine their operations.

It is crucial for commercial interior designers to be familiar with design thinking concepts and techniques as they can enhance their problem-solving abilities, promote collaboration with clients and stakeholders, and contribute to the overall success of their projects. By adopting a design thinking mindset, interior designers can drive innovation, deliver exceptional experiences, and create spaces that truly resonate with people.

Research Methodologies in Design

Research plays a crucial role in the interior design profession, going beyond the initial client interview and programming phase. While gathering information from clients and conducting site observations is an essential part of the design process, research expands the designer's knowledge and allows for a deeper understanding of their specialty and the project at hand.

The research process in interior design involves seeking answers to questions, exploring new knowledge, and conducting in-depth investigations. It goes beyond the immediate project requirements and aims to uncover insights, innovative ideas, and evidence-based solutions.

Research can take various forms, such as reviewing articles, books, and academic publications relevant to the field of interior design. This allows designers to stay updated on emerging trends, best practices, and new technologies. It also provides an opportunity to learn from the experiences and expertise of others in the industry.

In addition to accessing existing knowledge, research in interior design involves conducting investigations and exploring specific problems or ideas. This may include conducting surveys, interviews, or focus groups to gather data and insights from users, experts, or stakeholders. It could also involve analyzing case studies, conducting experiments, or exploring new materials and technologies. The research process generally follows a series of steps. It begins with identifying the research question or problem to be investigated. This helps focus the research efforts and set clear objectives. The next step involves reviewing existing literature and sources to gain a comprehensive understanding of the topic and identify gaps in knowledge.

Once the groundwork is laid, the research design is developed, outlining the methodology, data collection techniques, and analysis methods. This ensures that the research is conducted in a systematic and rigorous manner. Data is then collected, whether through surveys, observations, or other means, and analyzed to derive meaningful insights and conclusions.

The final step in the research process is the dissemination of findings. This may involve presenting research outcomes through reports, presentations, or publications, contributing to the collective knowledge of the interior design profession.

Research in interior design goes beyond the immediate project at hand, allowing designers to expand their knowledge, develop innovative solutions, and contribute to the advancement of the field. By embracing research as an integral part of their practice, interior designers can continuously enhance their skills, stay informed of industry developments, and deliver more impactful and evidence-based designs to their clients.

The Importance of Research in Design

The interior design profession, like any other, is built upon a body of knowledge that encompasses critical information, facts, and conclusions essential to the practice. This knowledge is derived through research, which contributes to the continuous growth and development of the field. A dynamic body of knowledge is crucial as it reflects the evolving nature of interior design and the advancements made through research activities, data collection, and publication. In interior design, the body of knowledge has primarily evolved through the execution of projects and subsequent evaluations of their outcomes. This type of research, known as applied research, involves gathering information and making decisions based on real-life problems encountered in design projects. On the other hand, pure research aims to expand the body of knowledge beyond problem-solving, often conducted by academicians to explore new avenues and generate insights.

However, there is a tendency in the industry to overlook the importance of project evaluations after completion. Interior designers often move on to new projects without taking the time to reflect on the effectiveness of their designs or whether they achieved the goals of the client. In today's commercial interior design landscape, projects have become increasingly complex, with a focus on addressing users' needs, sustainability, and well-being in spaces such as senior living facilities, hospitals, and hotels. Interior designers are also expanding their reach beyond local boundaries, working on projects in different states and even countries.

Interior design and architecture have a significant impact on the environment and the health of facility users. Design decisions should no longer be solely based on aesthetics but should also consider environmental implications and the use of renewable resources. Learning from both successful and problematic design decisions is crucial for designers and the profession as a whole. While practical, on-the-job research through experience is valuable, there is a need for better management and dissemination of this knowledge within design firms.

Specializing in a particular area of interior design can also benefit from organized research. Gathering information and developing case studies or white papers in their specialty can enhance a designer's reputation as an expert. These reports can be shared with potential clients to showcase expertise and add credibility. Collaboration between practicing designers and academicians is essential to strengthen the interior design profession. Engaging in research is not only vital for professional growth but also for improving the perception of interior design among the public, legislators, and others in the design and construction industry.

Research Steps

The design process and research process share similarities in their structured approach to problem-solving. While the design process focuses on creating solutions for design problems, the research process aims to gather information and generate new knowledge. Here are the steps commonly involved in the research process:

1. Define the problem and determine objectives: Just like in the design process, the research process begins by clearly defining the problem to be investigated. This involves understanding the research question or objective and identifying the specific information or knowledge gaps that need to be addressed.

2. Determine the methodology: Once the problem is defined, the next step is to determine the methodology or research approach. This involves selecting the appropriate research methods and tools to gather data and information. Research methods can include surveys, interviews, observations, experiments, literature reviews, or a combination of these approaches.

3. Determine the sample: In research, a sample refers to the subset of the population or target group that will be studied. It is essential to determine the appropriate sample size and selection criteria to ensure the findings are representative and can be generalized to a larger population. Sampling techniques vary depending on the research objectives and the characteristics of the target population.

4. Collect the data: Data collection involves gathering information through the selected research methods. This can include administering surveys, conducting interviews, making observations, collecting documents or existing data, or conducting experiments. The data collection process should be systematic, ensuring data reliability and validity.

5. Analyze the data: Once the data is collected, it needs to be analyzed to derive meaningful insights and draw conclusions. Data analysis can involve organizing and summarizing the data, applying statistical techniques, identifying patterns or trends, and interpreting the findings in relation to the research objectives.

6. Prepare the report or results: The final step involves presenting the research findings. This typically includes preparing a report or presentation that communicates the research process, data analysis, results, and conclusions. The report should be clear, concise, and effectively convey the research outcomes to the intended audience.

The subsequent stage involves identifying the appropriate methodology, which refers to the specific research approaches and tasks required to acquire the necessary information. Before delving into the details of various methodologies, it is crucial to highlight the distinction between primary and secondary research.

Primary research is the type of research that aims to discover new information that has not been previously known or explored. In the field of interior design and business, primary research often involves techniques such as questionnaires, interviews, surveys, and experiments to gather original data. For example, conducting a survey to measure client satisfaction with a design project would be considered primary research.

On the other hand, secondary research involves investigating and analyzing existing information and data that have been previously published or collected by others. It is often referred to as historical research since it relies on data that already exists. In the context of interior design, much of the research conducted is likely to be secondary research. For instance, comparing billing and time records of similar projects to assess profitability would be an example of secondary research in a business context. Similarly, comparing the pricing and performance of products specified for two similar projects is an example of secondary research in a design project. Students also frequently rely on secondary research when conducting literature surveys and preparing reports for their classes.

Both primary and secondary research play important roles in expanding the body of knowledge in interior design. Primary research allows for the exploration of new ideas, while secondary research helps build upon existing knowledge and insights. By utilizing both types of research, interior designers can gain valuable information, make informed decisions, and contribute to the advancement of the field.

Let's discuss different methodologies that can be utilized in the research process. The choice of methodology depends on the problem at hand and the objectives of the study.

1. Survey: This method involves collecting data through questionnaires, interviews, or surveys to gather new information. Surveys can be conducted with past clients, employees, or specific target groups. They can provide valuable insights but may be time-consuming and expensive to conduct.
2. Observation: Observational research involves discreetly recording behavior to gather primary research. It can involve techniques such as tracking customer movements in a store or counting the number of cars passing through a certain point. Observation can provide valuable information about user behavior.
3. Interview: Interviews are dynamic discussions where a researcher asks questions and records the responses. They can provide in-depth insights into specific topics and are often used during the programming phase when interviewing potential clients.
4. Historical survey and literature review: These methods involve reviewing existing data, literature, and historical information relevant to the research problem. Internet and library research can help gather information on various topics. These activities are associated with secondary research.
5. Case study: A case study involves in-depth analysis and review of a specific project or event to understand its successes and failures. It can involve data collection through surveys, questionnaires, or interviews.
6. Feasibility study: A feasibility study is conducted to determine the viability of a proposed project. Designers are often hired to conduct research and assess the project's potential success based on client-defined criteria. It can be an essential part of the early planning stages of commercial projects.
7. Experiment: While not commonly conducted by interior design firms, experiments involve manipulating variables to test hypotheses. This method is more often utilized by academicians.

Other methodologies may be applicable depending on the research problem, goals, and available resources. Further exploration of these methods can be done by referring to relevant books and resources.

After determining the methodology, the next step is selecting the sample for the research. The sample represents a small segment of the potential data options and needs to be carefully chosen to provide meaningful results. The sample's size and selection process should be clarified, considering the specific research objectives.

The data collection process follows, with the designated researcher carrying out the necessary data gathering activities. Depending on the chosen method, data can be analyzed using database software programs. In some cases, additional research may be needed if the initial results do not align with the problem definition. Finally, reports summarizing the study can be prepared for internal use within the firm or for external dissemination through the firm's website or publication in trade magazines.

EVIDENCE-BASED DESIGN

In commercial interior design, clients often seek evidence and verification to understand the rationale behind design recommendations. They want assurance that the proposed solutions will have a positive impact on their facility and justify the investment. To address this need, the research methodology of evidence-based design (EBD) has gained prominence.

EBD is a process that involves using current best evidence from research and practice to make informed design decisions in collaboration with the client. It emphasizes the use of valid evidence rather than relying solely on opinions or subjective judgments.

Originally rooted in the design of medical facilities, EBD has been focused on outcomes and addressing specific questions related to the impact of design decisions. For example, in healthcare design, EBD investigates whether certain materials used in patient rooms contribute to infections. By recording reactions and outcomes of design decisions on users, evidence is gathered to support the design process. While EBD has its origins in healthcare, it is increasingly being applied to other types of commercial facilities as well. It is worth noting that the research and data collection involved in EBD are often carried out by larger architectural and design firms due to resource limitations. The findings from such research provide valuable data to inform the decision-making process and support the design firm in making effective planning and specification decisions. This, in turn, helps clients understand and approve of the design choices being made.

Some designers may have reservations about EBD, fearing that it imposes rigid rules and compromises design aesthetics. However, proponents of EBD argue that it does not advocate for a one-size-fits-all approach or a loss of design creativity. Instead, EBD involves researching the effectiveness of similar projects to inform the current design process. It guides designers towards effective solutions while considering the unique factors and requirements of each project.

In summary, evidence-based design in commercial interior design involves incorporating research findings and best practices to make informed design decisions that are backed by evidence. It enhances the design process by providing a provable body of information and helping clients understand the rationale behind design choices. EBD does not promote cookie-cutter design but rather offers guidance for creating effective and tailored solutions.

Benchmarking

Benchmarking is a process that has gained traction in the business side of interior design practice. It involves studying and comparing the performance statistics of a design firm with those of other firms, particularly those that specialize in similar types of projects or are considered industry leaders in terms of best practices. The concept of benchmarking includes the idea of best practice, which refers to the successful methods and approaches used by top-performing firms. By measuring their own performance against that of the best firm in their specialty and adopting similar management principles, a firm can strive to improve its own performance.

Finding benchmarking metrics and best practice examples specific to the design industry can be challenging. Interior design and architecture firms are typically privately held, making their statistics less readily available. However, occasional metrics may be found in trade magazines or articles published by professional associations. Conducting internet searches on competing design firms may yield some useful information. Additionally, if a firm collaborates with another firm on a large project, there may be opportunities to share information and insights to some extent.

The benchmarking process should begin with gathering and analyzing the firm's own data. Internal documents can provide metrics such as billings, employee productivity, and the number of projects completed in a specific category or size over the past few years. While benchmarking is an excellent management tool, its application in the design industry may present certain challenges. Nevertheless, employing effective research techniques can still yield valuable insights and opportunities for improvement.

Goal Setting and Ideation in Project Journey

Setting clear goals for a project is crucial to its success. The client's goals are usually gathered during the programming interviews, and the designer works towards creating solutions that align with those goals. It's important for the designer to understand and discuss the reasons behind the client's goals. Goals in a project can encompass both aesthetic and functional aspects. While aesthetic goals influence visual choices, functional goals are focused on ensuring the facility works efficiently for its intended purpose. For example, in a luxury restaurant, aesthetic goals may involve creating an exquisite ambiance, while functional goals may include designing table spacing that allows waitstaff to move easily without disturbing diners.

Some goals may require a balance between aesthetics and functionality. In the luxury restaurant example, functional needs like wait stations must be carefully integrated into the dining room to ensure they don't detract from the overall ambiance. Uncovering goals can be done through various methods such as interviewing, using questionnaires, and making observations. These approaches help reveal both functional and aesthetic goals and provide insights for further discussions with the client.

During the conceptual stage, designers should be cautious about sharing sketches too early. Concepts are initially abstract ideas, and clients may become fixated on a particular sketch even if it's not the best solution. Instead, written concept statements are valuable tools that come out of concept discussions. Designers often prepare concept statements before creating sketches. These statements establish the likely direction of the design and provide a foundation for further refinement. As concepts are discussed and clarified with the client, sketches and preliminary material selections may follow. However, it should be emphasized to the client that these are preliminary and subject to change during later stages of the design process.

Once goals and concepts are agreed upon, the designer can proceed with the rest of the design process. Concepts and feasibility studies, which are often part of early programming tasks, are further discussed in later chapters that cover planning and design elements.

Design Process

The design process is likely familiar to most readers and is an essential research endeavor for interior designers. It involves a series of steps that need to be followed in order to successfully complete a project. While all projects have their complexities, commercial design projects tend to be particularly intricate due to their size, client requirements, code restrictions, bidding processes, and other factors that influence the final design. Having a well-defined process in mind helps mitigate potential issues and disputes.

The design process is universally recognized and accepted by interior designers, architects, and other professionals in the design/build industry. It applies to projects of various scales, including both commercial facilities and residential spaces. Even small projects, such as single-room specifications, can benefit from following the basic design process, highlighting its widespread applicability.

Outlined below are the fundamental steps of the design process, accompanied by common tasks associated with each stage. It's important to note that the task lists provided are not exhaustive but rather represent the most frequently performed activities. Additionally, throughout these phases, meetings with stakeholders and travel to the job site may be required to ensure successful project execution.

Programming: It is an initial phase of the design process that involves conducting thorough research and gathering information to understand the client's needs, site restrictions, code regulations, environmental considerations, security concerns, and economic impacts, among other factors. This phase often results in the development of written design concepts, program statements, reports, and preliminary sketched graphic drawings.

Key tasks involved in the programming phase include:
- Gathering comprehensive project information and conducting interviews with the client
- Determining the goals and objectives of the client's project
- Reviewing relevant codes, security protocols, and environmental guidelines
- Analyzing the site, considering its physical characteristics and limitations
- Assessing social, psychological, and cultural factors that may influence the design
- Conducting an inventory of existing furniture and equipment, if applicable
- Identifying preferences for new furniture and equipment
- Determining aesthetic preferences and desired design style
- Obtaining the base building plan or conducting site measurements
- Reviewing the lease agreement, if applicable
- Developing a scoping statement that outlines the project's scope and objectives.

These tasks collectively contribute to establishing a comprehensive understanding of the project's requirements and serve as a foundation for subsequent stages of the design process.

Schematic Design: During the Schematic Design phase, the programming information gathered in the previous phase is synthesized and translated into preliminary floor plans, elevations, and other visual representations that aim to explore and communicate the design concepts. This phase involves considering various factors such as building codes, building systems, sustainability, security, mechanical systems, and movable furniture and furnishings.

The tasks involved in the Schematic Design phase include:

- Interpreting the programming information to understand the project requirements
- Creating preliminary sketches and drawings of the space plan
- Developing initial drawings of elevations, details, and other visual representations
- Addressing environmental, human factors, and security considerations in the design
- Incorporating building codes, life safety regulations, and accessibility requirements into the plans
- Making preliminary selections of furniture, fixtures, and equipment (FF&E)
- Developing a budget that outlines the estimated costs of the project
- Finalizing the scoping statement or design concept statement that outlines the project's scope and design approach.

These tasks allow the designer to further refine and articulate the design concepts, taking into account the specific requirements and constraints of the project. The Schematic Design phase serves as a bridge between the initial programming phase and the subsequent stages of the design process.

Design Development: During the Design Development phase, the focus is on refining and finalizing the design based on the approved schematic design plans. The necessary orthographic drawings, furniture layouts, systems plans, and other detailed drawings are developed to ensure compliance with relevant codes and regulations. The specifications for furniture, fixtures, and equipment (FF&E) are also finalized, along with the completion of budget estimates. In this phase, sustainability criteria are applied as appropriate or desired for the project.

The tasks involved in the Design Development phase include:

- Finalizing the space plan, which involves making any necessary adjustments or refinements to optimize the layout and functionality of the space.
- Finalizing the furniture layouts, ensuring that the placement and arrangement of furniture and fixtures meet the requirements and objectives of the design.
- Finalizing other required orthographic drawings, such as detailed floor plans, sections, and elevations, to provide comprehensive documentation of the design.
- Addressing safety and environmental issues, considering factors such as accessibility, fire safety, and sustainable design practices.

- Confirming building systems and lighting requirements, ensuring that the design integrates with the appropriate mechanical, electrical, and lighting systems.
- Finalizing FF&E selections, specifying the exact furniture, fixtures, and equipment to be used in the project.
- Finalizing budgets, completing the financial planning and estimation for the design and construction process.

By the end of the Design Development phase, the design should be well-defined, incorporating the necessary details and considerations to proceed with the next stages of the project. This phase sets the stage for the production of construction drawings and documents in the subsequent phases.

Contract Documents: During the Contract Documents phase, the focus is on preparing the necessary documents and drawings that will guide the construction and installation of the interior design. These documents ensure compliance with applicable building codes, life safety regulations, and accessibility standards. The coordination of mechanical, electrical, lighting, and security systems is also addressed, either by the interior designer or in collaboration with consultants. If required by the design contract, bid documents and equipment installation drawings are prepared, taking into account any special installation requirements. Additionally, the specifications for furniture, fixtures, and equipment (FF&E) are finalized.

The tasks involved in the Contract Documents phase include:

- Preparing and finalizing construction drawings and documents, which provide detailed and comprehensive instructions for the construction and installation of interior nonload-bearing partitions and other design elements.
- Preparing construction specifications, which outline the materials, finishes, and installation requirements for various components of the design.
- Creating construction schedules that are specifically related to the interior designer's responsibilities, ensuring that the design process aligns with the project timeline.
- Developing other construction drawings as needed, depending on the specific scope of the project and any additional requirements.
- Coordinating consultant drawings with the construction documents, ensuring that all disciplines are aligned and integrated seamlessly.
- Preparing contract and bid documents, which outline the terms, conditions, and requirements for contractors and vendors involved in the construction and installation process.
- Coordinating design work with consultants, clients, and vendors, fostering effective collaboration and communication to address any design-related issues or modifications.

The Contract Documents phase is critical in providing the necessary documentation and instructions for contractors and vendors to accurately and efficiently execute the interior design. These documents serve as a contractual agreement and guide for the implementation of the design vision.

Contract Administration: During the Contract Administration phase, the interior designer takes on the role of overseeing and managing the construction and installation process to ensure that it aligns with the design intent and meets the client's requirements. The extent of the interior designer's involvement in this phase may vary depending on the jurisdiction and the specific project requirements.

In some cases, the interior designer can act as the client's agent in issuing bid documents, evaluating and qualifying bidders, and administering the bidding process. They may also be responsible for coordinating and supervising the installation work by vendors, ensuring that the plans, specifications, and requirements are followed.

Tasks involved in Contract Administration include:

- Analyzing bids and monitoring the bid process, which involves assessing and comparing the bids received from contractors to determine the most suitable option for the project.
- Observing the construction and installation work, regularly visiting the job site to ensure that the work is progressing according to the plans and specifications.
- Preparing change orders, which are modifications or adjustments to the original contract scope, specifications, or schedule, and ensuring that they are properly documented and communicated to the relevant parties.
- Managing the ordering and procurement of furniture, fixtures, and equipment (FF&E) if this responsibility falls within the scope of the interior designer's role.
- Inspecting the job site to verify the complete installation of FF&E and ensure that it meets the design requirements.
- Creating a punch list, which is a list of items, omissions, or damages that need to be addressed or corrected before the project is considered complete.
- Evaluating the post-occupancy performance of the interior design, which may involve gathering feedback from the client and occupants, assessing the functionality and effectiveness of the design solutions, and identifying any areas for improvement.

Throughout the Contract Administration phase, the interior designer assumes the role of project manager and collaborates with contractors, vendors, and other stakeholders to ensure the successful completion of the project, from client move-in to post-occupancy evaluation. Their objective is to maintain the quality and integrity of the design while addressing any issues that may arise during the construction and installation process.

Programming Elements

Programming is an essential part of the design process, particularly in commercial projects. It involves researching the client's needs, site restrictions, code regulations, environmental issues, security concerns, and economic impacts. This phase aims to gather project information and conduct client interviews to determine project goals and requirements.

The person in charge of the project may vary depending on the size and scope of the project. In commercial projects, the initial contact person may not be the primary decision-maker but can provide access to someone who has the authority to make decisions. It is important for the interior designer to understand the chain of command and work with the relevant stakeholders throughout the project.

The programming phase also involves assessing client needs and wants. Needs are essential requirements, while wants are desired but not necessarily essential elements. Through questioning and other programming techniques, the designer can identify the client's needs and wants and help reconcile any discrepancies, especially when there are budget constraints.

Asking questions is a critical part of programming. Questions help gather information, think critically, and understand the project in-depth. Designers should plan their questions in advance and actively listen to the answers provided. It is important to keep records of questions, answers, and client reactions for future reference.

Questions can be framed as open-ended or closed-ended, depending on the desired response. Open-ended questions encourage dialogue and detailed responses, while closed-ended questions seek specific and concise answers. A combination of both types of questions helps gather the necessary information for conceptualizing the project. Note-taking during programming is crucial to record important details and show respect for the client's ideas. However, designers should be mindful of the time taken for note-taking to ensure that meetings remain efficient and within the client's expectations.

THE OFFICE

Interior design firms are involved in designing a range of office facilities that cater to different business needs. These offices can be found in various industries, including retail stores, medical practices, bed and breakfast establishments, corporate offices, advertising agencies, accounting firms, and law offices, among others. The primary goal of office spaces is to facilitate specific tasks that contribute to the overall objectives of the business. However, it is important to recognize that not all office work is the same. The nature of work for an administrative assistant supporting a corporate executive differs significantly from that of a store manager. Therefore, it is crucial for designers to understand the unique requirements of each business and its respective office functions before initiating the design process.

Businesses face ongoing challenges and organizational changes that impact their operations and markets. Designers specializing in office design must be aware of these challenges and adaptable to incorporate any necessary adjustments during the design project. By comprehending the organizational dynamics, job roles, and equipment needs, interior designers can effectively create office facilities that align with the functional demands of diverse businesses, regardless of their size or industry.

Office Operations: A Comprehensive Overview

The office environment has experienced significant changes in response to evolving trends in how work is conducted. Advancements in technology, the increasing prevalence of remote work, and the growing importance of information have all played a role in reshaping the modern office landscape. Traditional hierarchical structures have given way to more flexible and collaborative work settings, as the need for physical office spaces for every employee has diminished with the rise of telecommuting and global connectivity. Instead, the focus has shifted towards knowledge workers who heavily rely on technology and information in their work. As a result, businesses now prioritize flexibility and adaptability in office design to accommodate changes both within and outside the organization. While socialization and collaboration remain important aspects, the increasing adoption of remote work options necessitates an understanding of diverse job functions and the varying needs of employees in order to create efficient and productive work environments.

In today's fast-paced business world, it is crucial for professionals at all levels to have a deep understanding of office operations. This overview aims to provide valuable insights into the current trends and practices that are shaping modern workplaces. From the integration of technology to the evolving dynamics of teamwork, this exploration of office operations offers a comprehensive perspective on the key factors driving success in today's contemporary office environment.

The Digital Transformation of the Workplace: Technological advancements have revolutionized office operations, giving rise to the digital workplace. This shift involves integrating digital tools, software, and cloud-based platforms to enhance productivity and efficiency. Automation and artificial intelligence (AI) streamline tasks, while cloud-based platforms facilitate efficient data management. The digital workplace empowers employees to collaborate seamlessly, automate routine tasks, and access information from anywhere, transforming office operations.

Flexible Workforce and Remote Collaboration: The modern workplace has embraced remote work and flexible arrangements. Remote collaboration and communication strategies are crucial for success in this agile workforce. Balancing productivity, work-life balance, and employee well-being is paramount. Digital tools enable seamless remote collaboration, enabling teams to work effectively regardless of their physical location.

Knowledge Workers and the Power of Information: The rise of knowledge workers has reshaped office dynamics, highlighting the importance of information in today's workplaces. Information is now recognized as a strategic asset that provides a competitive edge. Continuous learning and upskilling are crucial for knowledge workers, while effective knowledge management systems facilitate collaboration and informed decision-making. Embracing knowledge workers and leveraging information enhances productivity and drives success in the modern workplace.

Office Space and Design: Office spaces have undergone significant transformations to meet the needs of the modern workforce. Flexibility and adaptability are prioritized, allowing employees to personalize their workspaces and choose settings that suit their preferences and work styles. This shift has led to the creation of flexible layouts that can be easily modified and reconfigured to accommodate different tasks and collaboration needs. Collaborative spaces play a vital role in fostering creativity and innovation. Modern office designs incorporate dedicated areas such as open-plan workstations, breakout rooms, and communal lounges. These spaces are equipped with the latest technology and provide opportunities for spontaneous interactions, brainstorming sessions, and collaborative projects. By encouraging teamwork and idea exchange, these collaborative spaces boost employee engagement and drive innovation within the organization.

Sustainability and Employee Well-being: Sustainable practices and employee well-being are integral aspects of office design. Offices are designed with a focus on sustainability, incorporating energy-efficient lighting, recycling programs, and eco-friendly materials. This not only reduces the environmental footprint but also aligns with the values of employees and stakeholders. Additionally, employee well-being is prioritized through the inclusion of ergonomic furniture, access to natural light, and dedicated wellness areas where employees can relax and recharge. By reimagining office space and design, organizations create an environment that promotes productivity, collaboration, and well-being.

Evolving Team Dynamics and Collaboration: Team dynamics are evolving to embrace cross-functional teams, where individuals with diverse expertise collaborate towards shared goals. Effective communication and collaboration strategies are essential for the success of these teams, ensuring seamless information flow and open exchange of ideas. Organizations promote a culture of inclusivity and diversity, recognizing the value of different perspectives and experiences in driving innovation and problem-solving. While face-to-face interactions remain important, the integration of digital collaboration tools provides flexibility and enhances team collaboration, enabling seamless communication and cooperation regardless of physical location.

Operational Efficiency and Process Optimization: Organizations strive for operational efficiency by streamlining workflows and optimizing processes. This involves implementing agile methodologies, embracing data-driven decision-making, and promoting continuous improvement through lean management practices.

Agile methodologies enhance efficiency by enabling teams to adapt quickly, break down work into manageable tasks, and foster collaboration. Data-driven decision-making allows organizations to make informed choices based on data analysis, leading to optimized operations. Continuous improvement, driven by lean management practices, helps identify inefficiencies and reduce waste. Overall, operational efficiency is achieved through streamlining workflows, implementing agile methodologies, leveraging data for decision-making, and embracing continuous improvement practices.

Corporate Culture

Understanding the corporate culture of an organization is crucial for an interior designer when planning office spaces. Corporate culture encompasses policies, employee behavior, company values, the company's image, and assumptions about the world of work. It plays a significant role in the success of office design projects, especially when the company is undergoing a change in its interior design.

For example, transitioning from a hierarchical closed plan to an open plan requires a cultural change that may face resistance from employees, particularly leaders who are accustomed to private offices. To mitigate this resistance, involving and informing employees about the changes and their rationale is important. Effective interior design and planning of office areas and product specifications can either enhance or harm the corporate culture. When done correctly, it aligns employees in pursuing common beliefs and goals, resulting in improved customer satisfaction and a positive company image. Proper space allocation, planning, and product specifications based on functional needs rather than rank or status contribute to a productive work environment.

To avoid the costly mistake of designing an office facility that contradicts the corporate culture, interior design firms offer cultural audits as a pre-design service. A cultural audit helps identify the necessary activities to incorporate into the change process for a successful outcome. Key personnel and a random sample of employees working in the project area may be interviewed, and questionnaires or visual surveys may be used to gather information about space usage and communication patterns.

The insights gained from the cultural audit inform the interior designer's recommendations on space allocation, planning, and product specifications. By aligning the design with actual functional needs and employee preferences, the office environment becomes conducive to productivity. Involving employees in the process and communicating how the changes will improve overall effectiveness and individual work responsibilities helps facilitate a smoother transition.

Ultimately, office design serves as a catalyst for organizational change and enhances organizational effectiveness when employees are included in the process and understand the benefits of the new environment.

Types of Office Spaces

Office spaces are common in commercial interiors, and designing office facilities is a frequent task for interior designers. The term "office" can refer to the space where a person works or the various spaces used for professional and business activities. While not all businesses will have all types of office spaces, almost all commercial enterprises allocate space for office functions.

The planning of an office facility should align with the operational organization of the business. Businesses with structured operations often prefer a more formal office plan characterized by partitioned walled office spaces, also known as a closed office plan or conventional office planning. This layout provides privacy and is commonly favored by professionals such as lawyers, accountants, and medical practitioners.

On the other hand, businesses with a collaborative and team-oriented structure tend to adopt a space plan that utilizes movable furniture. Many businesses opt for a hybrid approach, combining closed offices for some staff members and open workstations for others.

A more collaborative organizational structure often leads to an open plan methodology, also called an open landscape. In its purest form, this plan eliminates private offices with full-height walls and doors, instead using movable wall panels and furniture items to divide the office space into work areas. Workstations, rather than offices, are used in team-oriented clusters, although semi-enclosed cubicles may still be necessary for specific job functions. This approach offers greater flexibility in layout and product specification.

In practice, many companies today utilize a modified open plan. This combines private closed offices for some staff members, typically along exterior walls or adjacent to the central core, with open workstations for others. This configuration allows for a mix of private and collaborative spaces within the office footprint.

Closed offices continue to exist due to various reasons, including status considerations. Some individuals who have climbed the corporate ladder over many years find satisfaction in achieving the status of a closed private office. Additionally, some workers believe they are more productive in closed offices or cubicles, although research suggests otherwise. Whether for privacy, status, or security, closed offices or "closed" cubicles still have a place in certain office environments as per individual preferences and requirements.

Different types of office spaces can be encountered in various organizations, whether they follow a more traditional or collaborative structure. These office spaces serve different functions and cater to the needs of employees at different levels. Here are some common types of office spaces:

- Executive office/suite: These offices are reserved for the highest-ranking individuals, such as the CEO, and are typically closed private offices. They may include a separate reception area and a receptionist to welcome visitors.
- Other executive offices: Offices for upper-level management positions are often grouped with the CEO's office. While they may not have a separate waiting area, a secretary outside the office is common.
- Small business owners or managers: These individuals may have their own versions of executive suites, with more spacious and strategically located offices.
- Department manager's offices and/or workstations: These offices are usually located on the same floor or near their respective department areas. They are smaller in size compared to executive offices and may have less luxurious furniture.
- Supervisor's offices and workstations: These offices are typically not private and are situated within the area where their subordinates work. The furniture used in supervisor offices is smaller and less extravagant than that of department managers.
- Workstations for general office job descriptions: The majority of office spaces are dedicated to various types of production employees, such as sales representatives and computer programmers. The size, configuration, and furniture requirements can vary based on the department's primary responsibilities.
- Ancillary or support spaces: These spaces are essential for supporting basic office work. While utility is prioritized over aesthetics, they serve important functions. Examples include conference rooms, duplication/copying rooms, filing rooms, reference storage areas, supply storage rooms, and employee lunchrooms or cafeterias.

It's important to note that the types of office spaces can vary significantly based on the specific needs and nature of each business. Specialized industries, such as advertising agencies or design-build firms, may require unique spaces to support their specific activities, such as storyboard creation or design review areas.

Essential Elements of Office Interior Design

The design of office interiors is a significant part of the commercial interior design industry, accounting for a large portion of design fees. Whether it's a small professional office or part of a larger commercial facility, understanding the functional needs, working relationships, and organizational structure of the office is crucial for effective design. While some office environments have maintained similar space and functional requirements over the years, others have undergone significant changes in response to evolving work dynamics. Innovative space planning, designs that accommodate diverse workforces, and suitable furniture products are key considerations in today's office environment. This chapter builds upon the previous discussion on designing office interiors and offers specific design guidelines for a generic general office. The first design application focuses on a traditional style of office organization characterized by predominantly case goods and closed planning. The second design application outlines guidelines for a generic office that primarily utilizes office systems products. Additionally, a new design application is introduced, discussing a small professional office. These chapters provide valuable insights and guidance for interior designers in creating functional and efficient office spaces, catering to the unique needs of different types of offices.

Planning and Design Elements

A crucial aspect of a successful office design project is understanding the communication patterns and functional interrelationships among employees. Even in a small office, arranging employees in proximity to each other based on their need to work together can significantly enhance the office's effectiveness. In larger corporations, the strategic arrangement of employees on each floor can have a profound impact on the overall success of the company.

The modern office environment has undergone significant changes, as discussed in the previous chapter. Social networks and technology now enable employees to work remotely, whether from home, while traveling, or even from a coffee shop, as long as their work is being accomplished. This shift has reduced the need for traditional hard offices, both in the form of individual private offices and offices designed with systems furniture. However, certain businesses still require private work areas with full-height walls to ensure privacy and security, such as law offices or accounting firms.

Open plan office environments have gained popularity as they promote easy interaction and collaboration among employees. This can take the form of grouped workstations with minimal separation and shared storage shelves. Collaborative spaces, equipped with tables, chairs, or lounge seating, provide areas where employees can gather and discuss ideas. The choice between open plan and private offices depends on the specific needs of the client, and as interior designers, it is our role to plan office spaces that best suit those needs.

The chapter introduces several terms, and their definitions are provided in the relevant sections where they are discussed in more detail. The chapter outlines the fundamental planning and design elements involved in office environments, covering feasibility studies, sustainable design criteria, safety and security considerations, code requirements, space allocation, circulation, furniture, materials, finishes, color, and mechanical systems. The chapter concludes with a section called "Design Applications," where generic projects are discussed in relation to the planning and design elements presented.

Space Allocation and Circulation

Space allocation and circulation are critical considerations in office interior design. During the programming phase, the designer gathers data to determine the amount of space required for each department and support spaces. Decisions regarding the office plan type (closed, open, or modified open), furniture selection, employee numbers, and required support spaces play a key role in determining space allocation. It is important to research building and accessibility codes to ensure compliance when determining space allowances.

In large businesses, there are often predetermined space allowances based on corporate policies. For example, different job functions may have specific square footage allocations, such as vice presidents having 250 square feet and secretarial staff having 48 to 64 square feet. Designers are typically required to plan the facility using these corporate standards or develop them if they do not exist. When corporate policies do not control square foot allowances, designers can determine them by creating typical plan sketches and understanding the furniture requirements for each space.

The space allowances for open plan environments are generally less than those for closed plans. The organization and configuration of components on panels in open plan workstations impact the square footage required for each employee's workstation. Status and work methodologies, such as teaming or individual work assignments, also influence square footage requirements. Support spaces are an essential part of office plans and include conference rooms, file storage areas, copy machine locations, and coffee areas. In high-rise buildings, support spaces are typically located adjacent to the central core, while smaller "neighborhood" support spaces may be included in larger footprints. Circulation paths are designed to move people through the office facility and connect different departments. In closed plans, circulation paths are considered corridors, while open or modified open plans have pathways through open areas.

Circulation paths generally require an additional 20 to 50 percent of floor space. Corridors must meet minimum width requirements specified by building codes, and aisles must be sized based on the occupant load. The width of major circulation paths and exit corridors may need to be larger depending on the number of occupants and accessibility guidelines.

Open office projects may require more space due to the need for extra aisles between workstations. The design of circulation paths can vary, including straight paths, maze-like layouts, or angled plans. Straight paths are more efficient, but designs with twists and turns or angles can add interest. The specific space requirements will vary depending on the type of systems furniture used and the chosen circulation path design.

The space allowances for workstations, offices, and support spaces constitute the net area required for planning the facility. However, additional architectural features and spaces such as columns, wall thicknesses, electrical closets, and circulation space should be considered. These elements are not included in the net area but are part of the overall required office facility.

Once space allocations are determined and functional adjacencies are clarified, the designer can proceed with schematic planning to test the gathered information and present potential layouts to the client.

Furniture

When it comes to office furniture, there is a vast array of options available, offering numerous choices in style, finish, fabric, size, and price point. These options include standard stock items, semi-custom items, and even custom-designed furniture. However, the selection process should prioritize the functional needs of the client and the project. Functionality should take precedence over pure aesthetics, although there can often be a balance between the two. It is essential to ensure that the furniture items meet performance criteria and satisfy the functional requirements of the space. For example, a desk should be of an appropriate size, and a file cabinet should accommodate the client's file folders.

Cost is an important consideration for corporate and business clients when choosing furniture. While the initial cost is often the primary concern, it is crucial to consider the long-term cost or life cycle cost, which includes maintenance and replacement. Budget-priced furniture may have a lower initial cost but may need to be replaced sooner and may not hold up well in high-use office environments. On the other hand, more expensive furniture items are typically better built, made of higher-quality materials, and designed to withstand wear and tear, resulting in less frequent replacement. Higher-quality furniture often comes with better warranties, providing additional economic benefits. It also tends to have superior design characteristics that align with the client's aesthetic goals. Many projects opt for mid-priced furniture, which offers a good balance between performance and aesthetics. The performance and quality of mid-priced furniture are generally high and suitable for a wide range of office interiors.

General use furniture, also known as conventional or freestanding furniture, is the most traditional category of office furniture. It includes desks, credenzas, bookcases, file cabinets, and seating. General use furniture is further divided into case goods (such as desks, credenzas, bookcases, and file cabinets) and seating. Some designers also consider tables as case goods, while others refer to them simply as tables.

In order to assist students and other readers who may be unfamiliar with certain terms, the following definitions pertaining to furniture and seating are provided.

Furniture Items:

- Case goods: Furniture items made of "cases," such as desks, credenzas, bookcases, file cabinets, and similar pieces.
- Conventional furniture: Includes desks, credenzas, file cabinets, and bookcases.
- Credenza: A storage unit with pedestals or cabinets, providing extra storage space.
- Double pedestal desk: A desk with two drawer units.
- Executive return: An additional desk unit at the same height as the main desk.
- Lateral file cabinet: A space-efficient file cabinet, typically 18" (457 mm) deep, available in various widths.
- Pedestal: A configuration of drawers, usually 15-18" (381-457 mm) wide, found in desks or credenzas.
- Return: An additional desk unit, usually 25" (635 mm) high, that creates an L- or U-shaped desk configuration.
- Single pedestal desk: A desk with only one drawer unit.
- Table desk: A desk unit without pedestals.
- Vertical file cabinet: The traditional filing unit, usually 15-18" (381-457 mm) wide and 28" (712 mm) deep.

Seating:

- Ergonomic chair: A diverse range of desk chairs designed in various styles to enhance user comfort.
- Executive chair: A desk chair with a wider seat and taller backrest compared to typical desk chairs, often featuring fully upholstered arms.
- Guest chair: A small-sized chair used by visitors at or near a desk.
- Posture chair: A desk chair specifically designed to promote better posture and provide increased comfort.
- Sled-base chair: A guest chair with a horizontal piece of metal or wood that connects the front and back legs, making it easier to move compared to chairs with separate legs.
- Task chair (also known as a secretarial or operational chair): A compact chair, with or without arms (recessed), designed for employees performing repetitive tasks such as typing.

The arrangement and configuration of furniture for each employee can vary significantly based on their position within the office hierarchy. Typically, higher-ranking employees have larger workspaces and furniture that is larger in size and configuration. For example, the CEO would have the largest office with high-quality furniture and a greater number of items. On the other hand, a middle manager would have a smaller office with relatively lesser-quality furniture and fewer items. Let's now explore the typical furniture items found in closed offices or those furnished with case goods.

Case goods desks come in various configurations and sizes.. The arrangement and size of pedestals and potential desk returns can be tailored to meet the functional requirements of each job position, and sometimes, to reflect the employee's status. It's important to note that not all desks and desk returns are designed to accommodate computers and keyboards adequately.

Credenzas are another common type of case goods furniture found in general office settings. They primarily serve as additional storage units and are typically designed with the same width as the desk. Credenzas are usually positioned behind the desk. Despite the increased use of digital storage, many companies still maintain paper files, making file cabinets essential. Files that need frequent access are often stored in desk or credenza pedestals, while other files required by employees are kept in separate file cabinets within the office or work area. File cabinets come in various sizes to accommodate letter-size and legal-size paper. Standard vertical file cabinets are commonly used, but alternative configurations are also available.

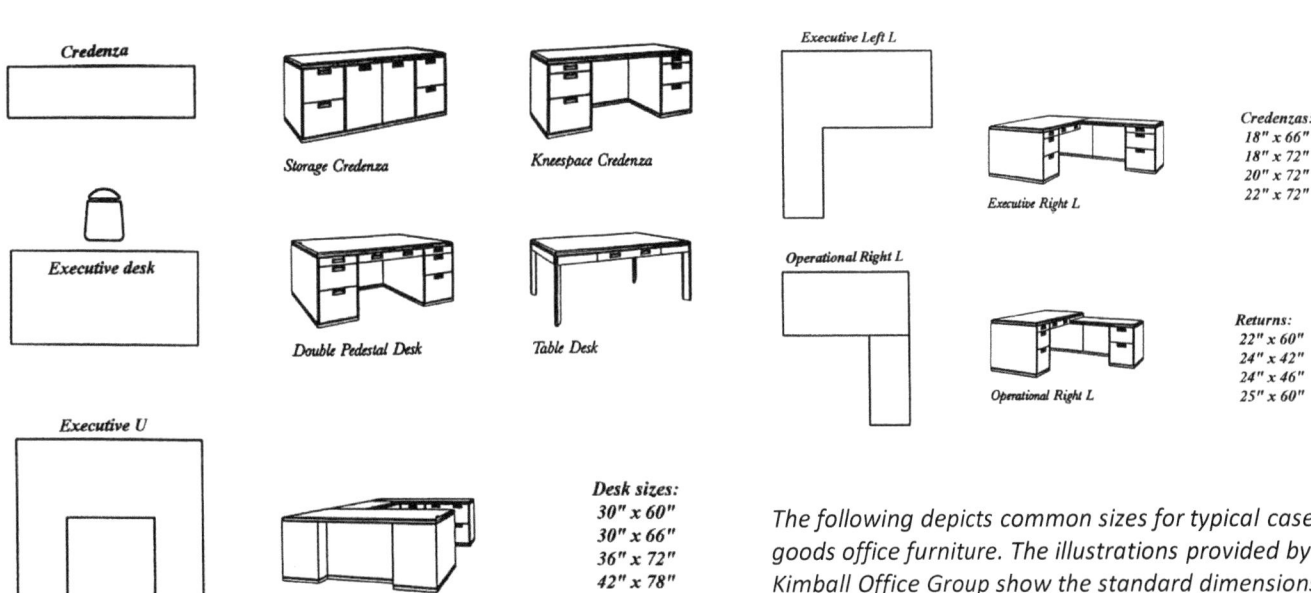

The following depicts common sizes for typical case goods office furniture. The illustrations provided by Kimball Office Group show the standard dimensions of these items.

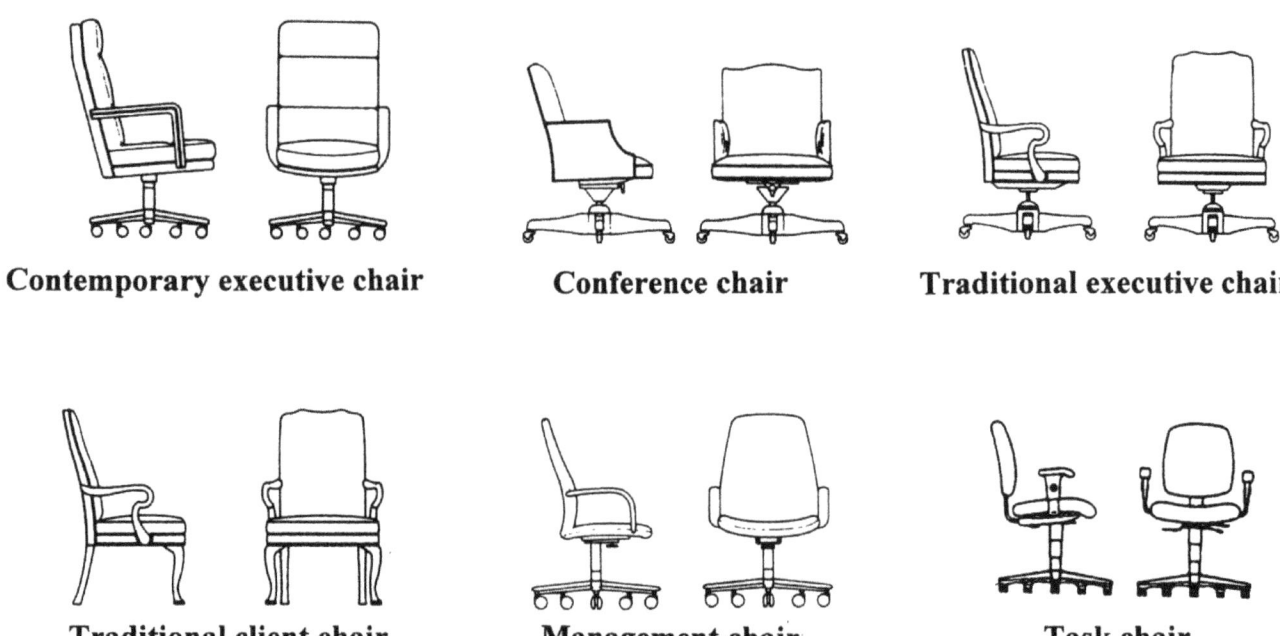

The image showcases standard office seating units available in both traditional and contemporary styles. The drawing is provided by Gunlocke.

Due to their large footprint, many designers and clients prefer to use lateral file cabinets instead of vertical file cabinets. Although they are not as deep, lateral files offer wider storage and better space efficiency. Of course, a desk chair is an essential seating piece for office workers. It goes by various names such as desk seating, posture chair, ergonomic desk chair, and more, depending on the manufacturer. Comfortable and supportive chairs are a requirement in office design, and ergonomic chairs have significantly improved comfort and functionality since their introduction in the 1970s.

There are different types of office seating available to meet various employee needs. Side chairs, guest chairs, and conference chairs are commonly used for office guests and in conference rooms. Other options include chairs designed for secretarial work, operational tasks, management positions, stools, high-back executive chairs, stacking chairs, sled-base chairs, and more. Soft seating is another category that includes lounge chairs, loveseats, settees, modular seating, and sofas, typically fully upholstered. Manufacturers offer a range of upholstery options to suit the aesthetic goals of interior designers and companies. Upholstery fabrics provided by manufacturers are guaranteed to withstand the heavy use of office seating. In some cases, with the approval of the seating manufacturer, interior designers can also use their own materials (COMs) sourced from other suppliers.

The Aeron chair is a well-liked office chair known for its ergonomic design. It comes in various sizes and configurations to accommodate different user preferences and needs.

The other category of office furniture is systems furniture, also known as open office furniture. This type of furniture is used when a company opts for an open or modified open plan for its office layout. Systems furniture consists of vertical panels that are shorter in height (not reaching the ceiling) and are combined with components such as shelves and work surfaces that are hung from the divider panels, creating workstations. To clarify the terminology related to open office systems furniture, the following terms are provided:

- Components: Individual items like shelves, work surfaces, and drawer units that are attached to or hung from the divider panels.
- Counter caps (or transaction surfaces): Used on low panels (ranging from 34 to 48 inches in height) in reception areas to create a more private transaction area across the counter.
- Divider panels: Vertical support units that form workstations and serve as the attachment points for components. The dimensions of divider panels are given in nominal measurements, with typical widths ranging from 12 to 48 inches and heights ranging from 30 to 85 inches.
- Pedestal: A set of drawers that can be attached to or stand independently from the work surface, functioning similarly to a pedestal on a case goods desk.
- Peninsula work surface: A work surface that connects to another surface at one end and extends into the workstation, resembling a desk. Storage
- shelves: Components available in different sizes, heights, and configurations, which can be open or enclosed.
- Systems creep (or panel creep): Refers to the need to account for the thickness of panels and connecting hardware when designing turns or corners in system furniture layouts.
- Systems furniture (or modular furniture): Furniture comprising of divider panels and components used to create functional workstations.
- Task lights (or shelf lights): Lighting fixtures that can be mounted beneath shelf units. Workstation: An individual work area or "office" formed by vertical divider panels and components.
- Work surface: The surface used as a desktop, available in various shapes such as rectangular, curved, corner, split-top, or curvilinear.

There is a wide range of options available in styles and configurations of systems furniture, giving interior designers ample choices to meet functional requirements, aesthetic preferences, and budget considerations. Systems furniture can be categorized into six main types, which may have different names depending on the manufacturer:

- Vertical divider panels: Simplest and most cost-effective way of using systems furniture, typically combined with freestanding desks, limited in terms of power and technology integration, and generally lower acoustic performance.
- Case goods product: Components attached to and supported by the sides of panels, creating a look similar to traditional furniture in an open plan setting.
- Modular component systems: Monolithic vertical panels that support a variety of adjustable components along their height, allowing for flexibility in customization.
- Frame and tile: Steel frame-based layout with horizontal tiles and components, offering an architectural aesthetic to the system furniture.

Other styles of systems furniture are available in the market, and manufacturers may have different names for them. It is recommended for readers to visit manufacturers' websites for more information on their specific products.

Systems furniture offers great flexibility, allowing for easy reconfiguration of workstations and adaptation to changing office technology. L-shaped, U-shaped, and open configurations provide ample surface space for equipment and paperwork. Components like overhead shelves and other accessories offer functional equipment equivalents to traditional case goods office setups in a more space-efficient manner. Open office projects are centered around divider panels that create workstations, define aisles, and provide varying levels of privacy. Depending on the product, components such as shelves, work surfaces, and file storage can be suspended from the panels. Panels also contribute to acoustic control and facilitate the distribution of electrical, telephone, and data transmission throughout the space. It is important to ensure the safe design of the station and proper use of components, following the manufacturer's instructions for open plan panel systems.

Using open plan or systems furniture comes with its own advantages and disadvantages. Here are a few key points to consider and discuss with the client.

Advantages

- Potential overall floor space savings: Workstations typically require less square footage compared to traditional built offices, allowing for more efficient space utilization.
- Lower build-out and construction costs: Fewer full-height partitions are needed, resulting in reduced construction expenses. Additionally, certain permanent mechanical systems construction can be minimized.
- Less downtime: Reconfiguring workstations requires less time compared to demolishing and constructing new hard walls, resulting in reduced disruptions to office operations.
- Flexibility: Workstations can be quickly reconfigured to meet the individual needs of employees, allowing for greater adaptability in the office layout.
- Energy savings: Open plans often lead to reduced costs for building and operating HVAC systems. Less ductwork, wiring, and other hard equipment are required during initial installation.
- Potential tax savings: Panels are considered furniture and may be subject to different accounting depreciation calculations than full-height walls.

Disadvantages

- Lack of privacy: The loss of private offices can be a concern for some projects, as open plans offer less privacy for individual employees.
- Noise: Open plans can be noisy if acoustical considerations are not properly addressed, potentially leading to reduced concentration and productivity.
- Lack of status: Workstations may have lower perceived status compared to individual offices. However, with the variety of furniture styles and finishes available today, designers can create distinctions in status within the workstation layout.
- Initial higher furniture costs: Panels and components for systems furniture can be initially more expensive compared to movable furniture and constructing walls. However, the cost-effectiveness of systems furniture increases when frequent space reconfiguration is required.

Materials, Finishes, and Color

Improvements made to the interior of an office building can significantly enhance its value for the owner. The choice of architectural finishes plays a key role in adding value to the asset. For instance, using marble floors in the executive corridors adds more value compared to carpet. When a client rents office space, the improvements made by the tenant belong to the landlord, which often leads to reluctance in investing heavily in special architectural finishes. Although the costs are borne by the tenant, the value is retained by the landlord.

Tenants typically receive an allowance from the landlord to cover specific improvements, including building standards and non-load-bearing structural elements such as partitions, plumbing, and architectural lighting fixtures. This allowance ensures some design continuity in both exterior and interior public spaces. If the interior designer wishes to deviate from the building standards or specify materials beyond the allowance, the client may approve the upgrade, with the client covering the cost difference. However, some improvements may be discouraged if they hinder the potential rental of the space to another tenant in the future.

Materials used for flooring, walls, ceilings, and window treatments must comply with applicable building codes and accessibility regulations for flooring materials. Architectural finishes must be durable and suitable for commercial use, considering the heavy wear and maintenance they will undergo. Let's examine flooring materials in more detail.

Carpeting is the most commonly used flooring material in office spaces. In certain areas such as mail rooms and storage rooms, resilient and hard-surface materials are also employed. Carpeting provides acoustic control and enhanced comfort. For high foot traffic areas and chair movement, it is advisable to select commercial-grade carpets with a tightly tufted or woven short-level looped surface that are easy to maintain. It's important to consider potential static electricity issues, which can damage computer equipment. Using carpet with static-inhibiting fibers or employing topical treatments can address this problem. Cut pile surfaces show traffic patterns more readily, unless they are highly dense carpets with a short nap. Plush surfaces can make it more challenging to move office chairs. In executive areas with lower wear, cut pile surfaces and more luxurious materials can be specified. Code requirements for carpets vary depending on the space they are used in, and compliance with National Fire Protection Association Class materials is generally necessary. It's essential for interior designers to consult the relevant jurisdiction for specific code requirements applicable to the facility.

Carpet tiles offer the advantage of creating interesting custom designs that may not be feasible with broadloom carpet. These tiles, typically tightly woven and bonded to a rubber base, can be either glued to the subfloor or installed as "free-laid" without adhesive. Carpet tiles are particularly beneficial in open-plan projects as they allow access to floor outlets and raised floor mechanical chases without causing damage. In fact, they are required when carpeting is installed over a raised floor. Carpet tiles come in sections measuring 18-24" square and can be installed with self-releasing or minimal adhesives, making them easy to replace if damaged or heavily worn. Although the initial cost of tiles is higher compared to broadloom carpet of similar quality, their versatility and practicality make them a popular choice.

Resilient and hard-surface materials, while less commonly used than carpet, find application in areas with heavy traffic, such as entrance lobbies, public corridors, and restrooms. In some cases, higher-end design specifications in executive suites may include wood, ceramic tiles, or stone flooring. Care must be taken when selecting resilient and hard-surface materials to ensure they are not slippery, posing a safety hazard. It's worth noting that these materials often require more maintenance to preserve their appearance, which can influence the flooring material selection. When it comes to materials for full-height partition walls, movable walls, columns, and other interior surfaces, their specifications are governed by their location within the project space. The applicable building codes will specify the required tests that the finish materials must pass. The specific test information can be obtained from the product manufacturer, while the codes will outline the necessary tests.

Most office partitions are built on-site, using either metal or wood studs covered with drywall that meets the code requirements based on the type of space being divided. For example, drywall used in exit corridors will have a higher rating compared to drywall used in regular office areas. Finish materials installed on exit corridor walls are also expected to meet higher ratings than those in office walls. When constructing stick-built partitions, it's important to consider the design aspect related to noise transmission. If the walls only go up to the dropped ceiling, conversations and noise can easily travel between adjacent spaces. For enhanced privacy, partitions should be built to the underside of the ceiling plenum.

Some clients opt for demountable walls as office partitions, which are pre-built partitions manufactured in specific sizes. These walls are held in place by tension through a gripper system at the bottom and attached to the T-bar in suspended ceilings at the top. Demountable walls offer the advantage of easy relocation when office space needs to be reconfigured. They can be finished with drywall and painted, but they are commonly adorned with vinyl or fabric wallcoverings that meet Class A fire code requirements. However, demountable walls do not provide significant acoustical control as they only extend to the ceiling tile. They can accommodate windows and doors, allowing for the creation of fully private offices of various sizes and configurations. Electrical and communications cables can be concealed within the wall sections, but plumbing is generally not accommodated in demountable walls due to their insufficient thickness to handle waste pipes.

When it comes to wall finishes, there are higher code restrictions and limitations on material types for walls in exit access corridors compared to walls creating private offices or conference rooms. In corridors and exit ways, only commercial-grade materials should be specified if a wallcovering is used. There is a wide variety of commercial wallcoverings available in different patterns and colors to create suitable backdrops for corridors and other partition walls in interior spaces. However, it's important to check with the local jurisdiction for any code restrictions when using textile wallcoverings. In some jurisdictions, textiles on walls may be allowed only if a sprinkler system is present or if the textile is treated with a fire-resistant chemical. Unfortunately, treating the textile with a fire-resistant chemical may alter its color to some extent. Architectural surfaces in office occupancies that are classified as businesses must meet specific classifications, such as Class A for enclosed stairways, Class B for other corridors, and Class C for other areas.

The most commonly used material for ceilings in commercial office facilities is suspended ceiling systems using fiberglass tiles. These tiles are installed in a metal ceiling grid that is suspended from the structural ceiling above. Fiberglass tiles are available in standard sizes of either 2 by 4 feet (610 by 1219 mm) or 2 by 2 feet (610 by 610 mm). Although primarily considered a background element, ceiling tiles can be specified and designed to provide design interest and can vary in their qualities of sound absorption and finish.

Mechanical systems such as HVAC ducts, electrical wiring, plumbing for fire sprinklers, and telephone and data cables are typically installed in the space between the acoustical tiles and the structural ceiling above, known as the plenum. Lighting fixtures can be easily installed by dropping them into the grid, or holes can be cut to accommodate various types of spotlights and can lighting.

In some cases, clients may opt to eliminate the suspended ceiling in certain areas and incorporate the appearance of mechanical systems into the design. While this can result in cost savings, it also means that the space will be noisier. Typically, the ceiling contributes to controlling 60 to 65 percent of sound, with 25 to 30 percent related to furniture and 5 to 10 percent to flooring. It is important to investigate and specify other factors that can enhance acoustical control to maintain a pleasant work environment.

Window treatments in commercial office interiors are often kept simple to maintain a uniform look from the outside. Vertical or horizontal blinds are the most common treatments used for this purpose. However, in areas such as executive offices, interior designers may specify fabric drapery in addition to blinds. It's important to note that local fire codes may restrict the use of textile window coverings in commercial offices unless the material meets high flame resistance standards or is treated with a flame-resistant chemical. Treating window coverings with flame-resistant treatments often alters the color and texture of the fabric.

Color plays a significant role in office interiors as it contributes to productivity and the psychological satisfaction of occupants. Interior designers have the flexibility to create various designs and calming backgrounds by utilizing color in office spaces. The Color Marketing Group (CMG) provides annual color forecasts that guide interior designers in determining emerging trends and suggesting cutting-edge design ideas to clients.

Color preferences in office facilities can vary greatly. Interior designers have a wide range of color schemes to choose from. Some businesses may have specific color standards based on corporate branding, which must be adhered to. Selecting a workable and pleasing color scheme, in conjunction with proper lighting, can enhance productivity and worker comfort. It is important to consider light reflectance factors when making color choices. Light values reflect a high percentage of light, while dark values reflect very little light. In areas with few or no windows, it is advisable to avoid dark colors. With careful planning and consideration of client preferences, almost any color combination can be successful in today's office facilities.

Mechanical Systems

The role of the interior designer in mechanical systems is primarily supportive. While the designer may provide lighting design services, in some cases, a specialty lighting designer may be involved to plan the lighting based on floor plans and equipment drawings. The designer can also specify certain elements of the equipment, but coordination with the architect or electrical contractor is necessary. In terms of electrical planning, the interior designer can create an electrical plan that indicates the locations of equipment and the requirements for outlets, switches, telephones, data units (such as computers), and other essential components. This type of plan becomes particularly important when incorporating open office systems furniture into the project.

Acoustic treatment is another aspect of mechanical systems that the interior designer must understand, especially in relation to the planning of systems furniture products. Even if the designer's involvement in the design of mechanical systems is limited, it is still essential to have a grasp of how these systems function and how they integrate into the overall office design.

This section aims to provide basic information on the design of mechanical systems in an office project. It will cover topics such as lighting design, electrical interfaces (with a focus on their impact on open plan systems products), data and telecommunications, and acoustics.

Lighting

Efforts to enhance energy efficiency in office lighting have led to a significant focus on reducing over-illumination. There are numerous options available to provide energy-efficient lighting that meets functional requirements.

When designing lighting for leased office spaces, interior designers often face challenges imposed by the building owner. The types, sizes, and even colors of lighting fixtures may be predetermined by the building standards. Upgrading these fixtures can significantly increase the costs for the tenant, who is responsible for the expenses. In such cases, the interior designer must carefully plan and specify colors, materials, and textures to create a functional and appealing space within the given constraints. The process of lighting specification begins by identifying the tasks to be performed in each area or room of the office facility. Standard lighting level guidelines, such as those provided by the Illuminating Engineering Society, are used in conjunction with this information to calculate the required lighting for different tasks and areas. Thorough research and specification of fixture types and placements are essential to achieve the desired lighting levels.

In office environments, lighting specification becomes complex due to the presence of computer monitors. Glare on monitors, which can cause eye fatigue, is a common issue resulting from light from windows or ceiling fixtures. Glare occurs when the brightness of the light exceeds the individual's visual comfort. For example, light reflecting on a computer screen from a window makes it difficult to view the screen properly. Similarly, direct ceiling fixtures that cast light downward can create challenges for office workers. This highlights the importance of the designer's careful consideration of both general and task lighting beyond simply specifying the fixtures.

Like many commercial interiors, offices typically incorporate three types of lighting to meet the needs of clients and interior designers. Ambient lighting, also known as general lighting, provides a uniform level of illumination that enables individuals to move around safely within the space. Various ceiling fixtures, including fluorescent fixtures, are commonly used for general lighting. Another approach to achieve ambient lighting is through indirect methods, where light is bounced off the ceiling from floor-standing fixtures, fixtures placed on shelves, or fixtures suspended from the ceiling, rather than directly illuminating from the ceiling. This indirect method is often employed when open plan layouts and systems furniture are utilized.

While ambient lighting serves as general illumination, it may not be sufficient for specific tasks. To address this, small movable fixtures such as desk lamps, floor lamps, or undershelf fixtures are used to provide task lighting in targeted areas. Task lighting ensures that each office worker has adequate light to work comfortably.

In larger office spaces, accent lighting may be incorporated for design purposes. Track lighting, soffit lighting, and spotlights are examples of accent lighting that add visual interest to the interior. Accent lighting can be used to highlight artwork in reception areas and conference rooms, install soffit lights in employee lunchrooms, or even serve as supplemental or primary ambient fixtures instead of fluorescent tubes. When considering accent lights, the designer must account for their contribution to the overall ambient light level.

Daylighting has gained prominence in office lighting due to the focus on energy conservation and sustainable design. Daylighting refers to the use of natural light from the sun, which enters a building through windows, skylights, or reflection off surfaces. Design plans that remove traditional full-height-wall private offices from the perimeter of the building allow more daylight to penetrate the entire office space. By factoring daylighting into the lighting load, companies may reduce the number of artificial light fixtures and modify the types of lamps used. However, daylighting has its drawbacks. Increased glare, heat from the sun through uncovered windows, unwanted reflections, and potential sun damage to furniture and finishes must all be considered when using daylight as a functional lighting source. Additionally, daylighting does not provide functional light during nighttime hours when offices need to be accessible to workers.

Electrical, Telephone, and Data Communications

In office projects that involve open office systems furniture, providing electrical, telephone, and data communications services becomes more challenging compared to closed plan setups with conventional furniture.

To understand the complexities involved, it's important to familiarize oneself with the following terms, which are applicable not only to open office systems but also to electrical services in other commercial facilities. The last three terms specifically pertain to data services:

- Access floors: Raised floors installed over a floor slab, providing space for electrical, telephone, and data cabling as well as HVAC ducts.
- Amperage: The measure of electrical current required to operate appliances or equipment.
- Armored or BX cable: Flexible cable consisting of two or more insulated wires and a ground wire covered by a flexible wound metal wrapping.
- Dedicated circuit: A separate circuit with its own hot, neutral, and ground wires that is not shared with any other circuit.
- Ethernet: A system used for connecting multiple computer systems to form a local area network (LAN).
- Flat cable: Also known as ribbon cable, it is electrical wiring flattened within a plastic material and shielded between thin, galvanized steel plates. Receptacle boxes can be attached along the flat cable strip. Flat cable is not suitable for use under broadloom carpet. Data and communications flat cable options are also available.
- Fiber-optic cable: A data cable that utilizes a thin glass filament wire for signal transmission.
- Local Area Network (LAN): A telecommunications network designed to prevent signal interruptions, typically confined to a small area such as a single building.
- Nonmetallic sheath or Romex cable: Two or more insulated wires covered by a nonmetallic, moisture-resistant sheath for electricity transmission.
- Rigid conduit: A heavy steel tube used to feed insulated wires and carry electrical wiring.
- Twisted-pair cable: A basic type of phone/data cable consisting of two copper wires twisted together and shielded by an insulator.
- Wi-Fi: Short for wireless fidelity, it allows for wireless networking between computers and other devices with a wireless chip.
- WLAN: Wireless Local Area Network, which is a wireless version of LAN.

When preparing a floor plan, the interior designer is typically responsible for locating office equipment and other small electrical equipment, such as a small refrigerator. They specify the locations for outlets and switches, as well as the types of these items, to ensure compatibility with the specified office equipment. However, the extent of the interior designer's legal ability to perform these tasks depends on local regulations. The overall design of the electrical system and adherence to electrical code requirements are the responsibility of the architect and consulting electrical engineer. The interior designer's electrical plans also include the locations for data and telecommunications equipment, which will be reviewed and finalized by the company providing telephone, internet, and data services.

Commercial buildings can have either single-phase or three-phase electrical service. Single-phase service, known as 240/120 V service, is the former standard found in older commercial buildings and is still used in many new construction projects. It supports two sets of 120-volt circuits. In contrast, three-phase electrical service, known as 208 Y/120 V service, is the present standard in newer commercial buildings and supports three sets of 120-volt circuits. This difference is significant when predominantly using open office furniture systems. Three-phase service is required to fully support open office furniture, while 480 Y/277 V systems are necessary for major equipment like air conditioning. Older buildings may require rewiring to accommodate systems furniture properly.

When working with systems furniture, the interior designer needs to understand the manufacturer's methodology for integrating electrical and data communications services with the panels. The most common method is the base feed system, where a trough along the base of each panel contains separate channels for electrical conduit and telecommunications cables. Code requires the separation of communications cables from electrical wiring. Another method is the belt-line system, where outlets and channels are approximately 30 inches (762 mm) above the panel's base, allowing for plug-ins above the work surface. A vertical channel along one side of the panel brings the service from floor entries or base feeds up to the belt-line feed unit, which is connected to the building's system using various methods. It's crucial for the designer to understand the wiring integration method specified by the furniture system to avoid costly mistakes.

To properly plan the electrical system, especially for projects involving panels, the designer must be aware of the amperage requirements of common office equipment that will be placed in the workstations. Amperage levels vary depending on the type of equipment used. For example, a stand-alone printer can consume between 1.0 to 7.0+ amps, and a computer monitor can range from 1 to 2.5 amps. The designer should verify the amperage of all office equipment to be used in the workstations and coordinate this information with the architect and electrical engineer involved in the project.

Acoustics

In an office environment, noise can be a significant issue, especially in open or collaborative workspaces. Noise from equipment, telephone conversations, and both business and casual conversations can disrupt work and decrease concentration. While the mere existence of noise is not necessarily problematic, it becomes a concern when it distracts individuals from their tasks. Loud or repetitive noises are particularly disruptive to concentration. However, the intelligibility of conversations beyond one's immediate work area is especially distracting. Intelligibility refers to the ability to understand and extract information from the sounds one hears. Even a small percentage of intelligible words in a sentence can convey the meaning of the entire sentence to the listener. When intelligibility drops below a certain threshold, typically less than 10 percent, understanding becomes nearly impossible. It's important for designers of open plan offices to manage intelligibility within specified zones while reducing other sounds to tolerable levels.

Sound is measured using decibel levels or dBA (decibel A-weighting). Different sounds have different decibel levels. For example, street noise can reach 100 dBA or higher, while a noisy office might be around 60 dBA. Normal speech between two people, taking place at a distance of approximately 36 to 42 inches (914 to 1067 mm), produces a decibel level of about 65 dB at the listener's ear. This level is so common that people tend to adjust their voice level or physical distance to achieve it. You may have noticed that restaurants can sometimes be exceptionally noisy due to numerous simultaneous conversations. Sound levels below 30 dB are considered very quiet, while levels above 85 dB are very loud, making normal conversation nearly impossible. Here are a few key terms related to office acoustics:

- Decibel (dB): The unit of measurement for sound. Higher numbers indicate louder sounds. Normal conversation typically has a rating of 65 dB at a distance of 3 feet.
- Noise Reduction Coefficient (NRC): A numerical value between 0 and 1 that represents the fraction or percentage of sound energy absorbed by a material. A rating of 0 means no sound is absorbed, while a rating of 1 means all sound is absorbed.
- Sound Transmission Class (STC): A single-number rating that describes an object's ability to block the transmission of sound. An STC of 0 indicates no reduction in sound level, while an STC of 50 means very little sound passes through the object.

Professionals in the fields of interior design, acoustics, and architecture do not aim for complete silence in office spaces. They recognize the importance of maintaining some ambient noise to avoid distractions. Interestingly, when a room is completely quiet, even the slightest sound can become disruptive. The goal is to create an environment that minimizes distractions rather than eliminating all noise. To achieve acoustical control, it is essential to manage the source of sound, the path it travels, and the experience of the listener.

In open-plan projects, careful consideration should be given to the arrangement of work groups, particularly those prone to generating noise. Implementing divider panels with strong acoustical properties around individuals who tend to speak loudly on the phone can be beneficial. Additionally, when direct communication is not necessary, orienting people away from each other in open-plan settings can help. It is also advisable to keep noisy work teams separate from individuals who require a quiet environment.

To control noise, it is important to thoughtfully select flooring, wall treatments, and ceiling materials. Carpets are superior to hard surfaces and resilient materials in terms of their acoustic properties. Therefore, specifying carpets with a Noise Reduction Coefficient (NRC) of around 0.40 is recommended. In areas with full-height partitions, insulating the walls can reduce sound transmission between offices or sections. For spaces that require strict sound reduction, it is necessary for partition walls to extend up to the next floor deck, rather than just the dropped ceiling, to prevent sound from transferring through the ceiling plenum. Vinyl wall coverings have better acoustic properties compared to painted walls. Ideally, the wall surface should be covered with acoustical materials from the floor up to 6 feet above the floor. It is important to avoid using lighting fixtures that replace absorptive ceiling tiles, as they can exacerbate acoustical issues. Instead, consider using parabolic or egg crate-style diffusers rather than flat lenses. Windows are often a significant source of noise unless they are covered with fabric drapes, although this is rarely practiced. Using window walls as traffic-aisle walls, rather than incorporating them into workstations, is a preferable solution.

Additionally, masking noise can help reduce its intelligibility. Masking does not eliminate or reduce noise; rather, it increases the overall sound level in a space. This can be achieved by using a non-distracting music system or, in more challenging situations where music is not suitable, an electronic noise-generating system may be necessary to create a background sound. Such systems are used when the existing background is too quiet to mask annoying sounds or to conceal speech sounds that should not be overheard. The sound produced by electronic masking systems often resembles a hiss and is referred to as white noise. It can be adjusted to appropriate levels throughout a large space, based on the needs of nearby occupants. Planning the implementation of masking systems should be done in consultation with an acoustician.

Design Applications

This section offers insights into the implementation of planning and design concepts in office environments. It aims to provide readers with an understanding of the essential spatial requirements and functional equipment needs for private offices, employing casework furniture and various support spaces commonly found in office-based businesses. Another section delves into design considerations specific to open office systems furniture. Although the layout may vary in an open plan setting, the spatial and product requirements remain largely similar. It's important to acknowledge that due to constraints, it's not possible to address every business type or individual job function in this chapter. Additionally, a new section focuses on the design of small professional offices, as it is a prevalent project in studio design.

Closed Office Plans

The traditional closed office plan, often considered outdated in modern office planning, still holds its significance. Many high-level executives in large corporations and professionals like lawyers and accountants prefer offices designed using traditional concepts. In some organizations, these traditional planning principles are favored to denote the status and even prestige of the office occupant. Closed office plans are created using full-height partition walls, either built on-site or utilizing demountable wall systems. They cater to individuals who require private offices or enclosed conference spaces. The closed office plan provides a sense of security for employees across various businesses.

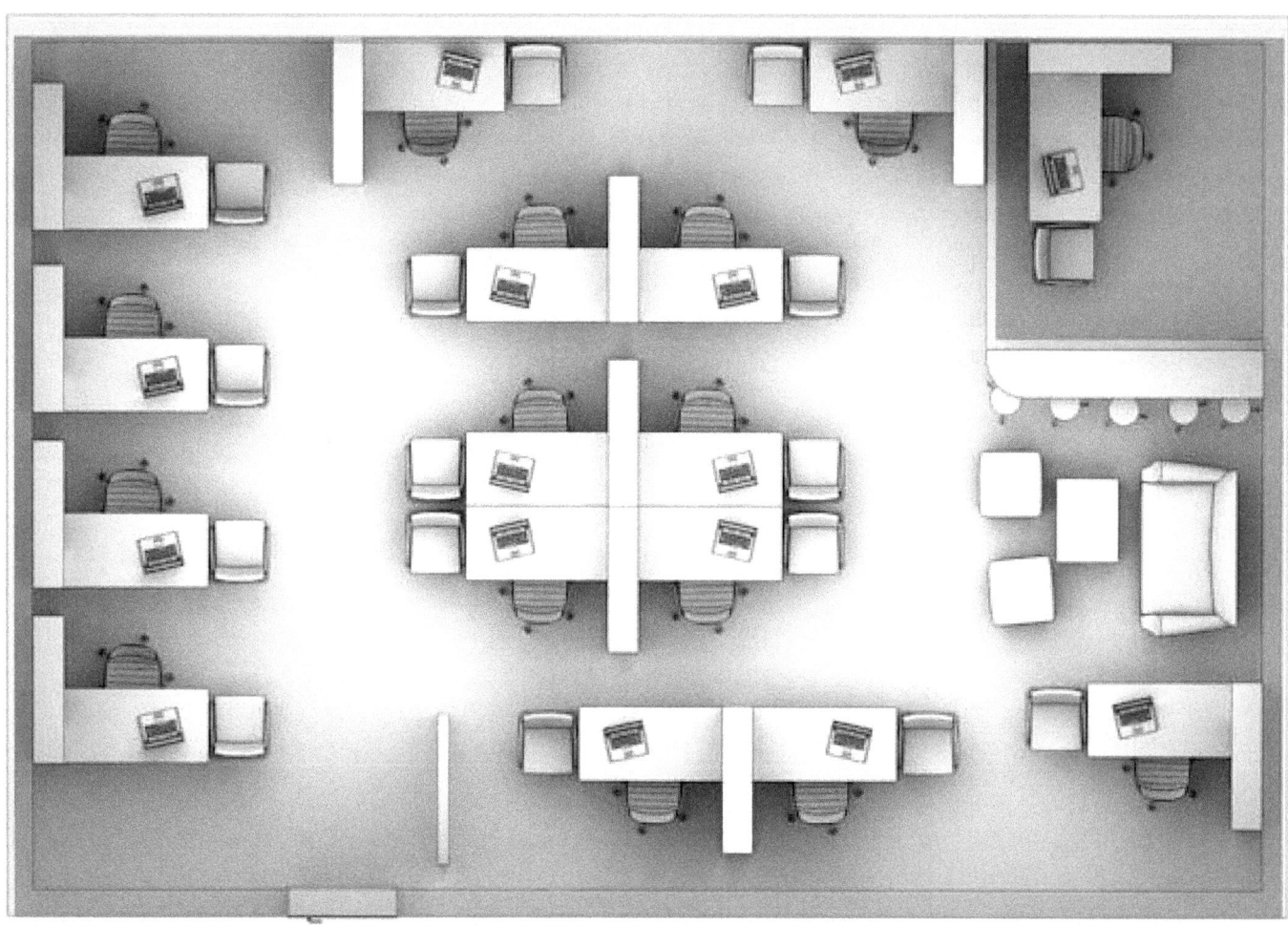

To familiarize readers with the allocation of space, furniture specification, and materials selection based on job responsibilities, a design application discussion is provided, focusing on a closed office plan. These concepts hold relevance not only for highly open and collaborative organizations but also for various other businesses. The discussion takes readers on a comprehensive journey, starting from the entry area and leading to the offices of executives or employees with whom visitors engage in business. It also includes concise design considerations for common support spaces found in general office settings. It's important to note that the discussion does not cater to specific types of professional offices, as covering the nuances of all business office variations would be impractical.

Entry Lobby

Within the premises of a large office building, an entry lobby serves as a welcoming space for visitors and often functions as the primary entry point for employees as well. Typically an open area, the entry lobby is minimally furnished, usually featuring only a security desk. However, in certain scenarios, a limited amount of seating in the form of soft seating units may be provided. Occasionally, guests may need to wait briefly in the lobby until an employee arrives to accompany them to the inner office area.

The security desk serves a specific purpose and is custom-designed as millwork. It also necessitates the inclusion of desk chairs for the security personnel, which are typically of stool height, approximately 30 inches (762 mm) high.

To facilitate easy navigation for guests, signage is installed in the entry lobby. These signs guide guests towards elevators and amenities such as coffee shops, which may be situated on the ground floor. The finishes within the entry lobby must comply with relevant codes, with a particular emphasis on the flooring's durability to withstand heavy foot traffic. Additionally, caution should be exercised to incorporate slip-resistant materials near entry doors. Incorporating a certain level of artwork seems fitting for the entry lobby, which could take the form of sculptures or appropriately sized paintings adorning the expansive walls. Smaller office buildings' entry lobbies share similar requirements, excluding the inclusion of a security desk. Some office buildings may even feature a coffee shop within the open space, necessitating a small seating area with tables.

Reception and Waiting Areas

Within business offices, a reception or waiting area serves as the designated space for receiving clients and guests, functioning as the entry point to the office facility itself. The size of the area is typically determined by the expected number of visitors who may need to wait for brief periods. A familiar comparison can be made between the spacious reception and waiting areas found in many medical office suites and the relatively modest waiting areas in small professional offices.

The design and specification of a reception and waiting area aim to create a favorable impression and introduce visitors to the business. As the size of the business increases, the reception area tends to become more elaborate. In contrast, smaller businesses may have a few chairs near the entrance. Interior designers face the challenge of creating a reception area that effectively represents the company while addressing the functional requirements of the space. To ensure security, the receptionist requires clear visibility of the entrance to the office suite from elevators or the exterior, depending on the office layout, as well as access to the back office entrance. The receptionist often juggles other responsibilities that may involve a telephone, computer, security monitors, and space for paperwork or sorting.

The furniture chosen for the receptionist must accommodate these various job functions and may include a custom-designed counter or desk in larger offices, while smaller offices may opt for a desk. Depending on the nature of the organization's business, accessibility guidelines may dictate the design of the counter. Receptionists, like most secretaries, typically have small armless chairs that can be easily pulled up to the desk or returned.

Visitor traffic from the reception area may require passage through doors into the general office space for security purposes. In some cases, such as in medical office suites, visitors may be required to approach a window within the reception area for signing in. Consequently, the receptionist is located in a separate room, distinct from the reception and waiting room. However, not all offices have this additional security measure that affects the planning process. Larger firms may position personnel offices, training rooms, and certain conference areas adjacent to the reception area, limiting the extent to which visitors can access the facility. Main corridors guide visitors from the reception area to different sections of the office facility.

It is common practice to use higher-quality furniture and materials in the reception and waiting area to establish the desired tone and image the company wishes to convey to its visitors. For small businesses, the products specified for the reception area may align with those used in other office areas rather than being upgraded. Seating units in reception areas often consist of chairs rather than sofas. Various styles of seating can be employed, ranging from the small chairs mentioned earlier to larger chairs that align with the design concept of the office complex. Additionally, a few end tables for magazines may be required, and some companies may choose to display their products in cabinets within the reception area.

Executive Offices

As businesses grow larger, executive office suites become more common for CEOs and vice presidents. Upper management in various office-based businesses, as well as owners of small professional businesses, also have their own private offices. Typically, it is the boss's or owner's office that is designed to make an impression on visitors conducting business with the firm. This section focuses on the executive office suite and the executive office itself.

An executive office suite is almost always designed as a closed plan to ensure the privacy required by these individuals. Additionally, a closed plan in this area helps create the desired status and image-focused design to impress visitors. The executive office suite is often strategically positioned on the top floor or another prime location within the building. In large corporations, it functions as a separate entity with private elevators to the executive floor, a dedicated reception area, and possibly amenities like a private dining room and lounge. In smaller facilities, business owners choose the location they consider prime, even if it means sacrificing the number of windows. The interior designer advises the client on the best location based on their specific needs and overall project goals.

Upon entering an executive office suite, visitors are greeted by a receptionist (often referred to as an administrative assistant) in a reception area. While this area may not be overly spacious, its functions are similar to any reception area in any business. It serves as a place to welcome suite visitors, provides a comfortable waiting area, and conveys a specific image. The furnishings in this area are similar to those in the main reception area, but they tend to exhibit higher style and quality. Beautiful fabrics, wall coverings, and accessories are selected to impart the desired sense of importance to the reception area. It is common for an executive suite to include a boardroom, which serves not only as a meeting space but also as a representation of the company's image and status. Boardrooms in large businesses often feature custom-designed conference tables crafted from exquisite woods, surrounded by large and comfortable chairs. Designers also incorporate projection screens, marker boards, and cabinets for beverage service and other essentials in high-level business meetings. In some cases, a separate projection room is provided behind the boardroom to house audiovisual equipment and setups for seamless presentations.

Visitors proceed through corridors to the appropriate executive office, where they are typically received by the executive's private secretary. Executive offices are often spacious, sometimes encompassing hundreds of square feet. There is no fixed standard for the offices of top executives, as they vary based on company policies and individual preferences. In a small business, the owner's office might span around 250 square feet (23.2 square meters), while larger companies may allocate at least 400 square feet (37.1 square meters) or more for the CEO. The workspace within executive offices typically begins with a desk, available in various sizes and configurations tailored to meet the functional requirements of each position. A large desk paired with a matching credenza unit, a posture chair for the executive, guest chairs positioned near the desk, a soft seating group comprising club chairs, loveseats, settees, or sofas and club chair arrangements, and additional storage units like bookcases, file cabinets, or display cabinets are commonly found in executive offices. In some cases, an executive office may also include a designated conference area. Furniture colors and styles are personalized to suit individual preferences within the executive suite.

The arrangement of furniture within executive offices is also crucial. Placing the desk to face the door, with guest seating positioned in front of it, conveys a more powerful statement compared to having the desk facing away from the door or against a wall. Alternatively, some opt for a non-power arrangement where the desk is placed perpendicular to the door. Soft seating groupings in L- or U-shaped configurations create a more casual atmosphere for conversations, while seating placed across from a coffee table contributes to a formal setting.

Color schemes in executive offices typically employ neutral tones for architectural finishes, with bolder colors and patterns utilized in upholstery. However, it's important to note that strong colors and large patterns are generally considered inappropriate for executive offices, as they are not hospitality facilities. Numerous resources delve into the specifics of hierarchy and design strategies to project power within executive offices.

Private Offices for Mid-Level Management

Now, let's explore important considerations regarding other private offices, specifically those for mid-level management staff. These individuals may also be assigned private offices with full-height walls. In smaller companies, work areas for job functions above staff positions are often situated within small private offices.

Typically, upper-level executives have an administrative assistant located just outside their office. This assistant is provided with a substantial desk or cabinet, accommodating a computer terminal similar to that of other clerical staff members. File cabinets to organize records for the executive are also commonly found. The size of other private offices can range from approximately 144 to 250 square feet (13.3 to 23.2 square meters), with variations based on job titles and company standards.

Furniture specifications for private offices generally include a desk, credenza, posture chair, and guest chairs as a minimum. At upper-management levels, options such as a conference table or a soft seating group may be added.

These offices are primarily furnished with smaller desks and credenzas compared to those provided to upper-level management. The credenza primarily serves as additional storage and is specified to have the same basic width as the desk. It is typically positioned behind the desk. Guest chairs are also necessary in this office. Mid-level managers who have frequent meetings might be provided with extra guest chairs or even a small conference table and chairs. However, it is uncommon for them to have a soft seating group.

Companies with numerous mid-level managers may introduce some variation by changing the color of fabrics on seating or the wall covering. It is not practical to specify a multitude of styles and colors throughout the facility, as the costs for individualized spaces can become prohibitive when dealing with large numbers. Office seating for executives and private offices should prioritize comfort and functionality while properly supporting the body. Manufacturers and chair designers offer a range of ergonomically designed seating options to meet the job functions and status requirements of employees at different levels.

Chairs used behind desks are typically specified with casters to allow for easier movement. Single-wheel casters are used for hard-surface floors, while double-wheel casters are more suitable for carpeted floors. Office chairs can also be specified to swivel and tilt. Guest chairs are available in various styles, offering functional and aesthetic choices. Manufacturers often provide several versions of the same chair style, enabling a single source for seating needs. When selecting upholstery, considerations should include maintenance requirements as well as aesthetics. Whenever possible, it is advisable to use fabrics offered by the seating manufacturer for optimal performance. Some seating companies may not accept customer's own material (COM) fabric, which refers to fabric that does not originate from the chair manufacturer, as the shape of the chair or fabric may not be flexible enough. Even if the fabric is accepted, the manufacturer may not guarantee the performance of COM. Specifying COM can increase the cost of seating units.

Conference Rooms

Conference rooms are essential auxiliary spaces in office complexes, regardless of whether the office is a small private company or a large conglomerate. These rooms serve as private spaces for various meetings, ranging from formal settings akin to boardrooms to more relaxed environments.

Conference rooms used for client meetings often feature higher-quality furniture and furnishings compared to those used solely by employees. These rooms serve multiple purposes, including employee meetings, training sessions, and client presentations. Generally, conference rooms are enclosed to ensure privacy and can be constructed using full-height stick-built walls or demountable walls. However, in open-plan projects, a conference space or team area may be open, without panels or walls surrounding the seating and table. This provides flexibility for the team's size, allowing it to expand or contract as needed.

The size of conference rooms varies based on their intended use. A conference room or area can be as small as 120-150 square feet (11.5-14 square meters) and comfortably accommodate four people with a small table approximately 36-48 inches (914-1219 mm) in diameter or 60 inches (1524 mm) long. As a general guideline, the designer should allocate approximately 30 square feet (2.8 square meters) per person for conference rooms that do not include storage cabinets or credenzas. The space should not feel cramped, providing ample room for the table, chairs, and circulation space. If presentations are made with a speaker standing at a podium or at the front of the room, additional space will be required. Even if a podium is not used, it is important to ensure sufficient circulation space for writing on a chalkboard or pointing at a screen.

As expected, conference rooms are furnished with tables and chairs. Round tables work well for small groups, although rectangular tables are also commonly used. In larger conference rooms, boat-shaped tables are employed. These tables resemble the plan view of a boat with flattened ends, allowing everyone seated at the table to have a clear view of one another. A common size for a rectangular table that accommodates eight people is 8 feet (2438 mm) in length, providing approximately 36 inches (914 mm) of table length per person on one side. It's important to remember that individuals will also be seated at both ends of the table. The size of the table should be proportional to the size of the chairs, with larger chairs requiring a larger table.

Chairs in conference rooms are often specified with casters or a sled base to facilitate easy movement. In more significant conference rooms, chairs may also be specified as swivel/tilt chairs to enhance comfort during extended seating. Small staff meeting rooms may have smaller chairs with fewer features compared to conference rooms where presentations to clients occur.

Depending on the purpose of the conference room or space, it may be necessary to consider and specify specialized equipment. Some examples include:

- Liquid writing surfaces, chalkboards, and/or tack boards.
- Projection screens.
- Audiovisual equipment.
- Screens and equipment for teleconferencing, including cameras, sound equipment, and monitors.
- Cabinets for storing various supplies.
- Small sink and refrigerator.
- Speaker's podium and sound system in larger conference or training rooms.

The increasing globalization of many large businesses has led to a higher demand for alternative conferencing solutions, including teleconferencing. Some manufacturers have developed specialized conference tables with data ports, pop-up screens, and other options to facilitate teleconferencing capabilities. With today's technology, teleconferencing can easily take place in workstations, offices, or conference rooms. When designing conference rooms for teleconferencing, special attention must be given to acoustics, lighting, and sightlines.

Acoustic control is crucial as sounds within the room can reverberate and make it difficult for remote participants to hear clearly. Additionally, ambient noise from outside the conference room can create challenges for those within. Therefore, these rooms should be treated as mini sound studios, with sound-absorbent materials on the walls and high-quality acoustical ceilings. Multiple lighting systems, such as recessed or surface-mounted fixtures for general lighting and dimmable spotlights for when audiovisual equipment is in use, are common lighting solutions in enclosed conference rooms. Lighting fixtures should be controlled by multiple switches and dimmers to allow for adjusting the lighting to meet occupants' needs. It's important to plan the furniture layout and lighting fixtures in a way that provides sufficient illumination on the table surface, avoiding backlighting of guests. Additional spotlights may be required for the podium or the front of the room to ensure proper visibility.

Additional Ancillary and Support Spaces

An office often requires various support or ancillary spaces that serve as workrooms or backup areas for the main office functions. It's important to note that not every office will have all of these functional spaces as separate rooms. For instance, a small office is unlikely to have a dedicated employee lunchroom. However, a designated counter area may be provided to accommodate a coffee maker, small refrigerator, and other items. While these areas are discussed within the context of a closed office plan, similar spaces will also be planned and specified for an open plan layout.

In a small or medium-sized office, a shared printer and copy machine are typically located in a storage room or along a corridor with sufficient space to accommodate the machines and allow for traffic flow. In larger facilities, strategically placed copy stations may be found throughout the space, complemented by a centralized copy center within the services core. Ample space should be allocated to accommodate the machines, as well as provide storage for supplies. This space allowance needs to consider the equipment itself, adjacent counters or tables required as work areas, and the necessary servicing space. It's also important to account for the floor space required for the machine operator and ensure adequate circulation space. The designer should consult with the client and the copy machine company to obtain specific information regarding size, weight, and mechanical systems specifications. It's worth noting that copy machines, excluding desktop models, may require a 220-volt electrical line and a separate circuit. These requirements should be clearly indicated on drawings and in the specifications.

Central filing areas are dedicated rooms that house file cabinets or filing systems for storing files that need to remain on-site. Despite the concept of the "paperless office" being discussed by design firms and office furniture manufacturers for many years, the storage of hard copy paper files continues to be a necessity for companies of all sizes. In recent times, archived files have been scanned and preserved on computer discs, with the paper files being stored in off-site storage facilities.

When planning the location of multiple file cabinets, weight becomes a crucial consideration. A building structure carries two types of loads: live load and dead load. The live load encompasses the weight of people, furniture, and equipment added to the building, while the dead load refers to the permanent structural elements of the building. It's important for the interior designer, in consultation with an architect or engineer, to estimate the total load imposed by these concentrated storage units.

To ensure the floor's structural integrity and prevent sagging or failure, the designer should obtain information on the live load limits of the floor from facilities managers, leasing agents, or the architect. If the estimated load of the concentrated storage units exceeds the safe load limits, necessary measures must be taken, such as reinforcing the floor or redistributing the storage units to multiple locations.

Another ancillary space worth mentioning is the designated area for storing resource materials. These materials, such as a law library in a law office, sample catalogs for interior designers, or advertising brochures for the marketing department, are often centralized in a dedicated resource materials area rather than being scattered throughout the facility. Similar to file cabinets, the load on the floor should be carefully considered when designing and locating these resource materials spaces.

Estimating the weight of books can be challenging due to their varying sizes. As a rough estimate, if a typical design reference book weighs around one and a half to two pounds, then approximately 15 books would weigh between 25 and 30 pounds. However, when designing spaces that house a substantial number of books, such as a law library or reference area, it is essential to collaborate with the architect to determine load limits specific to the location within the space.

Open Office Plans

Open office plans, compared to traditional case goods-oriented projects, exhibit similar spaces with some notable differences, particularly in the absence or reduction of full-height partition walls.

The conceptual planning of office and support spaces using office systems furniture remains consistent across different product lines. However, each product line has its own distinct characteristics in terms of panel sizes, component widths, and other factors that impact safe and logical planning. Even the way panels are connected to each other can affect the overall plan, as the size and thickness of panels and connectors can create a "systems creep" phenomenon. Systems creep refers to the need to account for the thickness of panels and connecting hardware whenever a panel run makes a turn. It is essential for the interior designer to seek information and guidance from manufacturers' representatives to ensure the most effective planning using the specific product.

In an open office layout, circulation space distinguishes between traffic aisles and traffic corridors. It's important to note that a corridor may be present if divider panels over 69 inches (1752 mm) in height are used on one side, while a full-height partition is used on the other side. In such cases, the corridor must have a minimum width of 44 inches (1118 mm) if the space's occupant load exceeds 50. Aisles, on the other hand, are circulation spaces between furniture items and partitions, provided that those partitions or divider panels are less than 69 inches (1752 mm) in height. The width of an aisle can be less than 44 inches (1118 mm) unless it serves a large number of occupants or needs to meet accessibility regulations. It's worth noting that in collaborative open spaces, aisles may not always be straight and may curve based on the specific requirements of the client's plan. Wider circulation spaces contribute to a more open and spacious atmosphere. The dimensions of main traffic spaces should be determined based on the occupant load and local code requirements.

In office design, there are several terms commonly used in projects involving systems furniture:

- Employee churn: Refers to turnover or movement of office staff within the organization.
- Free address: Unassigned workspaces available on a first-come, first-served basis without the need for reservations. Also known as hot desks.
- Guesting: Assigned or unassigned work area provided to a visitor from another company.
- Hoteling: System of unassigned workspaces that can be reserved by workers, similar to reserving a hotel room.
- Just-in-time: Open and flexible unassigned workstations that individuals or groups can use for varying periods of time.
- Shared assigned work areas: Workstations shared by two or more individuals, such as a secretarial station where multiple workers use the same workspace at different times.
- Unassigned office space: Office space not designated for a specific individual, available for use by any number of people on any given day. Reservations may be required.

In the market today, there is a wide range of products available for open office projects, making it impossible to discuss all the details of each product. The focus of this discussion is on planning concepts rather than specific product details, and it does not refer to any particular manufacturer's product line.

When visitors enter the office, they are typically greeted in a reception and waiting area by a receptionist. The receptionist's work area is often configured with system furniture, featuring a counter at a height of approximately 42 inches (1067 mm). This counter provides a work surface for paperwork, telephones, computer monitors, and other office equipment. The seating in the waiting area can vary, including appropriate chairs, benches, or sofas that align with the design concept and business goals in terms of the desired image.

While open offices are common, there are usually some private offices and cubicle-type workstations present. Private offices today often utilize demountable walls instead of traditional stick-built partitions. These demountable walls are full height and can be designed to match the dimensions of work surfaces and components used in open office systems. Upper-level executives in private offices may incorporate open office furniture components for their back desks instead of a traditional credenza, along with a table desk for their main workspace. Additional furniture choices in these offices depend on the client's preferences and requirements. The size of these private offices is typically similar to what was described in the section on traditional furniture planning. Ergonomic-style chairs are commonly used, and the workstation may include a small conference table and chairs or multiple guest chairs at the table desk. Other furniture pieces such as file cabinets and shelves may be included based on company policies and employee needs.

Staff offices in open office environments primarily utilize open office products. The configuration of staff workstations is determined through discussions with management and can include low panels or cubicles.

Workstations in staff areas are designed to accommodate the space and furniture items needed for each job function. In many cases, workstations are designed as typicals, meaning each category of workstation receives the same size space and components. This approach helps reduce costs as using multiples of the same product items is more cost-effective than individualized items. Some workstations may be assigned to specific employees who use them on a daily basis, while others may be unassigned stations used by employees who work remotely or have flexible work arrangements.

The size of workstations is determined based on job function and any company standards provided by the client. Staff workstations typically range from approximately 64 to 120 square feet, although larger sizes may be allocated based on specific needs and job ranks. The workstation is then furnished with the appropriate components for work surfaces, storage, and filing.

Common configurations for staff workstations include open and partially enclosed L-shaped, U-shaped, or even triangular layouts. These configurations are advantageous for placing computers in the corner and utilizing space on one or both sides of the computer for additional work areas. The shape of the workstation is defined by vertical panels, which separate the workstations. The height of these divider panels is typically low, around 42 inches (1067 mm), although they may reach up to 60 inches (1524 mm) if extra storage or partial privacy is desired. In some cases, the workstation is not fully enclosed like a traditional cubicle and may resemble an open Y-shaped configuration. However, employees usually face into the divider panel as the work surface is supported by the panels. The workstation may also include a shared side work area or table with the employee at the adjacent station. Lower panels encourage communication between employees, while higher panels provide some privacy and can accommodate storage components.

Lower panels in workstations not only facilitate communication but also allow more natural daylight to enter the office space. Small, movable conference tables can be included within or in close proximity to workstations, particularly in collaborative areas where one side of the workstation is not enclosed like a cubicle.

Divider panels come in various widths and heights to cater to employees' needs and functions. They can be fabric-covered, offering the opportunity to introduce color and patterns into the office environment. Alternatively, panels may be finished with wood laminates, selected melamine finishes, or other materials. Fabric-covered panels must meet Class A fire codes, and manufacturer-provided fabrics typically comply with these regulations. Custom fabrics may require treatment to be fire retardant.

Color and pattern can also be incorporated into workstations through tack boards, shelf covers, and seating. In some cases, panels are kept neutral, whether fabric-covered or made of hard surfaces, while color is introduced through seating materials and accessory items such as storage shelf fronts. Workstation finishes, such as wood veneer or laminates, may be specified to distinguish managers with higher status from lower-level employees. The workstation is completed with the appropriate configuration of components for work surfaces, storage, and filing.

Seating within workstations typically includes an ergonomic chair as the primary desk chair. These chairs are often specified without arms or with recessed arms, allowing workers to pull the chair closer to the desk for comfortable computer use. One or two small guest chairs are also common in workstations.

While open office configurations are prevalent, traditional cubicle planning still exists in many companies. However, modern cubicles feature lower panels, creating a more open and inviting atmosphere. Some companies and employees may choose to retain higher panels for a workstation design reminiscent of older cubicle concepts, with panels reaching approximately 58 inches (1473 mm) in height on at least two sides. Space allowances for workstations are determined based on client input, the configuration of component items required for the stations, and the designer's expertise and experience.

Collaborative spaces have gained significant popularity in office design, emphasizing teamwork and collaboration. While the concept of designing open office plans with a focus on teams is not new, the term "collaborative work" has emerged to replace "teamwork" in industry terminology. In this context, collaborative spaces refer to more open areas of workstations that provide conference, gathering, and interaction spaces for groups of employees working together on shared projects.

These spaces also serve as venues where employee interactions can foster the generation of ideas and solutions beyond the confines of specific work groups. Within the collaborative area, conference or meeting spaces can feature either lounge-type seating or traditional conference room seating, depending on the specific needs of the team. The selection of furniture and design elements in these areas is driven by the requirements and preferences of the work group.

When designing an area for a collaborative group, flexibility becomes a key concept in planning and specifying furniture. Major manufacturers of systems furniture offer a range of options designed to be flexible and customizable, catering to the needs of clients whose collaborative groups require personalized work areas and gathering spaces. To effectively plan work areas and select the necessary furniture items, it is essential for the interior designer to have a thorough understanding of how employees work.

The transition from cubicles to open collaborative workstations has brought about concerns regarding privacy, noise, and the potential loss of work focus in recent years. Some employees find it challenging to concentrate in very open workstation plans and integrated collaborative spaces. However, this doesn't mean that companies want to revert to cubicles and private offices entirely. Many companies believe that space plans emphasizing collaborative areas contribute to teamwork and the generation of ideas and solutions while also saving on square footage compared to cubicle plans with aisles. For many companies, a blend of collaborative spaces and areas that offer privacy, although not necessarily in the form of private cubicles or offices, provides the best of both worlds.

Today's office environments come in various configurations. Some companies remain hesitant about using office systems furniture due to concerns about its "industrial look." Others recognize the economic advantages and fully embrace the product. There are also those who see that the open office has evolved into a furniture product and planning process that aligns with the needs and technological work styles of the younger workforce. The interior designer's role is to understand these different approaches to office work, the availability of products, and the business goals of each client to create the most effective office space.

Designing a Small, Professional Office

The role of a commercial interior designer specializing in offices often involves designing small, professional offices for various types of professionals such as accountants, lawyers, consultants, real estate brokers, insurance agents, and architects, among others. While these offices can vary in size, this discussion will focus on an office space of approximately 3000 square feet (279 square meters) that is leased.

The specific space requirements and layout will depend on the nature of the office functions and the type of professional practice. It is important to consider that these offices are often small businesses owned and operated by the entrepreneur who started the business. They can also be satellite branches of larger corporations. Due to limited financial resources for leasehold improvements and furniture, cost-effectiveness is a key consideration for this type of facility. Functionality, efficient space utilization, and budget-conscious design and specifications are the primary concerns in designing an office for an entrepreneurial professional.

In a typical small, professional office, the following spaces are commonly included:

- Reception/waiting area: This is the entry point for clients, either directly from outside or from a building corridor. The reception area usually requires an allocation of approximately 144-180 square feet (13.4-16.7 square meters). It typically includes a reception desk, a few waiting chairs, end tables, and possibly display shelves or cabinets.
- Secretary/receptionist area: In a small office, the receptionist is often situated within the reception/waiting area rather than having a separate closed space. The receptionist's workspace should include a desk, space for a computer monitor and keyboard, and one or more file cabinets. It is important to ensure that the desk placement allows the receptionist to face the entry door.
- Principal's office: This is the office of the business owner or principal of the company. The size of this office may vary depending on the needs and preferences of the owner.
- Additional professional offices: There may be one or two offices allocated for other professionals who work as employees in the office. The size and number of these offices will depend on the specific requirements of the professionals and the nature of their work.
- Small conference room: Depending on the specialty of the office, a small conference room may be necessary. This space allows for meetings with clients or internal discussions. The size of the conference room will depend on the anticipated number of participants and the desired layout.
- Storage area: The office should include space for storage of supplies, a copy machine, file cabinets, and refreshment supplies. These can be accommodated in a single space or separate areas based on client preferences.
- Restroom facilities: At least one unisex accessible toilet facility should be provided within the office suite to comply with accessibility requirements.

In terms of circulation planning, there is typically one main corridor that leads from the reception/waiting area to the other offices and spaces in the suite. This corridor should meet building codes and accessibility regulations. In some cases, the corridor may include alcove spaces for shared amenities such as the copy machine, coffee area, or wireless printer. However, these functions can also be allocated to separate spaces based on the client's preferences and overall space allowances.

The office space allocated for the owner or principal of the business is typically the largest in size, ranging from approximately 144 square feet (13.4 square meters) to the desired size determined by the owner. The furniture in this office is typically of mid-price range and includes essential items such as a desk, credenza, posture chair, guest chairs near the desk, a computer cabinet, and additional file cabinets and shelves as needed. In larger offices, a small conference table with a few chairs may also be included.

In some cases, a second secretary may be required just outside the owner's office. This space will need to accommodate a desk or return for the computer monitor and keyboard, necessary filing cabinets and shelves, and a desk chair. Unlike the reception area, a guest chair is not usually needed for the secretary in a small, professional office. The arrangement of furniture in the office can vary based on personal preferences. Some owners prefer to position their desk so that they face the door, while others may opt for a layout facing windows if available. This layout preference should be discussed and determined during the programming phase.

The office for the second professional will generally be smaller than the owner's office, unless they are a business partner with equal status. In that case, both offices may have similar sizes. The furniture items needed will be similar if they are a partner, and slightly different if they are an employee. The essentials include a posture chair behind the desk, two guest chairs, a credenza, space for the computer, a file cabinet, and other storage items as required for the position.

It's important to note that office furniture layouts can be customized to meet the specific needs and preferences of the client, and furniture choices can be adjusted based on the budgetary considerations of a small, professional office.

If the client chooses, both the offices and the secretaries' work areas can be specified using system furniture. These components can be freestanding or wall-mounted and may include freestanding table desks or desks. The selection of finishes for the system furniture can be strategically chosen to create an executive look if desired. For the conference room, the space will typically accommodate a conference table seating four to six people, requiring a minimum of 144-150 square feet (13.4-14 square meters). The actual size will depend on the style and size of the chairs and table specified. Chairs on casters are commonly used, but other styles such as leg-based or sled-based chairs can also be suitable. A credenza or storage cabinet is appropriate for storing materials, and a marker board with a ledge can be useful for presentations. The specific items in the conference room will vary based on the type of office services provided.

During the programming phase, the designer will discuss size requirements and furniture preferences, including guest chairs, upholstery, and color choices. Furniture items for small professional offices are typically budget to mid-priced, with a range of styles from traditional to contemporary based on client preferences. While high-end items are less common, certain clients may require them based on the nature of their business. In terms of mechanical systems, the interior designer's responsibility mainly involves specifying lighting beyond the standard architectural ceiling lighting. Task lights for desk work and decorative lighting options can be considered in the reception area and conference room. The specific lighting choices will depend on the type of professional and the client's willingness to deviate from building standards.

The designer should research code restrictions for walls and floors based on whether the office suite is in a freestanding building or a multi-story office building. The designated building standard materials for wall and floor finishes will meet code requirements. Modifications to these finishes must also comply with code regulations if the designer encourages the client to upgrade to higher quality and more visually appealing options. In small office spaces, finishes are typically standardized throughout the office, except for the owner's office where different wall coverings or upgraded flooring may be approved. Durable, low-level loop carpeting that is glued down is ideal for withstanding chair casters and high traffic, while carpet over padding can be an upgrade for the owner.

The designer should also encourage the use of upgraded sustainable products for finishes and upholstery. Building standards may not include low-VOC paints and nontoxic glues for carpeting, so it is important to prioritize environmentally friendly options. Achieving LEED status may be challenging for a small professional office housed in a leased space within an office building, as many sustainability factors are beyond the client's and interior designer's control. However, incorporating sustainable practices and materials to the extent possible is still beneficial.

Home Offices

Designing a home office requires thoughtful planning and consideration, as it blends residential and commercial interior design principles. Here are some key tips to keep in mind:

- The location of the home office within the house will determine the level of interaction with family issues during work hours. Ideally, it should be in a separate bedroom or a private space to minimize distractions.

- Image is important even in a home office. If clients visit the home office, it is advisable to use higher-quality furniture and furnishings to create a professional impression.

- Furnish the home office with standard office furniture that meets functional needs and budget constraints. Some clients may opt for custom cabinets and desks, while others may prefer commercial furniture at an appropriate price point.

- In the case of employees working from home, the company may provide furniture and other office products for the home office setup.

- Effective space planning is essential to accommodate necessary office furniture and equipment in the home office.

- Ergonomic adjustable chairs are crucial for maintaining proper seated posture, even in a home office where long hours of work are common.

- Light and neutral colors are recommended for home offices, as they create an open and less confining atmosphere in typically small rooms filled with furniture and equipment. Choose colors and materials that enhance the office space without creating discomfort.

- Retrofitting electrical, telephone, and internet services may be necessary in older homes. Consider installing a dedicated circuit for the computer to protect against power surges.

- Task lighting is essential to ensure adequate lighting in work areas within the home office.

When transitioning an office to a home setting, it is important to consider applicable codes and regulations. Building codes generally do not impact a home office unless it is located in a converted garage or an addition to the house. However, homeowners' associations and local laws may impose restrictions on running a business from a residential property. It is crucial for homeowners to research and comply with these regulations, and designers should also investigate zoning and building code restrictions before undertaking a home office project.

RETAIL FACILITIES

Retail stores are constantly being built or renovated to cater to the needs of consumers. Whether independently owned, part of a retail chain franchise, or owned by corporate groups, these stores rely on effective interior design to drive their success. The design and layout of a store are crucial in guiding customers through the space, showcasing the merchandise in the best possible way, and ultimately encouraging them to make purchases.

To create an effective retail interior design, it is important for designers to have a thorough understanding of the client's business. While personal shopping experiences can provide inspiration, they are not sufficient for creating a functional and successful retail design solution. This chapter aims to provide an overview of the key considerations and methodologies involved in planning and designing a retail store. The focus is on functional design elements that contribute to a positive customer experience.

A retail store's primary goal is to sell merchandise to the end user or ultimate consumer. This chapter follows a similar structure to previous chapters, starting with an overview of the retail business and then delving into generic planning and design elements. Additionally, design application discussions for a clothing store, gift store, and jewelry store are included to provide further insights into the design process for specific types of retail spaces.

Retail Business Operations

The success of a retail facility's design relies heavily on the designer's understanding of the client's business and the operations of the retail industry as a whole. Retail operations are multifaceted and go beyond creating an attractive environment to showcase products. Therefore, interior designers should not make final design decisions without considering the background information about the client's specific business.

The primary goal of retailing is to attract customers and generate sales, regardless of the type of products being sold, whether it's jewelry, clothing, or tires. The design and layout of a retail store are intended to guide customers through the space, helping them easily find and purchase goods. Retailers have specific concerns that include allocating sufficient space for merchandise display, preventing theft, minimizing liability risks, cultivating a favorable brand image, and fostering business growth.

While the design of a retail facility is crucial, marketing and merchandising also play vital roles in the success of a retail business. To better understand the business side of retail and its connection to interior design, here are some key terms commonly associated with retail operations:

- Hard goods: Heavy merchandise typically made of metal or wood, such as furniture, appliances, and sporting goods, also known as hardlines.
- Marketing channel: The network involving producers, wholesalers, retailers, and consumers that facilitates the flow of goods or services from the producer to the final consumer.
- Marketing concept: The belief that the primary goal of every business is to meet consumer needs while

generating a profit.
- Merchant: An individual or entity that buys and sells commodities for profit, including vendors who sell to retail sellers or stores.
- Retail sale: The purchase of a product by the ultimate consumer.
- Retailer: A middleman merchant who primarily sells goods to the end consumer. Retailing: The business activity of selling goods or services directly to the final consumer.
- Soft goods: Lightweight and soft merchandise, such as clothing, linens, towels, and sheets.

When determining which products to offer for sale, merchants take into account various factors. Firstly, they consider the benefits that consumers seek in products. Secondly, they assess whether the products satisfy physiological, safety, or psychological needs. They also evaluate the advantages of supplementary services, such as delivery, installation, and alterations, that can enhance the customer experience.

Consumers' purchasing decisions are directly influenced by their needs and wants. Needs refer to essential physiological and psychological requirements necessary for their well-being. Physiological needs are crucial for survival and basic comfort, such as food, clothing, and housing. Safety needs pertain to security and stability, such as a cellular phone or a car alarm. Esteem needs are related to self-respect, admiration, and achievement, and the goods that fulfill these needs vary depending on the consumer's background. Examples of esteem-need goods include antique furniture, a new car, or designer jewelry.

Wants, on the other hand, are conscious desires to acquire objects that promise some form of reward. Many goods that satisfy esteem needs can also fulfill wants.

Understanding these needs and wants is essential for store owners to determine their product offerings and develop a retail plan that aligns with the overall design concept and feasibility study. The retail plan encompasses activities crucial for successful business operations, answering questions regarding what, when, where, why, and how specific retail activities will be accomplished. It considers the right message, appeal, and services as part of the retail planning process.

The retail plan consists of five important stages:

1. Defining retail environments.
2. Controlling financial, organizational, human, and physical resources.
3. Identifying and selecting retail marketing and sites.
4. Developing and managing products.
5. Creating and implementing promotion strategies.

The retail plan also guides the conceptual interior design of the store, similar to the design concept used in hospitality projects. It is crucial for the interior designer to understand the underlying philosophy of retail planning for each project to deliver an effective interior design for the facility.

Store owners or management teams are responsible for developing the merchandise blend, finding the best location, operating the store, and managing various aspects such as purchasing, pricing, controlling, and promoting merchandise. They also provide the interior designer with ideas for the store's interior design. Current interior store design focuses on creating a streamlined and organized ambience with wider aisles, better sight lines, and the use of flexible fixtures, moving away from the earlier approach of crowded merchandise displays. Collaborating with the store owner, the interior designer considers how the store's environment will influence customers and encourage purchases. The store's image plays a significant role in attracting customers to the merchandise within a specific setting. The store's image encompasses its location,.

interior design, product presentation, pricing, and public relations. The interior design helps set the stage for merchandise presentation and creates an appropriate image that aligns with the type of products offered. For instance, the interior design of a luxury jewelry store would differ significantly from the jewelry section of a large retail chain. In addition to specifying finishes, colors, and graphics, the interior designer's space planning of fixed and flexible merchandising areas influences sales and contributes to the store's overall image.

An emerging trend in retail design and business is the incorporation of experiential opportunities. Experiential retail focuses on creating experiences for customers, allowing them to interact with and experience the merchandise firsthand. It goes beyond simply viewing products and offers customers the chance to touch, hold, and engage with the merchandise in the actual environment where it will be used.

Traditionally, customers have been able to touch and hold certain types of merchandise like clothing. However, the shift is occurring in the environment where the merchandise is being sold. Retailers are recognizing the importance of the interior environment in setting the stage for the purchase and enhancing the overall shopping experience. For example, in a food store, enticing odors from baked goods or the deli section can tempt customers to make impulsive purchases beyond their shopping list. Grocery stores often provide free samples to encourage customers to try specific products, creating an experiential opportunity that can lead to a purchase. Sporting goods stores like Cabela's may have features like climbing walls, allowing customers to test products or walk around in boots to assess their fit. These interactive elements enable customers to see and experience the products firsthand.

Theme appeal is another design approach used in retail stores. It involves creating an environment that directly relates to the product, holidays, or special events. Examples include the use of Christmas decorations and seasonal displays in stores, as well as special displays tied to local events. By aligning the store environment with a specific theme, retailers can enhance the overall shopping experience and create a sense of excitement and engagement for customers.

Indeed, creating a cohesive and effective design for a retail store requires careful consideration of all the factors involved, including the retail plan, the merchandise being sold, and the overall brand image. The design must effectively communicate to customers that this store is the right place for them to make their desired purchases, whether it's a camera, jewelry, clothing, or any other item.

The physical appearance of the store, including its location and design, should complement and enhance the presentation of the merchandise. Any disconnect or mismatch between these elements can negatively impact the store's profitability and potentially lead to its downfall. Therefore, it is crucial for interior designers to have a deep understanding of the retail business before embarking on the design process.

Before engaging in specific space planning or design specification activities, designers must familiarize themselves with the merchandising methodology of the retail store. This involves gaining knowledge about the store's target customers, the desired shopping experience, the product displays and arrangement, and the overall brand identity. By understanding these key aspects, designers can align the interior design with the retail strategy, ensuring that the store's layout, aesthetics, and functionality support the desired shopping experience and effectively showcase the merchandise.

The interior designer's role is not only to create an aesthetically pleasing space but also to contribute to the success of the retail business by designing an environment that attracts and engages customers, encourages purchases, and enhances the overall brand image. A thorough understanding of the retail business is vital in achieving this goal and avoiding any potential mismatch between the design and the merchandising strategy.

Types of Retail Facilities

Retail stores can be categorized based on the type of merchandise they sell and their operational characteristics:

- Single store: An independent store selling a specific product or range of products from a single location.
- Chain store: A retail store with multiple locations, either independently owned or owned by a larger chain, and can be managed locally. It may also operate as a franchise store.
- Department store: Retail stores offering a wide variety of brands and products. These stores often serve as anchor stores in shopping centers or malls and may have dedicated sections for specific brands or product categories.
- Magnet store: Well-known chain stores that attract a large number of customers to malls or shopping centers. They are also referred to as anchor stores.
- Hypermarket: Large retail stores spanning over 200,000 square feet (18,581 square meters) and offering a diverse range of general merchandise and/or food products. Although some hypermarkets are discount stores, not all fall into this category.
- Supermarket: Large stores primarily focused on selling groceries and household items.

The single store model is relatively straightforward, with the owner working directly with the interior designer. The design choices can vary as they are based on the owner's preferences and vision. Chain and franchise stores have specific design policies established by corporate entities, and designers may have more restrictions in their design process. Department stores create appealing environments to showcase merchandise, and some incorporate dedicated sections for particular brands. Hypermarkets, such as Walmart and Target, have a significant impact on retailing by offering a wide range of products in open and simple store layouts. Warehouse stores, like Costco, which require membership, also fall under the hypermarket category.

Understanding the characteristics of each retail store type helps interior designers create effective designs that cater to the specific needs of the business and enhance the overall customer experience.

There are various other types of retail stores that are worth mentioning, including boutique and specialty stores, dealerships, and supermarkets. Boutique and specialty stores typically have a smaller footprint and focus on a specific product niche, while dealerships refer to stores that specialize in selling certain types of products, such as automobiles or electronics. Supermarkets, on the other hand, are larger stores that primarily sell groceries and household items.

Retail stores can also be classified based on their location. One type is the freestanding or stand-alone store, which is housed in a single building and can sell a wide range of merchandise. Many retail stores are located within shopping centers, which are collections of retail stores often accompanied by offices. Some shopping centers are referred to as strip centers because they are built in a linear fashion rather than clustered around a central courtyard.

Shopping centers are often developed as mixed-use properties that combine retail stores with food service facilities, offices, and other service providers. They can serve as community gathering places, especially when located near residential areas. Some shopping centers in urban areas may even include hotels. In recent years, there has been a focus on redeveloping existing properties and revitalizing shopping centers.

Another trend is the development of large regional shopping centers that feature a wide variety of specialty stores along with one or more anchor stores. These regional centers attract customers from a broad area and often include amenities such as sports facilities, movie theaters, and entertainment venues. The design of these centers incorporates landscape and hardscape features to create an inviting environment. Adequate parking and access to public transportation are important factors in attracting customers to regional shopping centers.

Malls are similar to regional shopping centers but are typically enclosed. They offer a comprehensive range of shopping services and amenities, including specialty stores, anchor stores, food service facilities, and entertainment venues like movie theaters. Larger regional malls in suburban areas often feature multiple anchor stores and a greater variety of specialty stores. Some regional malls may also include hotels and recreational facilities on the outskirts of the mall.

Open-air village concepts have gained popularity as a retail shopping option. These projects emulate small-town business districts, with shops lining narrow streets. Parking may be located in front of or behind the stores, reminiscent of old-town shopping areas. Pedestrian paths, plazas, and town squares are common features of these retail centers, which may also incorporate spaces for offices, community services, dining, and entertainment.

In addition to these traditional retail options, there are newer nontraditional options that cater to consumer convenience. Pop-up stores are temporary retail spaces that exist for a limited period, often seen during seasonal events like Halloween. Kiosks have become prevalent in shopping malls and other retail locations. E-tailers are businesses that operate online, allowing customers to shop through online ordering, catalogs, or television. While these nontraditional options may not typically involve the hiring of interior designers, they are worth mentioning as alternative business models in the retail industry.

Planning and Interior Design Elements

The design of a retail store is influenced by the merchandise it sells, the target market, and the price point of the products. Different age groups and consumer segments have varying preferences and purchasing power, so the layout, materials, and colors used in a store catering to younger buyers will differ from those used in a store targeting older buyers. It is essential to consider the needs and preferences of different generations, including the influential baby boomer generation, when designing retail spaces.

Luxury boutique stores selling high-end products require a distinct design approach. These stores use upscale materials, sophisticated lighting techniques, and carefully planned layouts to create an environment that exudes elegance and extravagance. The installation of expensive materials may require specialized project management to ensure flawless execution. On the other hand, small, budget-priced stores may not use expensive materials but should still aim to create a cohesive design that complements their merchandise.

This section provides an overview of the fundamental planning and design elements for small retail stores, which can also be applied to larger stores. The specific nature of the store's specialty will influence how these elements are implemented. The section covers concept and feasibility studies, store merchandising, sustainable design, security, building codes, space allocation, traffic patterns, furniture selection, materials and finishes, and mechanical systems. These topics are essential considerations in creating functional and visually appealing retail spaces.

Retail Store Exterior Design

The exterior design of a retail store plays a crucial role in attracting customers and making a positive first impression. Whether seen from the street or within a mall, the storefront should capture attention, showcase the products effectively, and maximize visibility of the selling areas. Several design concepts contribute to the exterior appearance of the store, including the overall architectural design, entrance design, store window displays, and signage.

The configuration of the storefront greatly influences its ability to draw customers into the store. The straight front configuration is common and provides ample display windows, allowing shoppers to easily see inside. Another popular configuration is the angled front, where the two windows closest to the entrance are angled to guide window shoppers towards the doors. The arcade front features recessed windows, increasing the window display area but slightly reducing the interior selling space.

Each configuration offers its advantages. The straight front maximizes selling space while still allowing for window displays. The angled front provides multiple views of displayed merchandise, reduces glare, and enhances visibility. The arcade front increases the store's window display area, attracting attention with its recessed windows.

The entrance door of a store is an opportunity to brand and market the business. Stores often place logos on doors to help identify themselves. The number of entrance doors required depends on the store's interior footprint and compliance with local codes. Store window displays are essential in enticing customers. Apparel shops often utilize large windows to showcase clothing on full-sized mannequins. Jewelry stores, on the other hand, may prefer smaller display windows, placed at eye level, to showcase smaller objects. Some retailers combine merchandise displays with a view into the store's interior, using ramped windows that have a higher display floor in the back, creating a wedge or tiered shape. This approach is common in shoe and accessory stores.

Store signage is another key element in attracting customers. Store signs have a long history of helping customers identify the type of merchandise available from a particular merchant. Many signs incorporate the store name along with the type of products being sold, while others rely on strong branding to instantly convey the merchandising concept. Chain stores often have standardized signage and logos that ensure instant recognition. Smaller stores also aim to design their signage in a way that helps customers understand their product offerings, whether it be gifts, clothing, or auto parts.

Retail Store Exterior Design

To increase the chances of success for a new retail store, conducting a feasibility study and developing a concept are important business tactics. This process is similar to feasibility research conducted for other commercial facilities and helps the store owner gain a clearer understanding of their concept and its potential reality. By being proactive in assessing risks and rewards, the owner can make informed decisions.

The feasibility study begins with the ideas and vision of the store owner, which are then expanded upon by the interior designer. In larger facilities like department stores, the involvement of a consultant may be necessary. Unlike feasibility studies for other commercial interiors, the product mix is crucial to the success of a retail store. Extensive marketing and merchandising research is necessary to identify the products that will attract customers and entice them to visit the store. Some key topics that should be researched and studied include:

- Business idea (e.g., clothing, gifts, jewelry)
- Product mix and price point
- Target customers and their demographics
- Competition in the market
- Potential customer traffic flow
- Demand for products in the desired location
- Type of service offered (full or self-serve)
- Store location
- Merchandise display strategies
- Budget allocation for fixtures, interior finishes, initial inventory, and technology.

Engaging in "retail store research" is essential. This involves visiting and observing existing stores, as each store has its own story to tell the customer. The entrance, materials, finishes, colors, fixtures, and lighting choices all contribute to the narrative. The type of products, their price points, and the level of customer service provided by the sales team also convey important messages. While retail research should not be the sole means of learning about retail design, it should be recognized as a valuable tool in the designer's toolkit.

Store Merchandising

The planning and interior design of a retail store are greatly influenced by the type of merchandise being sold and the target customers. The specific mix of merchandise impacts the layout of the store, including traffic paths, display fixtures, architectural finishes, and furniture choices. Different layouts, display methods, and fixtures are required to showcase jewelry, clothing, or sporting equipment.

There are key terms associated with store merchandising that are important to understand:

- Merchandising: The overall sales promotion activities, including market research, product development, manufacturing coordination, effective advertising, and selling.

- Merchandising blend: The combination of the retailer's merchandise and the decision-making process used by consumers in making their selections.
- Non-selling space: Areas in the store not designated for direct merchandise display or sale, such as the stockroom and store office.
- Selling space: The designated area for displaying merchandise and facilitating interaction between customers and store personnel.
- Vignette: A display of furniture and accessories that is created to resemble an actual room.
- Visual merchandising: The presentation of merchandise in store windows and other locations within the selling space.

Merchandise is often categorized into three types: demand, convenience, and impulse. Demand merchandise refers to necessary items that drive people to shop, such as clothing or furniture. Convenience items are regularly used products, like hosiery or lamps, while impulse items are unplanned purchases often displayed at the point of purchase, such as candy at a grocery store checkout counter.

When allocating space for merchandise, the interior designer should be aware of two approaches: the model stock method and the sales/productivity ratio method. The model stock method determines the floor space required to stock a desired amount of merchandise, while the sales/productivity ratio method allocates selling space based on sales per square foot for each merchandise group. The retailer decides which approach to use, and it directly influences the placement and space planning of fixtures and the arrangement of merchandise in the store.

Visual merchandising plays a significant role in promoting sales once customers are in the store. It involves displaying merchandise in store windows and other areas within the selling space. Visual merchandisers or display designers are hired to handle this aspect of merchandising. A talented and creative display designer can attract customers based on the reputation of their show windows and displays.

Visual display is a powerful tool in merchandising that serves multiple purposes. It not only generates interest and exposure for products but also enhances their visual appeal, provides information, facilitates sales transactions, and ultimately boosts sales. In addition, many merchandising displays can double as storage space, utilizing backup stock within the display itself. Visual merchandising plays a crucial role in creating a store's image and brand identity, effectively functioning as a form of non-media advertising.

For interior designers, working as visual merchandisers presents an excellent opportunity to rapidly develop and expand their portfolio. It is particularly beneficial for entry-level designers seeking to gain valuable work experience and accumulate a diverse range of portfolio items.

Sustainable Design

In retail store design, sustainable efforts can be focused on energy efficiency, water conservation, and the use of environmentally friendly materials. While certain aspects of building construction systems are beyond the control of the interior designer, there are opportunities to make an impact in terms of energy conservation and interior finishes.

Common fixtures in retail stores, such as cabinets, shelving units, and storage units, are often constructed using materials that may off-gas toxic fumes, such as plywood and laminate finishes. However, custom-made display cabinets and fixtures can be created using green products and techniques. Exploring materials that do not produce toxic fumes is important for these types of products. In some cases, metal shelves can be a suitable alternative. However, it's essential to consider the appropriateness of materials based on the nature of the store and the target market. For instance, metal shelves may not be suitable for a store selling high-end luxury products.

Repurposed materials have gained popularity in store designs, such as using barn wood as paneling in a sporting goods store. Mosaic wall treatments and repurposed furniture pieces are other examples. Resources like GreenSpec from BuildingGreen can help designers find environmentally friendly products for their projects.

The Forest Stewardship Council (FSC) certification ensures that wood comes from responsibly managed forests. Using FSC-certified wood for paneling and furniture items promotes sustainability in retail store design.

Green interior design treatments often include exposed concrete flooring, unfinished ceilings, and the use of low-VOC (volatile organic compounds) paints for walls. Selecting low-VOC flooring materials and adhesives, as well as energy-efficient lighting fixtures with compact fluorescent lamps (CFLs) or LED lamps, contribute to energy and lighting efficiency in retail settings.

In retail, there are customers who prioritize purchasing green or natural products and are willing to pay extra for them. Stores that embrace green design and sustainable concepts can attract environmentally conscious consumers. Examples of successful retailers with a focus on sustainability include REI for sporting goods and Whole Foods for groceries.

LEED (Leadership in Energy and Environmental Design) certification provides a framework for designers to meet sustainable design specifications for retail stores. Information about LEED for Retail can be found on the U.S. Green Building Council website under the Building Design and Construction category.

Security and Safety

Security and safety are essential considerations in retail store design, both for the customers and the store owners. Customers want to feel safe when visiting any type of store, regardless of its size. Security measures such as security cameras and other devices can help deter potential robbers and create a sense of safety. Architects and designers play a crucial role in designing retail spaces that prioritize customer safety and security.

Store owners also need to implement their own security measures to prevent theft and shrinkage (loss of inventory). Shoplifting and employee pilfering are common concerns in retail, and various security measures can be utilized to address these issues. Examples include placing large convex mirrors in blind corners, having employees walk through the store to maintain customer contact, employing fitting room attendants, implementing procedures to limit the number of items in fitting rooms, and designing display fixtures that do not obstruct visual control from the cash register. Careful layout planning can also prevent high-priced items from being located too close to the front entrance where they are more vulnerable to theft.

Video surveillance systems are widely used in retail stores, regardless of the merchandise being sold. These systems allow store owners to monitor activities throughout the store, particularly areas such as the cash register and where high-value items are displayed. Video surveillance can also extend to the parking lot to provide customers with a sense of security, especially during nighttime shopping. Some stores and shopping malls may incorporate exterior barriers to prevent thieves from crashing into entrances, particularly in electronics, convenience stores, and drug stores.

At the cash wrap register area, security measures should be implemented to protect the store and customers from data breaches. The point of sale (POS) system should be locked when not in use, and the credit card swipe unit should be positioned in full view of the customer to prevent fraudulent activities. Display cabinets in the cash wrap area, where high-value items are often showcased, should be lockable to deter theft.

Electronic article surveillance (EAS) systems and exit pedestals are highly effective security measures. EAS tags, attached to merchandise, contain circuits capable of emitting radio signals. If the tags are not removed or deactivated during the sale, an alarm is triggered at the exit, alerting the sales staff to potential theft. EAS tags can be attached as separate devices or integrated into price tags. Other electronic tags or marking devices can encode prices onto tickets, and optical character recognition (OCR) systems can process specific tags. Advances in anti-theft technology continue to help minimize losses in retail business.

Additionally, safety considerations such as aisle sizes, fire sprinklers, and accessible counters are defined by codes and regulations and must be addressed in the store design process.

Code Requirements

Building and fire safety codes, as well as accessibility regulations, play a crucial role in ensuring the safety of customers and store owners/property owners in retail stores. Compliance with these codes is essential in the interior design and space planning process of a retail store, regardless of its size or type. It is important to note that code requirements may vary depending on the location and type of building in which the store is situated, so it's necessary to verify local code requirements for each specific project.

Retail stores are typically classified as Mercantile facilities according to the International Building Code and the Life Safety Code. This classification applies to spaces primarily intended for the display and sale of goods.

However, some stores that primarily provide services, such as beauty shops, may fall under the Business classification. Department stores, grocery stores, showrooms, and wholesale stores (excluding warehouses) are other examples of facilities classified as Mercantile. Malls, which often comprise multiple stores and may include restaurants and entertainment spaces, can have specific code requirements.

In retail stores, full-height partition corridors are less common, and traffic paths are typically in the form of aisles. Aisles in retail stores are considered exit-access passageways and must be wide enough to accommodate the occupancy load. The minimum clear width for aisles is typically 36-44 inches (914-1118 mm). Space requirements between movable fixtures are determined by local codes. Material and finish selections in retail stores must adhere to fire and building codes. Wall and ceiling finishes are generally required to be Class A or B in terms of fire safety, while flooring must meet Class I or II standards. Lighting fixtures must be carefully located and specified to prevent fire hazards and avoid interference with sprinklers and smoke detectors, considering the combustible nature of merchandise in stores. Decorative treatments should be chosen with fire safety in mind and must comply with local codes.

Retail stores must also comply with accessibility guidelines, which can impact the design of cash wrap counters, display fixture heights, dressing room sizes, and entrance clearances. Stairs and raised floor areas must be designed to ensure accessibility and safety. Accessible dressing rooms typically require a minimum width of 54-72 inches (1370-1829 mm) if a door is used. Railings are necessary for raised areas, unless a variance is allowed by local jurisdiction. Ramps are required to provide accessibility to raised areas. Different materials on stairs leading to raised areas may be necessary to indicate the raised areas and prevent falls, as per accessibility regulations. Local code officials should be consulted for specific requirements related to raised areas in retail stores.

Toilet facilities are also a requirement for retail stores. Small stores may only need to provide a unisex toilet facility, while larger stores must have separate toilet facilities for men and women, with one or more fixtures. Separate facilities for employees and the public are not required in Mercantile occupancies. All toilet facilities must comply with accessibility standards, including the provision of at least one accessible toilet facility for each sex as necessary.

It is important for the interior designer to prepare drawings and specifications that meet the applicable local codes for the specific retail establishment and its location. This brief overview does not cover all the code requirements for retail stores, so it is crucial to consult with local authorities to ensure compliance.

Space Allocation and Circulation

The allocation and layout of space in a retail store are crucial considerations for both the retailer and the designer. Retail space is typically divided into selling space and non-selling space. Selling space refers to the area dedicated to the display of merchandise and customer interaction, while non-selling space includes areas such as the stockroom and office that are not directly involved in merchandise display or sales.

During the programming phase, the designer will discuss various guidelines and factors that influence the space plan of the store. These considerations include the feasibility of the store footprint, the merchandise mix, fixture types and locations, architectural finishes, signage placement, and the layout of selling and non-selling space.

Key guidelines related to selling space include:

- Prime location: The most valuable space in a store is typically near the front, where it attracts the most customer attention.
- Aisle placement: Display space on main or central aisles is more valuable than space on peripheral or side aisles.
- Eye-level display: Eye-level space is highly desirable as it is more likely to catch the customer's attention, particularly for new items.
- Floor level: Space on the first floor is generally more valuable than raised or upper-floor space.
- Aisle significance: Space along the aisles is more valuable than peripheral corner space.

Circulation and traffic patterns play a crucial role in determining the layout of aisles and fixture positioning. Research has shown that people tend to turn right when entering a store, so it's important to attract customers to the left as well to promote two-way traffic. One strategy is to position demand merchandise away from the entrance, forcing customers to pass convenience and impulse items before reaching their intended purchases. Convenience items are typically placed in the midsection of the store, while impulse items are often located near the sales counter or close to the entry.

There are various store layout options depending on the size and type of store. Smaller stores may have limitations but still aim to maximize merchandise visibility, while larger stores and department stores have more flexibility in their layouts. Some common store layouts include:

1. Straight plan: This is an economical layout suitable for various types of stores. Wall fixtures and display devices are arranged along the perimeter walls, and other fixtures are placed within the space to facilitate smooth traffic flow from the front to the back of the store. Niche areas along the walls or raised areas can be used to add visual interest and enhance merchandise display.
2. Boutique system: This layout divides the sales floor into individual semi-separate areas, each focused on a specific shopping theme or product category. It is commonly used in high-end stores to create a personalized and unique shopping experience.
3. Diagonal plan: This layout encourages customer movement throughout the entire store. It is effective for self-service stores, as it guides customers to explore different sections and view a wide range of merchandise.

These are just a few examples of store layouts, and there are other arrangements that may be suitable depending on the store's specific needs and objectives. Further resources can provide additional insights into various store layout options.

The free-flow system is a floor plan style that allows for flexible traffic patterns and placement of fixtures. It is particularly advantageous for small stores as it encourages browsing and impulse buying. This system allows for easy changes to displays and fixtures, making it adaptable to the volume of merchandise in stock. In stores with numerous columns, the grid system is often used to work around these structural elements. This system creates a straight plan due to the column locations and is commonly employed in larger stores like department stores. While it offers limited flexibility due to the constraints of the columns, the grid system simplifies the arrangement of fixtures and aisles within the overall space.

In larger stores, multiple planning concepts may be utilized, depending on the department. Techniques are often employed to guide customers from one department to another, and factors such as stairs, escalators, and elevators play a role in facilitating traffic flow. The placement of these elements is typically planned by the architect or in consultation with them. Escalators are commonly installed in pairs and situated in the center of the sales area, while elevators are typically located towards the rear of the store.

For easy access, it is important to ensure a clear path from the store entrance to all sections of the store. In small retail stores, a single aisle extending the length of the store, known as the straight plan system, is often employed. In larger stores, minor aisles may branch off from the main aisle, whether it runs through the center of the store or creates a radial layout with a circular traffic pattern.

When determining the placement of different types of items, factors such as cost, theft prevention, and security are important considerations. Merchandise placement is highly flexible and varies based on the merchant's preferences and the product mix. The final decision on placement is influenced by the need for merchandise exposure (such as impulse versus convenience items) and the retailer's target customer profile, including age group and shopping frequency.

When planning non-selling space in a retail store, it is important to consider several factors:

- The amount of back storage for reserve stock should be determined by the store owner, as it will impact the available selling space. It is essential to strike a balance between having enough stock readily accessible and maximizing the selling area.
- Adequate space should be allocated for a desk or office for the store manager in the back area. This provides a dedicated workspace for administrative tasks and managerial responsibilities.
- Consider how new merchandise will be brought onto the sales floor without disrupting customer traffic. Designate specific pathways or timing for restocking to ensure a seamless shopping experience for customers.
- In freestanding or strip center stores, provision should be made for store delivery trucks to load and unload items in a separate receiving area. This helps maintain organization and efficiency in the back of the store.
- Certain products may require preparation before they can be displayed on the sales floor. Clothing stores, for example, often need to open shipping cartons, steam or press garments, and hang them on hangers before they are ready for sale. Allow space for these preparatory tasks.
- Consider how deliveries made by rapid-ship companies will be handled, as they may not be delivered to a designated freight door. Plan for a convenient and efficient process to receive these deliveries within the store.
- Additional storage may be necessary to handle off-season stock that was not sold during the season. This allows for proper organization and rotation of merchandise, ensuring that the sales floor remains visually appealing and well-stocked.
- For clothing stores, space will be needed for alterations and fitting rooms. Allocate an area where customers can try on garments and have them adjusted if necessary.
- Non-selling spaces such as custodial supplies and employee restrooms are important considerations. Local codes will dictate if a restroom for customers is required in addition to employee facilities.
- In larger stores with many employees, a break room or designated area for employees to store personal items should be planned. Providing a comfortable space for employees can contribute to their satisfaction and overall well-being.

By carefully considering and planning non-selling spaces, the interior designer can ensure that the back-of-house operations run smoothly and efficiently, supporting the overall functionality of the retail store.

Fixtures and Furniture

In a retail store, the furniture primarily consists of various merchandise display fixtures that are essential for showcasing products. The selection and arrangement of these fixtures depend on the nature of the merchandise and the store's requirements. Here are some common types of display fixtures used in retail stores:

- Cash wrap desk: This is the counter area where the cash register and other point-of-sale (POS) equipment are located for conducting sales transactions.
- Cubes, pedestals, and showcases: These custom-designed items are used to display merchandise or showcase valuable products.
- Freestanding fixtures: These floor-standing fixtures allow customers to access merchandise from all sides. Examples include two-way and four-way fixtures, gondolas, spirals, and rounders. Two-way and four-way fixtures typically consist of a flat metal bar supported by a round post.
- Gondolas and cabinets: Gondolas are open-shelved units with access from all sides. They can be made of custom or stock millwork and are commonly used to display various merchandise in different types of retail stores.
- Island fixture: This three-dimensional counter is used for displaying a wide range of accessories such as jewelry, scarves, handbags, and cosmetics.
- Mannequins: These human-like figures are used to display clothing items. They come in different sizes and levels of realism, from lifelike to simplified representations.
- Rounders: This type of fixture consists of a round tube above a stand, allowing merchandise to be hung from clothes hangers. Rounders are often used to display items on sale.
- Slatwall fixture: Brackets are used with slatwall panels to display various merchandise, including apparel. Different types of brackets can be used to optimize the display of the store.
- Spiral fixtures: These vertical curvilinear fixtures, typically made of metal, have evenly spaced hooks for holding clothing accessories like belts or scarves.

When designing the retail space, the interior designer's goal is to provide creative planning in the selection and specification of these merchandise display fixtures. The fixtures should optimize the use of selling floor space, be flexible in their arrangement, and easily accommodate the store's merchandise. In some cases, custom cabinetry and fixtures may be required, and the interior designer will need to produce detailed drawings for their manufacture.

Flexibility is an important aspect of store fixtures, allowing them to be modified and adjusted to accommodate different sizes and types of merchandise. Shelving units, for example, can have adjustable shelves that can be rearranged as needed. Gondolas and cabinets often have built-in storage capabilities to accommodate stock while also providing display space.

The cash register and cash wrap areas require specific cabinet designs to house the necessary equipment and supplies. These cabinets are typically custom-designed to meet the store's specific requirements. They should provide space for one or more POS computers, a counter for wrapping or bagging items, storage for bags and boxes, and any other specific needs defined by the client. Accessibility requirements should also be considered when designing these custom cabinets. Depending on the type of merchandise being sold, additional furniture items may be needed in the selling spaces. For example, shoe stores may require chairs for customers trying on shoes, jewelry stores may need chairs or stools for customers examining jewelry pieces, and clothing stores often provide seating units for customers waiting for someone to try on merchandise. These additional furniture items are tailored to the specific needs and comfort of the customers and can vary based on the merchandise mix and store concept.

Materials, Finishes, and Color

The choice of materials and finishes in a retail store can significantly impact the shopping experience and the presentation of merchandise. Owners of smaller stores, boutiques, and department stores are seeking more than just a functional space—they want an engaging and visually appealing environment. Unusual materials, creative use of textures on walls, and well-designed lighting can enhance the overall atmosphere and contribute to the desired shopping experience.

While store finishes are not typically changed annually, many retailers opt to remodel their stores every few years to keep up with evolving trends and maintain a fresh look. It's important to select materials and finishes that can easily blend with seasonal changes in merchandise and can be updated or refreshed through simple changes like paint.

Soft and porous materials absorb sound, while hard and rigid materials reflect it. Consider the level of traffic and wear and tear in different areas of the store when selecting materials. High-traffic areas may require more durable and resistant surfaces to withstand the abuse.

Building and fire safety codes will dictate the permissible materials for walls and floors. The choice of wall treatments will depend on the extent to which walls are used for merchandise display and the types of fixtures involved. Paint is often a cost-effective option for highlighting products on walls. Graphics and signs can also be incorporated to identify products and guide customers within the store.

Floor treatments should take into account aesthetics, noise reduction, and safety. In climates with harsh winters, it's important to avoid slippery surfaces near entrances. Hard-surface materials are suitable for many store types, but in a boutique clothing store, a quieter and more elegant atmosphere can be achieved with high-density, low-pile carpeting. However, carpeting requires maintenance and consideration for the placement of electrical outlets for vacuum cleaners.

Color selections in a store can be influenced by corporate guidelines for chain or franchise stores, or by the retailer's established logo and color scheme. Dark colors can create dramatic interiors, but it's important to consider how they may impact the appearance of merchandise. In clothing stores, where the colors of merchandise change frequently, neutral colors are often used as a backdrop to avoid conflicting with the changing colors of the products. Ultimately, the choice of materials, finishes, and colors should align with the retailer's brand image, target customers, and merchandise mix to create an appealing and harmonious shopping environment.

Mechanical Systems

he interior designer plays a crucial role in the specification and placement of lighting fixtures in retail stores. The primary objective of lighting is to enhance the display of merchandise and create a positive shopping experience. Proper lighting design can significantly impact consumer perception and increase merchandise sales.

In the sales area, there are four main categories of lighting:

- General (ambient) lighting: This provides overall visibility in the store and can be achieved using various fixtures. The lighting levels should range from 20 to 60 foot-candles, depending on the type of store and merchandise.
- Accent lighting: This type of lighting is used to draw attention to specific displays and create visual impact. Track lights and spotlights are commonly used to highlight key merchandise. Accent lighting can be compared to the sparkle lighting used in food service facilities.
- Case and shelf lighting: These lights are placed within display cases and above or along shelves to showcase specific products. It's important to ensure that the lighting fixtures are hidden to prevent customers from accidentally coming into contact with hot lamps.
- Peripheral lighting: This lighting is used to attract attention to wall displays and merchandise. Recessed lights and wall washers are commonly employed for peripheral lighting.

Lighting fixtures are not frequently replaced due to their cost and the potential need for rewiring. Therefore, it's essential to select fixtures that offer flexibility, allowing for easy adaptation to changes in display layouts. Improperly chosen fixtures and lamps can adversely affect the colors of merchandise, potentially leading to customer dissatisfaction and returns.

It's important to comply with building codes and safety regulations regarding exit and egress lighting levels. Local codes may also impose restrictions on energy usage, particularly for large stores that are limited in terms of watts per square foot. Smaller specialty stores may have higher allowances based on the type of merchandise they sell. State regulations can impact lighting design requirements for energy conservation. The designer must ensure that the lighting plan not only meets functional needs but also aligns with energy efficiency guidelines set by the jurisdiction.

Other mechanical systems in a retail store include technology for the point-of-sale (POS) system, security systems, and sound systems for background music. Lighting design can influence the HVAC system, so close collaboration between the interior designer and architect is necessary to optimize energy efficiency.

Design Applications

Design applications in retail stores can vary depending on the type of merchandise being sold. While many elements of store planning remain similar across different types of stores, this section will focus on design applications for small clothing stores and gift stores, which are common examples. Additionally, a brief section on hardline stores will be included.

In small clothing stores, the layout and display of merchandise are crucial. Considerations such as the placement of racks, shelving units, and fitting rooms need to be carefully planned to optimize the browsing and shopping experience for customers. Creating attractive and visually appealing displays that highlight the clothing items is essential. Lighting plays a significant role in showcasing the merchandise, and attention should be given to selecting fixtures and lamps that enhance the colors and textures of the clothing. Additionally, providing adequate storage space for inventory and designing functional cash wrap areas are important considerations.

For gift stores, the design application focuses on creating an inviting and engaging atmosphere. Display fixtures such as shelves, cabinets, and showcases should be designed to showcase a variety of gift items in an organized and visually appealing manner. Custom millwork or stock millwork can be used to create unique displays that align with the store's theme or branding. Attention should be given to incorporating elements such as signage, graphics, and themed vignettes to help customers navigate and explore the store. Lighting should be used to create a warm and welcoming ambiance.

Hardline stores, which sell products like appliances, furniture, and sporting goods, require a different design approach. Space planning becomes crucial to accommodate the size and arrangement of larger items. Showrooms and product demonstration areas can be incorporated to allow customers to interact with the merchandise. Attention should be given to providing clear and informative signage and product information. Additionally, durable and functional fixtures and storage solutions should be designed to handle the weight and display requirements of the hardline products.

Generic Small Clothing Stores

The layout and design of a clothing store are crucial aspects that revolve around the store owner's merchandising concept. The strategic grouping and placement of merchandise within the store serve the primary objective of maximizing sales. Moreover, these groupings play a significant role in guiding customers as they navigate through the store in search of specific items. For instance, it is common practice to display complementary accessories like belts near pants, facilitating convenient outfit coordination for customers.

Space Allocation and Planning

The arrangement of a small clothing store incorporates similar elements of spatial planning as larger clothing stores. The store layout is formed by strategically allocating space into logical groups of fixtures to showcase the merchandise. This plan encompasses the sales area, traffic flow, fixture selection, and placement. Additionally, the designer will determine the positioning of fitting rooms and non-selling areas, as well as specify colors, materials, and lighting for architectural surfaces.

In a small clothing store, maximizing the utilization of space for merchandise display and sales is crucial, as the selling space generates revenue. Therefore, the retailer will prioritize using the maximum square footage for displaying and selling items, while allocating a smaller portion of space for non-selling functions.

Given the variation in apparel stock and quantities, flexible and functional planning is essential. The designer must create a layout and fixtures that offer the store owner or manager flexibility in displaying merchandise. In clothing stores, it is common to group items that are used together by customers. For example, in a women's store, blouses and tops are placed near skirts, pants, jackets, and accessories such as belts and scarves. Similarly, ties, belts, and dress pants are positioned near dress shirts in men's stores. This concept, known as "in close proximity," ensures that related items are placed near or next to each other. This principle can be applied to other types of stores and facilities as well. The proximity of products facilitates easy access for sales clerks and increases the potential for selling complementary items. Mirrors on the sales floor can also assist customers in quickly visualizing how different items coordinate before trying them on in the dressing room.

Space planning is also influenced by the volume and combination of demand, convenience, and impulse goods in the clothing store. Demand merchandise, such as coats, dresses, and suits, convenience items like gloves, sweaters, ties, and socks, and impulse items such as costume jewelry, scarves, handkerchiefs, and other accessories, each require different types of display fixtures in clothing stores.

The circulation and traffic paths within a clothing store are designed to guide customers through the store and allow for flexible placement of fixtures. The spacing of display fixtures and counters is influenced by jurisdictional codes and accessibility requirements. Movable fixtures are considered furniture, allowing some flexibility in aisle sizes. However, it is advisable to follow accessibility guidelines, with a recommended width of 36" (914 mm) for aisles. In most small retail outlets, a single straight center aisle extends the length of the store. The width of the main aisle is typically 6' (1829 mm), while minor aisles range from 3 to 4' (914–1219 mm), depending on fixture placement. If raised areas are included, accessibility requirements must be met. In larger clothing stores, the accessibility and convenience of stairs, escalators, and elevators play a crucial role in determining the flow of traffic. Another significant category is children's clothing stores, which generate substantial revenue. The fundamental concepts discussed above apply to children's clothing stores as well, but with adjustments made for smaller-scale furniture and dressing rooms that accommodate both children and parents.

Dressing rooms, also known as fitting rooms, are considered part of the selling space. Each dressing room should be equipped with a stool, chair, or bench, a shelf for handbags or accessories, several hanging hooks, and a full-length mirror. The size of dressing rooms will vary based on the store's price point, with luxury stores typically offering more spacious dressing rooms.

Privacy is an important consideration when planning dressing rooms. The entrances to dressing rooms should be screened from the main sales floor while being under the control of staff. In many clothing stores, a three-way mirror may be positioned adjacent to the dressing rooms, allowing sales clerks to suggest additional items that enhance the outfit. It is essential to ensure that at least one dressing room meets accessibility standards.

Non Selling Space

In any clothing store, regardless of its size, a certain amount of non-selling space is essential. Careful planning of non-selling space is crucial to avoid wasting valuable selling space. Non-selling areas in clothing stores may include:

- Space for receiving and signing for incoming stock.
- Area designated for unpacking and inspection of merchandise.
- Dedicated space for layaway items.
- Designated area for prepping merchandise, such as ironing and steaming.
- Space for temporarily hanging new items on racks before they are moved to the sales floor.
- Area for administrative activities, such as office tasks and managerial responsibilities.
- Storage space for administrative files and records.
- Secure location for employees to store personal belongings.
- Space for storing back stock of merchandise.
- Area for storing cleaning supplies, boxes, vacuums, and other related items.
- Space allocated for mechanical equipment like HVAC systems.
- A public restroom, which may be required by code, is essential for customers.
- Additionally, a restroom for staff members is necessary and must meet code requirements.

These non-selling spaces play a vital role in supporting the efficient operation of the clothing store while ensuring that the primary selling areas are optimized for merchandise display and sales.

Fixtures and Furniture

Once the merchandise mix, zoning, and traffic paths are established, fixtures are selected accordingly. Flexibility is key, as merchandise volumes change with each season. The following are commonly used flexible fixtures in clothing stores:

- Two-ways: Fixtures with two arms, allowing items to be displayed on both sides.
- Four-ways: Fixtures with four arms, providing multiple display options.
- Spirals: Fixtures with a spiral design, maximizing the use of vertical space for displaying garments.
- Rounders: Circular fixtures for hanging clothes, enabling easy browsing.
- Slatwall and modular perimeter frames: Wall-mounted fixtures with slotted panels for attaching various accessories and shelving.
- Gondolas: Freestanding fixtures with shelving, commonly used for displaying folded items like shirts or sweaters.
- Mannequins: Human-like models used to showcase complete outfits or specific garments.

In clothing stores, it is common to provide seating near dressing rooms and mirrors for the convenience of accompanying individuals. The type and style of seating should align with the overall store design and price point. Upholstered seats are more commonly found in stores selling higher-priced and upscale merchandise, as they provide greater comfort.

The cash wrap desk or counter holds significant importance. In small stores, it is often strategically located to have a clear view of the store, especially the entrance. Besides facilitating sales and returns, the cash wrap desk can serve as a display area for small impulse purchase items. To design the cash wrap desk effectively, the interior designer should gather as much information as possible from the retailer regarding its specific usage and requirements. Typically, the cash wrap desk is a custom-designed cabinet, approximately 42" (1067 mm) high, featuring a writing surface for customers. An interior countertop, 36" (914 mm) high, houses the point-of-sale (POS) computer, cash drawers, cash register, and a wrapping area. The higher counter ensures better security for the cash register or drawers. However, accessibility standards may necessitate a portion of the customer's side of the counter to be no higher than 34-36" (864-914 mm), or an auxiliary counter with a maximum height of 36" (914 mm) may need to be provided. Adequate storage space should be incorporated into the cash wrap desk for items such as shopping bags.

In children's stores, precautions must be taken to ensure fixtures cannot be easily tipped over. Access to small items like costume jewelry should be restricted. Additionally, the materials used for floors, walls, and seating should be easy to maintain. Some stores may include a small play area, but careful design is necessary to ensure security and minimize liability. An unsupervised play area where children may get injured poses potential risks. Furthermore, implementing a point-of-sale (POS) system can assist store owners or managers in performing various management control functions. In addition to printing receipts, the computerized system maintains accurate inventory records and expedites merchandise ordering processes.

Materials and Color

When it comes to finishes and color specification for a clothing store, several factors should be considered. Flooring choices should prioritize both safety and aesthetics. If the entry is directly from outside, flooring near the door should be specified as slip-resistant, and a floor mat might be necessary. Carpeting is a popular choice for its comfort and style, commonly found in many clothing stores. Carpet tiles offer a sustainable option as worn areas can be easily replaced compared to broadloom carpeting. However, patterns should be used sparingly as they can detract attention from the merchandise. Area rugs should only be used in locations where they won't pose a tripping hazard. It's important to note that wood floors, although visually appealing and warm, require additional maintenance.

Wall treatments offer various material options. Keep in mind that fixtures will typically display merchandise against the walls. Paint is the most cost-effective option and easily changeable. However, painted walls are prone to damage and scratches, requiring more frequent repairs. Wallpaper and similar products are also susceptible to damage, and there may be code considerations when using them. It's crucial to select colors and materials that won't reflect a tint onto the merchandise, as this can alter their perceived color. Neutrals are generally recommended for large surface areas within the interior to avoid color distortion. Accent colors, such as those behind the cash wrap counter, can be used to add visual interest.

The careful selection of finishes and colors ensures that the store environment enhances the presentation of merchandise without compromising its true appearance.

Mechanical Systems and Codes

Lighting design and specification are crucial elements in a clothing store, and it can be beneficial to involve a lighting designer to ensure optimal results for the wide range of products found in retail clothing stores. Proper lighting is essential for accurate color rendition of merchandise and protecting certain fibers from fading. The interior designer should collaborate in specifying the luminaires used in the store.

Here are some general guidelines for lighting specification in stores:

- Recommended lighting levels: Cashier checkouts should have around 50 foot-candles, merchandise feature displays require approximately 100 foot-candles, and general merchandising areas benefit from around 30 foot-candles.
- The lighting plan should guide customers to move seamlessly between different areas of the store.
- Retail lighting can be creative and utilize theatrical lighting effects to add interest and excitement.
- Color-correcting lamps are important to enhance the colors of the apparel.
- Energy-efficient light fixtures and lamps should be specified.
- Spotlights on tracks offer flexibility in directing light.
- Care should be taken to avoid fixtures that blind customers, and baffles can help refract the light.
- Lighting should wash the merchandise with even light distribution, avoiding hot spots.

Code compliance is a crucial consideration in the design of a clothing store. Clothing stores are typically classified as mercantile (M) occupancies under the International Building Code (IBC). This applies to both freestanding stores and those within shopping malls. Specific code issues include the size of aisles between fixtures, accessibility considerations, and restrictions on architectural materials. At least one dressing room must meet accessibility standards, and additional accessible dressing rooms may be required based on the store's square footage. Toilet facilities must also comply with accessibility regulations, even if they are not made available to customers.

Ensuring compliance with codes and regulations is vital for the safety and accessibility of the clothing store, while effective lighting design enhances the shopping experience and showcases the merchandise effectively.

Generic Small Gift Store

The design of a small gift store presents unique challenges compared to clothing stores. Gift items are typically small and require specialized display fixtures to showcase them effectively. Additionally, the display of gifts often requires varying viewing heights to accommodate different types of products. Stores that sell high-value or fragile items, such as jewelry or crystal gifts, may require specific fixture treatments and closed case fixtures or cabinets for enhanced security.

When planning the interior of a gift store, the merchandise mix serves as the foundation. The nature and size of the items will influence the layout and specification of fixtures. It is crucial to establish zoning and carefully consider the placement of products in collaboration with the store owner during the programming phase.

Window design and display play a vital role in attracting potential customers and enticing them to enter the store. Some gift stores utilize closed window displays, such as shadow boxes, to create an exclusive and attention-grabbing presentation of merchandise. Other stores, particularly those selling larger gift items, opt for open window displays that provide a glimpse into the rest of the selling space, giving passersby a preview of what awaits inside.

Space Allocation and Fixtures

Circulation and traffic patterns in a gift store are determined by the placement of fixed features like wall cabinetry, the cash wrap counter, island fixtures, and gondolas. The store layout typically includes a central aisle or main aisle that is around 6 feet wide, with minor aisles measuring 3 to 4 feet wide. The choice of store layout, such as the straight plan or diagonal plan, depends on the type of fixtures needed for displaying the gift items.

The placement of the cash wrap counter is an important consideration in the store design. It is usually positioned toward the rear or at least one-third into the selling space. The location of the cash wrap counter is determined based on the owner's preferences, with clear lines of sight to the entrance and the entire store for security purposes. The counter may be a pre-made fixture from vendors or a custom-designed cabinet by the interior designer to meet specific needs and aesthetics. Accessibility requirements must also be taken into account when designing the cash wrap area.

The overall store layout, fixture specification, and design aim to create a stage that highlights the gift items and invites customers to explore the merchandise. Through discussions with the store owner, the designer organizes the layout to ensure customers have a clear path to view all the products available. Proper fixture positioning ensures that customers are exposed to a majority of the items for sale.

Non-selling space is also necessary in gift stores, although it is typically smaller in size compared to clothing stores. The specific needs for non-selling areas will be clarified by the store owner, and they may include requirements for storage, office space, and other functions. For a list of common non-selling space considerations, refer to the "Generic Small Clothing Stores" section.

Cabinetry plays a crucial role in gift stores and is often designed and manufactured specifically for the retail industry. Ready-made cabinets in various styles, as well as custom-designed cabinets, are available from specialized vendors. Glass-top cabinets, gondolas with open or closed shelving, wall shelving units, and base cabinets with open or closed storage are commonly used in gift stores. Pedestals, cubes, and glass cases may also be utilized for displaying certain items. Flexibility in shelf arrangement is important to accommodate seasonal changes in merchandise.

Slatwall fixtures are popular in gift stores due to their versatility for hanging, display, and shelving purposes. The use of slatwall fixtures and accessories provides endless possibilities for arranging and presenting merchandise. Considering viewing levels is crucial when specifying fixtures, with higher-priced or new products typically placed at eye level for easy viewing. However, accessibility should be taken into account, as lower shelving may be harder to reach for customers with mobility needs or seniors.

Code compliance is a significant consideration in gift store design. Gift stores are classified as mercantile occupancies in the International Building Code. Depending on the location of the gift store, such as within a hotel or hospital, architectural finishes may be subject to stricter regulations. Accessibility requirements must also be met, ensuring that the store design, including the cash wrap desk, complies with accessibility standards. In existing facilities, the cash wrap area may require redesign to meet accessibility requirements.

Finishes, Lighting, and Other Systems

In gift stores, the selection of materials and finishes should strike a balance between creativity and practicality. The focus should remain on the merchandise rather than overwhelming it with excessive interior design elements. Neutral background colors are typically preferred for walls and cabinetry, allowing the items to take center stage. However, strategic use of color can be applied in specific areas or alcoves to highlight special merchandise or create visual interest. It's important to consider the ability to incorporate temporary finishes, such as in cabinets or behind wall shelves, to accommodate changing displays for new or seasonal merchandise.

Flooring choices in gift stores often favor carpeting, especially in higher-end stores and jewelry shops. High-density, low-pile carpeting is commonly used to provide a soft and luxurious feel. Keep in mind that carpeting may show traffic patterns more quickly and require regular cleaning. Small to medium-sized patterns can help camouflage wear. Alternatively, hard-surface flooring options like marble or travertine can create a sense of luxury, although they tend to be noisier and may require specific maintenance.

Lighting plays a crucial role in gift stores, serving both functional and aesthetic purposes. General lighting is used for overall visibility and monitoring of the space, while ambient lighting is employed to draw attention to the walls. Pendant lighting can be utilized to designate specific areas, while task lighting is used to highlight products and work surfaces. Track lighting fixtures and pendant fixtures can attract attention to specific displays or areas. Pendant fixtures at the cash wrap counter serve the dual purpose of providing task lighting and emphasizing the point of sale. Flexibility in lighting design allows the store owner to achieve the desired focused lighting effects that entice customers. Colored lights and sparkle lighting can also contribute to creating an exciting environment. The selection of lighting fixtures should align with the store's image and design concept, as they can convey different moods and styles. While energy efficiency is important, the priority in gift stores is often choosing fixtures and lamps that best showcase the merchandise. Compliance with energy codes may require incorporating some energy-efficient systems. It is advisable to involve a lighting consultant in the planning process, especially if the interior designer lacks experience in retail store lighting design.

Security is an important consideration in gift stores, given the small size and value of the items. Despite electronic tagging and alarm systems, theft can still occur. Security cameras placed in inconspicuous areas of the store can be effective without compromising customer privacy. Convex mirrors are a cost-effective monitoring device that enhances visibility and deters theft.

Generic Jewelry Stores

The design of a jewelry store is heavily influenced by the type of jewelry being sold, whether it is high-end gems and fine jewelry or costume accessories. This distinction will impact various design recommendations for the store. The focus of this discussion is on mid- to high-end jewelry stores.

When customers enter a jewelry store, they expect an environment that exudes elegance and sophistication. This is particularly important when the store specializes in selling precious stones, gold, and fine jewelry. The store's image and ambiance play a significant role in attracting and engaging buyers. Materials used for walls, floors, and display cabinets should reflect this desired elegance.

Displaying jewelry in a captivating and beautiful manner is crucial for successful sales. Display cases, gondolas, island fixtures, and cabinets designed for gems and fine jewelry should be enclosed to ensure security. Display cases are typically set at a height of 36" (914 mm) to allow customers to comfortably sit and examine items. However, jewelry display cases are generally 40" (1016 mm) high, featuring glass tops and fronts. If the store also offers lower-priced costume jewelry, these items can be displayed without lockable cabinets.

Additional fixtures may be necessary in a jewelry store, such as lockable display kiosks, small racks, or units that sit on top of cabinets. The specific fixtures required will depend on the store owner's preferences and the programming information gathered. Here are some specific tips for designing a small jewelry store:

- Floor plan layouts can vary but commonly include straight or diagonal arrangements.
- The location of the cash wrap and register will be determined by the store owner's preferences, either at the back of the store with a view of the entire space or near the front to allow staff to monitor the entrance.
- The floor plan should accommodate a space for jewelry repair, typically on the main selling floor.

- Lighting design is of utmost importance to showcase the sparkle and brilliance of the jewelry items. Lighting should be specified for the closed cabinets as well as for general illumination and highlighting other fixtures in the store.
- Security systems play a critical role in jewelry stores, considering the high-value nature of the merchandise.
- Very high-end jewelry stores may have a vestibule area with a separate locked door for entry, enhancing security measures.

Hardline Stores

Hardlines are a category of merchandise that consists of durable and non-textile items. Examples of hardlines include furniture, major appliances, consumer electronics (such as computers), automotive items, sporting goods, toys, hardware, housewares, and household appliances. There are also other items that can be classified as hardlines, including cosmetics, lighting fixtures, plumbing fixtures, and certain food items.

In contrast, softlines or soft goods primarily consist of textile-based products that are foldable, such as clothing, linens, towels, gloves, and footwear.

Hardline products are commonly sold in large stores, big box stores, and specific sections of department stores. Due to the physical size and nature of these products, they require more square footage for display purposes. Some items like furniture and major appliances may only be displayed as samples, with customers needing to place back orders or special orders to obtain the merchandise. On the other hand, products like consumer electronics and sporting goods are typically available for immediate purchase and can be taken home by the customer.

One common characteristic of hardlines is that they are often packaged in boxes or hard packaging. This necessitates additional storage space in both the selling area and stock rooms of the store. For instance, in consumer electronics stores, open display items are accompanied by extra boxes of the same product stored underneath the display. This practice assures customers that they are purchasing a new product.

In many cases, hardline products have related ancillary items that are displayed nearby. These ancillary products are complementary to the main items and may include items such as cables and inks for computers and printers, organizer bins for refrigerators, sporting apparel for sporting goods, and car wash products, oil, and car floor mats in a tire store. It is important for the store designer to have thorough discussions with the store owner regarding all the products that will be sold, including any ancillary or impulse items that will require dedicated display space and fixtures. For instance, stores selling home appliances may showcase the appliances with custom or semi-custom cabinets to demonstrate how they would look in a real-life setting. Similarly, furniture stores often create vignettes or product groupings that replicate the atmosphere of a bedroom, living room, or other living spaces.

Effective space planning is crucial when designing a store for hardline merchandise. The layout must consider the size of the products on display as well as the ancillary items the owner intends to sell. Ample space should be provided in the aisles to allow customers to step back and view the hardline items from a comfortable distance. Additionally, the aisles should be wide enough to facilitate the movement of merchandise to and from the sales floor. Typically, a minimum aisle width of 4 feet is recommended for traffic paths. It is important to ensure that the aisle layout complies with building codes and accessibility guidelines to ensure customer safety.

Here are several general tips to consider when designing a store or department that sells hardlines merchandise:

- Space planning: Ensure that the layout allows enough space for customers to view all sides of a product, especially for items like furniture and appliances.
- Display fixtures and materials: Select display fixtures, methods, and finish materials that align with the type and price point of the merchandise. Use materials that enhance the perceived value of the products. For example, high-end kitchen appliances may be showcased on displays incorporating marble, while a hardware store may opt for more appropriate materials.
- Custom-designed fixtures: Hardline stores often require specialized or custom-designed fixtures that can support the weight of the products being displayed and prevent items from falling off the shelves.
- Experience-driven displays: Consider incorporating displays that allow customers to interact with the products or demonstrate their utilization. This can enhance the shopping experience and create a more engaging environment. For example, sporting goods stores may provide secure areas where customers can try out items like bows and arrows.
- Brand influence: The design of the store may be influenced by the brands of merchandise being sold. This can impact product placement, color schemes, and the use of graphics within the store.
- Color usage: Hardlines stores often have more space, allowing for more color incorporation. However, exercise caution to prevent overwhelming the products with excessive bright or bold colors. Find a balance that complements the merchandise without overshadowing it.
- Lighting: Since these stores tend to be large with high ceilings, lighting is primarily focused on providing adequate general lighting to optimize visibility of the products. Creative aesthetics can take a backseat to functional illumination.
- Support space: Allocate a sufficient percentage of the floor area for support spaces that accommodate stock storage. Even items like cameras may require display gondolas or cabinets to hold stock inventory.

These tips provide a starting point for designing a store or department that sells hardlines merchandise. Keep in mind that each store's requirements may vary, and it's essential to tailor the design to the specific needs and goals of the store owner.

SUSTAINABILITY – THE INDOOR ENVIRONMENT

The significance of Indoor Environmental Quality (IEQ) in buildings is widely recognized, although the exact understanding of what it entails may be unclear to many. While Indoor Air Quality (IAQ) is a major component of IEQ, there are other important factors to consider. These include thermal comfort, acoustical comfort, and access to daylight and views.

Indoor Air Quality (IAQ) plays a vital role in maintaining a healthy indoor environment. When people breathe in clean and uncontaminated air, their well-being and overall performance improve. However, IAQ is just one aspect of IEQ. Other factors, such as thermal comfort, refer to maintaining appropriate temperatures and humidity levels that promote comfort for building occupants. Acoustical comfort focuses on reducing noise levels and creating a peaceful environment, while daylighting and views involve maximizing natural light and providing occupants with connections to the outdoor environment.

Indoor air pollution can pose greater health risks than outdoor air pollution. Since indoor pollutants are confined within the building, exposure to contaminants can be more concentrated compared to outdoor environments. Additionally, indoor air pollution is often invisible, unlike the visible smog that can be observed in urban areas. To ensure a healthy and comfortable indoor environment, it is important to address all aspects of IEQ, including IAQ, HVAC, acoustical comfort, and access to daylight and views. By prioritizing these factors, buildings can contribute to the well-being and productivity of their occupants.

Enhancing Indoor Air Quality: The Role of Interior Design

When it comes to interior design, the first step towards ensuring a healthy indoor environment is to prioritize indoor air quality (IAQ). IAQ plays a vital role in controlling and minimizing indoor pollutants, which directly impacts the well-being, productivity, and satisfaction of occupants. In today's world, employers and building owners expect design professionals to address IAQ concerns as part of sustainable design practices.

While sustainable design often emphasizes energy efficiency and environmental conservation, it's important to avoid inadvertently compromising IAQ in the process. Design professionals, along with owners and other stakeholders involved in green interior design, material selection, and building operation, must be aware of potential sources of indoor pollution and the adverse effects they can have on human health. Neglecting IAQ can lead to building-related health issues, legal complications, and reputational damage.

The good news is that we have a better understanding of IAQ issues and can adopt basic principles to achieve and maintain good IAQ. This involves considering proper ventilation systems, effective air filtration, thoughtful material selection, and regular maintenance practices. By incorporating these principles into the design process, interior designers can create healthier indoor environments that promote occupant well-being and align with sustainable design objectives.

The Consequences of Poor Indoor Air Quality on Building Occupants

Poor indoor air quality (IAQ) can have significant impacts on the health and well-being of building occupants. The indoor air is a dynamic mixture of various chemicals, particles, microorganisms, and allergens. Here are some major types of indoor air pollutants, their sources, and potential health impacts:

1. Chemicals: Pesticides, formaldehyde, volatile organic compounds (VOCs), and semi-volatile organic compounds (SVOCs) can be emitted from building materials, furniture, cleaning products, and other sources. They may cause respiratory irritation, allergies, headaches, dizziness, and even long-term health effects.

2. Particles: Dust, fine particles, and other airborne particulate matter can originate from outdoor air, as well as indoor sources like smoking, cooking, and cleaning activities. These particles can exacerbate respiratory conditions, trigger allergies, and contribute to poor respiratory health.

3. Microorganisms: Viruses, bacteria, mold spores, and allergens such as dust mites can thrive in indoor environments with high humidity or water damage. They can cause respiratory infections, allergies, asthma exacerbations, and other health issues.

4. Moisture: Excessive moisture can lead to mold growth, which releases spores and produces allergens. Prolonged exposure to damp and moldy environments can cause respiratory symptoms, allergic reactions, and even respiratory infections.

Building occupants spend about 90 percent of their time indoors, with a significant portion of that time being in their own homes. However, exposure to indoor air pollutants does not automatically result in adverse health effects. The following factors play a role in determining the impact on occupants:

- Sensitivity: Some individuals may be more sensitive to certain pollutants, such as those with pre-existing respiratory conditions or allergies.
- Concentration and Duration: Higher concentrations of pollutants and longer exposure durations increase the likelihood of health effects.
- Ventilation: Inadequate ventilation can contribute to the buildup of pollutants and compromise IAQ.
- Overall Health: The general health status of individuals can influence their susceptibility to the effects of poor IAQ.

To mitigate the impact of poor IAQ, it is crucial to address the sources of pollutants, ensure proper ventilation and air filtration, maintain moisture control, and promote good indoor hygiene practices. By proactively managing IAQ, designers and building owners can create healthier indoor environments that support the well-being of occupants.

Indoor Pollutants: Categories, Sources, and Health Impacts on Occupants

Pollutants	Sources	Potential Health Effects
Formaldehyde, aldehydes	Building materials and combustion	Cancer and respiratory irritation
VOCs (e.g., formaldehyde, toluene, and 1,4-dioxane)	These pollutants can originate from various sources such as building materials, textiles, furnishings, finishes, consumer products, pesticides, fragrances, personal care products, cleaning products, and processes, as well as dust accumulation.	Health risks from indoor air pollution include irritation of the senses and respiratory system, gastrointestinal discomfort, hormone disruption, cancer, as well as reproductive and neurological/developmental problems.
SVOCs (e.g., phthalates, halogenated flame retardants and siloxanes)	Common indoor sources of these pollutants include plastics, insulation materials, upholstered furniture, textiles, and electronics.	Exposure to these pollutants can lead to reduced fertility, learning disorders, birth defects, and disruptions in hormone levels.
Viruses, bacteria	Originates from HVAC systems, various surfaces, and even people themselves.	Exposure to these pollutants can increase the risk of respiratory and gastrointestinal illnesses.
Allergens, endotoxins	Originates from Dust mites, cockroaches, pets, rodents	Causes Allergy, asthma attacks, respiratory irritation, cardiovascular disease
Dust and fine particles	Originates from Ubiquitous, combustion sources, print devices	Allergy, asthma attacks, cardiovascular disease

Indoor mold growth	High levels of moisture in walls, ceilings, HVAC systems, basements, and crawl spaces can result in the proliferation of mold and mildew.	This can trigger allergies, asthma attacks, as well as cause sensory and respiratory irritation. Additionally, it can increase the likelihood of respiratory infections.

The impact and risks associated with indoor air pollutants depend on various factors, including the concentration and relative exposure to the pollutants, potential synergistic effects, personal characteristics (such as age, gender, weight, and general health), route of exposure (inhalation, contact, ingestion), and the duration of exposure. Longer exposure generally increases the risk of health problems, which can manifest acutely or chronically over time.

As technology and health knowledge advance, new challenges and solutions will emerge in relation to indoor air quality. Some of these challenges include:

- Energy conservation measures: The need for increased energy efficiency has led to tighter homes and buildings with reduced ventilation rates, potentially resulting in elevated pollutant levels.

- Climate change: Extreme environmental conditions may lead individuals to spend more time indoors for refuge, necessitating the use of new temperature- and moisture-resilient materials and construction techniques. These changes can introduce new pollutant exposures and present additional indoor environmental challenges.

- Chemical usage: Synthetic chemicals are commonly found in construction materials and furnishings, and a significant percentage of these chemicals have not been thoroughly evaluated for potential toxicity. Scientific research suggests that even low levels of exposure to certain chemicals can have biological effects. As new methods for measuring toxicity emerge, material selection will become more precise and informed.

It is crucial for designers, building professionals, and individuals to stay informed about the evolving understanding of indoor air quality and to implement appropriate measures to mitigate potential health risks associated with indoor pollutants.

Reducing Indoor Pollutants: Effective Strategies for Cleaner Air

To protect the indoor environment and ensure good indoor air quality (IAQ), several key principles can be followed:

Source control: The most effective approach to managing IAQ is to eliminate or control sources of indoor air pollution. This involves selecting construction materials and furnishings that emit low levels of volatile organic compounds (VOCs), semi-volatile organic compounds (SVOCs), and particles. It is important to choose products that have been verified to meet criteria set by credible public health agencies and third-party certifiers. Care should be taken, as some products labeled as "green" may be rated based on their VOC content rather than their actual emissions. To ensure low VOC emissions, it is recommended to refer to listings by third-party IAQ certifiers or review test reports that demonstrate compliance with VOC criteria.

Ventilation: Adequate ventilation is crucial for maintaining good IAQ. The HVAC system should be designed, operated, and maintained to bring in clean outdoor air in sufficient quantities to prevent the buildup of indoor pollutants. Regular cleaning of the HVAC system is important to prevent dust accumulation and the growth of biological pollutants like mold, bacteria, and viruses in ducts. High-efficiency particle filters should be used to capture smaller particles that can be irritating to occupants, and they should be cleaned and replaced regularly. Flushing out the building with fresh air before occupancy can help remove high VOC levels from new building materials and finishes. Operating the HVAC system at slightly positive pressure relative to the outdoors can also help inhibit moisture intrusion and condensation, which are key factors in indoor mold growth.

Moisture control and preventing mold growth: Dampness in buildings is associated with respiratory diseases, and mold growth can be a significant issue. Mold requires warmth, an organic food source, and moisture to grow. It is important to address sources of moisture within the building and select materials and finishes that allow for the movement of air and moisture. Building tightness should be balanced to allow for moisture to escape and prevent water infiltration from outside. Controlling moisture generation from building occupants and activities is also important. Selecting materials with appropriate permeability properties can help facilitate vapor pressure diffusion and prevent moisture accumulation within the wall system.

Protecting from Outdoor Air Pollution: Protecting from outdoor air pollution is crucial for maintaining good indoor air quality. Outdoor air often contains pollutants such as particles, ozone, carbon monoxide, nitrogen oxides, and aromatic hydrocarbons, which can be harmful to human health. Urban areas tend to have higher levels of air pollution compared to rural areas, requiring extra measures for protection.

Proper Filtration Systems
One effective strategy for protecting indoor air quality is to implement proper filtration systems. These systems should be designed to remove pollutants like ozone and fine particles from the outdoor air brought into ventilation systems. It is important to ensure that the filtration systems are designed and maintained to effectively clean the outdoor air and provide a clean and healthy indoor environment.

Consideration for Heavily Industrialized Areas
Buildings located in heavily industrialized areas may face additional challenges due to specific pollutants present in the outdoor air. In such cases, specialized considerations may be necessary to address these pollutants and minimize their impact on indoor air quality. This could involve the use of advanced filtration technologies or specific ventilation strategies tailored to the unique environmental conditions of the area.

Importance of Clean and Healthy Outdoor Air
Regardless of the location, it is imperative that the outdoor air being brought into a building is clean and healthy. This is particularly important considering that people spend a significant amount of their time indoors, where exposure to outdoor air pollutants can occur. By ensuring that the outdoor air is free from harmful pollutants, the indoor environment can be safeguarded, promoting the well-being and health of building occupants.

Filtration for Maintaining Indoor Air Quality :

Filtration plays a critical role in maintaining good indoor air quality (IAQ) by removing unwanted particles and contaminants from the air. While the concept of air filtration is straightforward, the approaches used can be diverse and complex. Properly fitted and regularly changed filters are essential for ensuring clean and healthy indoor air, but the topic is not without controversy. In buildings with air-handling equipment, some level of filtration is necessary to keep ducts, blowers, and other equipment clean. Specific environments, such as surgical rooms in hospitals and clean rooms in electronics manufacturing, require high levels of air filtration. However, determining the filtration requirements for other spaces can be more challenging.

Balancing Filtration Efficiency and Energy Consumption

One challenge with air filtration is finding the right balance between filtration efficiency and energy consumption. While higher filtration efficiency leads to cleaner air, it also increases resistance to airflow. This can reduce the delivery of conditioned air, increase energy consumption, and potentially damage mechanical equipment. The Leadership in Energy and Environmental Design (LEED) certification program has further complicated this issue by requiring higher value MERV (minimum efficiency reporting value) air filtration for certain points, which can impact energy use.

Understanding MERV Ratings

MERV is a standardized measure of filter efficiency, ranging from 1 to 20, with higher values indicating greater particle removal ability. For example, a MERV 14 filter is 95 percent efficient and commonly used in hospital HVAC systems, while a MERV 13 filter is considered above average for commercial applications with 85 percent efficiency. In office buildings, filters in the MERV 4 to 5 range are typically standard. Designers aiming for optimal IAQ can work with mechanical, electrical, and plumbing (MEP) professionals to determine the highest MERV value suitable for the system's capabilities and budget.

Precautions During Construction

During construction, it is crucial to use MERV-8 filtration if the HVAC system is in use. Measures should be taken to protect equipment, ducts, grilles, plenum, access floors, and other openings from moisture, dust, and odors. Prevention of contamination through the use of low-VOC materials, negative pressure, and barriers to contain construction dust is key to achieving clean indoor air. Following construction and before occupancy, both mechanically and naturally ventilated buildings should undergo a two-week flush-out procedure with outside air to eliminate airborne contaminants. However, the feasibility of flush-outs may be limited by factors such as time constraints, climate conditions, and cost.

Source Control as a Better Strategy

Indoor air pollutants originate from various sources, including tobacco smoke, mold, building materials, cleaning products, and electronic equipment. Minimizing the presence of contaminants within buildings requires effective source control measures. However, this task is not without challenges, as there are no federally regulated standards for indoor air quality (IAQ), and obtaining accurate information on certain products can be difficult due to conflicting voluntary standards and greenwashing practices by manufacturers. Nevertheless, prioritizing source control to prevent the introduction of pollutants into indoor spaces is a more effective and cost-efficient strategy compared to attempting to remove pollutants once they are already present.

Volatile Organic Compounds (VOCs): Understanding Their Significance and Impact

Volatile Organic Compounds (VOCs) are a group of carbon-containing chemicals that readily evaporate at room temperature, releasing gases into the air. They can originate from natural and human-made sources and are commonly present in everyday products such as paints, solvents, cleaning agents, adhesives, and fuels

The term "volatile" indicates the tendency of these compounds to vaporize. Being "organic compounds" means that they contain carbon atoms. VOCs have notable implications for the atmosphere, as they contribute to the formation of ground-level ozone, which poses risks to both human health and the environment.

Indoors, the accumulation of VOCs can be concerning as they can reach high concentrations. Elevated levels of VOCs can lead to various health problems. Symptoms of exposure to high indoor VOC concentrations include nasal congestion, eye irritation, throat irritation, and headaches. Prolonged exposure to VOCs indoors can result in respiratory issues, allergies, and other health complications.

VOCs encompass a wide range of compounds, including Very Volatile Organic Compounds (VVOCs), VOCs, and Semi-Volatile Organic Compounds (SVOCs). Monitoring total volatile organic compounds (TVOCs) in air samples provides an overall assessment of indoor air quality. Concentrations of VOCs are typically higher in newly constructed spaces before materials have had a chance to off-gas and disperse. The levels of TVOCs can fluctuate as new products are introduced or removed.

VOCs are ubiquitous and found in numerous products, spanning building materials, furnishings, cleaning agents, and cosmetics. They are often associated with distinct odors, with the "new-car smell" being a recognizable example. Formaldehyde, a common VOC, emits a noticeable odor and is used as a preservative in various products, including paints and personal care items. It is also present in urea formaldehyde resins used as binders in plywood, particleboard, and composite products. While formaldehyde occurs naturally in plants and animals, high concentrations of it indoors can cause irritation and potentially contribute to carcinogenic risks.

Strategies for Selecting Low-Emitting Materials

Pollutant source control has become more manageable, thanks to the availability of numerous low-emitting materials in the market. These products, including paints, coatings, adhesives, floor coverings, and substrates, have replaced high-emitting alternatives and contribute significantly less to indoor air pollution. The emergence of low-emitting materials is a response to the growing awareness of severe reactions caused by poor indoor air quality.

When it comes to selecting low-emitting materials, it is essential to consider their volatile organic compound (VOC) content. VOCs are a group of chemicals that can easily vaporize at room temperature and are found in everyday products such as paints, solvents, adhesives, and cleaning agents. To regulate VOC emissions, there are VOC content limits expressed in grams per liter (g/L). Design professionals can refer to LEED v4 and LEED v4.1 standards to determine the acceptable VOC limits for various materials.

For instance, interior paints are subject to specific VOC limits based on their type and application. Flat paints used on non-wood substrates must adhere to a VOC limit of 50 g/L, while those used on wood substrates have a limit of 100 g/L. Similarly, adhesives used for interior installations, such as carpet and resilient flooring, have their own VOC limits ranging from 50 g/L to 200 g/L, depending on the type of adhesive.

In practice, when specifying materials, consider the following recommendations:

- Paints and Coatings: Opt for low- or zero-VOC paints and coatings to minimize the emission of harmful chemicals into the indoor air. These products have improved significantly and are now comparable in both price and performance to high-emitting counterparts.

- Adhesives and Sealants: Choose low-VOC adhesives and sealants for installing flooring products, reducing emissions of harmful chemicals during and after construction.

- Flooring Materials: Consider low-emitting alternatives such as hardwood, bamboo, or natural stone flooring, which release fewer volatile chemicals into the air. If carpets are preferred, select those with low VOC emissions that meet recognized certification standards.

- Composite Wood Products: Look for composite wood products, such as plywood and particleboard, that comply with stringent emission standards like CARB Phase 2 or are certified as having low formaldehyde emissions.

- Cleaning Products: Opt for environmentally friendly, low-VOC cleaning products or explore alternative cleaning methods like steam cleaning or using natural cleaning solutions.

By following these guidelines and prioritizing the use of low-emitting materials, design professionals can contribute to creating healthier indoor environments with improved air quality and enhanced occupant well-being.

To make informed choices and select low-emitting products, design teams can follow a few steps. Firstly, it is crucial to be knowledgeable about high-emitting materials and actively avoid them by opting for low-emitting alternatives. Design professionals can refer to the Residential Interior Design Chapter, specifically under the Sustainability x Materials section, for more information on low-emitting materials. This resource provides comprehensive discussions and guidance on the selection and use of low-emitting materials.

Noise Pollution: Recognizing the Impact of Unwanted Sound

While often overlooked, acoustics play a crucial role in indoor environmental quality. Excessive noise can have a significant negative impact on the well-being and performance of individuals in various settings, including offices, hospitals, hotels, and schools. Unfortunately, many people have little control over the unwanted sounds they are exposed to, whether it's construction noise outside their window or footsteps from the floor above.

Factors such as open collaborative environments, smaller workstations, unfinished non-acoustical ceilings, raised floors, mechanical air distribution, and the prevalence of electronic devices have contributed to the increased negative effects of noise. The World Health Organization published a report highlighting the relationship between environmental noise and health effects, including cardiovascular disease, cognitive impairment, sleep disturbance, tinnitus, and annoyance. The findings serve as a warning about the significance of addressing noise-related issues. The good news is that most common acoustical design problems can be effectively resolved through integrated planning. It is essential to involve all relevant team members, including manufacturers whose products will play a critical role in the solutions, such as ceiling, sound masking, furniture, and carpet systems.

One recommended approach to achieving acoustical success is the "ABC" approach: absorb, block, and cover. The performance of all installed systems should be assessed based on their ability to absorb, block, and cover sound. Ceilings, fabrics, and carpets are rated using a noise reduction coefficient (NRC), which indicates their sound absorption capabilities. Higher NRC ratings indicate greater sound absorption. Studies have shown that products with cut pile and cushions, as well as permeable carpet backings with greater height and thickness, offer better acoustical control. Lighting fixtures and air diffusers, which are part of the ceiling system, should also be selected with acoustic properties in mind.

Furniture systems, panels, walls, partitions, and glass play a role in blocking sound transmission between spaces and are rated according to their sound transmission class (STC). Office installations commonly have ratings between 40 and 53. Higher partitions and panels provide better sound blocking, but it's essential to balance this with the occupants' access to daylight and views. Glass can be an effective solution as well.

Sound masking, also known as "white noise," is an effective acoustical control strategy. It can be as simple as utilizing the fan noise from the HVAC system to mask other sounds. However, there are more advanced electronic masking technologies available in the market that can be integrated into the overall design. Privacy apps for computers and cell phones can also contribute to reducing the impact of noise.

By considering acoustics from the early stages of a project and involving all relevant stakeholders, integrated planning can effectively address noise-related issues. The selection of appropriate materials and systems, along with the implementation of sound-absorbing, sound-blocking, and sound-covering strategies, can significantly improve the acoustical environment and enhance the well-being and productivity of occupants.

Sound Control in Buildings: Essential Principles for Managing Acoustics

Effective management of sound and noise in buildings is crucial for creating a comfortable and productive environment. Design strategies and the use of appropriate acoustical materials play a significant role in optimizing acoustic performance. Here are some key considerations:

1. **Speech Privacy**: Good acoustic design focuses on controlling the transmission of speech through solid structures (walls, roofs) and air channels (ducts, conduits) to ensure privacy.

2. **Speech Intelligibility**: In spaces like schools and performance venues, intelligibility is essential. Controlling reverberation helps enhance speech clarity and comprehension.

3. **Noise Transmittance**: Unwanted noise, originating from building equipment or external sources, can be disruptive. Managing noise transmission is crucial for maintaining a peaceful environment.

To address these acoustic issues effectively, certain design strategies should be implemented early in the design process:

- **Strategic Building Orientation and Layout**: Placing quiet areas such as classrooms and conference rooms away from outdoor noise sources and noisy spaces like gyms or staff rooms. Open office layouts should incorporate sound-isolated spaces for private conversations and meetings.

- **Right-sizing of Rooms**: Optimal speech intelligibility can be achieved by designing smaller rooms that minimize excessive reverberation commonly found in larger spaces.

- **Noise Source Reduction**: Thoughtful HVAC and ducting design can help minimize disruptive mechanical system noise. Areas requiring quiet should be isolated from noise-generating spaces like data centers.

- **High-Performance Building Envelope**: A high-insulating and airtight building envelope not only enhances energy efficiency but also reduces external sound infiltration.

Supplementing these strategies, the selection of specialized sound-absorbing or sound-blocking materials should be considered, taking into account the following metrics:

- **Reverberation Time**: This metric measures the echo in a space. A shorter reverberation time (around 0.6-0.7 seconds) reduces echoing and improves speech intelligibility.

- **Noise Reduction Coefficient (NRC) and Sound Absorption Average (SAA)**: These metrics indicate the sound absorption capabilities of materials. NRC ranges from 0 (e.g., marble) to 1 (specialized acoustical padding). For classroom ceiling tiles, a minimum NRC of 0.70 is often recommended to control reverberation.

- **Sound Transmission Class (STC) Rating:** STC measures sound isolation by assessing the transmission loss through walls, ceilings, or other interior assemblies. Higher STC values indicate better sound isolation. Classroom partitions typically require a minimum STC rating ranging from 45 to 60, depending on the adjacent space.

- **Outdoor-Indoor Transmission Class (OITC):** Similar to STC, OITC measures transmission loss at lower frequencies associated with traffic noise. Recommended OITC values for school roofs and walls may range from 30 to 56, considering outdoor noise levels.

In some cases, the addition of sound may be necessary. Techniques such as sound masking (typically using white noise to provide speech privacy in open offices or medical settings) and noise canceling (using sound waves to counteract specific noise frequencies) can be employed to achieve effective noise management and control.

Harnessing Natural Light

Making use of natural daylight in building interiors offers numerous benefits, including reduced reliance on electric lighting during the daytime, energy savings, cost savings, and improved occupant well-being. When properly managed and complemented by pleasant views, natural light becomes a powerful element of green interiors, making a significant impact on the overall design. However, it is crucial to handle daylighting effectively to create a positive experience for building occupants.

The concept of "cool daylighting" is gaining popularity, as it combines the natural essence of sunlight with a modern and environmentally conscious approach. According to the Daylighting Collaborative, cool daylighting leverages the abundant energy from the sun, which has been shining for billions of years, while also aligning with contemporary trends in environmental sustainability and technological advancements. Daylit buildings are considered more environmentally friendly, technologically advanced, and socially aware than traditionally lit buildings. They signify a commitment to building science, energy efficiency, occupant comfort, and environmental preservation.

The implementation of daylighting strategies is interconnected with other design considerations, as discussed in the previous chapter on lighting. In her subsequent essay, Nancy Clanton delves into the interplay between the physical characteristics of a building, opportunities for energy savings, and lighting and daylighting solutions. These interconnected aspects play a vital role in optimizing the benefits of daylighting while ensuring efficient and sustainable design practices.

Challenges in Daylighting Design

Daylighting, as a form of illumination, poses unique challenges due to its variability, dependence on occupant behavior, and its impact on various aspects of a building.

Harnessing the power of daylight can be a complex endeavor. Even in prestigious green buildings designed by renowned architectural firms, issues such as glare, overheating, decreased productivity, and excessive reliance on artificial lighting persist. The prevalence of closed blinds and constant use of electric lights counteract the potential benefits of natural light. Rediscovering how to effectively utilize daylight in our buildings proves to be more challenging than expected. Modern daylighting systems must seamlessly integrate with electric lighting and mechanical systems while considering the prevalence of computer screens in workspaces and multimedia learning environments in educational settings. Paradoxically, advancements in building envelope efficiency may inadvertently trap solar heat gain from daylight, resulting in increased cooling loads. As daylighting is deeply rooted in architectural history, innovative strategies are necessary to address these contemporary circumstances.

Daylight typically enters buildings through windows or skylights, and often the interior design is limited by the available natural light. In buildings with northern orientations, constrained by neighboring structures or featuring small and deeply recessed windows, the design team has limited control over daylight penetration. However, buildings with southern, western, and eastern exposures present excellent opportunities for daylighting, requiring the implementation of control strategies. These strategies may include light shelves, shades, louvers, and window films to effectively manage the entry and distribution of daylight within the space.

The Importance of Daylighting

Incorporating daylighting into building design offers numerous long-term advantages, including improved environmental quality and energy efficiency. The allure of harnessing free solar energy becomes even more compelling as energy costs continue to rise. Traditional buildings prior to the widespread use of electricity relied heavily on daylight as their primary source of lighting. Today, we have the advantage of leveraging design principles and advanced materials to maximize the benefits of daylight while mitigating its potential negative effects, such as excessive heat gain. Successful daylighting design begins with a well-conceived concept that is supported by effective strategies and techniques. By embracing daylight as a valuable resource, we can create healthier and more sustainable built environments.

The Sunny Side of Economic Success

The incorporation of effective daylighting in building designs proves to be a highly cost-effective approach. When taking into account long-term advantages like energy savings, it becomes evident that it is a worthwhile investment. Studies have revealed that the financial gains resulting from enhanced productivity and increased profitability can far outweigh the overall costs incurred over the lifespan of the building.

In addition to energy savings, incorporating quality daylighting in building designs offers several other economic advantages.

1. Increased Productivity: Natural daylight has been linked to improved productivity and overall well-being of building occupants. Research shows that exposure to natural light enhances mood, concentration, and cognitive function, leading to higher productivity levels. Employees working in well-lit environments tend to be more alert, focused, and efficient, resulting in increased output and potentially higher profits for businesses.

2. Health Benefits: Daylighting contributes to the overall health and well-being of occupants. Exposure to natural light helps regulate circadian rhythms, promoting better sleep patterns and reducing the risk of health issues associated with disrupted sleep cycles. A healthier workforce translates to lower healthcare costs, reduced absenteeism, and improved employee morale and satisfaction.

3. Enhanced Retail Sales: Daylighting has been shown to positively impact retail environments by attracting customers and influencing their purchasing behavior. Well-lit retail spaces create a more inviting and pleasant atmosphere, leading to increased foot traffic and potentially higher sales. Natural light can enhance the visibility and appeal of products, making them more enticing to customers.

4. Brand Reputation and Marketing: Incorporating daylighting strategies in building designs demonstrates a commitment to sustainability, environmental responsibility, and occupant well-being. This can enhance the brand reputation of businesses and organizations, appealing to environmentally conscious consumers and attracting positive attention in the market. It can also serve as a unique selling point for businesses, differentiating them from competitors.

Overall, the economic benefits of incorporating quality daylighting extend beyond energy savings, encompassing improved productivity, reduced healthcare costs, increased retail sales, and enhanced brand reputation. By considering these factors in building design, organizations can create spaces that are not only visually appealing but also economically advantageous.

Conceptual Strategies for Building Design

The orientation and layout of a building form the foundation for effective daylighting design. Determining the size and placement of windows is crucial in optimizing the quantity and quality of natural light, while incorporating pleasing views enhances occupant satisfaction and productivity.

Proper building orientation is key to unlocking the full potential of daylight. Fortunately, the path of the sun remains constant, allowing designers to strategically position the building for optimal natural light throughout its lifespan. To minimize solar heat gain and glare, an orientation that maximizes southern and northern exposures is recommended. Southern-facing glazing can provide up to 45 percent of daylight, while northern exposures offer glare-free illumination.

Building Orientation and Geometry:

Proper building orientation is fundamental to effective daylighting design. By aligning the building to maximize southern and northern exposures, designers can minimize issues such as solar heat gain and glare. Southern-facing glazing can provide up to 45 percent of daylight, while northern exposures offer softer, glare-free illumination. Taller ceilings and high windows facilitate deeper penetration of daylight into the interior space, creating a more visually comfortable environment. Incorporating daylight from multiple directions further improves the uniformity of lighting distribution.

Glazing Size and Placement:

Strategic selection of glazing size and placement is critical in optimizing daylighting performance. Windows on the north and south facades offer the best-quality daylight. To reduce contrast between the brighter window areas and the surrounding walls, larger windows are preferable over smaller "punched" windows. By analyzing factors such as climate conditions, shading, solar heat gains, and specific daylighting goals, designers can determine the optimal amount of glazing to incorporate in the building's design.

Toplighting Strategies:

Toplighting, which involves introducing natural light through skylights or roof windows, is particularly effective in large single-story buildings and central interior areas. By allocating a portion of the roof area to toplighting, designers can ensure consistent and uniform lighting throughout the space. Generally, dedicating around three to five percent of the roof area to toplighting is recommended for achieving desirable lighting conditions.

Expanding on the Benefits:

Integrating these conceptual strategies into building design brings various benefits. Effective daylighting not only reduces the need for artificial lighting during the day, resulting in energy savings, but also enhances the overall environmental quality of the space. By harnessing free solar energy, building occupants can enjoy a connection to the outdoors and experience the positive physiological and psychological impacts of natural light. Additionally, research has shown that daylighting can improve productivity and profitability, which further contributes to the long-term economic success of a building.

By implementing these conceptual building design strategies—considering building orientation, optimizing geometry and window placement, and incorporating toplighting techniques—designers can leverage the inherent advantages of daylighting. This approach not only promotes energy efficiency but also creates visually appealing and comfortable indoor environments, positively impacting the well-being and productivity of building occupants.

Taking Advantage of Views:

Having quality views is highly desirable and beneficial for various tasks. Access to views has been shown to reduce stress for teachers, promote faster recovery and reduce the need for pain medication in healthcare settings, increase productivity and reduce health complaints among office workers. Corner offices with two windows are particularly coveted. Views of nature are more beneficial than overlooking a parking lot and also minimize reflected glare. If a building site lacks natural views, incorporating landscape elements and flowers can significantly enhance the overall environment.

Technical Fine-Tuning:

Once the design has considered building orientation, geometry, and glazing placement, the next step is to address specific technical aspects of daylighting. This includes selecting appropriate glazing types, implementing shading systems to control direct sun penetration, and integrating the design with electric lighting and controls.

Glazing Types and Considerations:

When choosing glazing, several factors need to be considered. One consideration is the desired amount of visible light transmission through the window. View windows should provide adequate light without being overly bright or tinted to alter the color perception. Windows that primarily serve for daylight penetration, but are not within the normal field of view, can have higher visible transmittance values. Another important factor is the solar heat gain coefficient (SHGC), which indicates the amount of solar heat that passes through the glazing into the building. Opting for a lower SHGC value improves thermal comfort and reduces cooling loads, resulting in more efficient HVAC system sizing.

Shading for Windows and Skylights:

Most windows and skylights require shading to minimize glare and solar heat gain from direct sun penetration. External shading devices such as awnings, porches, light shelves, and vertical fins are effective in preventing solar heat gain from reaching the window. Horizontal shading is particularly important for southern facades, while vertical shading and landscaping can help mitigate direct sunlight on east and west facades. Skylights also require shading to control glare and solar heat gain. Techniques such as splayed ceiling openings, reflectors beneath skylights, and high-performance skylights can be employed to manage direct sun penetration. Additionally, internal user-controlled shading may be necessary for task areas, especially in buildings that are not aligned with orthogonal coordinates.

Supplementing Daylight with Electric Lighting:

An integrated design approach is to ensure that electric lighting supplements daylight rather than duplicating it. On cloudy days, when daylight appears flat, some direct lighting is necessary to introduce shadows. Lighting vertical surfaces, such as interior walls, helps balance the brightness of glazing and creates a visually comfortable scene. Fortunately, less artificial lighting is generally required during nighttime activities. Designing the electric lighting system to meet the needs of cloudy days and nighttime usage can result in reduced equipment requirements. Moreover, considering that internal heat generated by electric lighting, occupants, and equipment contribute to cooling loads in many buildings, effective daylighting can lead to long-term energy and cost savings.

Dimming Decision: A Question of Illumination

An essential technique for effective lighting control is the combination of personal controls and automatic controls. Personal controls empower occupants to adjust lighting according to their individual needs, allowing them to turn lights on or off and dim them as desired. On the other hand, automatic controls rely on technologies such as daylight sensors, motion sensors, and building energy management systems.

Personal controls are ideal for areas where people work, meet, or teach, such as offices, classrooms, and conference rooms. These spaces can be equipped with manual dimming controls that have predefined upper limits to ensure that lights are not unnecessarily bright when ample daylight is available. Additionally, occupancy sensors can be integrated to automatically control lighting based on occupancy patterns.

In public areas like hallways, restrooms, lunchrooms, and lobbies, automatic controls such as daylight sensors and occupancy sensors work effectively and discreetly to manage lighting. These sensors ensure that lighting is activated only when necessary, optimizing energy efficiency.

While personal and automatic controls offer significant benefits individually, their combination provides the best overall lighting control strategy. For building-wide control, it is recommended to use an automatic energy management system that primarily focuses on emergency conditions, allowing lights to be turned off or dimmed as required. Properly designed lighting systems with daylight and occupancy sensors will seamlessly integrate into the building's energy management system, automatically minimizing lighting loads during both daytime and nighttime operations.

By implementing a comprehensive approach to lighting control, occupants can enjoy personalized lighting settings while achieving energy savings and maximizing the overall efficiency of the building's lighting system.

Blending Aesthetics and Engineering:
The Artful Science of Daylighting Design

Daylighting design is a harmonious blend of artistic vision and scientific understanding. By employing simple yet effective techniques, remarkable results can be achieved. For complex buildings, the expertise of a daylighting consultant may be sought to assist with various aspects such as orientation, geometry, glazing specifications, shading devices, and the use of daylight models to refine the design solutions. The following steps serve as the foundation for successful daylighting design:

1. Maximize the utilization of south and north façades to take advantage of the best daylighting opportunities.
2. Incorporate high ceilings and tall windows to facilitate deeper penetration of daylight into the space.
3. Prioritize quality views in areas where tasks are performed and ensure equitable distribution of daylight.
4. Calculate the optimal size and number of windows and consider top lighting to achieve uniform illumination while minimizing heat gain.
5. Select high-performance glazing that strikes a balance between daylight transmission and thermal control.
6. Employ fixed shading devices and view-preserving blinds on south, east, and west façades to mitigate direct sunlight and glare.
7. Mitigate direct sunlight in task-oriented areas such as offices, classrooms, and conference rooms.
8. Opt for high-reflectance surfaces to enhance the distribution and diffusion of daylight within the space.
9. Integrate electric lighting and controls seamlessly with daylighting design to maximize energy savings and ensure optimal lighting conditions.

From an artistic perspective, daylighting design embraces the direction and quality of light, as well as the interplay of shadows and highlights, to create visually captivating environments. Architects and designers employ various elements such as skylights, windows, light shelves, and light-diffusing materials to effectively control the entry and distribution of natural light, resulting in dynamic and aesthetically pleasing spaces.

On a scientific level, daylighting design recognizes the physiological and psychological effects of natural light on building occupants. Extensive research has demonstrated that exposure to daylight can enhance mood, productivity, and overall well-being. It helps regulate the circadian rhythm, promotes healthy sleep patterns, and contributes to energy conservation by reducing the reliance on artificial lighting during daylight hours.

Successful daylighting design involves achieving a delicate balance between maximizing daylight and controlling glare, ensuring even distribution of light throughout the space, and considering the specific requirements and functions of each area within the building. It necessitates a meticulous examination of site orientation, building layout, window placement, and the careful selection of appropriate materials and shading solutions.

In essence, the art and science of daylighting design strive to create indoor spaces that are visually appealing, sustainable, and conducive to occupant comfort and well-being. By harnessing the abundant natural light available, architects and designers have the power to transform interior environments into vibrant and healthy spaces that positively impact the experience of those who inhabit them.

CHARTING A SUSTAINABLE PATH: OVERCOMING OBSTACLES

Whenever we embark on new and unfamiliar terrain, it can be a bit overwhelming. This is particularly true when it comes to adopting and promoting sustainable design practices, which can be especially challenging due to the need to persuade clients who may not yet be convinced of their benefits. Despite the hurdles that come with this process, it may be that the greatest barriers to overcome are those that reside within the designers themselves.

Ignorance

The belief that what we do not know cannot cause harm is dangerous, especially when it comes to sustainability. As the world faces the consequences of the overconsumption and degradation of natural resources, there is an urgent need for education and information. The destruction of rainforests, warming of the oceans, and health hazards caused by VOC emissions from common products are just some of the consequences of our actions. To combat this, we should visit websites of organizations such as the Natural Resource Defense Council, the Worldwatch Institute, Conservation International, the World Resources Institute, or the Earth Policy Institute to learn about these issues. The cure for ignorance is knowledge, but we must act on this knowledge to prevent negligence.

Detachment and Denial

Despite the increasing public awareness of global environmental issues, such as global warming, water scarcity, species extinction, and resource depletion, some individuals still refuse to accept the scientific evidence supporting these claims. Others acknowledge the problem but avoid taking responsibility for it, instead placing blame on others. It is concerning that although some designers specify only certified wood for their projects, others choose to use endangered tropical hardwoods for furniture and flooring, prioritizing their personal satisfaction over environmental responsibility.

Inconvenience

Often, we find ourselves short on time and opt for the easier solution, which can have significant ecological consequences. Instead of separating our trash for recycling, we throw everything in one big can, or we dispose of discontinued carpet folders instead of returning or donating them. Similarly, we might choose to send damaged furniture to the landfill instead of refinishing it, or we might discard used inkjet and toner cartridges rather than returning them for refill. Although these actions may seem small, when viewed collectively, they can have a significant impact on the environment. Therefore, it is important to take the time to make sustainable choices and consider the long-term effects of our actions.

Lack of Education & Experience

Design schools now include green design in their curriculum, and most design professionals have some understanding of sustainability. However, some newcomers to the field may feel overwhelmed by the vastness and complexity of green design. Interior designers acknowledge that certain technical energy and mechanical issues are beyond their scope and are the responsibility of engineers. But the key to successful green design is collaboration among all project participants from the beginning. Designers must acquire a fundamental understanding of sustainability principles and the science and technology necessary to provide valid services and advice to their clients. They should also continually seek professional development opportunities and stay informed of current environmental events. Research has shown that more experienced team members with a better understanding of green design and construction processes lead to more successful projects. Above all, collaboration among project participants is crucial for the success of green projects.

Resistance to Transformation

Due to the comfort associated with familiarity, humans have a tendency to stick to established practices, even when there's potential risk involved. For instance, it may feel safer to write specifications based on boilerplate models that have been used for years rather than experimenting with newer ones. It's common for people to be less anxious about specifying products and technologies that have been tried and tested, as opposed to newer and more ecologically responsible ones. This reluctance to change is not unique to any particular profession or field, and is often seen in various areas. In the design industry, for example, contractors have been known to disregard specifications provided by designers, either out of fear or ignorance, thereby refusing to consider more environmentally friendly processes or products.

Exclusive interest

Trade associations have a mission to safeguard and promote the industry they represent, and they are typically helpful resources for design practitioners seeking technical information. However, some trade associations focus primarily on lobbying efforts, urging lawmakers to act in ways that are beneficial to their industry but may go against ethical practices. For instance, the American Chemical Council pressured members of Congress to stop using the LEED rating system in government buildings, arguing against proposed changes that would reveal and restrict toxic hazards. Although this effort was unsuccessful, the credit additions to LEED v4 were ultimately modified to accommodate industry concerns. Regulations may be written with lenient requirements, or compliance measures may be relaxed, to enhance the sales of trade association members. USGBC President and CEO Rick Fedrizzi criticized these associations as "scoundrels" who disregard scientific evidence and rely on obfuscation and innuendo to maintain a status quo that favors themselves rather than others. For people who lack knowledge about the complexities and challenges that impact a particular industry, it can be challenging to discern truth from falsehood.

Absence of Laws, Principles, and Understanding

In the early years of the green building movement, designers experimented with different strategies and practices without much knowledge, figuring out what worked and what didn't. However, this changed with the release of LEED (Leadership in Energy and Environmental Design) by the U.S. Green Building Council in 2000, which provided a green building rating system. Although LEED is constantly evolving, it has faced controversy, causing the USGBC to delay the release of LEED v4 for a year due to concerns about proposed changes. In particular, the Materials & Resources category needed refinement as approaches to material selection had changed significantly. Incorporating life cycle analysis (LCA) into materials selection is also a challenge as there is no consensus on how to frame the protocol, despite its importance in evaluating the ecology of a product.

Aesthetics

In the past, the term "green design" was associated with unattractive and uninteresting designs. However, this perception has largely disappeared, and green designers are celebrating this progress towards sustainability. Chapters 8 and 9 showcase some of the most beautiful and inspiring green projects. As interest in creating green interiors that are aesthetically pleasing and inspiring grows, manufacturers have jumped on board by developing sustainable products. This has provided designers with a wide range of stunning choices for furnishings and finishes.

Time and money limitations

The belief that "green design is expensive and time-consuming" is often repeated so much that it has become a common saying. Although there is some truth to this statement, green design is a skill that can be learned, and with practice, it becomes natural and valuable. Initially, the process may seem daunting, involving researching a product's environmental properties, understanding energy-efficient technologies, and asking manufacturers about their environmental performance. However, these efforts are intellectually stimulating and rewarding.

Some clients are reluctant to certify their buildings according to the LEED Green Building Rating System because of the associated costs and time commitment. A survey of 700 executives by Turner Construction Company in 2012 found that only 48 percent were likely to seek LEED certification when building green buildings. This was a decrease from previous years, with the main reasons cited being the cost, staff time, and overall difficulty of the certification process.

However, regardless of whether they seek certification, these executives are increasingly adopting recognized green building practices. A majority of executives (56 percent) are very committed to environmentally sustainable practices, and an additional 34 percent are somewhat committed. They also have a growing understanding of green building methods, with over half of executives who are not likely to seek LEED certification preferring to use their own company's green building standards.

Operational constraints

Certain materials may have excellent performance but are too hazardous to use. Asbestos and PVC are two well-known examples. In the field of interior furnishings, PVC is particularly problematic because designers are used to specifying vinyl flooring, furnishings, and window treatments, and struggle to find suitable alternatives. Nevertheless, it is possible to install PVC-free products that maintain quality and performance, as many innovative practitioners have demonstrated.

Concern of litigation

Green building lawsuits raise designer concerns over contractual assurances. To mitigate risks, designers collaborate with legal counsel, employing provisions and disclaimers to prevent warranties and subjective compliance guarantees. Transparent communication with clients and regular goal reassessment ensure alignment. Safeguarded by proactive measures, designers navigate sustainable design and building performance while minimizing litigation risks.

Dispelling Myths and Misconceptions

Despite the progress made in the development of sustainable products, there are still some common myths and misunderstandings that persist. These misconceptions often prevent the widespread adoption of sustainable alternatives. To clear the air and set the record straight, let's take a closer look at the reality behind some of the most prevalent myths surrounding sustainable products. By dispelling these misconceptions, we can gain a better understanding of the true status and potential of sustainable products in our daily lives.

Are sustainable products truly inferior in quality compared to standard products?

Sustainable products are not inferior in quality to standard products. Today, they meet the same performance requirements and often exceed them. Early issues related to quality were not due to their sustainable characteristics. Manufacturers have made significant advancements, investing in the development of high-quality sustainable products. The shift towards sustainability has led to improved manufacturing processes, resulting in durable and visually appealing products. Let's debunk the myth that sustainable products are of lower quality and embrace their positive impact on the environment.

Do sustainable products fall short of meeting aesthetic standards?

The appearance of a product alone is not enough to determine its sustainability. While some sustainable products may have a visually appealing design that aligns with eco-friendly values, it is important to look beyond appearances. Today, it is difficult to identify sustainable products solely based on their looks. Genuine sustainable products are backed by comprehensive certifications, transparent labeling, and adherence to specific environmental standards. It is crucial to consider reliable information and certifications to make informed decisions about sustainable purchases.

Is it true that sustainable products come with a higher price tag?

While some sustainable products may have a higher upfront cost, the long-term benefits, such as durability and reduced maintenance expenses, often make up for it. Additionally, advancements in manufacturing technologies have led to more competitively priced sustainable options, debunking the misconception that all sustainable products are more expensive.

Are sustainable products difficult to find and not readily available in the market?

Manufacturers have recognized the demand for sustainable products and are actively embracing environmental stewardship. As a result, the availability of sustainable products is no longer a concern. Manufacturers are not only capitalizing on the sales opportunities presented by green building practices, but they are also taking responsibility for their environmental impact.

Sustainable products are exclusive or unavailable from competitive manufacturers

The collaborative nature of the industry has contributed to the continuous improvement of sustainable products, with manufacturers embracing responsible practices and innovation. This commitment has ensured that a diverse range of high-quality, environmentally friendly options are readily accessible to meet the needs of green building projects.

Building a Sustainable Design Practice: Integration is Key

The sustainable design movement has had a profound impact on the design community, prompting us to critically examine the consequences of our work on both humanity and the natural environment. The evidence of our negative impact on the ecosystem is undeniable, and there is a growing recognition that we have the power to change our trajectory. We are discovering that there is a better way to live, conduct business, and design. Design firms are increasingly embracing integrated sustainable approaches for a variety of reasons. Some are motivated by the desire to differentiate their services or stay in line with current trends, while others recognize it as the right thing to do. Informed clients are demanding green design, and many are even seeking LEED certification, particularly institutional clients. Design firms must be prepared to respond if they want to remain relevant in today's industry.

To effectively integrate sustainable thinking into a design practice, a commitment must start from the top leadership of an organization. Sustainability should not be treated as an optional add-on service but rather as an integral part of the firm's overall design philosophy for true success. Just as it wouldn't make sense to design some projects without considering accessibility for people with disabilities, it also doesn't make sense to design some projects that are eco-friendly while others harm both people and the environment. As designers of the built environment, we have a responsibility to prioritize the health and well-being of both individuals and the natural world.

While young designers often exhibit a universal enthusiasm for sustainable design, they cannot be solely relied upon to drive the shift towards sustainable practices within a firm. Successful integration of sustainable design requires a genuine commitment from the firm's leadership. It is crucial for firm leaders to understand and appreciate the benefits of sustainable design in order to foster a meaningful shift in mindset.

In the design profession, learning by doing is key. One effective way to promote a transition towards sustainable design within your firm is to find a client who is interested in building a green project. This may be easier than expected, and repeat clients can present the best opportunities as they already trust your expertise and know that you have their best interests at heart.

Personnel responsible for marketing within the firm need to have a solid understanding of sustainable design and be able to effectively communicate its value to clients. Entrusting this task to a recently LEED-accredited intern may not inspire much confidence. Clients want assurance that firm principals genuinely believe in sustainability and are committed to delivering successful integrated designs.

Like any new project type, taking on green design requires a learning curve and additional time and effort. However, it should be viewed as an investment in a new area of market differentiation for your firm. While individual efforts to learn green practices are commendable, design firms seeking substantial change must make a firm-wide commitment. Without such a commitment, the firm may risk losing its self-taught environmental experts to another firm with a genuine dedication to sustainability. Therefore, allocating resources for office-wide professional development programs focused on sustainable design is crucial.

Firm leadership plays a critical role in keeping sustainable design at the forefront of the firm's mindset and culture. They must ensure that the momentum towards sustainability is maintained and prevent a regression into old ways of thinking. Evaluating new products based on their environmental impact, functionality, and cost should be a standard practice. Regular in-house professional development meetings can be an effective way to share knowledge and stay updated on new green products entering the market. It is important to encourage staff members to ask tough questions of manufacturers and discern genuine sustainability from mere "greenwashing."

Design is the harmonious combination of beauty and functionality, with functionality measured by how well programmatic requirements are met. In addition to operational efficiency, durability, image, and value, programmatic requirements must also include consideration for environmental impact and human well-being. By integrating these aspects into the design process, firms can create spaces that not only meet the needs of occupants but also have a positive impact on the environment and promote well-being.

Ways to integrate sustainable practices into your design firm:

- **Establish a Sustainability Vision**: Define and communicate a clear vision for integrating sustainable practices throughout your design firm, making sustainability a core value in all aspects of your work.

- **Educate and Train Staff**: Foster a culture of continuous learning and awareness by providing ongoing education and training to your staff on sustainable design principles, techniques, and best practices.

- **Incorporate Sustainable Design Guidelines**: Develop and implement specific sustainable design guidelines that integrate strategies, standards, and benchmarks into the design process and project evaluations.

- **Collaborate with Experts**: Engage with sustainability consultants, experts, and organizations to gain insights and expertise in sustainable design, fostering partnerships that promote innovation and sustainable solutions.

- **Embrace Life Cycle Thinking**: Adopt a holistic approach by considering the environmental, social, and economic impacts of materials, construction methods, and operational aspects throughout the life cycle of each project.

- **Utilize Green Building Certifications**: Seek recognized green building certifications, such as LEED, to ensure adherence to sustainability standards and work towards achieving higher certification levels.

- **Foster Collaboration and Stakeholder Engagement**: Encourage collaboration with clients, contractors, suppliers, and stakeholders to incorporate sustainable practices into all project phases, fostering open dialogue and shared responsibility.

- **Emphasize Energy Efficiency and Renewable Energy**: Prioritize energy-efficient design strategies and promote the use of renewable energy sources, exploring innovative technologies and approaches to minimize energy consumption.

- **Promote Sustainable Material Selection**: Encourage the use of environmentally friendly and responsibly sourced materials, considering factors like durability, recyclability, and embodied carbon.

- **Measure and Track Performance**: Implement systems to measure, track, and report the sustainability performance of projects, identifying areas for improvement and showcasing the positive impact of sustainable design practices.

- **Integrate sustainable design strategies in all projects**: Make sustainable design a standard practice by incorporating equal- or low-cost strategies into every project, highlighting their value and long-term return on investment.

- **Engage in professional development**: Stay updated on sustainable design trends and practices by actively participating in green building organizations, attending conferences, workshops, and seminars.

- **Lead by example**: Demonstrate your firm's commitment to sustainability by encouraging principals to achieve LEED accreditation, setting an example for the staff and showcasing your dedication.

- **Support staff in obtaining LEED accreditation**: Invest in staff development by covering LEED exam costs, offering incentives or rewards for achieving accreditation, and providing opportunities for further knowledge enhancement.

- **Pursue green projects**: Seek out green projects or advocate for incorporating sustainable strategies with established clients, emphasizing the benefits and alignment with their goals and values.

- **Research green products**: Dedicate time to research green products and materials, creating a designated resource area for easy access by project teams.

- **Engage with manufacturers**: Invite manufacturers of green products to provide lunchtime presentations, encouraging critical discussions and enhancing the team's understanding of sustainable products.

- **Collaborate with sustainable consultants**: Involve consultants committed to sustainable design from the early stages, leveraging their expertise for effective and holistic solutions.

- **Stay informed**: Subscribe to green design publications to stay updated on industry trends, case studies, and innovative approaches to sustainable design.

- **Personal commitment**: Encourage staff to adopt environmentally friendly habits, fostering a culture of sustainability within the firm.

Implementing sustainable design practices requires leadership and a commitment to doing what is right for the community and the environment. It involves educating clients about the benefits of sustainable strategies and designing in ways that prioritize human well-being. Each design firm will have its own set of goals, resources, and constraints, so it's important to take a customized approach. What works for one firm may not work for another, and strategies will vary based on factors like location, size, and company maturity.

I recommend that design firms embark upon a thorough assessment of their goals, available resources, and limitations. This introspective examination will serve as the foundation for developing and implementing bespoke green initiatives that align precisely with their individual needs. By consciously selecting actions that harmonize with their unique circumstances, I firmly believe that firms can gradually propel themselves towards a realm of more sustainable practices.

Undoubtedly, the journey towards greening a design firm is an ongoing odyssey, one that necessitates an unwavering commitment, adaptability, and an insatiable thirst for knowledge. By wholeheartedly embracing the timeless principles of sustainable design and seamlessly integrating them into every facet of their work, I posit that design firms wield an unparalleled ability to manifest transformative change within the very fabric of our built environment.

Let us remember that this pursuit of sustainability is not a destination but a perpetual voyage, wherein each step taken forward represents a conscious choice to contribute positively to the world. As I immerse myself in this noble endeavor, I implore design firms to join me in this collective mission, embracing the inherent responsibility we bear and ensuring that our creative endeavors foster a more sustainable and resilient future for generations to come.

www.ingramcontent.com/pod-product-compliance
Ingram Content Group UK Ltd.
Pitfield, Milton Keynes, MK11 3LW, UK
UKHW052121230426
12049UKWH00010BA/150

9 789359 894638